REREADING

Rereading

MATEI CALINESCU

Yale University Press   New Haven & London

PN
98
R38
C35
1993

Designed by Nancy Ovedovitz and set in Sabon type by Keystone
Typesetting, Inc., Orwigsburg, Pennsylvania. Printed in the United States of
America by Vail-Ballou Press, Binghamton, New York.

Library of Congress Cataloging-in-Publication Data

Calinescu, Matei.
    Rereading / Matei Calinescu.
        p.   cm.
    Includes bibliographical references and index.
    ISBN 0-300-05657-5
    1. Reader-response criticism.   2. Literature—Appreciation.
    3. Books and reading.   I. Title.
    PN98.R38C35   1993
    801'.95—dc20   92-28229
                                                           CIP

A catalogue record for this book is available from the British Library. The
paper in this book meets the guidelines for permanence and durability of the
Committee on Production Guidelines for Book Longevity of the Council on
Library Resources.

10   9   8   7   6   5   4   3   2   1

Reading . . . does not hurry past us with the speed of oral delivery; we can reread a passage again and again if we are in doubt about it or wish to fix it in the memory. We must return to what we have read and reconsider it with care. . . . We should read none save the best authors and such as are least likely to betray our trust in them, while our reading must be almost as thorough as if we were actually transcribing what we read. Nor must we study it merely in parts, but must read through the whole work from cover to cover and then read it afresh.

QUINTILIAN
Institutio Oratoria

· · · · · · ·

Any book which is at all important should be reread immediately.

ARTHUR SCHOPENHAUER

· · · · · · ·

We have to admit that we owe more to Tolstoy, Flaubert, and Hardy than we can measure; that if we wish to recall our happier hours, they would be those Conrad has given us and Henry James; and that to have seen a young man bolting Meredith whole recalls the pleasure of so many first readings that we are even ready to venture a second. The question is whether, if we venture ourselves a second time with *Vanity Fair,* the Copperfields, the Richardsons, we shall be able to find some other form of pleasure to take the place of that careless rapture which floated us along so triumphantly in the first instance. The pleasure we shall now look for will lie not so obviously on the surface; and we shall find ourselves hard pressed to make out what is the lasting quality, if such there be, which justifies these long books about modern life in prose.

VIRGINIA WOOLF
"On Re-reading Novels"

· · · · · · ·

I had an experience with the 18th century poet Klopstock. I found that the way to read him was to stress his metre abnormally. When I read the poems in this new way, I said: "Ah-ha, now I know why he did this." What had happened? I had read this kind of stuff and had been moderately bored, but when I read it in this particular way, intensely, I smiled, said: "This is *grand,*" etc. But I might have said

anything. The important fact was that I read it again and again. [...]
What are expressions of liking something? Is it only what we say or
interjections we use or faces we make? Obviously not. It is, often,
how often I read something or how often I wear a suit. Perhaps I
won't even say: "It's fine", but wear it often and look at it.

LUDWIG WITTGENSTEIN
Lectures and Conversations on Aesthetics,
Psychology and Religious Belief

· · · · · · ·

Kafka's whole art consists of compelling the reader to *reread*. The
denouements of his stories—or their absence of a denouement—
suggest certain explanations, but these are never clear enough. We are
thus required to reread his stories from a new angle, an angle from
which these explanations may appear better justified. Sometimes
there is a double or a triple possibility of interpretation, whence the
need for two or three readings. But one would be wrong to try to
interpret everything in Kafka in detail. A symbol always has a certain
generality and the artist gives us only a rough translation. There is no
word-for-word or crib here. Only the movement is rendered.

ALBERT CAMUS
Carnets

· · · · · · ·

One cannot *read* a book; one can only reread it.

VLADIMIR NABOKOV
Lectures on Literature

· · · · · · ·

The words were where they should be, and the books told a
story you could follow; you could re-read, and, on re-reading, re-
encounter, enhanced by the certainty that you would encounter
those words again, the impression you had felt the first time. This
pleasure has never ceased for me; I do not read much, but I have
never stopped re-reading Flaubert and Jules Verne, Roussel and
Kafka, Leiris and Queneau; I re-read, and each time it is the same
enjoyment, whether I re-read twenty pages, three chapters, or the
whole book: an enjoyment of complexity, of collusion, or more
especially, and in addition, of having in the end found kin again.

GEORGES PEREC
W or the Memory of Childhood

CONTENTS

. . . .

. . .

CONTENTS

· · ·

CONTENTS

. . .

PREFACE

· · · · · · ·

When I think of rereading I often turn to a metaphor of haunting. First, there are texts that haunt us, that cannot and will not be forgotten, texts that seem to have strong if often mysterious claims over our memory, attention, and imagination and that urge us to reread them, to make them present to our mind again and again. Second, there are texts that haunt other texts, in the sense that they appear in them as expected or unexpected visitors and even, one might say, as phantoms or specters, if such notions could be freed of their sinister connotations. Since this meaning of haunting is indeed broadly metaphorical, one has little difficulty accepting the possibility not only of historically earlier texts haunting later ones, but also of later texts haunting earlier ones. (Parodies haunting their models, commentaries haunting the originals that inspired them, Proust haunting Ruskin as much as Ruskin haunts Proust, Kafka "creating" his precursors, as Borges famously put it.) Such circular haunting suggests one of the major recurrent themes of my book: the essential circularity of the time of reading. It is because of this circularity that I often speak of reading and rereading as a single (if double-faced) entity, and that I occasionally use what might look like an orthographic oddity or manneristic affectation: the word *(re)reading*. Textual haunting, in this second sense, is just one instance—but a very important one—of the larger phenomenon of intertextuality. The third meaning of my metaphor suggests that it is we, active

· · ·

rereaders, who are haunting the texts. We revisit them to understand why they attract us or to enjoy the surprise of rediscovering them, of reexperiencing their ability to come alive and renew themselves.

But how important is it to distinguish between reading and rereading? The dichotomy is not simple (few critical dichotomies are) and it rests on a tenuous theoretical basis, although it is intuitively compelling. Every avid reader of literature has a clear sense of what rereading is, having personally experienced the fascination that certain books exert over us in time, the desire to return to them, the exquisite pleasure of doing so (but also the occasional disappointment). We all have, alongside an open list of books we would like to read, our list or "canon" of books that we would like to reread, that we occasionally do reread, that we sometimes make a special point to reread periodically in a sort of private ritual. Remarkably, such informal, subjective, idiosyncratic canons tend to coincide, at the core if not always at the margins, with the canon of literary classics. And reading the classics, as Italo Calvino once observed, is always an act of rereading; even though "every rereading of a classic is as much a voyage of discovery as the first reading" (*The Uses of Literature*, p. 127).

Why then distinguish between reading and rereading? Precisely, I would argue, in order to be able to come to terms with paradoxes of the type Calvino proposes: How can one reread a book one has never read? How can one read freshly, as if for the first time, a book one knows well? Another reason for maintaining the distinction has to do with our fuller understanding of the fundamental process of literary reading itself, about which so much has been written in the last two or three decades—from the point of view of the (German) aesthetics of reception, from that of (French) structuralism and poststructuralism, and from that of (Anglo-American) reader-response criticism. When one looks at the rich critical literature on reading one is surprised at how little independent work has been done on rereading. Studies of literary reading do occasionally take up the question of rereading and offer tantalizing insights into it. But there is no comprehensive attempt to compare more systematically the processes of reading and rereading and to analyze the complicated, sometimes complementary, sometimes sharply conflictual relationships between them, as well as those situations in which the two are hard to distinguish at all.

A more sustained reflection on rereading (as a special case in a larger phenomenology of repetition: of remembering, reevoking, reviewing in retrospect, retracing, thinking back and rethinking, rediscovering and

· · ·

revisiting) can improve our understanding of the reading process itself in at least two areas that current theories of reading appear to neglect. Most current theories seem to assume a uniform quantity and quality of attention on the part of the reader. The reader may be variously conceived as a "competent reader," an "implied reader" (a role that is inscribed in the text), a "postulated reader," a "real reader," or a composite of all these; the question of attention is very rarely addressed. One of the advantages of distinguishing between reading and rereading is that the problem of attention is immediately brought to the foreground. Reflective rereading presupposes attention of an obviously different kind from the one involved in the curious, "mimetic," linear perusing of an engrossing text, which is sometimes taken as paradigmatic, at least in studies of reading fiction. The attention proper to reflective rereading may give us a hint as to what Proust meant, in one of his essays on Ruskin, when he stated that reading, while not yet a spiritual act (as Ruskin thought), could be at once a form of self-understanding and a preparation or training for the spiritual. Such dimensions of (re)reading, which are usually ignored by contemporary studies of literary reception or reader response, reveal their full significance only in light of the history of reading, an area of study that has thus far attracted historians but surprisingly few literary critics or theorists.

This brings me to the second advantage of considering reading in terms of the proposed dichotomy: the natural opening of the subject to historical understanding. Historically—and paradoxically—in the Western world reading was preceded by rereading. I think that Jacques Derrida once said, both jestingly and in earnest, that "at the beginning was repetition." The priority of rereading offers one partial illustration of this paradox. Before writing and rereading there was even more repetition in oral cultures, in which the "tribal encyclopedia" (Eric A. Havelock) had to be memorized in the form of oral poetry. Reading in the post-Reformation modern age of print and of increasingly accessible books started by separating itself (never perfectly, though) from rereading—from the constant rereading of religious or devotional texts, from the secular rereading of the classics of antiquity, from the "intensive" reading habits bequeathed by the manuscript culture of the Middle Ages and temporarily reinforced, although in different ways, in the Roman Catholic world of the Counter-Reformation and in the Protestant world in which mass reading truly began as mass rereading of the supremely rereadable text, the Bible. The dichotomy between reading and rereading allows us to see in a new light

. . .

certain revealing "accidents" in the history of literary (re)reading in the West, starting with *Don Quixote,* a novel in which the problem of reading and rereading is fully and wonderfully developed.

A final note. The "reader" or "rereader" generically referred to in this essay is usually a *hypothetical construct.* I see reading—that is, *(re)reading*—as a process of continuous hypothesis building and revising; of continuously making smaller or larger "abductions," as Charles Peirce would phrase it, and recasting or replacing them; or, to use Umberto Eco's terms, of ceaselessly making forecasts and taking "inferential walks"; or of constructing provisional frames within which the text acquires motivation, coherence, and meaning. To read is to make guesses based on expectations and assumptions and to modify them as the reading proceeds, and sometimes even long after the reading has been completed. When such guesses refer retrospectively to a read text they naturally lead to rereading, the activity I focus on in this book. In an important sense my essay then is concerned with what happens *after* reading. In other words, it deals largely with the expectations, assumptions, and guesses of someone who returns to a known text. My generic rereader, then, does not exist in reality: he or she is no more than a hypothetical embodiment of the hypothesizing vocation of reading itself. With respect to the real readers who might be interested in the questions raised by my essay, I should perhaps add that no special preparation is needed to read it, except a willingness to bring the acts of reading and rereading into the focus of one's consciousness and to seek introspective validation for those approaches and insights that are not and cannot be validated otherwise. It is in view of such nonspecialist potential readers that I have tried to keep jargon or technical language to a bare minimum and, in those cases in which technical terms were unavoidable, that I have done my best to explain them and use them as lucidly as I could.

Over the four years I worked on this book many colleagues and friends professionally or personally interested in the reading and rereading of literary works have read the manuscript wholly or in part and have offered candid criticism, suggestions, and encouragement. Among them I feel especially indebted to Willis Barnstone, Adriana Calinescu, Marcel Cornis-Pope, David M. Hertz, Michael Holquist, Kenneth R. Johnston, Giuseppe Mazzotta, Breon Mitchell, Thomas Pavel, Marjorie Perloff, Claude Rawson, Alvin H. Rosenfeld, Scott Sanders, Mihai I. Spariosu, Nicolas Spulber, and Meir Sternberg.

. . .

The writing was helped by research grants and a sabbatical leave from Indiana University and by a research stipend from the National Endowment for the Humanities, to which I wish to express my gratitude.

Special thanks for consistent support and thoughtful advice go to my editor at Yale University Press, Jonathan Brent. I am grateful to Richard Miller for his extremely careful reading and rereading of my manuscript.

. . .

. . . .

PART ONE

Models of Reading

. . . .

Rereading Borges's "The Aleph"

I am always rereading rather than reading.
JORGE LUIS BORGES
Borges at Eighty

. . . .

My choice of examining a story by Borges to begin my essay on rereading should not come as a surprise. Borges, who has often spoken of his passion for rereading, is famous as an author of texts that are at once highly lucid and readable—albeit at a slow pace, dictated by their rich, quirky, often sly intertextuality—and compulsively rereadable: texts not only haunted by other texts but in their turn haunting, beckoning the reader to revisit them in a renewed search for their hidden, tantalizingly elusive meanings. In fact, the two operations, the linear (curious, end-oriented) movement of reading and the to-and-fro, back-and-forth, broadly circular (reflective and interpretive) movement of rereading are often indistinguishable in the actual experience of reading Borges. One might say, paraphrasing Roland Barthes, that the author of "The Aleph" forces us to reread his texts from the outset. Or, if one were to use Wolfgang Iser's concept of the implied reader, one might speak of the Borgesian text as postulating not a reader but, paradoxically, a rereader,

. . .

someone who would feel the need to read it over again and would enjoy it more fully on rereading.

"The Aleph" is one of Borges's most characteristic texts and a brilliant illustration of his cult of brevity. Its evocative title names but a single letter, Aleph, the first of the Hebrew alphabet, which in Kabbalistic lore stands for and mysteriously participates in the infinity of the godhead. Read straight through, "The Aleph" yields a relatively simple plot which culminates, near the end, in the fantastic vision of an Aleph (a small brilliant microcosmic sphere which mirrors the entire universe seen from every possible angle) in the basement of a Buenos Aires house in late October 1941. A first more or less "naive" reading of the story will naturally try to make sense of the text in narrative terms, to identify the main storyline, to get the essential "facts"—that is, to establish what is fictionally true in the fictional world of the story. On this primarily anecdotal level of "what happens," the text could be summarized as follows:

A first-person narrator, who later identifies himself as "Borges" (the quotation marks are used to distinguish him as fictive author from his homonym, the real author),[1] relates that, after the death of Beatriz Viterbo, he had made it a habit to pay a visit to her house on Garay Street every April 30, the anniversary of her birth. The narrator, we understand, had been deeply in love with the somewhat vulgar Beatriz, but his feeling had not been reciprocated. Once she was dead, "I could devote myself to her memory, without hope but also without humiliation" (*Borges: A Reader,* p. 155). So every April 30, between 1929 and 1941, that is for twelve years in a row, he would pay a visit to her first cousin, Carlos Argentino Daneri, who lived in the Garay Street house. On the last of "these melancholy and vainly erotic anniversaries" (p. 155), Daneri, slightly tipsy, launches into an eulogy of modern man and modern technology, and then explains his great project, a poem entitled "The Earth," from which he reads aloud several stanzas, commenting on them with pompously erudite enthusiasm ("I saw . . . that Daneri's real work lay not in the poetry but in his invention of reasons why the poetry should be admired," p. 157). Two weeks later Daneri invites "Borges" to a new saloon-bar just opened by his landlords, Zunino and Zungri. There, after reading again fragments from the "pedantic hodgepodge" of his poem, Daneri asks "Borges" to obtain a foreword for it from Alvaro Melián Lafinur, a man of letters of (we infer from the context) slightly dubious reputation. "Borges" agrees and promises to speak to Lafinur on the coming Thursday, after a meeting at the Writers' Club. We are in May, but

. . .

Daneri does not call the narrator until the end of October, when he seems to have forgotten about the Lafinur foreword (which "Borges" had not bothered to ask for anyway). Daneri speaks in a stammering voice about the impending demolition of his house: his landlords, "under the pretext of enlarging their already outsized 'saloon-bar,' were about to take over and tear down his house" (p. 158). Daneri is furious and makes plans to have his lawyer (Dr. Zunni) sue Zunino and Zungri. During the same long telephone conversation, he reveals that in the cellar of the house there is an Aleph (one of those "points in space that contains all other points," p. 159) and that without it he will be unable to finish his poem. Daneri wants to show "Borges" the Aleph and the latter, even though he thinks that the bizarre proposal might come from a madman, accepts. In the utter darkness of the cellar, "Borges" is afraid that Daneri might want to kill him. But then—suddenly, unexpectedly—he does see the mystical Aleph. Its description is one of Borges's most poetic and subtle pages:

> The Aleph's diameter was probably little more than an inch, but all space was there, actual and undiminished. Each thing (a mirror's face, let's say) was infinite things, since I distinctly saw it from every angle of the universe. I saw the teeming sea; I saw daybreak and nightfall; I saw the multitudes of America; I saw a silvery cobweb in the center of a black pyramid; . . . I saw a ring of baked mud in a sidewalk, where before there had been a tree; I saw a summer house in Adrogué and a copy of the first English translation of Pliny—Philemon Holland's—and all at the same time I saw each letter on each page (as a boy, I used to marvel that the letters in a closed book did not get scrambled and lost overnight); I saw a sunset in Querétaro that seemed to reflect the color of a rose in Bengal; . . . I saw all the ants on the planet; I saw a Persian astrolabe; I saw in the drawer of a writing table (and the handwriting made me tremble) unbelievable, obscene, detailed letters which Beatriz had written to Carlos Argentino; I saw a monument which I wor-shipped in the Chacarita cemetery; I saw the rotted dust and bones that had once deliciously been Beatriz Viterbo; I saw the circulation of my own dark blood; I saw the coupling of love and the modification of death; I saw the Aleph from every point and angle, and in the Aleph I saw the earth and in the earth the Aleph and in the Aleph the earth; I saw my face and my own bowels; I saw your face; and I felt dizzy and wept . . . I felt infinite wonder, infinite pity. (p. 161)

"I saw *your* face"—this abrupt appearance of the second-person pro-noun, this startling disclosure that the reader's face, inclined as it is over this very page of "The Aleph" at the moment of perusing this very

· · ·

sentence, had already been reflected in the infinite mirror of the Aleph—can create in an attentive first-time reader a subtle temporal shock. The Aleph becomes the text itself and the reader is absorbed into it through this strange pronominal hole. This paradox of reading—of reading "The Aleph," a text that has self-consciously anticipated every reader who has ever gone through it—constitutes the delicately uncanny effect produced on us by this fantastic story. It is the veritable moment of epiphany: the reader sees himself or herself in the mysterious universal/textual Aleph that "Borges" describes. After this experience of universal wonder, the return to ordinary reality can inspire only a sense of infinite pity. What follows is of a more playfully satiric and parodic (including self-parodic) nature.

Once out of the cellar, "Borges" hears the "hated and jovial voice of Daneri" telling him, "You couldn't pay me back in a hundred years for this revelation. One hell of an observatory; eh, Borges?" But "Borges," bent on taking revenge for what he has just learned about his beloved Beatriz and Daneri, refuses to recognize that he has seen anything and makes a point to treat Daneri as if he were crazy ("I embraced him and repeated that the country, fresh air, and quiet were the great physicians," p. 162). There follows a "postscript" (dated March 1, 1943), from which we learn that, six months after the demolition of the Garay Street house, Daneri published some of the Argentine sections of his poem (for which he got the Second National Prize of Literature). "Borges" goes on to discuss, with a display of great erudition, the name and nature of the Aleph. For the name, he refers the reader to the Kabbalah (in which "that letter stands for the *En-Soph,* the pure and boundless godhead") but also to the mathematician Moritz Cantor, who uses it as "the symbol of transfinite numbers" (p. 162). As for the nature of the particular Aleph he had seen, he concludes that, "Incredible as it may seem, I believe that [it] . . . was a false Aleph" (p. 163). The story ends with a comment on inescapable forgetfulness: the narrator is "losing, under the wearing away of the years, the face of Beatriz" (p. 163). The last word, as we see, is the name of Beatriz. This had also been, if not the first word, the first name to be mentioned in the very first sentence of the story: "On the burning February morning Beatriz Viterbo died . . ." (p. 154).

The foregoing summary, which I could not have made without rereading Borges's text several times, not only over the years but even as I was writing these pages, constitutes what I think could be taken as a rough approximation of the main "facts" which an attentive first-time reader of

· · ·

"The Aleph" would normally be expected to retain. One thing should be immediately clear: when I *write* about what the first reading of a literary piece is like (was like, should be like), I cannot but place myself in a perspective of rereading. This may sound paradoxical but it is, in fact, quite normal. What, as a writer, as a critic, I call "first reading" is already much more than a pragmatic or a phenomenological first acquaintance with a literary text: it is a constructed hypothesis which presupposes a certain degree of accuracy, and therefore a certain amount of checking (rereading). A purer sort of first reading (but one still available for inspection, and therefore not the entirely private act that reading often is) could be achieved in a psychological laboratory, where a subject would be given an unknown text to read and would be asked to recount what he or she has read right away and without being allowed to look at the text. A recording of the subject's words would constitute the "virtual text" of a first reading—quite interesting to examine from a psychological point of view.[2] There is a sense in which not even this kind of first reading can be considered truly "first" (in the sense of "virginal" or "innocent")—but this question need not detain us here. Suffice it to say that when I speak of first reading—of the first reading of "The Aleph," for instance—I mean a *hypothetically* linear reading, continuous, fresh, curious, and sensitive to surprising turns or unpredictable developments (which include unpredictable intertextual associations), to limit the description of this hypothetical construct to just a few obvious features.

A first-time reader of "The Aleph" with some literary background will realize sooner or later that Borges's text may loosely allude to an author whose name is never to be found among the many mentioned in "The Aleph" (from Homer and Hesiod to Spenser and Michael Drayton and Shakespeare, from Lucian of Samosata and Pliny to Goldoni and Xavier de Maistre and Paul Fort): is not the dead Beatriz, so insistently, so obsessively present to the mind of the narrator, somehow related, and not merely onomastically, to Dante's famous and quasi-mythical Beatrice Portinari? Emir Rodriguez Monegal, in his brief commentary to "The Aleph" in *Borges: A Reader,* notes that Borges himself has explicitly denied any concealed parodic intention with regard to Dante's *Divine Comedy* but that, in spite of such denial, "the story is about a man ("Borges") who is hopelessly in love with a woman called Beatriz and who is guided to a vision of the world, contained in a cellar, by a poet called Carlos Argentino Daneri (*Dan*te's surname was Aligh*ieri*). To compound things even further, Daneri is writing a poem describing the entire world"

. . .

7

(p. 351). "The Aleph," Rodriguez Monegal adds, in agreement with earlier Borges scholars, must then be related to an article on Dante that Borges wrote at about the same time as the story: "In presenting Dante's love for his Beatrice as hopeless and viewing the actual encounter between the two in Purgatory as a real nightmare, B. gives away the concept behind his story. Being a parody—that is, an inverted and displaced version of the original—his story makes the meeting of the two lovers even more impossible and humiliating" (ibid.).

A reading of Borges's essay "The Meeting in a Dream" (which is a commentary to *Purgatorio* 30–33) shows that the last part of Dante's *Purgatorio,* in the idiosyncratically literal interpretation that Borges proposes, could be one of the key intertexts of "The Aleph." Of course, once we have recognized this, once we have discovered the target of the (possible) secret parody, we have moved into the area of rereading. Searching the text of "The Aleph" for parodic allusions or analogies to Dante clearly involves an act (be it purely mental or mnemonic) of reperusing Borges's story, of refocusing our attention from certain details, which struck us the first time around, to others, or even to the same details, but reassessed in the new light of the Dante intertext, which reveals itself only to the attentive rereader. Like the notion of first reading, that of rereading is in large part a theoretical construct, a hypothetical model meant to help us get a better grasp of certain experiences with which we are familiar (we actually reread much more often than we suspect) but of which we are usually unself-conscious. Rereading in this sense is the repetition of a previous act of reading, but more importantly it is the rediscovery of an already known text from a different vantage point, for example its reconsideration within intertextual frames whose relevance has become clear only after the completion of a first reading. The hypothetical nature of rereading thus conceived is quite apparent: what really could differentiate a first reading of "The Aleph" triggered by a perusal of this essay from what I have called rereading? But the distinction between reading and rereading, even if diluted to the formula of (re)reading—the parenthesis indicating its floating, optional character—remains useful. At least heuristically, it is justifiable to speak of a linear first reading and of a metaphorically circular rereading, specifying that the latter's circularity is naturally expansive, that the circles of understanding it draws around the center of a particular work are increasingly large and involve reading and rereading other works, many other works, ideally (in a Borgesian spirit) all other works, the totality of what has been written.

· · ·

To give just a few examples of rereading "The Aleph" in terms of Dante: an incidental characterization of certain Italian survivals in the personality of Daneri ("At a remove of two generations, the Italian 's' and demonstrative Italian gestures still survived in him," p. 155) may take on some importance, even though one would be hard put to define it in more precise terms. More significantly, Carlos Argentino will be seen as a hilarious analogue to Dante's Virgil, as a "tenth-rate Virgil . . . who leads the narrator downward into a pitlike cellar" where he has the vision of the Aleph.[3] The occurrences of the name of Beatriz, in their immediate narrative context, will be pondered anew; the name Viterbo (also the name of a city in Italy, located northwest of Rome and mentioned in Dante's *Inferno*)[4] will acquire a subtle new resonance; and the name Elena, given to Beatriz when "Borges" addresses her portrait in a "seizure of tenderness" ("Beatriz, Beatriz Elena, Beatriz Elena Viterbo, darling Beatriz, Beatriz gone for ever, it's me, it's Borges," p. 160), will perhaps be seen in terms of Dante's treatment of Helen of Troy in *Inferno 5*, where she is condemned to the infernal circle of the lascivious (Elena thus links the invocation to the "unbelievable, obscene, detailed letters Beatriz had written to Carlos Argentino," p. 161).[5]

A careful rereading of "The Aleph" within the frame created by a (re)reading of the last three cantos of Dante's *Purgatorio* and of at least some of Borges's own essays on Dante (starting with "The Meeting in a Dream")[6] will certainly lead to the discovery of other interpretive possibilities which a first reading, by hypothesis unaware or imperfectly aware of the Dante intertext, would have missed. Such a rereading of "The Aleph" will also suggest some broader features of Borges's art, including his own peculiar ways of (re)reading other texts—in the event allegorical texts— and of weaving them obliquely, almost unrecognizably, into his own complicated textual tapestries.

"The Meeting in a Dream" confirms Borges's ambivalent attitude toward allegory. Interpreted logically, an allegory, he believes, is little more than an abstract equation (essentially simple, if not tautological) presented as a puzzle; interpreted literally, it may strike one as bizarre and even repulsive (as in Dante's procession at the end of *Purgatorio,* featuring "animals whose wings are studded with open eyes, a green woman, a crimson one, one that has three eyes, a man that walks in his sleep, etc.," pp. 211–12). Borges tries to explain the ugliness of these symbols, as well as the great severity of Beatrice to Dante, in the key scene of their encounter in the Earthly Paradise, by speculating that

· · ·

To fall in love is to create a religion with a fallible god. That Dante professed an idolatrous adoration for Beatrice is a truth that does not bear contradicting; . . . Dante, when Beatrice was dead, when Beatrice was lost forever, played with the idea of finding her, to mitigate his sorrow. I believe that he erected the triple architecture of his poem simply to insert that encounter. Then what usually happens in dreams happened to him. . . . He dreamed of Beatrice, but he dreamed her very austere, he dreamed her inaccessible, he dreamed her in a chariot drawn by a lion that was a bird. . . . A nightmare . . . is set forth and described in the following canto [32]. Beatrice disappears . . . ; a giant and a harlot usurp Beatrice's place." (p. 212. Allegorically, the giant is Philip IV; the harlot, the church.)

Could a reading of Dante—or rather a subtle, deliberate misreading—be at the origin of Borges's idea of making Beatrice, in her ironic twentieth-century disguise as Beatriz Viterbo, a more or less literal harlot? Would it then be legitimate to claim that "The Aleph" is indeed a secret parody of the *Divine Comedy,* reduced to the dimensions of a short (very short) story?

"The Aleph" can be seen as a parody of the *Divine Comedy* in another, more extensive and more intensive, sense as well. In this view, "The Aleph" would not be a rewriting of just one scene from Dante's vast poem but a compression, a "parodic miniaturization" (in Rodriguez Monegal's words), or an extreme serio-comic contraction of the whole work. Such a revisionary mode of rewriting has been linked to a Hebraizing tendency in Borges's work, and more specifically to a certain "dialectical cabalistic posture . . . producing fictions that . . . derive from time-honored writings (the Bible, the *Iliad,* Dante, Shakespeare, Cervantes, Kafka, and others)."[7] Read or reread in such terms, "The Aleph" relates a supernatural vision, comparable but at the same time contrastable to Dante's, for Borges does not see any afterlife, any divine hierarchy, any road to salvation; his infinity is an immanent one and it is actually nothing but the sum of possible perceptions of this world. Hence the curious reaction of the narrator: infinite wonder (the original has *infinita veneración,* which is closer to reverence than to wonder, but I definitely prefer the notion of wonder here) and infinite pity.

Borges's own denial that "The Aleph" is a parody of Dante must be taken seriously, I believe, even when the intertextual importance of the *Divine Comedy* is recognized. "The Aleph" may be a secret commentary, or an independent meditation on a motif from Dante, or a variation on the Beatrice theme, or the description of an alternative and more pessimistic vision of the world—all possibilities which exclude the commonly de-

. . .

rogatory (reductive, diminishing) connotations of the term *parody*. But Borges's denial could be taken seriously also in another, more radical, sense. Whatever the genetic relationship between "The Aleph" and Dante, one would perhaps be better off reading or rereading Borges's story without even considering *The Divine Comedy,* or considering it only as a marginal reference among many others. One could thus start by (re)reading the story against the directly suggested background of the Kabbalah and Kabbalistic mysticism, in which case "The Aleph" would be primarily just that, as I already pointed out—an Aleph, a microcosmic concentration of cosmic multiplicity, a reflection of the universe (both physical and moral) in one letter, a magic abbreviation of the world, the world itself being nothing but "the result of multiple combinations of the twenty-two letters of the Hebrew alphabet," as stated in *Sefer Yetsirah (Book of Creation).*[8]

Perhaps the most remarkable consequence of such an approach is, as Jaime Alazraki notes in his *Borges and the Kabbalah,* an awareness that "Borges challenges the reader to activate his resources, to become himself a Kabbalist" (p. 50). The Kabbalistic Aleph, as another Borges critic reminds us, is not only "useful to Borges in his attempt to abbreviate the universe in literature, but . . . also meaningful to the reader as a symbol of all Borges' writing."[9] Seen as a résumé or mirror of the writer's oeuvre, "The Aleph" can profitably be (re)read with other Borgesian fictions in mind, and particularly those centering around universal symbols or images, even if they be intolerable, such as "The Zahir."

"The Zahir" (first published in 1947) is a sort of negative of "The Aleph" (note that *Zahir* starts with *z,* the last letter of our alphabet and the symmetrical opposite of *a*). The story harks back to "The Aleph" also by its central motif, the death of a loved woman (Clementina Villar, Theodelina in a later version). In a preciously self-ironic style, the narrator—again identified as "Borges"—tells us that Clementina "on June 6 . . . committed the solecism of dying in the very middle of the southern district. Shall I confess that I—moved by the most sincere Argentinean passion, snobbery—was enamored of her, and her death moved me to tears?" (*Borges: A Reader,* p. 198). The Zahir—an ordinary coin worth twenty centavos—comes into the possession of "Borges" on the dawn of June 7, when, after the wake for Clementina, he walks into a bar to buy himself a drink and gets the Zahir in the change. On November 13, the day of writing, he hopes to wear away the obsessive Zahir still in his possession "simply through thinking of it again and again. Perhaps behind

· · ·

the coin I shall find God" (p. 202). In the meantime, the Zahir has magically acquired all the contradictory meanings and qualities attributed to it in various cultures and languages, including, in Arabic, the sense of "notorious" or "visible," which is "one of the ninety-nine attributes of God." In short, the Zahir has become an unbearable symbol of infinite, painful circularity, an obsessive counterpart of the elusive Aleph.

"The Aleph" can also be reread from the point of view of the central symbol of "The Handwriting of God" (first published in 1949), namely, the Wheel: the wheel of life, certainly, but also the wheel of fire and water, which becomes a wheel of torture—the wheel on which Tzinacán, the priest of Moctezuma, is tormented by the Spaniard Pedro de Alvarado before he gets to understand "the script of the tiger" and to discover the fourteen magic words that could make him all powerful but that he shall never utter because in the meantime he has forgotten his identity.[10] Other stories, essays, and poems, particularly those of direct Kabbalistic inspiration, could also serve as frames for (re)reading "The Aleph." When the reader becomes a Kabbalist—which can happen even during a reading that is empirically first—he or she becomes in fact a rereader. Instead of a linear reading, the Kabbalist will try various other methods of (re)reading, vertical or circular, intratextual or intertextual. These should not necessarily be aimed at discovering some nebulous hidden doctrine; what their users are normally content with is to realize the secret necessity of the text itself, particularly when this necessity is concealed under the appearances of chance. From early in his literary career, Borges was fascinated by what he took as the fundamental assumption of the Kabbalists and tried, in his own words, to vindicate not "the doctrine, but rather the hermeneutical or cryptographic procedures which lead to it. These procedures, as is well known, are the vertical reading of sacred texts, the reading referred to as *boustrophedon* (one line from left to right, the following line from right to left), the methodical substitution of certain letters of the alphabet for others, the sum of the numerical value of letters, etc. It is easy to scoff at such operations. I prefer to attempt to understand them" (*Borges: A Reader,* p. 22).

The justification for such methods—which may easily slip into apparently absurd applications[11]—lies in the absolute character of the sacred text, a text in whose composition chance has by definition played no role whatsoever. Interestingly, Borges thinks that ordinary (profane) texts may also be judged by the greater or lesser "amount of chance" they contain and that they should be read accordingly (the lesser the amount of chance

. . .

the more justified the use of methods of interpretation close to those of the Kabbalists). Borges distinguishes three types of texts: journalistic, consisting of simple reports of "facts," of "ephemeral utterances," in which both the meanings and the length and acoustics of the paragraphs are purely contingent or accidental; poetic, consisting of verses that "subject meaning to euphonic necessities" ("what is accidental in [such verses] is not the sound: it is the meaning," as in certain poems by Tennyson, Verlaine, and Swinburne); and texts produced by "a third writer—the intellectual. He certainly has not eliminated chance, either in the handling of prose (Valéry, De Quincey), or in that of verse, but he has denied it as much as possible, and limited its incalculable concurrence. He remotely resembles the Lord, for whom the vague concept of chance holds no meaning" (p. 24).

There can be little doubt that Borges, as both a prose writer and a poet, saw himself as a representative of the third group. We must therefore assume that he attempted to reduce the role of chance in his own writings, to limit "its incalculable concurrence" (or, to put it differently, to make the effects of chance *calculable*, to subject them to rules, as in certain games of ingenuity and absorption).

This assumption would justify the application to his writings of certain hermeneutic or Kabbalistic methods of reading, even though the results would never be conclusive. In regard to "The Aleph," as careful rereaders of the text, we might thus indulge in speculations concerning the recurrence of certain letters in the names of the characters. Is the "B" (not only in "Borges" but also in Beatrice) to be interpreted as playing a role similar, or ironically similar, to the Kabbalistic *beth*, the second letter of the Hebrew alphabet, but the one with which the sacred text, the Torah, actually begins? Is there anything to be made of the "Z" with which the names of Daneri's landlords (the clownish-sounding Zunino and Zungri) begins? And how about the "Z" in the name of Daneri's lawyer? The narrator confesses that "Zunni's name impressed" him (p. 159) because his law firm (in spite of its "unlikely address") was "an old and reliable one." Have the *z*'s in these names anything to do with the Lurianic concept of *zimzum* ("condensation" or "contraction")?[12] Do they allude to the *z*'s in the title of the story "Emma Zunz," which has been discussed in terms of the Kabbalah?[13] (One also notes that Zunz, the name of a great nineteenth-century scholar of Judaism, is quoted in Gershom Scholem's studies of the Kabbalah.) Do these *z*'s also somehow allude to the *z* in the title of "The Zahir"? Is there any special significance to the fact that

· · ·

13

Daneri first speaks of the existence of an Aleph in the cellar of the Garay Street house during a discussion about the lawyer Zunni? The passage about Zunni (another clownish-sounding name) reads like a factual report in "journalistic style," that is, a style attempting to record neutrally events in the (random) order in which they happen and lacking any inner necessity: "I asked him whether Zunni had already been hired for the case. Daneri said he would phone him that very afternoon. He hesitated, then with that level, impersonal voice we reserve for confiding something intimate, he said that to finish the poem he could not get along without the house because down in the cellar there was an Aleph" (p. 159). A Kabbalistically minded reader, however, will look beyond the apparently arbitrary succession of reported actions and words to seek a principle of inner coherence, clues to a rigorous secret logic which might use chance as a disguise.

The question of concealed meaning—of both the why and the how of concealment—haunts the act of rereading, particularly as it comes to focus on tiny textual details, idiosyncratic formulations, letter combinations, patterns of occurrence of names and dates, and other such matters. The Kabbalistically minded reader will, in other words, always reread for the secret, ultimately not so much for the sake of penetrating the secret per se (although this is always a challenge and therefore an important motive) as for the sake of eliminating chance, of reducing the "noise" of randomness, of gaining access to a zone of transparency of meaning. The operation of (re)reading would thus be symmetrical to the operation of writing as conceived by Borges in the case of his "third writer," the intellectual (who sees his or her task as limiting "the incalculable concurrence" of chance). In the light of such considerations, is there any relationship between the z in the names Zunino, Zungri, Zunni (which also share the initial group of three letters, *zun*) and the *a* of the Aleph?

(Re)reading for the secret or, in Borges's sense, (re)reading Kabbalistically (against chance), will generate a host of other questions which a first, linear, trusting reading can at best entertain only fleetingly. Foremost among them in "The Aleph" are the questions raised by the punctiliously precise dates of which the text of the story is full. (Such dates are one of the most prominent features of journalistic style which, as Borges puts it in "A Vindication of the Kabbalah," reports that "yesterday's irregular assault took place on such-and-such a street, on such-and-such a corner, at such-and-such an hour of the morning.") Does the date of Beatriz Viterbo's death (on an indeterminate "burning February morning" in 1929) have a

. . .

hidden significance? Does her birthday mean anything?[14] What could be the significance of the day of Sunday, April 30, 1941, the day when Daneri first speaks about his poem and reads from it? What shall we make of the fact that exactly "two Sundays later" (that is, on May 14) Daneri calls up "Borges" and invites him for cocktails at the saloon-bar that the "forward-looking Zunino and Zungri" have just opened next door? Is there anything special about the fact that "Borges" sees the Aleph on an evening toward the end of October 1941? How is one to account for the fastidiously precise dating of the postscript, March 1, 1943? What is one to make of the fact that the narrator's anniversary visits occur exactly thirteen times (over a period of twelve years)? Are there other numerological implications hidden in the dates, the names, or elsewhere in the text? Or could all of these dates and numbers be totally meaningless? The last hypothesis is theoretically hard to accept in regard to a text that is extremely carefully written in the "third" Borgesian style, the one that tries to limit the role of chance. On the other hand, it is no less hard to find out with any degree of certainty what such dates or numbers might mean. Could they have a purely private significance?[15] Might most of them have been used as screens or false clues to mislead the reader as to the veritable hidden significance of one or two? Or could they conceal a more objective symbolic meaning? In the latter case, their symbolism would probably be tied to the dates of certain important holidays (might not the birthday of Beatriz, April 30, be connected in some fashion, seriously or ironically, with the Christian or Jewish sacred calendar, and more specifically with such celebrations as Easter or Passover?). Or might their hidden symbolism be linked, as I suggested earlier, to certain historical dates? It is not important here to find answers to these questions—I am not trying to propose a full-fledged interpretation of "The Aleph" or to offer a commentary, but simply to show what kinds of questions could arise in the mind of a (Kabbalistic) rereader and what kinds of details would call attention to themselves as one keeps returning to a mysteriously haunting text. A similar set of questions could be asked regarding the connotations and possible symbolism of the toponyms used in the story (the parts of Buenos Aires, starting with Garay Street, that are mentioned by name, the significance of the north/south opposition, and so on). Sometimes such questions lead to a specific interpretation or interpretive suggestion.[16]

(Re)reading and interpretation (in the active sense of *interpreting*, making interpretive guesses and decisions)[17] are mental operations so closely related that they often appear to be indistinguishable. No wonder

. . .

then that in many usual, informal contexts, reading and interpretation function as interchangeable synonyms: when I speak of "my reading" of this or that key passage in a book or even, more broadly, situation, what I mean is the same thing as "my interpretation." By extension, rereading has come to signify reinterpretation in the sense of a new or newly revised interpretation: various book series or titles of individual critical studies, such as "rereading nineteenth-century fiction" or "rereading author X or work Y" convey this meaning. But there are circumstances in which (re)reading and interpretation may be usefully distinguished. One possible difference between the two might be formulated as a difference between process and result. To repeat: it is true that reading and rereading are activities that always take place within a larger hermeneutic horizon and that they involve myriad minor and major interpretive guesses, decisions, and revisions; but interpretation presupposes not only a completed reading and many rereadings of the work but also an attempt to answer in a new, original manner at least some of the major questions raised by the text, questions that readers or rereaders can afford to leave unanswered without diminishing the *pleasure* they derive from going through the text. In other words, to interpret in this sense involves being aware of other interpretations and of conflict among them and trying to offer a better interpretation—one that is tighter, better argued, and resolves or transcends old conflicts by offering new frames of meaning-making.

My focus throughout this study is on reading and rereading as processes, as time-bound activities, as explorations, as visitings and (perhaps nostalgic) revisitings of texts, as walks through textual places, pleasure trips, rambles, or pilgrimages. From the point of view adopted here interpretations—and unavoidably there have been many of them in my (re)reading of Borges and many more are to come in my more or less extensive (re)readings of other authors from Cervantes to Henry James, Proust, or Nabokov—should be seen as means toward an end: the end being the continuation of reading and its expansion into rereading (and, as we shall see, into writing and rewriting). Here I do not read or reread in order to interpret; I interpret (among many other things) in order to read and reread and understand (re)reading.

. . .

Temporal Flow or Spatial Form?

Wait for the dust of reading to settle; for the conflict and the questioning to die down; walk, talk, pull the dead petals of a rose, or fall asleep. Then suddenly without one willing it, . . . the book will return, but differently. It will float to the top of the mind as a whole. And the book as a whole is different from the book received currently in separate phrases. Details now fit themselves into their places. We see the shape from start to finish; it is a barn, a pig-sty, or a cathedral. Now then we can compare book with book as we compare building with building.

VIRGINIA WOOLF

. . . .

Reading (Diachronically), Rereading (Synchronically)

Some modern writers and critics have dealt with the processes of reading and rereading in terms of temporal versus spatial metaphors (these latter being drawn from the perceptual field of the visual arts). At the root of such oppositions is our sense that, while the first reading of a literary work is an unavoidably linear-temporal process, a second reading, even though it takes place in time as well, enables the rereader to apprehend each part of the work within a simultaneous, "spatial" awareness

. . .

of the whole. This in fact is never the case, as we shall see. But even so, spatial metaphors applied to rereading (in contrast to the linear-temporal metaphors applied to reading) are interesting to consider: they help us to bring into focus one of the most puzzling aspects of the temporality of reading and rereading, namely, our intuition that the essential successiveness of the first reading of a literary work can be reversed in a second reading, and that this reversal may result in a spatial consciousness of the work as a "landscape." Or, in other words, a rereader might feel that a work with which he or she is already familiar is available to understanding not only as a past, remembered diachronic unfolding, but also as a present synchronic structure. On closer inspection, however, such spatial metaphors ("landscape," "structure") reveal their ultimate inadequacy. Rereading is less a matter of "space" than a matter of time, albeit a special time, a circular or quasi-mythic time, which remains to be described in more specific terms.

A series of larger theoretical questions confronts us at this point. What exactly is the status of the distinction between reading and rereading? Is there such a thing as a pure first-time reading of a literary work? When can we legitimately speak of rereading? Can the mental operations involved in reading and rereading be separated with any degree of precision? Or are the two terms essentially fuzzy concepts and the distinction between them fluid? And if so, can they be used as "ideal types"—not for the sake of a merely abstract discussion but for specifiable analytical purposes? And then what are these purposes, how are they to be defined, and what can we expect by way of results? These are only some of the questions that I will address and readdress throughout this essay. While it would be premature to try to answer them here, however briefly, a statement about my general strategy in dealing with them is in order. To put it bluntly, the distinction between reading and rereading, which seems empirically and pragmatically so obvious, is theoretically both untenable and unavoidable. My strategy will be to acknowledge its untenability (in a variety of specific cases and in as precise analytic terms as possible) while taking critical advantage of its unavoidability, of the need to reaffirm it in spite of all its aporias, and of the often paradoxical insights into the process of reading that such reaffirmation may produce.

What should be clear is that reading and rereading often go together. Thus, under certain circumstances the first reading of a work can in fact be a *double* reading; that is to say, it can adopt, alongside the prospective logic of reading, a retrospective logic of rereading. Such a double reading

. . .

consists, naturally, of the sequential temporal movement of the reader's mind (attention, memory, hypothetical anticipation, curiosity, involvement) along the horizontal or syntagmatic axis of the work; but it also consists of the reader's attempt to "construct" (note the building, spatial metaphor) the text under perusal, or to perceive it as a "construction" with certain clearly distinguishable structural properties.

This double (first) reading is one in which two radically different kinds of attention and interest are involved (one diachronic, the other synchronic), and in which the "normal" linear reading is already "shadowed" by a sort of tentative rereading. The key element here is the ability of the mind to adopt a perspective characteristic of rereading in the course of the very first reading of a text. This ability is more common than we tend to think. Of course, in the ordinary first reading of most works, including literary works, the "structural" component of attention plays only a marginal role. But this same component becomes quite important when the first reading is done by someone with a deeper engagement, personal or professional. Personally, to take an example, one may have a special attachment to a particular author, and then one will read his or her newest book with the full double attention characteristic of double reading. As an author's latest book is always also a rewriting of earlier ones, an informed reader will be in a position to read and reread at the same time. Professionally (consider the case of a literary critic or student of literature), one may be involved in a certain area of research and thus one will read new works within that area with the sharpened structural attention characteristic of rereading. Paradoxically, such a structural reading of a nonliterary work by a professional (a work, say, of literary scholarship perused by a literary scholar) may be very fast: the specialist will skip all the background information he or she is already familiar with and will try to "see" the central argument of the work and assess its quality. Only significant originality of approach and insight will slow down the reading and result in the reader's absorption in subtle details and nuances. Normally, the (double) first reading of a literary work will be slower than a single linear reading, because in literature little details, which can easily be overlooked or forgotten, may always turn out to play a huge structural role.

This kind of double reading is not without drawbacks, particularly in the case of literature. On occasion, the sharpened attention it demands may spoil the more naive pleasures associated with a first, linear, curious, engrossing reading, which certain fictional texts keep in store for the happy "ordinary" reader. On the positive side, a good background and a

. . .

19

demonstrated aptitude for structural reading will reduce to a minimum the "messiness" of many first readings, especially those of older literary classics, which often require hard mental work before they disclose their "secrets." But the diachronic and synchronic types of attention involved in double reading do not always coexist easily or peaceably: the values of reading may come in conflict with those of rereading. Both the history and the phenomenology of religious-literary reading offer many examples of such conflicts, which we shall consider as we go.

Nabokov's Paradox and Spatial Metaphors

One way of approaching the conflict between literary reading and rereading is to take a closer look at the temporal categories applied to reading-for-the-first-time, in contrast with the spatial-visual metaphors sometimes used, even if not entirely adequately, to describe rereading. The conflict is intriguingly articulated in what I would call Nabokov's paradox: "One cannot *read* a book: one can only reread it."[1] The paradox is an amusing reformulation of the famous quandary of the "hermeneutic circle," namely, that in order to understand a whole one must have a prior understanding of its parts, but in order to understand each part one must have a prior understanding of the whole. Nabokov explains:

> When we read a book for the first time the very process of laboriously moving our eyes from left to right, line after line, page after page, this complicated physical work upon the book, the very process of learning in terms of space and time what the book is about, this stands between us and artistic appreciation. When we look at a painting we do not have to move our eyes in a special way. . . . The element of time does not really enter in a first contact with a painting. In reading a book, we must have time to acquaint ourselves with it. We have no physical organ (as we have the eye in regard to painting) that takes in the whole picture and then can enjoy its details. But at a second, or third, or fourth reading we do, in a sense, behave towards a book as we do towards a painting. (*Lectures on Literature*, p. 3)

To grasp the larger significance of Nabokov's paradox we must recall the distinction, familiar in aesthetics since Lessing's *Laokoon,* between the inescapably successive character of our understanding of poetry (meaning broadly literature), which Lessing ranges among the temporal arts, and our instant apprehension of visual artistic objects such as paintings or sculptures, which belong to the qualitatively different category of spatial

. . .

arts. Nabokov contradicts Lessing's insight: when we reread, he suggests, we transform the temporal relations (established in a first reading) into spatial or quasi-spatial ones.

Nabokov's intuition about a "spatialization" of literary perception in the act of rereading seems to be confirmed by those students of the reading process who pay (usually scant and incidental) attention to the question of rereading. On the whole, even among the so-called reader-response critics, those who *explicitly* address the problematics of rereading are surprisingly few, and still fewer are the practical critics (of whatever persuasion) who operate with the distinction between reading and rereading. But, significantly, those who do tend to elaborate it in terms of temporal/spatial analogies. Thus, Albert J. Guerard, in his *The Triumph of the Novel* (1976), after deploring the critics' failure to realize how important it is to distinguish between reading and rereading ("I find it very strange that so few critics ever make this distinction or, if they do, fail to indicate which reading they are describing"), goes on to speak of reading and rereading in precisely temporal/spatial terms: "Talk of suspense, of exciting plot, of dizzying ambiguity, of the pleasures of incessant surprise refers to a hypothetical first reading. But talk of unity and satisfying relation of the parts to the whole, of subtle reflexive reference, of foreshadowings, refers either to a subsequent reading or implies an exceptionally competent retrospective spatial contemplation of a first reading" (*The Triumph of the Novel*, p. 20).

Guerard further distinguishes among several possibilities of "second readings," but they can easily be reduced to two basic ones, which again can be described in diachronic/synchronic terms: (1) a reexperiencing of the fictional text "serially, continuing to care about the characters, even though we now see them differently. . . . We again move from first page to last with pleasure and even excitement" (p. 21); and (2) an essentially synchronic-spatial view of the text, which enables us to "see the novel as a whole, laid out before us as a complex artifact, a structure." Interestingly, Guerard believes that such a synchronic perspective can have an ultimately distorting effect: "To the degree that this spatial reading sees the novel as inert and fixed it may be regarded as less faithful than the others. For mobility and even continuing indeterminacy would seem to be the essence of great fiction" (p. 21). In fact, however, a purely spatial rereading that would "freeze" the inherently temporal perception of a text is an utter impossibility.

The special affinities between rereading and spatial perception are

• • •

noted in Joseph Frank's influential essay, "Spatial Form in Modern Literature," originally published in 1945. Frank shows how Lessing's classical dichotomy between the arts of successiveness (poetry, music) and the arts of simultaneity (painting, sculpture) has come to be challenged in modern literature by the sophisticated use of "spatial form" in the works of poets like Ezra Pound and T. S. Eliot, or in novels by Gustave Flaubert, Marcel Proust, James Joyce, and Djuna Barnes. In the composition of Joyce's *Ulysses,* Frank observes, a crucial role is played by the use of various techniques of suggesting simultaneity (such as the deliberate fragmentation of narrative structure). And he adds, in a formulation that closely resembles Nabokov's paradox, "This, it should be realized, is the equivalent of saying that Joyce cannot be read—he can only be reread. A knowledge of the whole is essential to the understanding of any part" (*The Widening Gyre,* p. 19). Frank is aware that a spatial apprehension of a work of the length and complexity of *Ulysses*—given the extended time, the intensity of sustained attention, and the quality of memory needed for its achievement—would place an "insuperable burden" on the reader. "But the fact remains," he writes, "that Joyce . . . proceeded on the assumption that a unified spatial apprehension of his work would ultimately be possible" (p. 19).

If Joyce indeed proceeded on this assumption he could do so only by attributing to his reader's memory the angelic capacity of absolute recall. On a human level, such a capacity would appear as a pathological feature or a "monstrosity," as Borges wryly suggested in his essay "A Fragment on Joyce." A person capable of really reading and understanding *Ulysses* in its entirety would be, he insists, a sort of "Funes the Memorious." In other words, the reader postulated by Joyce would closely resemble Borges's fictional creature (and possible ironic self-projection) Ireneo Funes, who "knew the forms of the southern clouds at daybreak on April 30, 1882, and in his memory he could compare them to the seams of a book bound in Spain that he had once handled as a child. He could reconstruct all his dreams, all his daydreams. . . . I have mentioned him because the consecutive undeviating reading of the 400,000 words in *Ulysses* would require analogous monstrosities" (*Borges, A Reader,* p. 135; Borges himself, as he confesses, was never able to read *Ulysses* in its entirety).

Incidentally, if the reader's memory were angelically infallible, the very notion of rereading would be inconceivable and all the typically Joycean joys of intertextual allusion, derived from the constant play of reading and rereading (including the numerous interruptions to consult dictionaries,

· · ·

commentaries, and specialized Joyce glossaries, and even to read or reread fragments of countless works alluded to in the text, starting with *The Odyssey*), would be forever lost. As things stand, though, *Ulysses,* irrespective of whether its form is spatial or not, is one of those books that, as Frank himself is ready to admit, effectively cannot be read, but only reread. It is perhaps the quintessential modern book designed specifically for rereading.

Joseph Frank's ideas about spatial form in literature were the object of renewed critical interest in the late 1970s as a result of the publication in *Critical Inquiry* of Frank's "Spatial Form: An Answer to Critics" (the critics being Frank Kermode, Philip Rahv, Roger Shattuck, Walter Sutton, and Robert Weimann). This was followed, in the same periodical, by Frank's "Spatial Form: Further Reflections," a more broadly theoretical overview of new literary practices (such as the French *nouveau roman*) and new critical approaches (structuralist poetics from Roman Jakobson to Gérard Genette), which appeared to lend support to Frank's concept of spatial form. Referring to Genette's *Figures III,* which develops a model of narrative analysis on the basis of examples largely drawn from Proust, Frank is gratified to find numerous instances of a fully self-conscious use of spatial terminology. (This should not come as a surprise, given structuralism's built-in and well-known *parti pris* for synchronic, spatial relations as opposed to diachronic-historical relations.) Especially relevant is Frank's citation, and enthusiastic endorsement, of the following passage from Genette (which I reproduce in Frank's own translation):

It is not true that reading is only that continual unfolding . . . and the author of *A la recherche du temps perdu* no doubt knew this better than anyone— he who demanded of his reader an attention to what he called the 'telescopic' character of his work, that is, to the relations at long distance established between episodes far removed from each other in the temporal continuity of a linear reading (but, it should be noted, singularly close in the written space, in the paginated thickness of the volume), and which requires for its consideration a sort of simultaneous perception of the total unity of the work, a unity which resides not solely in the horizontal relations of continuity and succession, but also in the relations that may be called vertical or transversal, those effects of expectation, of response, of symmetry, of perspective, which prompted Proust himself to compare his work to a cathedral. To read as it is necessary to read such works . . . is really to reread; it is already to have reread, to have traversed the book tirelessly in all directions, in all its dimensions. (p. 290)

. . .

As important as the connection between the perception of literary "space" and the necessity of rereading is Genette's reminder that Proust used to compare his monumental novel to a cathedral.[2]

Proust, the Cathedral and the Book

This famous Proustian simile is worth considering more closely for a moment. Its obvious architectural meaning (with all its connotations of majestic but carefully organized space, harmonization of remote details within a unified structure, and so on) is by no means more important than the simile's indirect and subtly temporal intent, achieved through its reference to the world of reading. For in claiming that *A la recherche du temps perdu* was designed as a cathedral, Proust certainly had in mind the close symbolic affinities between a cathedral and the Book (the Bible) as a powerful paradigm of reading. More specifically, he could not have failed to think of the biblical sense of the word "cathedral" indicated by both the title and the central topic of John Ruskin's *The Bible of Amiens* (that is, the thirteenth-century Gothic masterpiece which is the cathedral of Amiens). Proust, a longtime reader and admirer of Ruskin, had translated *The Bible of Amiens* in 1904 and had written in the preface to the volume (consisting mainly of two articles on Ruskin published a few years earlier): "what Ruskin refers to in particular as the Bible of Amiens [is] the West Porch. 'Bible' is taken here in the literal and not in the figurative sense. This porch of Amiens is not merely a stone book, in the vague sense in which Victor Hugo would have understood it: it is 'the Bible' in stone. . . . [A] cathedral is not only a beauty to be felt. Even if it is no longer for you a teaching to be followed, it is at least still a book to be understood" (*On Reading Ruskin*, pp. 19–20).

Even though he insists on the "literal" sense of his use of "Bible," Proust's preface is highly metaphorical and freely draws on the elements of two symbolic-associative series: the first derived from the notion that a cathedral is another way of *writing* the same Book, the second from the notion that the Bible is a sacred (and thus exemplary) text. A good illustration of the first metaphorical series (the cathedral as writing) is the following sentence: "Here ends the teaching that men of the thirteenth century came to seek at the cathedral, a teaching which . . . it continues to offer in a kind of open book, written in a solemn language where each letter is a work of art, a language no longer understood" (p. 27). As for the second series (the cathedral as a locus of the sacred), it is exemplified by Proust's

. . .

extraordinary treatment of Ruskin's own text, and indeed of his whole oeuvre, as a new Bible or exemplary frame of reference, related to both the real Bible and the Bible (the cathedral) of Amiens: "It was the soul of Ruskin I went to seek there, which he imparted to the stones of Amiens as deeply as their sculptors had imparted theirs. . . . I went to Amiens . . . with the desire to read the Bible of Ruskin there. For Ruskin, having believed in those men of another time because in them was faith and beauty, also happened to write his Bible as they had written theirs" (p. 28).

Proust's phrase "the Bible of Ruskin" conveys, beyond its two obvious references (Ruskin's own text and the cathedral which is the subject of this text), a third and more important meaning. "The Bible of Ruskin" suggests a model of reading and indeed rereading (the Bible being the archetypal book for rereading in the Western world, as we shall see in more detail in chapter 6). The model is one of reading the way Ruskin does, whether one reads words or stones, with one's eyes and mind or with one's action: Proust's own pilgrimage to Amiens, as described in the preface, was itself a form of rereading Ruskin.

The ultimate purpose of such reading is self-reading as a way to self-knowledge. This latter implication becomes clearer if we consider Proust's belief, reinforced by his contact with Ruskin, in reading as self-scrutiny, a belief he articulated many times in his great cathedral-novel, *A la recherche du temps perdu*. In the last part, *The Past Recaptured*, he writes, "In reality, every reader is, while he is reading, the reader of his own self. The writer's work is merely a kind of optical instrument which he offers to the reader to enable him to discern what, without this book, he would perhaps have never perceived himself" (*The Past Recaptured*, pp. 163–64; *A la recherche du temps perdu*, vol. 3, p. 911).

We are now in a better position to see that the Proustian comparison of *A la recherche* with a cathedral refers both to the explicit architectural-spatial aspect stressed by Genette (and endorsed by Frank) and to the spiritual-temporal dimension of any worthwhile act of reading, as concretized in the double image of the cathedral-as-Book and the Book-as-cathedral.[3] Finally, the cathedral metaphor relates to the idea of time in an additional and less expected sense. The builder of a grandiose work (be it a cathedral or a great book) may well not be granted sufficient time to finish the job: "How many great cathedrals remain unfinished!" exclaims Proust, thinking obviously of his own novel, which was indeed to remain unfinished. But under such circumstances unfinishedness is something to be proud of.[4]

. . .

Reading: A Timeless Sequence?

It should not come as a surprise that students of the visual arts support the intuition that our mind needs to achieve some sort of spatial simultaneity or "synopsis" in order to fully apprehend sequentially given objects of understanding. Rudolf Arnheim, the psychologist of visual perception in art, writes, "In order to comprehend an event as a whole, one must view it in simultaneity, and that means spatially and visually. . . . The curious paradox [is] that a piece of music, a drama, a novel, or dance must be perceived as some kind of visual image if it is to be perceived as a structural whole (*New Essays in the Psychology of Art,* pp. 79–80). Arnheim goes so far as to maintain the essential "timelessness" of many events, including reading, based on the sharp distinction he draws between "sequence" and "temporality": "By no means all sequences are temporal. The sequence of the letters of the alphabet does not involve time, nor does the sequence of numbers. . . . What counts is the order of things, regardless of whether the sequence dwells in simultaneity or occurs in succession" (p. 85). Arnheim's example of a sequence without time— on the level of the understanding consciousness—is the "spatial character of memory" (*Art and Visual Perception,* p. 307).

Arnheim's apparently paradoxical position (stressing the ultimate timelessness of certain temporal unfoldings) is based on a restrictive definition of time, derived from a model of *waiting* or *acting toward a goal.* A typical temporal situation, according to this definition, is that of a person waiting for something to happen (for instance, for the water in the kettle to boil, which will always confirm the proverbial truth that "a watched kettle never boils") or that of a person moving toward a goal, for instance running to catch a train. When there is no waiting, with its inherent frustration and impatience, time simply vanishes. Thus, Arnheim writes, echoing Bergson, when we look at the clock after an exciting conversation with a friend, "we are surprised that several hours have passed. A day of inspired work or an evening of concentrated reading produces the same effect" (*Art and Visual Perception,* p. 306). In this logic, literary reading would be a (consciously) temporal activity only in the case of reading a suspenseful narrative—a narrative, that is, which stimulates the reader's impatient curiosity about the outcome of certain actions or about whether his or her inferences and guesses in regard to the solution of certain enigmas are correct.[5]

But Arnheim's concept of time as a function of impatience is of limited

. . .

use when we want to deal with the more subtle kinds of temporality involved in reading and rereading or, for that matter, in the experiencing of music, theatrical events, or dance. Phenomenologically, the temporality of reading and of rereading is so pervasive, and indeed so clearly constitutive of its object (particularly when this object is aesthetic: a poem of some length or a novel or a drama, offering themselves to us as modes of using time), that "timeless" spatial concepts as models of understanding the processes of reading or rereading are ultimately untenable.

Spatial approaches to (re)reading, beyond the special sense in which alphabetical writing and reading have to do with space (a text being a form of artificial memory, or storehouse of information, created by the reduction of speech sounds to space, that is, to the two-dimensional letters inscribed on the surface of the page), do have heuristic value and call attention to important aspects of literary understanding, such as those regarding the compositional structure or the architectonics of a work. But time remains of the essence in the very act of apprehending a literary text of any length and complexity (both reading and rereading take time, and this fact never totally escapes consciousness). Even the clearly spatial concept of the architectonics of a work (for instance Proust's cathedral-novel) does not exclude time as a dimension of understanding: architectural works themselves reveal their "value" (aesthetic, spiritual) only in time, after many revisitings and "rediscoveries" in different moods and from different perspectives. And if rereading is indeed more "spatial" than first-time reading, it can also be, when it is a labor of love and of deeper commitment (not unlike Proust's "Ruskinian pilgrimages") an even more emphatically temporal activity than reading: a way of giving a spiritual dimension to time.

To posit, as Arnheim does, that the concept of a sequence outside time, as exemplified by the ideal sequence of natural numbers in arithmetic, applies to such arts as music and literature is to make a plain phenomenological impossibility into a requirement of understanding. Even in purely theoretical terms such a position is untenable, as Roman Ingarden convincingly argued as far back as the 1930s, when he wrote his seminal phenomenological studies of the literary work of art and its cognition. Thus, in *The Cognition of the Literary Work of Art* (1937), after emphasizing the inescapable "temporality of the literary aesthetic object" and insisting that under no circumstances can this object "be constituted all at once," and that, once constituted, it inexorably "passes away . . . and afterwards is accessible only to memory," he wrote in regard to the notion of an ideally simultaneous (or timeless) sequentiality:

. . .

27

The claim might be advanced that the aesthetic concretization of a literary work of art is intentionally determined by the work all at once, since all parts of the work exist once they are recorded in writing. This view is untenable, however, because no aesthetic concretization of a literary work of art is intentionally determined by the work alone but requires a codetermination by the reader in order to be supplemented by those determinations which correspond to the places of indeterminacy and the potential elements of the work. And then the constitution of the literary aesthetic object can be accomplished only in a temporally extended process. (p. 387)

This passage contains some of the key concepts of Ingarden's phenomenology of literature, which has exerted a profound influence (particularly through the work of Wolfgang Iser) on modern theories of aesthetic reception. The definition of the literary work and of its existential mode as a "purely intentional object" (or, to translate this technical expression: as a fictional object created in an act of consciousness) had been established in Ingarden's earlier book, *The Literary Work of Art* (1931), in which, as the subtitle indicates, he had involved himself, along the lines of Husserl's phenomenology, in "an investigation on the borderlines of ontology, logic, and the theory of literature."

Time, Concretization, Structure

As a purely intentional object, the literary work of art differs radically from both real and ideal objects in that it lacks "ontic autonomy." As Ingarden puts it, the literary work of art is "ontically heteronomous," which is to say that it cannot exist independently from a creative projection of intentional thought (by an "author") and, then, from an act of "concretization" by a reader. No two concretizations of the same work, even by the same reader, can ever be identical, primarily because of the temporal-historical dimension in which all reading occurs. Seen from this point of view, each act of reading is "absolutely individual" (*Cognition*, p. 402) and as such is incommunicable. Hence, in order to make a reading experience communicable, the necessity to reread and thus try to limit the individualizing effect of (personal) time and history:

> If we want to transmit to others the content of the aesthetic object we have constituted, we must try to grasp it without regard to the temporal *quale*. This is possible insofar as we ourselves can compare several aesthetic concretizations of the same literary work which we have constituted at different times and find what is constant in them, what remains, despite the varying

. . .

temporal *quale*. Of course, what we obtain in this way is no longer so strictly individual. It is the common aspect of several concretizations, provided that we succeed in constituting them all in the same way—which is, of course, not easy. The comparison usually takes place with the essential help of acts of memory, which, of course, involve various dangers of deception and error. (p. 403)

Such difficulties and dangers are not insuperable, however. Literary cognition is possible, Ingarden argues, because the literary work of art itself is stable in its "schematic structure." Of course the text—if taken to mean the words on the page, the graphic marks on the paper surface—is stable, but Ingarden means much more than that. Seemingly unaware of the contradiction, he speaks almost in the same breath of the "absolute individuality" of each concretization and of something that is "absolutely identical" in two temporally distinct readings of the same work, namely, its schematic structure (*Cognition,* p. 402). But how can one be sure that this identity is, as Ingarden so emphatically states, absolute? Is the schematic structure—the apprehended structure of "gaps" to be "filled-in" by the reader—something that can be ascertained with complete and incontrovertible objectivity?[6] How can such objectivity be achieved? Why would the schematic structure, which is accessible only through reading— that is, only through an inherently temporal and successive process—be free from the individual variations, from the unpredictable turns, felicities and vicissitudes, of any reading?[7]

Such unanswered questions point to an unresolved conflict that underlies Ingarden's phenomenology of reading, a conflict that brings us back to the main question dealt with in this chapter, namely, the uses of temporal and spatial models of understanding in accounting for reading and rereading. The suggestion that the literary work is, as a work of art, essentially an immobile and recoverable "schematic structure" appears to be just another static, spatial metaphor, perhaps less easily recognizable than those previously examined because it is more abstract. The theoretical implications of this spatial metaphor (the work as "structure" or "skeleton" should be apprehended with perfect accuracy) are incompatible with Ingarden's own predominantly temporal approach to reading (for which see in particular the chapter "Temporal Perspective in the Concretization of the Literary Work of Art," in *Cognition,* pp. 94–146), so rich in insights and intuitions.

As to the general status of the spatial metaphors that are often used to describe what happens in the rereading of a literary work as distinct from

. . .

its original reading, I think it could be profitably approached from a different angle, an angle from which such spatial metaphors appear to be approximations of an underlying conflict between two extreme positions in modern literary hermeneutics: one strongly privileges the first reading of a text (to the point that it gives it an exemplary and theoretically normative status); the other privileges rereading.

. . .

THREE

First-time Reading
as Norm

Literary Readability and Its Aesthetic Significance

The notion of literary readability rests on a paradox. To sustain the interest of a reader, a text of some length must be at once accessible and difficult or, in terms of the Russian Formalists' theory of "defamiliarization," familiar and unfamiliar. This paradox is well known to students of narrative. As Shlomith Rimmon-Kenan observes:

> There is one end every text must achieve: it must make certain that it will be read. . . . The text is caught here in a double bind. On the one hand, in order to be read it must make itself understood, it must enhance intelligibility by anchoring itself in codes, frames, *Gestalten* familiar to the reader. But if the text is understood too quickly, it would thereby come to an untimely end. So, on the other hand, it is in the text's interest to slow down the process of comprehension by the reader so as to ensure its own survival. To this end, it will introduce unfamiliar elements, it will multiply difficulties of one kind or another . . . or simply delay the presentation of expected, interesting items. (*Narrative Fiction*, pp. 122–23)

We might add that the delay of interesting items must be achieved skillfully, seductively, by the introduction of independently or intrinsically interesting information. It is in this area that truly great writers particularly excel: they are capable of working miracles of detail, of riveting

· · ·

the attention of the reader to vivid little side-scenes, to digressions containing arresting insights, to suggestive language effects, so much so that the reader temporarily forgets the larger expectations created by the text, the eager anticipations, the curiosity to find out what happens next. Otherwise, the reader will remorselessly skip whole passages and get to the end in no time. A text must insure that it is read in its *entirety*: the various delaying devices must be compatible with this overall goal.

Looking at the matter from the point of view of the polarity between reading and rereading, it is obvious that certain types of difficulties or delays can enhance the first reading (as in the case of a detective story of the puzzle type or in that of a fantastic story),[1] often to the detriment of the text's rereadability. At the other extreme, there are calculated, strategic textual obstacles (leaving aside unpredictable difficulties arising from historical-cultural gaps in the individual reader's background) that are designed to make the first reading harder and "messier" while mysteriously persuading the reader that a second reading of the work would be much more revealing and rewarding than the first. Sometimes, the mere credibility of such a promised reward the second time around offers one a sufficient incentive to go through an otherwise difficult text: the actual rereading may be postponed indefinitely.

Among the problems raised by the complex temporality of reading, one of the most intriguing, from the point of view of a theory of *re*reading, is the aesthetic significance of the first reading of a literary work in relation to its second, third, or nth reading. The still-prevailing aesthetic consensus, based on the core of reading habits formed in school in contact with the classics of literature, tends to grant primacy to a first linear, ideally uninterrupted reading of a rereadable text (the assumed definition of a classic being that it is at once highly readable and indefinitely rereadable). This ideal type of literary reading (which could be seen as the generalization of nineteenth-century enlightened educational standards derived from the reading of great "realistic" fiction from Dickens and Balzac to Flaubert, Tolstoy, and Dostoevsky) has been internalized by most of us to the point that it underlies some of our most elementary, usually unexamined, expectations in matters of literary reading and readability, including rereading and rereadability.

What are these expectations? First, we take it for granted that a literary text should make sense or be coherent (both semantically and formally) when properly read for the first time. We also assume that the text should convey, however indirectly, some kind of message, or at least stimulate the

· · ·

reader to reflect on some deeper themes (such as life, death, love, friendship, justice, art, society, and so on). A literary text, we believe, should possess a degree of transparency from the very beginning and become even more transparent in the process of its reading.

Another significant expectation is that the text offer internal means for solving the difficulties and problems with which it confronts the reader. Thus the meaning of rare words should be graspable from the contexts of their occurrence (we resent having to use a dictionary too often), enigmas should be worked out and queries answered (neither too early nor too late, of course, for otherwise the reading would become either uninteresting or frustratingly slow-going), and loose ends should be tied up or, at the least, the text should contain suggestions as to how they might be tied up. The reader may occasionally enjoy tying up the loose narrative ends in imagination, if the work suggests a range of possibilities from which to choose; and if the text satisfies all the other expectations of coherency, transparency, self-sufficiency, and so forth with skill and charm, it may itself offer fully written-out alternative or even mutually exclusive endings, as John Fowles's best-selling *The French Lieutenant's Woman* demonstrates. What the reader normally wants is not closure as such but only the imaginative possibility of closure.

Finally, we expect that once our mind has managed to tune itself to the text's tone, style, ways of handling imagery, and other particularities, the reading may proceed at a certain more or less constant speed. This expectation is supported by our broader experience of reading as a self-adjusting process: any new text, in fact, requires a slower, more laborious reading at the beginning; but once we grasp its inner logic (or, in the case of a novel, once we have entered its fictional world), we take it almost for granted that our reading can achieve a cruising speed and that the initial slowness, resulting from an effort of orientation in the new world of the book, will lead to some kind of sustained involvement.

All these expectations presuppose that the literary work itself be constructed in such a way as to be aesthetically apprehensible on a first reading, even when its high aesthetic value fully justifies its rereading (or reflective reexperiencing) many times over. Roman Ingarden's position on this question is worth considering more closely. It represents one of the most sophisticated articulations of the paradigm of what we might call "classical" readability, which is a product of an advanced literate culture whose main patterns of reading were established, as suggested above, in the nineteenth century. The ideal reader Ingarden postulates in *The Liter-*

. . .

ary Work of Art and subsequently in *The Cognition of the Literary Work of Art* (which deals more directly with questions of reading) is a reader who experiences a work aesthetically on the first reading. We must assume that the work is canonic or classical since Ingarden's examples do not include disruptive modernist or avant-garde works nor—and this goes almost without saying—works of no aesthetic merit. In his view, a critical rereading can deepen the perception achieved on first reading, correct mistakes made the first time around, and lead to new analytical-reflective insights, but cannot add anything aesthetically fundamental to the first reading. Ingarden's approach closely approximates the "natural" ideology of reading characteristic of a secular (time-conscious, progressive, enlightened) culture in which the essential linearity of writing/reading has been fully internalized by a large reading public.

Roman Ingarden and the "Classical" Paradigm of Reading

The "classical" paradigm looks "natural," even though it is historically circumscribed (it did not exist before the eighteenth century and it became widespread in the nineteenth) and is quite relative. A highly literate earlier culture, dominated by religious modes of thought (those of the Reformation, and more specifically Calvinism, with its emphasis on the individual reading of the Bible for purposes of saving one's soul) was no less "naturally" in favor of rereading and the rereadable, and often sternly censored and dismissed the merely readable. Arguably, such a culture had little if any use for an aesthetics of first reading. Even in a predominantly secular and pluralistic culture like ours, with its broad toleration of all sorts of beliefs and practices including religious and quasi-religious ones, what appears to be intuitively and generically "normal" is, on closer analysis, only a very rough and often misleading approximation.

There are circumstances, institutional (for example, the university and the teaching profession) or personal (such as a serious commitment to an ideology or to a style of writing or to a particular group of writers), in which rereading offers a better model of understanding the ideal literary work than does its first reading. Also, in a dynamic cultural situation, with diverse trends and countertrends and audiences, certain movements (one immediately thinks of modernism) can promote rereading as a polemical weapon against, or as an antidote to, what is thought to be a purely consumptive and essentially passive first-and-only reading—reading just to "kill time." Of course, this latter kind of reading-to-kill-time, the *bête*

· · ·

noire of avant-garde movements which formulate their creative strategies in total opposition to what they perceive as sheer kitsch, has nothing to do with the "classical" theory I am now focusing on, in which the first reading of a work is given, above and beyond its self-evident chronological priority, an aesthetically normative status.[2] Ingarden is fully aware of the many possible shortcomings of a first reading and of the important corrections a second reading might bring to it, but, he posits, "the first reading has the advantage over all following readings that it decides in large measure whether one will succeed in a correct apprehension of the work at all. The first reading is particularly important for literary works of art, which are perceived in an aesthetic attitude and which make possible the constitution of the aesthetic object" (p. 145). Similar formulations are repeated throughout *The Cognition of the Literary Work of Art* and developed into an elaborate dichotomy between a first, "ordinary" reading (a reading "which is to provide guidelines for the later cognition of the work by means of analytical consideration," p. 287) and a second, "analytical," "reflective," or "investigative" reading, which should strive to correct the errors or distortions that may have occurred in the first reading. But for Ingarden the first reading remains decisive even though its results are in no way binding; and the second reading will always be "secondary" in an aesthetic sense, even though it can produce an improved, richer, and deeper understanding of the work.

Ingarden's bias in favor of the first reading pervades his use of the dichotomy between reading and rereading. This bias is apparent in the very choice of the basic "simplifying conditions" or methodological assumptions which underlie his theory of reading: all are premised on the notion of a first ideal, unimpeded, transparent, continuous, and uniform reading, in keeping with the "classical" paradigm as outlined above.

What are these assumptions? Here is a list (based on *The Cognition of the Literary Work of Art,* pp. 15–16): (1) the reader is presented with a work that is complete or in a definitive state; (2) the work is written in the native language of the reader (translations are therefore excluded); (3) the language of the work is contemporary with the reading and is thoroughly mastered by the reader (in other words, the work is both linguistically and, by implication, culturally transparent to the reader); (4) the reading of the work is "solitary" (that is, "without consultation with other readers and hearers" and generally free of any external influence, including any knowledge by the reader of existing interpretations or critical opinions about the text); (5) the reading is linear, irreversible, and *uninterrupted;*

· · ·

35

this last condition is essential, as Ingarden insists: "Lengthy interruptions in reading, the repetition of certain parts of the work during reading, referring back to parts which have already been read and have sunk into the phenomenal past—all this disfigures the aesthetic concretization of the literary work of art and its aesthetic value" (p. 165); (6) the work is short enough to be read in its entirety in a single act of reading from beginning to end;[3] and (7) the speed of reading is uniform. What is remarkable about Ingarden's first-reading ideal type is its profound, inescapable, but also perfectly happy temporality. Essential for understanding his position properly is his concept of irreversibility, an irreversibility which is both a necessity and a norm (remember his strictures against "referring back") and whose sense persists even when an unusually vivid act of recollection seems to have suppressed any "temporal distance" between the present and the past. Ingarden notes that in the temporal perspective of ineluctable but completely felicitous irreversibility, and irrespective of subjective variations in the experience of temporal distance

> there is the independent phenomenon of the constant sinking into the past which is bound up with the duration of the psychological subject in time. Even when we bring a past event closer to us in memory . . . diminishing its temporal distance, we still have the peripheral awareness that it is constantly and inevitably sinking deeper and deeper into the past. . . . As a necessary consequence of the accumulation of constantly new actualized present moments, this phenomenon of "sinking into the past" is inevitable and irreversible and has thus absolutely no correlate in spatial perspective. . . . If it were possible to relive our life without losing our memory of our first life, then that would be a second, later life, in relation to which the first would sink further and further into the past. (pp. 117–18)

Within this framework, a spatial artistic form, such as a painting which we can see as a whole in a single glance, and a literary (or musical) work, which we can apprehend only in time, are separated by a truly unbridgeable gap. Ingarden stresses:

> After the reading is concluded, the work ceases altogether to be actual. It can be revived only in active memory or in acts of recollection but, even then, only in condensed form or by running through its successive parts in recollection. Otherwise, it can be apprehended only in a single temporal perspective, namely, in the one we have at the end of the work; this is a temporal perspective which is perhaps very important or even the most important for the cognition of the work, but it gives us the work only in a considerably foreshortened form. In order to accomplish a cognition of the

. . .

literary aesthetic object, the cognizing subject . . . would have to lean for support on the results of a vivid and maximally adequate memory. . . . But, as a result, new dangers threaten, of deception or error in remembering, and, in addition, new secondary temporal perspectives begin to intervene as the cognizing subject becomes distant from the phase of aesthetic experience. (pp. 302–3)

One may ask why the first reading of a work—ideally under the conditions spelled out above—would enjoy the aesthetically exemplary status that Ingarden grants it. The only instance I recall in which he deals directly with this question occurs in the concluding chapter of *The Cognition of the Literary Work of Art*. To the crucial question of what precisely makes the first reading so preeminent that one should not "base the cognition of a literary aesthetic object on a new aesthetic experience in a new reading," his answer is little more than a hint that the first reading has the advantage of newness, of providing fresh experience, as opposed to a second reading which, being a repetition, could not completely avoid a sense of *déjà vu* (or, we might say, *déjà lu*), or a certain dullness or staleness. In Ingarden's own words, "it is always questionable whether and to what extent the reader succeeds in achieving a new, fruitful aesthetic experience of a literary work of art with which he is already familiar" (p. 399). Without elaborating, he concludes the paragraph with the puzzling statement that "this possibility should be left uninvestigated" (ibid.).

We are left to speculate that Ingarden privileges the first reading of a literary work—the reading which, according to him, constitutes the work as an aesthetic object—in the name of a freshness of impression, of a feeling of surprise or wonderment generated by the original contact with a literary work of art. It is a pity that he does not explore this area further. For it is, after all, in terms of newness that we can best assert the significance of the first reading of a work and that we can construct the ideal type, or the operational fiction, of a pure and purely constitutive aesthetic first reading. (But does not a sense of newness, of a perhaps more unsuspected and paradoxical newness, also appear in the act of rereading truly great texts? And is not this second newness, this surprise in recognition, this revelation of difference in sameness, the finest reward of rereading?) It matters little whether the newness of the first contact is equated with "defamiliarization" (to use the concept of the Russian Formalists), or whether it is analyzed in terms of expectations that are skillfully manipulated, "disoriented" and subtly "reoriented" in the process of reading (as Ingarden's main continuator, Wolfgang Iser, does in his insightful discussion of the

· · ·

"wandering viewpoint" in reading). What remains certain is that if reading is conceived within a purely linear and irreversible temporal perspective, as Ingarden does (with the major exception of his self-contradictory belief that the schematic structure of a work can be objectively perceived and must therefore be exempt from the effects of temporality), then chronological priority becomes the key element of a normative frame within which a second reading is bound to become secondary, even in a pejorative sense.

Although the temporality of reading is intuitively obvious to all of us *when we think of it,* the fact is that we do not think of it very often, because reading is such a highly automatized and therefore unself-conscious activity. It is still surprising that most critics and literary theorists have traditionally ignored the temporal dimension of reading, all the more so as it is an important consideration in the writer's composition of the text and construction of the text's intended reader. Things have changed only in recent decades, with the emergence of reader-oriented criticism. Before it, the major twentieth-century schools of criticism—from Russian Formalism through the Anglo-American New Criticism to French structuralism—paid little attention to the reader or to the process (as opposed to the interpretive results) of reading. There were of course important exceptions, among which Ingarden's phenomenology of reading or, in the United States, the rhetorical criticism of a Kenneth Burke were outstanding. But, since I have been speaking of Ingarden at some length, we might note that precisely his analysis of reading was overlooked even by those New Critics who were directly influenced by him—such as René Wellek, who developed Ingarden's ideas about the work of art as a "schematic structure" but largely ignored his views on the reading process.

The New Critics, as Steven Mailloux observes in his *Interpretive Conventions,* "tried *to produce readings* rather than describe reading, and the readings it produced focused on the text's 'total structure,' its 'set of organic relationships'" (p. 67). (Such "holistic," atemporal readings resulted, in terms of my opposition between reading and rereading, from an optical illusion characteristic of unself-conscious rereading, which is what the New Critics' "close reading" actually is.) The adoption of a temporal reading model by some reader-response critics—the best known of whom is Stanley Fish—was an important contribution to understanding an essential aspect of reading.[4] This model has, in my opinion, one major limitation: it is exclusively a first-time reading model and thus ignores rereading and the actual interpenetration of the first reading and rereading, or reading with a foreknowledge of what is to come (Fish's reading of

. . .

Paradise Lost has been criticized for its artificial linearity). This model nevertheless constitutes a significant step forward with regard to the concept of reading implied in older forms of holistic criticism. What the notion of (re)reading can add to it—although this can create new tensions and paradoxes—is the model of a metaphorically circular time and a consciousness that (re)reading can be described, and indeed must be described, in both linear and circular terms. At any rate, the temporal model of reading developed within reader-response criticism has its place within what I have called the "classical" paradigm of reading, whose first phenomenological description was given to us by Ingarden. This brings us back to the question of the secondariness of rereading, considered from this paradigm.

Critiques of the "Classical" Paradigm

One way of rejecting the notion of the secondariness of rereading could invoke the spatial argument. As I pointed out in the previous chapter, the attempts to give a spatial dimension to reading, specifically to the second reading of a work, may be seen as a reaction against an exclusively linear-temporal model of reading, that is, against a model in which a text as a whole can never hope to be fully copresent with its parts in a reader's mind. Spatial metaphors are metaphors of simultaneity and presence, and thus of transcendence, be it for only a moment, of the constant "sinking into the past" of all that we read and reread and, in a more general way, of all temporal experience. But such metaphors, suggestive as they may be, cannot cast serious doubts on the essential temporality of both reading and rereading.

Another way of questioning the secondariness of rereading without denying its temporal character is to stress its qualitatively different temporality. This approach, for which I have argued directly or indirectly all along, has the advantage of making the distinction between first-time reading and rereading more flexible and phenomenologically more accurate, while preserving its analytical power. What rereading does is to add a circular twist (and sometimes more than a mere twist—an imaginatively new, mysterious, mythical dimension) to an otherwise inescapable linearity. A more sustained and sustainable critique of the linear-irreversible view of reading presented by Ingarden (a view that is acceptable to our common intuition of time and time-bound activities) will thus take a definitely nonspatial course.

. . .

This course can be exemplified by two distinct developments in contemporary criticism. The first is represented by some members of the Konstanz school of "reception aesthetics," as well as by some literary semioticians in the structuralist tradition. This first position on the dichotomy between reading and rereading will be examined in the specific cases of Hans Robert Jauss and Michael Riffaterre. The second is the poststructuralist approach to textual analysis, for which the work of Roland Barthes, a critic who specifically recognizes the temporal circularity of rereading, will serve as example in the next chapter.

By and large, Jauss remains a defender of the first reading, but only in terms of what he calls its "aesthetic priority" and within the broader framework of a triadic theory of "horizons of reading," a theory explicitly grounded in Hans-Georg Gadamer's view of the three constitutive moments of the hermeneutic process. These moments are *intelligere* or what in traditional hermeneutics was called *subtilitas intelligendi* (or understanding, which Jauss equates with the aesthetic comprehension achieved in a first reading of a literary work), *interpretare* or *subtilitas explicandi* (or interpretation, by which Jauss refers to the reconstruction, in a second reading, of the meaning of the sequential parts of a work in light of the whole), and *applicare* or *subtilitas applicandi* (or application, which Jauss conceptualizes as the reader's awareness, in a third critical-historical reading, of the different significations the work has been given throughout the history of its reception, from its first readers to the most recent ones). An example of analytical use of these wide-ranging concepts is Jauss's essay on Baudelaire's poem "Spleen II," which begins by distinguishing "the horizon of a first, aesthetically perceptual reading . . . from that of a second retrospectively interpretive reading . . . to which I will add a third historical reading that begins with the reconstruction of the horizon of expectations in which the poem 'Spleen' inscribed itself with the appearance of the *Fleurs du mal*, and that then will follow the history of its reception or 'readings' up to the most recent one, that is, my own" ("The Poetic Text within the Change of Horizons of Reading," in *Toward an Aesthetic of Reception*, p. 139).

All this looks quite promising. But when he turns to the practical discussion of Baudelaire's poem, Jauss seems to have a hard time applying his neatly established triad. It soon becomes apparent that only two elements of the triad play a major role in his argument, and that these are easily reducible to the dichotomy between the first reading, which concretizes the work within "the progressive horizon of aesthetic perception,"

. . .

and the second, "reflective" reading, with its "retrospective horizon of interpretation" (p. 143). The question then is: what constitutes the "first-ness" or "priority" of this reading? Jauss leaves no doubt that such "sec-ondary" activities as rereading and "historicist understanding" (which presupposes a large amount of reading *about* and *around* the work, about how it was understood by other reader-critics, about the circumstances which surrounded its production, and so on) have a significant bearing on his notion of first reading. We must then conclude that Jauss is using an entirely artificial concept of first reading, one which has not only aban-doned all claims to temporal priority but openly admits its nature as a pure "hermeneutic reconstruction."

In Jauss's actual analysis of Baudelaire's "Spleen II," his three main categories (treated, somewhat misleadingly, in three separate sections of the essay which purport to deal with a first, second, and third reading of the poem) keep overlapping. Thus, what Jauss proposes as a first reading of Baudelaire's poem is in large part a combination of speculative histor-icist reconstructions (and not from one but from two distinct points of view: that of a would-be reader of Baudelaire's own time and that of a "historical reader of the present"). And as we read into Jauss's essay, it becomes difficult to see why a first, "perceptual-aesthetic" reading of Baudelaire's poem should be primarily concerned with a formal-stylistic analysis of sound patterns (rhythms, rhymes, accented and unaccented syllables, long and short vowels), as he suggests. Such a peculiar focus becomes actually possible only after many careful rereadings of the poem, and results from a highly specialized type of critical attention and knowl-edge: why then attribute it to a "first" reading (even when the word "first" is purged of any chronological suggestions)? Do sound patterns have such an obvious aesthetic advantage over imagery, tropes, and other linguistic figures?

Is There Such a Thing as a First Reading?

Ingarden, as we saw, proceeded on the assumption of a pure ("soli-tary," uninfluenced, pristine, and, as it were, virginal) first reading, an assumption which comes so naturally to us that we tend to grant it without examination. But as soon as we look at it more attentively, as Jauss urges us to do, the basic plausibility of Ingarden's model evaporates. The concept of a virginal first reading, so appealing to our naive intuition, cannot withstand critical reflection.

. . .

41

Even before I decide to read a book, I have not only certain expectations, shaped by my generic acquaintance with the kind of book I have selected from a great many available books, but quite probably some more specific assumptions about the chosen book itself. This is obvious in the case of classic works or authors, surrounded as they are by an atmosphere of diffuse cultural knowledge: before one has the opportunity to read, say, *Hamlet* or *King Lear,* one is likely to have heard all sorts of things about Shakespeare and his most famous plays. Fame manifests itself in the form of such foggy, tantalizing, sometimes irritating, almost always misleading hearsay knowledge, which may lead to a good reading experience but also to many a letdown. So when I make up my mind to read a book (not necessarily a classic), I most likely already know something about it: I may have been advised by a friend or a reviewer to read it, or perhaps forbidden to read it by an authority figure or censor; I may have been given reasons why I should, or perhaps should not, read it; or I may have simply heard it mentioned informally as an enjoyable book, or as being original, topical, scandalous, etc. Even the first book of a new author cannot be read totally "innocently." If I buy it or borrow it after having seen a review of it in a newspaper, can I really say that I read it for the first time in Ingarden's strict sense of an uninfluenced reading? Even when I pick a new book by an unknown author on a whim, I am better informed about it than I might suspect. This information (which may well turn out to have been misleading) is derived from where the book in question is sold (at a discount bookstore chain, a small specialty bookseller's, or the airport newsstand); from the books that immediately surround it (current best-sellers, mysteries, fiction, science fiction); from the title; from the book jacket; and quite likely from a general impression gained by quickly glancing through the pages.

Jauss does not address these questions as such, but since he deals with a well-known poem by an illustrious writer, the sheer impossibility of a properly called first reading must have struck him from the outset. When Jauss renders problematic the notion of a chronological first reading (by distinguishing it from what he calls an aesthetic first reading), he seems to refer to the chronology or "history" of individual readers, of their first encounter with specific texts, and to have in mind primarily the category of reader-scholars to which he himself belongs. Thus the question of a first, "virginal" reading is fraught with unresolvable difficulties. What would count for a scholar of French literature like Jauss as his first reading of a poem by Baudelaire? A first-acquaintance reading done in his student

. . .

days and now probably forgotten (unless it was the occasion of some memorable epiphany)? The first rereading done in view of preparing a course or writing an essay—a first rereading that in practice cannot be separated from the numerous rereadings that come after it? An imaginary, purely hypothetical first reading? Jauss avoids these problems by replacing the notion of temporal priority with that of aesthetic priority.

But still, the temporality of reading is such that considerations of firstness in time, however flimsy or slippery the grounds on which they are usually made, cannot be abandoned altogether. No matter how much I may have heard or read about Tolstoy's *War and Peace,* there is a first time when I actually read it, when I discover its world, feel its rhythms, experience its moods, and come under the spell of its almost miraculous details. Furthermore, there is a sense in which great novelistic classics like *War and Peace* seem to urge us to reverse Nabokov's paradox ("One cannot *read* a book; one can only reread it") and to say: One cannot reread *War and Peace;* one can only read it for the first time. With great literature, we may justifiably say, each time is the first time.

Things are of course very different in the case of short poetic texts. A poem like Baudelaire's "Spleen II" can be read and reread many times in a single sitting—and this can be supplemented by the reading, in the same sitting, of selected critical commentaries and interpretations, which are routinely included in good critical editions of the classics of poetry. Poems are thus rereadable not only paradigmatically (texts constructed in view of repeated reading or hearing) but also practically and literally, so much so that in the matter of poetry the distinction between first reading and rereading is hard to sustain in phenomenological terms and almost naturally tends to acquire a purely methodological-analytical character.

The distinction, in this latter sense, may end up giving rise to a veritable imperative of rereading: poetry must be reread! As Michael Riffaterre has convincingly argued, in order to read a poem adequately one has to read it twice: first, by deciphering the "single, linear text" and adopting an attitude in which the text functions as if it were "mimetic" (or, in more ordinary words, as if it were referring, however obscurely or obliquely, to states of affairs in the real world); and, second, by submitting it to a "retroactive" or "hermeneutic" reading in which the previously hidden significance of the poem reveals itself, but only to the reader who successfully "leaps the hurdle of the real" and thus manages to get beyond "mimesis" and reach the higher level of "semiosis."[5]

· · ·

· · · · · · · ·

FOUR

Rereading as Norm

Tensions between Reading and Rereading

The moot question of phenomenological (temporal, chronological) first reading versus rereading can be profitably avoided in the case of short poetic texts—Riffaterre's reading and rereading of poetry are structural-semiotic operations to which the dimension of real time is essentially irrelevant. This ceases to be true of the reading of longer texts, whether poetic or in prose. Even a short novel or novella (for instance Thomas Mann's "Tristan," to stay with one of Ingarden's examples), which can be read uninterruptedly in one sitting of two or three hours, cannot be read and reread the same way a short poem in Riffaterre's model is first *read* (in a linear, "mimetic" deciphering of its text) and then immediately *reread* (in a slower, more reflective, retroactive hermeneutical mode). The time element starts making itself felt in different ways and with wide-ranging consequences. An interruption of some length almost unavoidably occurs between the act of first reading and that of rereading. This means that the memory of the first reading—whose tasks have already been complicated by the much larger quantity of information to be assimilated—will surely be less accurate or sharp than in the case of a short poem, however difficult or hermetic the latter might be. The first reading itself (a relative notion, as we saw in chapter 3, since a "pure" or "virginal" firstness simply does not exist in literary reading) extends over a longer period and thus can be

· · ·

conceived as a straight, continuous, purely sequential "linear decipher-ing" with more difficulty than in the neat methodological assumption of Riffaterre's semiotics of poetry.

An obvious complicating factor is the interplay of anticipations and retrospections. From early on in the first reading of a longer work, one can speak of a "dialectic of protension and retention" (Wolfgang Iser, *The Act of Reading*, p. 112), which normally plays a more limited role in the reading of short poems. In this dialectic the reader's mind, as it moves through the text, adopts a "wandering viewpoint." Along the axis of protension (or anticipation) the reader's expectations are constantly mod-ified in light of what he or she has just read; along the axis of retention (memory), the inscribed images resulting from the first, as yet incomplete, reading are subject to a permanent revision or transformation in light of what is being read, of the new (unexpected) information provided by the text. To make things even more complicated, the first reading does not exclude a "structural" type of attention. On the other hand, rereading does not exclude the "linear" attention and involvement characteristic of the first reading—as in the rereading of a work of fiction for purposes of replaying the game of make-believe it proposes. Also, in a second reading, the "dialectic of protension and retention," far from being abolished, takes on new and more subtle forms. Along the axis of protension, the rereader usually experiences the unexpected in those miraculously fresh details which are part of the texture of great prose. Along the axis of retention, the understanding of the work as a whole is constantly reap-praised also in light of such miraculous details, whose retroactive effects can be breathtakingly profound.

The real problem is not, as I have already suggested in my discussion of Ingarden, to recognize that there is a distinction and indeed a conflict of implied values between the first and second readings of a literary work, but to decide which one offers better, more reliable criteria of apprecia-tion, in other words, which one should be given an aesthetically normative status. But why choose between the two? Why not regard them as comple-mentary phases of a larger process of understanding? Because, I would answer, considerations deriving from the social and cultural history of reading, as well as from the psychology of literary reading, make such a position very tenuous. Perhaps a model of literary reading that integrates or reconciles the values of first reading with those of rereading is not impossible. But before envisaging that possibility, one should try to be-come fully conscious of the hidden tensions between the two seemingly

. . .

continuous activities. These can be better exposed by a close examination of the position in favor of rereading as norm, for which Roland Barthes's work will serve as an example.[1]

Roland Barthes: A Paradigm of Rereading

To begin with, as a radical thinker with an inclination toward some sort of philosophical anarchism, Barthes was particularly intent on contesting the traditional privileges of the One, in which he saw a symbol of authority, and asserting the rights of the Many. From this general standpoint, the outstanding characteristic of his theory of reading is his insistence on multiplicity and plurality, and on the need for what he calls a "plural" reading of a "plural" text, in contrast with Ingarden's general emphasis on the solitary ideal, uninterrupted, first reading in which the aesthetic object is constituted. (The other model of reading which I have presented, Jauss's, is less beholden to the idea of unity and more sensitive to the importance of historical-contextual variations, but it still retains, as we have seen, the notion of an aesthetic, if not temporal, priority of the first reading.)

Barthes's model of rereading is best understood as an almost point-by-point reversal of the "classical" view of a normative first reading as conceptualized by Ingarden. Essential to his approach is the distinction he makes between readable and rereadable texts and thus between readability and rereadability, which are seen as the terms of a polarity. There are, as he argues in the opening pages of S/Z, two kinds of texts, "readerly" (*lisible*) or "classical," on the one hand, and "writerly" (*scriptible*) or avant-garde, on the other. Corresponding to these two kinds of texts are two antithetical types of reading: the first is passive and singular (a onetime affair) and reflects "the commercial and ideological habits of our society, which would have us 'throw away' the story once it has been consumed ('devoured')" (p. 15); the second is active, productive, ultimately playful, and it truly involves the reader in the pleasure of (mentally) writing or rewriting the text. Significantly, this second type of productive reading is nothing but rereading. The single and irreversible reading or the using up of "readerly" texts—texts conceived to be commercially exciting on a first-and-only reading basis—becomes plainly an antimodel.

It might be helpful to relate Barthes's semiology of reading to the historical background from which it emerged as one of the most elegant

· · ·

manifestations of a way of thinking widespread among the French intelligentsia in the 1960s and early 1970s. This way of thinking, and the whole intellectual climate surrounding it, has virtually disappeared from the France of the 1980s and 1990s, but it still seems to stir up intense if belated passions in American academic milieux. It hardly needs saying that Barthes's seminal insights into the process of reading—some of which are used in the present study—cannot be reduced to a historically and sociopolitically circumscribed pattern of thought, such as the one that Luc Ferry and Alain Renaut have labeled *la pensée 68* or "the thought of '68." A summary description of that pattern, however, can serve to explain the recurrence of certain themes and concepts and render explicit the political sensibilities they imply; among the themes and concepts I have in mind are textuality, ideology, structure, "mythology" in the peculiar sense of "petit-bourgeois" mystification or deception, and the Saussurean opposition "signifier/signified" (but with an un-Saussurean bias in favor of the signifier).

Barthes's interest in the phenomenon of reading dates from the latter part of his career, starting in the late 1960s. Earlier, in the 1950s, he had been involved in a quasi-Marxist critique of ideology, whose most interesting results were articulated in *Mythologies* (1957). During the next decade he embarked on the construction of a scientific semiology (part of which would have been a "science of literature"), a project inspired primarily by the linguistic, anthropological, and psychoanalytical versions of structuralism that came to dominate the French intellectual scene of the 1960s. Increasingly aware of the limitations and rigidities of orthodox structuralism, he started to develop a more free-wheeling theory of reading and textuality, first fully presented in the book-length analysis of a short story, "Sarrasine," by Balzac (*S/Z*). This third phase in his intellectual biography has sometimes been characterized as "poststructuralist." Less constrained by the requirements of "objectivity" and "scientificity," Barthes now shows himself ready to explore *The Pleasure of the Text* (1973), the territories of autobiography (*Roland Barthes by Roland Barthes*, 1975), and even the literary sentimentalities of *A Lover's Discourse* (1976).

But even after the shift of critical focus from "structure" to "text," his work continues to express some of the core ideas shared by the radical intellectuals of the time, ideas which had also inspired the leaders of the May 1968 student uprising in Paris. As late as 1974 he wrote: "Concerning . . . the ideological commitment of Semiology, I believe the stake has

. . .

grown considerably larger: what Semiology must attack is not only, as in the days of *Mythologies,* the petit-bourgeois good conscience, but the symbolic and semantic system of our entire civilization; it is not enough to seek to change contents, we must above all aim at *fissuring* the meaning-system itself: we must emerge from the Occidental enclosure, as I postulated in my text on Japan" (*The Semiotic Challenge,* p. 8). I note in passing the irony, at least from the perspective of the 1990s, of making Japan, a country which has technologically out-Westernized the West, the model for breaking away from "the Occidental enclosure": this is certainly no more than one of those quirks or moments of wrong-headedness that are not seldom observed in brilliant minds such as Barthes's.

With the benefit of hindsight, we can say today that the 1960s were in French cultural life the heyday of an acute leftist ideological criticism which was in fact directed much less against "bourgeois" or "petit-bourgeois" values—as the critics themselves believed—than against the values of a newly emerging modern mass-democratic society with its attendant consumer culture. In other words, France was in a process of modernization (it had failed to modernize in the interwar years and it needed over a decade to recover fully from the trauma of World War II), and its intellectuals were less than eager to face a situation in which their social prestige was sure to suffer a degree of erosion. What is remarkable, but not completely surprising, is that many of the country's more radical intellectuals expressed their discontent by resorting to highly indirect rhetorical strategies and elaborate forms of discourse, thus giving a new lease on life to an old, aristocratic French form of linguistic exclusiveness, namely, *préciosité.*

What were the essential components of the "thought of '68"? In terms of political thought, it should be noted that earlier Marxist and neo-Marxist directions (usually in sharp disagreement with the Stalinist line of the French Communist Party) tended to merge with home-grown varieties of radicalism. These included a powerful streak of anarchism, whose history in France goes beyond Georges Sorel's turn-of-the-century anarcho-syndicalism, or Proudhon's mid-nineteenth century individualist anarchism, all the way back to the sixteenth century of Etienne de la Boëtie's *Discours sur la servitude volontaire,* one of the scriptures of the more philosophically inclined anarchists. This complex of radical ideas, transformed into a pervasive strain of leftist sensibilities, found an unexpected intellectual ally in the newly discovered "demystifying" power of psychoanalysis, a doctrine whose influence in France had been culturally negligi-

· · ·

ble before the 1950s. Psychoanalysis, through the work and teaching of Jacques Lacan, became so influential in the 1960s that its cultural impact could be described not only as "revolutionary" (what is immune to the "revolutionary" cliché?) but even as somehow comparable with that of the French Revolution.[2] Another unexpected but quite useful ally of the "thought of '68" was structuralism, whose scientific prestige (due in large part to the impressive anthropological work of Claude Lévi-Strauss) led many intellectuals working in the "human sciences" to use it not only as a method of research but also as an instrument of cultural criticism (following the example of Lévi-Strauss himself). To wind up this admittedly oversimplified sketch of the French intellectual scene in the 1960s, we also have to take note of the renewed philosophical influence of Martin Heidegger, specifically his antimetaphysical and antihumanist ideas, which were turned against the "humanist" postwar existentialism of Jean-Paul Sartre as they were reelaborated and made intellectually fashionable by such *maîtres à penser* of the period as Michel Foucault and Jacques Derrida.

These were the years of the critique of the subject (history was a "subjectless process," as an intellectual guru of the time put it), the "textual years" in which the French intelligentsia were enthralled by what Marcel Gauchet has described as a sort of linguistic idealism that took itself for a materialism ("a materialism of the signifier"). Was this a case of "a literary caste hallucinating that it could hold on to a world which escaped it, by identifying that world with something over which it exerted undeniable mastery"? (This caste's area of mastery was of course language, writing, books, to which it attempted to reduce everything.) As Gauchet goes on to say, the hypothesis that the French intelligentsia of the time were indulging fantasies of linguistic control of reality, "even if false, has the merit of bringing out clearly what remains to be properly understood: the exorbitant character of the intellectuals' conviction ("cette conviction de clerc") that the world is made to end up in a Book, that society is a Text, that Writing is History, that Discourse is Praxis, and Being, Language."[3]

The echoes of the ideological, methodological, and philosophical polemics that surrounded the "thought of '68" can be identified throughout the work of Roland Barthes, who himself achieved an uncontested status as a *maître à penser* in matters of literary and, more broadly, cultural criticism. In his semiology of reading, for example, these echoes are clearly heard in the contemptuous tone and vocabulary he adopts when speaking

. . .

of the "readerly"; they are equally distinguishable in the positive tone in which he extols the virtues of the "writerly" and more generally of the avant-garde.[4] Another survival of the spirit of the 1960s in Barthes's thought, and notably in his later poststructuralist phase, is his tendency to apply the notion of "text" indiscriminately to any complex phenomenon that happens to elicit his approval. Such metaphoric extensions are of course possible, and sometimes suggestive (as is the very metaphor from which the word *text* itself was born: the weaving metaphor of *texere* or that of *textus,* originally a web or texture) but they hardly justify a "textualist" view of the world. Barthes's own "textualism" is rather capricious. "The Text," he typically writes, "exceeds the old literary work; there is, for example, a Text of Life" (*The Semiotic Challenge,* p. 7). From this we infer that the "old literary work," whatever its drawbacks and weaknesses, is salvageable insofar as it is "text." But it is harder to follow Barthes when, in order to preserve the honorific status of textuality, he is willing to accept such absurd propositions as that some literary works (ones he obviously does not care for) are no texts at all: "There can be 'Text' in a very old work, and many products of contemporary literature are no texts at all" (*The Rustle of Language,* p. 57). In the latter case, what Barthes considers bad literature is simply placed in the limbo of an undefined nontextuality.

I have elsewhere touched on some problems raised by the promotion of textualism to a general model of history and reality.[5] It is not that I reject textual metaphors (I actually think that events can sometimes be profitably seen as textual webs that demand to be read) for the sake of older parental metaphors which are implied in the more traditional concept of history as a generative unfolding in which the past determines the present. The questions I would pose to a textualist or a pantextualist are of a purely pragmatic order: why, when, and how are textual metaphors better (more enlightening, more satisfying intellectually) than generative metaphors—or, for that matter, biological-organic metaphors, or mechanical metaphors?[6]

Needless to say, the foregoing historical-critical remarks are not meant to detract from the valuable core of Barthes's theory of reading. The importance of his semiology, as I see it, is that it deliberately overturns not only the naive model of reading but also the highly complex phenomenological one proposed by Ingarden and argues in favor of a new model based on the notion of rereading—a rereading that is understood, refreshingly, not in spatial but in temporal terms; and a rereading whose

. . .

beginning can thus coincide, however paradoxically, with the beginning of reading itself.

Rereading from the Outset

Barthes's approach and Ingarden's ideal model of reading offer an almost perfect parallelism of contrasts. In terms of the fundamental dichotomy between the first reading of a work and its rereading, Barthes decidedly favors the second reading. A text, he expressly stipulates, should be read "as if it had already been read." (Is he suggesting, by the way he uses the phrase *as if,* that rereading might be a special case of a highly sophisticated and self-conscious game of make-believe in which the reader would pretend to be a rereader?) Barthes adds:

> Rereading is here suggested at the outset, for it alone saves the text from repetition (those who fail to reread are obliged to read the same story everywhere), multiplies it in its variety and plurality: rereading draws the text out of its internal chronology ("this happens *before* or *after* that") and recaptures a mythic time (without *before* or *after*); it contests the claim that would have us believe that the first reading is a primary, naive, phenomenal reading which we will only, afterward, have to "explicate," to intellectualize (as if there were a beginning of reading, as if everything were not already read: there is no *first* reading, even if the text is concerned to give us that illusion . . .); rereading is no longer consumption, but play. (*S/Z*, p. 16)

Since for Barthes the very notion of a first reading is largely based on an illusion, the critical (re)reading recommended by him will not necessarily seek to reconstruct a supposedly phenomenal-virginal first reading, some kind of original, "fresh," pristine experience tied to a first contact with the text. (Or when it will have to reconstruct the "first" reading of a particular work for textual-analytical purposes, as we shall momentarily see, the stress will be not on such romantic notions as originality, freshness, or authenticity, but on notions derived from the logic of theoretical thinking, such as making guesses and inferences, having expectations that are confirmed or disconfirmed, settling indeterminacies, or recognizing points of undecidability.) Nor will rereading try "to *describe* the structure of a work." What it will attempt to do is to produce "a mobile structuration of the text (a structuration which shifts from reader to reader down through History)" (*The Semiotic Challenge*, p. 262). The operational rules to be followed in this kind of plural rereading for purposes of commentary include: reading very slowly, "as slowly as necessary" (no concern then for

· · ·

an ideal uniform reading speed) and "stopping as often as one must . . . , trying to locate and to classify *without rigor* not all the meanings of the text (which would be impossible, for the text is open *ad infinitum*: no reader, no subject, no science can exhaust the text), but the forms, the codes which make meaning possible" (Ibid.). Frequent interruption, which Ingarden found objectionable from the point of view of an aesthetic reading of the work, is strongly recommended (among other things as an antidote against the "ideology of totality"): "The tutor text will ceaselessly be broken, interrupted without any regard for its natural divisions . . . ; the work of the commentary . . . consists precisely in *man-handling* the text, *interrupting* it" (*S/Z*, p. 15).

But in an important sense, and without necessarily contradicting himself, Barthes reconfirms that the temporal sequence of the text is essential and must be taken into account. What he calls "textual analysis" is "based on *reading* rather than on the objective structure of the text," which is to say that it proceeds in the "natural" temporal order of reading a text (from beginning to end) and retraces—reflectively—the steps of a first hypothetical "naive" reader, who learns how to find his or her way through the work. Thus, analysis will try, among other things, to identify the points of indeterminacy of the text, the ambiguities and amphibologies encountered by the reader, and will discuss the ways in which they can be solved or must be left unsolved when the text turns out to be properly undecidable. All this amounts to reintroducing the notion of a first reading, that is, of a reader who is at least theoretically new to the text (although this newness does not carry any particular advantages) and who gets acquainted with it gradually in a first "ordinary" reading.

The real difference between Ingarden and Barthes is that Barthes relativizes the concept of first reading (asserting that an absolute first reading, a completely "innocent" first contact with a work, cannot exist) and refuses to grant it any special status beyond that of a methodological hypothesis. As he makes clear, textual analysis has as its object the "structuration of reading" as a process and therefore will "follow the text *as read*"—which is to say that it will unfold in the precise order (linear, irreversible) in which the text is given, starting with the beginning (the title, the inaugural words of the text) and ending with the conclusion: "We shall allow our analysis to follow the text *as read;* quite simply, this reading will be *filmed in slow motion*. This way of proceeding is theoretically important: it signifies that we do not aim at reconstituting the text's structure, but at following its structuration" (*The Semiotic Challenge*, p. 264).

. . .

It is only in the complex play of rereading that the multiplicity and indeed the "infinity" of the text can be discovered. This infinity is derived from "intertextuality," that remarkable feature by which a text always refers to (or cites) other texts of the same type, including, but not limited to, its direct sources of inspiration or its polemical (parodic) targets. Barthes considers that the notion of intertextuality is "particularly valid for literary texts, which are woven of extremely varied stereotypes, and where, consequently, the phenomenon of reference, or citation, to an anterior or ambient culture is very frequent" (*The Semiotic Challenge,* p. 231). And he adds this important comment, which introduces a new dimension to the complex temporality of (re)reading: "In what is called intertextuality, we must include texts which come *after*: the sources of a text are not only *before* it, they are also *after* it. This is the point of view so convincingly adopted by Lévi-Strauss when he says that the Freudian version of the Oedipus myth belongs to the Oedipus myth: if we read Sophocles, we must read Sophocles as a citation of Freud; and Freud as a citation of Sophocles" (Ibid.). This suggests that in the world of (re)reading, the chronological-historical flow of phenomenal time actually is reversed insofar as we recognize the essential circularity of citation. Citation, in the sense in which Barthes uses this notion, requires the broader frame of reference of a "mythic time without *before* or *after,*" of a time, I would argue, in which *before* and *after* become interchangeable, in which priority and posteriority have lost the absolute character they have in our inner time consciousness and in the abstract consciousness of historicity and historical, unidirectional, irreversible time.

A Mythic, Circular Time

In the later Barthes, the related notions of intertext and mythic time acquire an interesting personal, even intimate dimension. I have in mind, for instance, the aphorism included in *The Pleasure of the Text* (1973) in which he speaks of the circularity of the reader's time as opposed to our habitual historical consciousness of an inflexibly linear, unidirectional time. In this aphorism, which reads like an undated entry in a (reader's/ writer's) personal diary, Barthes describes some of his typical, recurrent reading experiences. While reading a minor work by Stendhal (*Mémoires d'un touriste*), he is struck by the Proustian ring of some phrases; likewise, while reading Flaubert, he cannot help discovering something Proustian in Flaubert's description of the blooming apple trees in Normandy. This

. . .

spontaneous tendency to read "à partir de Proust" makes Barthes realize that

> Proust's work, for myself at least, is *the* reference work, the general *mathesis,* the *mandala* of the entire literary cosmogony—as Mme de Sévigné's letters were for the narrator's grandmother, tales of chivalry for Don Quixote, etc; this does not mean that I am in any way a Proust "specialist"; Proust is what comes to me, not what I summon up; not an "authority," simply a *circular memory.* Which is what the inter-text is: the impossibility of living outside the infinite text—whether this text be Proust or the daily newspaper or the television screen: the book creates the meaning, the meaning creates life. (*The Pleasure of the Text,* p. 36)

Such a circular model of a reader's memory, and of reading time in general, is an open challenge to our conventional-historical way of thinking. But no matter how paradoxical it may appear in some of its implications, the circularity of this mythic/literary time is not in conflict with intuition and was a subject of reflection long before Barthes noticed it. It is central, for instance, to T. S. Eliot's argument (in his 1919 essay "Tradition and the Individual Talent") that the "aesthetic" past, unlike the purely "historical" past, is "altered by the present as much as the present is directed by the past." In other words, what happens when a new work of art is created is something that happens simultaneously to all the works of art that preceded it (*Selected Prose,* p. 38).

Eliot speaks from the perspective of an "objective" if constantly changing order of tradition, but his insight seems equally justifiable from the perspective of an individual reader. Within a personal circular model of "aesthetic" time, the "supervention of novelty" (the discovery of a new book, of a new literary universe) cannot be tied to any fixed external chronology. This means that, from the point of view of an individual reader, any work, irrespective of its age, can perform the function of Eliot's "new work" once it is (re)read in an "inspired" or "creative" fashion and given, however temporarily and partially, the prestigious status of general mathesis or mandala mentioned by Barthes or, to put this in simpler terms, once it is taken as a frame for organizing the literary associations stored in the reader's memory. Such a work will modify the perception of the works that preceded it (in the memory of the reader) and will determine, at least for a while, future reading expectations, choices, reactions, and "discoveries." The unrelatedness between the mythic/personal time of the reader and the conventional one-way time of literary

. . .

history can give rise to all sorts of apparent surprises and unexpected possibilities, depending of course on the angle from which they are viewed (conventional time from the perspective of reading time or vice versa). One of these surprising possibilities is that of chronological "reverse influence" (Proust on Flaubert, as we just saw; or Proust on Ruskin—at least for this writer).

This latter possibility is explored in Borges's essay "Kafka and His Precursors" (1941), in which Kafka serves as an example of how a great writer can "create" (in a metaphorical but at the same time logically very rigorous sense) his literary ancestors. "At first," writes Borges, "I thought [Kafka] was as singular as the fabulous phoenix; when I knew him better I thought I recognized his voice, or his habits, in texts of various literatures and various ages" (*Borges: A Reader*, p. 242). The texts he cites for their Kafkaesque note are weirdly heterogeneous (Zeno's paradox against movement, an apologue by the ninth-century Chinese writer Han Yu, a religious parable by Kierkegaard, the poem "Fears and Scruples" by Robert Browning, a short story from Léon Bloy's *Histoires désobligeantes,* and a horror tale by Lord Dunsany), but the identification of Kafka's timber of voice is carefully circumscribed and convincing. The conclusion offers a lucid formulation of the notion of reverse chronological "influence" in the world of reading. As Borges points out, all the texts examined in the essay

> resemble Kafka's work; . . . not all of them resemble each other, and this fact is the significant one. Kafka's idiosyncrasy, in a greater or lesser degree, is present in each of these writings, but if Kafka had not written we would not perceive it; that is to say it would not exist. The poem "Fear and Scruples" by Robert Browning is like a prophecy of Kafka's stories, but our reading of Kafka refines and changes our reading of the poem perceptibly. Browning did not read it as we read it now. The word "precursor" is indispensable in the vocabulary of criticism, but one should try to purify it from every connotation of polemic or rivalry. The fact is that each writer *creates* his precursors. (p. 243)

I would add that in creating their precursors (creating and *not* imitating or emulating them; in effect, making the precursors look like imitators or emulators of their own work), great writers in fact force us to reread both their work and that of their precursors. We return to their texts with new insights, new perspectives, and new, unexpected intertexts. The consciousness of intertextuality always implies some form of rereading—or at least the project to reread. By the same token, rereading is always

· · ·

intertextual, even when the intertext is nothing but the remembered virtual text of a more or less distant and foggy first reading. If one can
(re)read Flaubert or Ruskin "à partir de Proust," one certainly can reread
Proust himself the same way, taking the memory of earlier readings as a
point of departure and a frame of reference.

But can one ever say that one has grasped any specific part of *A la
recherche du temps perdu* in terms of the whole work in an act of simultaneous vision? The purely spatial-visual metaphor is inadequate. And if the
architectural simile of the *Recherche* as a cathedral, proposed by Proust
himself, is more appropriate, it is not only because architectural space has
a complex temporal depth, a "fourth dimension" in time, but also because
a cathedral is at once an *imago mundi* and the locus of a potential
transformation of both ordinary space and time into their mythic homo-
logues. Certainly Proust does not use this key metaphor because a cathedral is a vast building (after all, he did not compare his work to a large
palace or to a railway station). It is, in other words, the cathedral's being a
place of *pilgrimage* (a pilgrimage is always double-sided: everyday and
mythical, temporal and trans-temporal), and not simply a large-scale
spatial object, that gives Proust's comparison its more profound, spiritual
justification.

But the mythical circularity of the time of (re)reading and remembrance, even though it can weaken the sense of irresistible linearity and
unidirectionality of both textual time and biological time, remains inscribed in it and, together with all other temporal experiences, is subject to
the inexorable law according to which whatever occurs in phenomenal
time cannot but sink further and further into the past. One obviously does
not grow younger while reading or rereading a book. Even so, one's ability
to imagine and explore through reading a mythically circular time constitutes a significant enrichment of one's temporal experience and of the
ways in which one can understand and give meaning to time.

. . .

PART TWO

History, Psychology, Poetics

FIVE

To Read or to Reread?

> There is no doubt that whatever amusement we may find in reading
> a purely modern novel, we have rarely any artistic pleasure in
> rereading it. And this is perhaps the best rough test of what is
> literature and what is not. If one cannot enjoy reading a book over
> and over again, there is no use reading it at all.
>
> OSCAR WILDE
> "The Decay of Lying" (*The Critic as Artist,* p. 300)

Critiques of Pure (Fictional) Readability

The Oscar Wilde quotation in the epigraph represents one of the paradoxical critical conclusions of nineteenth-century aestheticism. Even though it is couched in the hedonistic language of pleasure and enjoyment, the aphorism brings to mind, through the central notion of repetition ("reading . . . over and over again"), the universe of mythical recurrences and of timeless—ultimately religious values. The paradox, illustrating one of Wilde's typical rhetorical modes, is deliberate: an apparently frivolous formulation is charged with a highly serious and even mysterious meaning. The rejection of the modern novel should come as no surprise in the broader context of Wilde's aesthetics in which the works to reread are by Plato or Keats ("In the sphere of poetry, the masters not the minstrels, in the sphere of philosophy, the seers not the *savants*"), Dante or Baudelaire.[1] Modern novels "are so like life that no one can possibly believe in their probability"; they are little more than depressing testimonials to "our monstrous worship of facts," often compounded by "the bad habit of uttering moral platitudes"; and even if individually they may have "many good points, as a class, they are quite unreadable" (p. 297).

That the movement of art for art's sake aspired to institute a new religion of art in a period when the traditional Christian worldview was undergoing a profound crisis has been affirmed many times and need not be elaborated here. Within this frame, Wilde's emphasis on the concept of rereading, coupled with his devaluation of mere reading, presents intriguing parallelisms with the religious valorization of the act of repeated meditative reading of sacred texts in opposition to mere superficial reading, particularly in post-Gutenberg and post-Reformation Europe, when books, both religious and secular, became available to an ever-broader reading public. But before getting into more specific questions of the history of reading—including the great European model of intensive (re)reading, the Bible—let us consider some of the more striking instances of the conflict between reading and rereading in its various aesthetic, moral, religious, and political guises.

Wilde's derogatory remarks about the novel were echoed by his younger French friend and admirer, André Gide. In 1913, already famous, Gide was invited by a large Parisian daily paper to comment on his ten favorite French novels. Without any particular enthusiasm, he listed works by Stendhal, Laclos, Madame de La Fayette (quite reluctantly), Abbé Prévost (hesitatingly), Fromentin, Balzac (halfheartedly), Flaubert (with significant reservations), Zola (because one cannot omit him), and, finally, a novel that he had not yet read but that he was at least hoping to enjoy, *La Vie de Marianne* by Marivaux. Clearly, Gide had not been very happy with the question. In fact, not unlike Wilde, he did not really care for the novel as a genre and, to make things worse, he thought that in comparison with other nations the French did not particularly excel in it. Had he been asked to list his favorite ten books in the whole of world literature, "not one of these [French novels] would be among them."

The 1913 *enquête* reminded Gide of a literary game he used to play in high school with his classmate Pierre Louÿs:

> It was Jules Lemaître, I think, who brought into style the little game Pierre Louÿs and I used to play when we were in the upper classical form at school:

· · ·

"Supposing you had to spend the remainder of your days on a desert island, what twenty books would you want to take with you?" Twenty books! For us that was too few . . . so we used to write down the names of authors rather than the titles of works; for example, we used to name simply Goethe and thus were not forced to choose among *Faust, Wilhelm Meister,* and the poetry; then we had recourse to trickery: . . . we chose Leconte de Lisle, whose translations [from Homer and other poets of antiquity] seemed to us then to be of unsurpassable beauty. In this way, we brought our library of twenty authors up to three or four hundred volumes. I have kept several of these lists, which we used to draw up anew every semester. In vain do I look for the name of a novelist. The novel, last born, is most favored today. In literature as a whole, and particularly in French literature, it has a small place; we were not so shortsighted as to fail to recognize this fact even then. (*Pretexts,* pp 243–44)

It is obvious that the criterion of selection used in Gide's game is one of rereadability as distinct from, and even opposed to, mere readability. In an imaginary wilderness, with a theoretically inexhaustible supply of spare time but severely limited reading material (this being the main rule of the game), one would of course select rereadable books, reusable and all-purpose classics for all seasons. Typical novels, as Gide saw them at the time, would not qualify.

One notes that emphatically rereadable novels like Joyce's *Ulysses* or, even closer to the limits of the unreadable, *Finnegans Wake* (the latter perhaps is the ideal choice for a desert island) were not yet written. As for the great French novel for rereading, Proust's *A la recherche du temps perdu,* its first two volumes were published in 1913 by Grasset, but only *à compte d'auteur,* having been rejected by Gallimard on advice of none other than Gide himself! Gide's implicit objection to the novel as a genre was that it was simply too readable and, thus, insufficiently rereadable. Wilde had formulated the same objection explicitly, more than two decades earlier, when he relegated the "purely modern novel" to the limbo of literary works that were merely readable (and perhaps even amusing) but definitely unrereadable and therefore not worth reading.

Don Quixote's Library

The contrasts and conflicts between reading and rereading are more directly and more dramatically present in the opposite of the desert island game: the game of imaginary censorship. If in the first the players are

. . .

asked to select the few books whose exclusive repeated reading would make them happy for an indefinite time, in the second they are called upon to eliminate, from an existing overstock of books, those volumes they deem to be bad, harmful, confusing, or simply worthless. This is perhaps a game we would not care to play nowadays (for the idea of censorship is utterly repellent to us), but it was popular for many centuries.

There are illustrious literary examples of such games of fictive censorship. Consider the most famous one, the sixth chapter of Part I of *Don Quixote* (1605), in which the personal library of Alonso Quijano/Don Quixote is being purged by his friends, the priest and the barber. The aim of the purge is to prevent Don Quixote not from reading but actually from rereading the chivalric romances that are held responsible for his madness. The scene of censorship, the "great and diverting scrutiny which the curate and the barber made in the library of our ingenious gentleman," is just one of the many references to the *libros de caballerías* made in a novel that is at once a sweeping parody of the chivalric genre and the most comprehensive and detailed account of that genre to have come down to us from the Spanish Golden Age—a veritable encyclopedia of chivalric writing and lore.[2]

The scene takes place just after the first sally and misadventure of the self-imagined knight. Badly battered, Don Quixote is brought back to his house by a charitable farmer and falls asleep, while his old friends, urged on by his niece and housekeeper, are preparing an auto-da-fé of books of chivalry. Three positions emerge concerning the degree of blame to be placed on Don Quixote's books. The most intransigent and most ignorant is the stance of the niece and the housekeeper. They are so incensed against Quixote's books that they want them all placed in a heap and burned immediately. The author or the third-person narrator, who recounts the scene in a good-natured manner, is the most indulgent (at one point he in fact exonerates the books on trial by calling them "innocent"). The curate (a homespun, village version of religious common sense) and the barber (standing perhaps for lay common sense) take an intermediate stance: they are quite willing to condemn some—actually most—of Don Quixote's books, but not indiscriminately.

Some twenty-odd titles in Don Quixote's library of about three hundred volumes are specifically commented upon. Saved from the flames is, significantly, *Amadis of Gaul*—the first book of chivalry to be printed in Spain (in 1508)—which is, as the barber puts it to the initially hostile priest, "better than all the other books of this sort that have been com-

. . .

posed, and . . . unique of its kind." Of course Don Quixote knows this book—like most of the others—almost by heart and keeps quoting from it and reenacting scenes from it in hilariously inappropriate circumstances. But irrespective of its apparent ill-effects on our hero, the book is spared not only because of its originality and uniqueness, but also, one suspects, because of its century-old unabated popularity. Popularity, an undeclared criterion, should not be underrated. Cervantes himself, in the very parody of the genre introduced to Spain by *Amadis,* clearly hoped to achieve an equally broad-based popularity, and he saw no point in offending the admirers of *Amadis,* whether they were well-educated, knowledgeable readers *(discretos)* or whether they belonged to the *vulgo* or the ignorant "mass" (if one can speak, even metaphorically, of a mass readership in early seventeenth-century Spain).[3] Parody, incidentally, does not exclude admiration for, and even emulation of, certain features of its target; and it occasionally includes an oblique eulogy thereof.

At any rate, *Amadis* was, after Fernando de Rojas's *La Celestina* (1499), the second greatest fiction "best-seller" of the Spanish Golden Age. The word *fiction* should be emphasized here, since in absolute terms both were easily overtaken in popularity by a nonfiction "how-to" book: Fray Luis de Granada's instructional manual on how to pray.[4] (This was, after all, the time of the Counter-Reformation.) Why were chivalric books so attractive? It is safe to say that they were read primarily for the imaginative involvement they promised or for their fantasy content, and not for the didactic-moralistic features claimed by their authors, who had to justify their suspect works (which many religious moralists condemned outright) before the censors of the Inquisition. This is not to say that chivalric romances did not contain serious teachings. One notes, however, that boring as they may seem to today's improbable reader, such teachings (in *Amadis,* for instance, the lengthy expositions of the chivalric honor code and the extensive descriptions of exemplary chivalric behavior, manners, and speech) were directly involved in the larger exercise in castle building invited and guided by the chivalric novel: one got acquainted with the lore of a dream world.

Structurally, as examples of what might be called daydream literature, the chivalric novels were not so different from such more recent analogues as, say, Ian Fleming's James Bond novels.[5] In other words, they were designed—however encumbered their design may appear to us today— for an early type of fast, involved, or "extensive," reading, rather than for a reflective, insistent, "intensive" (re)reading. They offered themselves to a

. . .

potentially addictive sort of reading for purposes of escape. That was why moralists were so opposed to them. But of course they could be read (and reread) differently—more seriously, symbolically, and even allegorically. *Amadis of Gaul,* the archetypal novel of chivalry, the classic of the genre in Spain, was readable in both modes and, as Cervantes implies in saving it from the fire, also worth rereading.

But who were the actual readers of run-of-the-mill romances of chivalry? Did the romances' vaunted popularity translate into anything approaching a mass audience, an audience in which distinctions of high and low become unimportant, or were they rather addressed to a more limited readership of aristocrats who could afford them (economically) and make sense of them (culturally)? Such questions have received contradictory answers.[6] My own view has already been suggested: chivalric romances belong to the category of popular ("readable," "formulaic") literature, if not in a historical, then in a structural sense. Even though they could be read only by the members of a small elite in a country in which more than three-quarters of the adults were illiterate, chivalric books share significantly more features with the genres of today's mass literature (Westerns, fantasy, science fiction, and so on) than with those of "high literature."

One must also keep in mind that chivalric romances in sixteenth-century Spain were popular in a particularly strong aristocratic-Catholic culture, one that was virtually immune to the Reformation and that was to become a model of the Counter-Reformation, with its characteristically flamboyant baroque style. These novels could not help but reflect the moral, political, and religious values of the larger culture. Thus, in Montalvo's preface to *Amadis of Gaul,* the reader is urged to understand the feats of arms allegorically, even inspirationally, as relating "to our own salvation" and as "wings whereby our souls may rise to the height of the glory for which they were created." The story itself has a strong religious background: devout Christian knights move in a time "measured in monastic terms," in a world where they "frequently meet with hermits and regularly keep vigil, confess, and hear mass."[7] Does this mean that chivalric novels were actually read along Christian-allegorical lines? At least in some cases—rare but significant—they must have been. We do know that in sixteenth-century Spain there existed, in certain religiously oriented circles, a fashion to read lay chivalric literature "a lo divino."[8]

Many Spanish religious figures—great saints like Loyola or Teresa of Avila—are known to have been addicted to chivalric literature in their youth. How did such mystic natures respond to the popular romances?

. . .

What did they preserve from such early readings in their later imaginative life? Was there any relationship between their perception of chivalric ideals and that of Don Quixote? Particularly Loyola's youthful passion for chivalric literature has evoked certain Quixotic analogies, analogies on the strength of which "it was once proposed that Cervantes was thinking of Loyola when creating Don Quixote."⁹ Is it possible to see Don Quixote as a failed saint? And what would a true saint have found in those *libros de caballerías* that drove Alonso Quijano to take himself for Don Quixote?

Saint Teresa of Avila's autobiography provides us with precious information about the ways and contexts in which chivalric novels could be read (at least by certain readers, such as her mother and herself as an adolescent) and about the place they occupied in the imaginative life of an outstanding sixteenth-century mystic. The reading biography of Teresa, as documented in *Libro de su vida* (written in the 1560s), is of great interest to the student of the history of reading. Quite remarkably, as a child Teresa became an avid reader of the lives of saints and wanted to imitate them: at the age of seven she planned to flee with her favorite brother Rodrigo to the land of the Moors, where she dreamed of being put to death: "I had one brother about my age. We used to get together to read the lives of saints. . . . We agreed to go off to the land of the Moors and beg them, out of love of God, to cut off our heads there (*Collected Works*, vol. 1, p. 33).

The episode illustrates what might be called a case of child Quixotism, that is, of naive symbolic misreading and mistranslation into action (or projected action) of an idealistic-heroic text. After the failure of the attempt to flee, Teresa's fantasy of religious self-sacrifice satisfied itself (more adequately?) through play: "When I saw it was impossible to go where I would be killed for God, we made plans to be hermits. And in a garden we had in our house, we tried as we could to make hermitages piling up some little stones which afterward would quickly fall down again . . . . When I played with other girls I enjoyed when we pretended to be nuns in a monastery" (p. 34).

Such remarkable make-believe derived from religious childhood reading shows, in Teresa's case, a single-mindedness which was to be fully reconfirmed in her mature life as a nun, a mystic, and an intensive reader of devotional books which helped her to prepare for contemplation and prayer. The two distinct but structurally similar periods in her reading biography are separated by her adolescent infatuation with romances of chivalry. It was from her mother that Teresa got the habit of reading such

· · ·

books. Her mother "loved books of chivalry," which provided her with an essentially harmless pastime because she read them as they were meant to be read ("to escape thinking of the great trials she had to bear," p. 35) and they never interfered with the performance of her duties. For younger Teresa, however, the consequences of such reading were less harmless. Having no particular worries or burdens to forget, she got addicted to books of chivalry for no other reason than to satisfy the needs of her youthful imagination: "I was so completely taken up with this reading that I didn't think I could be happy if I didn't have a new book." (How nicely her sentence captures the logic of "extensive" reading: the insatiable hunger for novelty within the confines of generic predictability!) Even worse, she started imitating the vain behavior of certain female characters in chivalric fantasies ("I began to dress in finery and to desire to please and look pretty").

But chivalric literature need not be read only along such lines. Like the Arthurian legends of the Round Table from which they derive, the sixteenth-century *libros de caballerías* are variations on the two fundamental themes of archetypal initiation: the quest (for the Grail, the ultimate secret of life) and the test. The involved reader of heroic and fantastic chivalric adventures might never become conscious of this deeper initiatory dimension. Even so, chivalric books provide the reader—including the most naive literal reader—with a rich and inherently ambiguous imagery of castles, fortresses, weapons, valiant knights undergoing all sorts of tests, imprisonments, escapes, enchantments, and dangerous illusions created by demonic wizards. Aside from unstructured daydreaming, such imagery could be summoned independently for purposes of symbolic expression of or meditation on a moral-religious problem. It has thus been suggested that Saint Teresa's use of images such as *castle* (as in her famous "interior castle"), *fortress, crystal,* and *cavalier,* as well as the terminology of love (with the concrete image of the heart at its center), could be tied, at least in part, to her memories of reading chivalric novels.[10] It is true that many identical or closely similar images also occur in the Bible, or in devotional works based on Biblical imagery. But such coincidences might in fact reinforce the possibility of giving chivalric images a more exalted spiritual significance.

If there is any basis to such a view, if indeed Teresa was able to spiritualize the chivalric images stored in her memory from the days of her adolescence, it may be that her renunciation of the "bad books" of her youth and her turning to "good books" (like the *Letters of Saint Jerome* or

. . .

Francisco de Osuna's *Third Spiritual Alphabet*) was somehow smoother than she thought. What is remarkable is that reading, as a specific kind of mental activity having to do with images, remained important throughout Teresa's life. Her autobiography develops a whole theory of "spiritual reading" as an aid to meditation and prayer. For people affected by a certain "dryness" of the imagination, among whom she numbered herself, meditation or "discursive reflection" might be too arduous a task without the *imaginative* help offered by reading (one notes the implicitly mediating role assigned to *images*). For many years in her life as a nun, Teresa confesses, "I never dared to begin a prayer without a book." And she continues: "For God didn't give me talent . . . for a profitable use of the imagination . . . [which] is so dull that I never succeeded . . . to think about or represent in my mind . . . the humanity of the Lord." A further discussion of the problematics of spiritual reading—or what Michel de Certeau has called "absolute reading"[11]—would take us too far from the subject at hand. It suffices here to note that spiritual reading was part of the response of the Counter-Reformation to the reading revolution brought about by the Reformation (more about this in chapter 6).

Returning now to the scene of censorship in *Don Quixote,* let us focus on another book that is saved from the flames of the auto-da-fé, and saved, like *Amadis,* because of its rereadability: the famous Catalan classic *Tirant lo Blanch*. This romance by Johanot Martorell (published in 1590) receives at once the curate's most lavish eulogy and, puzzlingly, some of his most devastating criticism:

> "Well, bless my soul!" cried the curate . . . "Let me have it, my friend, for I cannot but remember that I have found in it a treasure of contentment and a mine of recreation. . . . Tell the truth, friend, and admit that in the matter of style this is the best book in the world. Here knights eat and sleep and die in their beds and make their wills before they die and do other things that are never heard of in books of this kind. But for all that, I am telling you that the one who needlessly composed so nonsensical a work deserves to be sent to the galleys for the rest of his life. Take it along home with you and read it and see if what I say is not so." (p. 55)[12]

In the priest's argument, then, *Tirant* would be a paradoxical example of a good bad book: a rare rereadable, well-written exemplar of a merely readable (that is, popular, naively fantastical, escapist, shallow) genre, a book whose very qualities magnify its generic defects. In short, *Tirant* is a strange hybrid: an unpopular popular book. (Indeed, historically it ap-

. . .

pears that it did not fare well with contemporary readers—so much so that, unlike virtually all of the other *libros de caballerías,* it is probably more widely read today, as a classic, than it was in its time.) The priest's critical view is in this case intriguingly sophisticated: the novel is praised for its literary qualities but criticized for putting those qualities at the service of the fabulous, absurdly unrealistic logic of the chivalric genre. In this novel, for once, knights convincingly eat, sleep, or die in their beds. If he could write so well about true life, why did the author of *Tirant* need to use the chivalric frame? To provide his reader with an opportunity of escape? But if the purpose was mere escape, why put so much vigorous talent into the book? The priest seems to come close to accusing Martorell of not having written a version of *Don Quixote!*

Be that as it may, in contrast to *Tirant lo Blanch, Don Quixote* succeeds in keeping the escapist, wish-fulfilling logic of chivalric fiction *external* to the plot: the reader is never asked to accept it or attribute "fictional truth" to it, even occasionally or partially (as was the case in *Tirant*). The chivalric mentality is from the outset the target of a lively parody, but a parody that becomes increasingly complex in Part II, in which Don Quixote is aware of his own story as told in Part I. Part II abounds in spectacular paradoxes of infinite regress, of fiction within fiction and imitation within imitation; paradoxes of the parody of a parody (whose principal effect is to confer a certain mysterious sublimity on the character of the Don, a sublimity that has haunted and puzzled generations of interpreters).

Other genres represented in Don Quixote's library, such as the pastoral, are in principle less harmful (less violent and suspenseful, less exciting and involving—in a word, less compulsively readable) than the chivalresque. But even they are not completely safe from misreading. As Don Quixote's niece points out, her uncle might well be cured of the chivalry sickness only to pick up, from pastoral poems, a different version of the same mimetic disease. By reading bucolic fantasies he could "take it into his head to become a shepherd and go wandering through the woods and meadows singing and piping, or, what is worse, become a poet, which they say is an incurable disease and one that is very catching" (p. 56).

Here and throughout *Don Quixote* it is understood that books, even the most "innocent" ones, can pose a threat of mimetic contagion to certain vulnerable readers. This brings me to the crucial questions: What kind of reader, or rather misreader, is Don Quixote? What kinds of books are especially dangerous to him? And why? Don Quixote, as I have

· · ·

already suggested, is a typically intensive reader of texts ostensibly designed for extensive reading. Or, to put it differently, he brings characteristically intensive, passionate, and deeply serious (quasi-religious if not plainly religious) reading habits to secular fictional texts that are meant mainly for entertainment and escape. Don Quixote treats fictions and fictional games of make-believe as if they were exemplary (mythical or sacred) models. An exceedingly thoughtful and attentive reader, he consistently misuses and misapplies the religious logic of imitation (as in the imitation of saintly models or the notion of *imitatio Christi* so prevalent in the late medieval Catholic world) in relation to secular and fantastic heroes, such as those who populate the world of chivalric romances. His particular problem stems from a failure to keep separate two distinct mental frames: one for responding to fictional (symbolic) information, the other for dealing with the everyday and the practical. This problem is of course compounded by his obsessive rereading/reenacting of chivalric fantasies and by his inability to understand the symbolic other than in the most iconic-literal terms.

Don Quixote, we may conclude, is the reader as hero—admittedly a special kind of comically sublime hero whose extraordinary adventures are (parodically, hilariously, endearingly, mysteriously) nothing but adventures of reading, rereading, misreading, and misrereading. Cervantes's novel thus raises at the very beginning of the history of the modern novel the crucial question of reading, and more precisely that of the ethics of reading or rereading fiction, which has remained, even though in less overt forms, a major concern of both novel writing and novel criticism to this day.[13]

An Attack on Reading in the Age of Enlightenment

A similar conflict between the demands of reading and those of rereading, but seen from a less imaginative, sterner, and indeed more authoritarian perspective, is illustrated in another book burning which occurs nearly two centuries after the purging of Quixote's library. With the proliferation of books of all types during the French *siècle des lumières,* the notion of a generalized surfeit of reading as a real intellectual danger begins to preoccupy some of those radical *hommes de lettres* in whom Tocqueville was later to see the precursors of the French Revolution of 1789. Louis-Sébastien Mercier was one of them. An influential disciple of Jean-Jacques Rousseau and a widely known writer in his own time who counted Goethe

· · ·

and Schiller among his admirers, Mercier wrote prolifically in many genres, from bourgeois drama to political journalism. Today, however, he is remembered almost exclusively for his curious literary dream of a holocaust of libraries, which would mark the beginning of a radiant utopian era: "We should all join in writing together the first page of the book which will render all of these books absolutely useless.... One could set fire in imagination to all the libraries of the world and, by saving only forty volumes, preserve all that the human spirit needs to know" (*Dictionnaire d'un polygraphe,* p. 272). In such a sweeping condemnation of writing and books the metaphor of writing (the first page of the book of a bookless future) conveys an involuntary irony. Mercier's recurring fantasy finds its most elaborate expression in his utopian novel *L'An 2440, rêve s'il en fût jamais* (1771), translated into English as *Memoirs of the Year 2500* (1772). In twenty-fifth-century Paris, the time-traveling narrator of 1771 visits the king's library and is surprised to find a vast empty building containing only a small number of books: "I ventured to ask if some fatal conflagration had not devoured that rich collection. 'Yes,' they replied, 'it was a conflagration; but by our hands it was designedly illumined'" (pp. 167–68).

Mercier's spokesman for the future dwells on the ills brought about in the past by false and deceptive books and recounts the scene of the huge book-burning that inaugurated utopia: "By an unanimous consent, we brought together, on a vast plain, all those books which we judged either frivolous, useless, or dangerous; of these we formed a pyramid, that resembled, in height and bulk, an enormous tower; it was certainly another Babel.... This tremendous mass was set on fire, and offered as an expiatory sacrifice to veracity, to good sense, and true taste" (p. 170).

The books that have escaped the flames are, unsurprisingly, established classics, although not without exceptions. Of the Greeks, the library of the twenty-fifth century had preserved Homer, Sophocles, Euripides, Demosthenes, Plato, and Plutarch (no mention is made of Aeschylus); but "they had burned Herodotus, Sappho, Anacreon, and the vile Aristophanes" (p. 172). Of the Latin authors, Virgil, Pliny, and Livy had been saved, but "they had burned Lucretius, except for some poetic passages, because they found his physics false, and his morals dangerous.... Ovid and Horace were purged.... Catullus and Petronius had vanished in smoke" (pp. 172–73).

There is little point in examining in detail the list of authors whose works are saved, purged in part, or eliminated *in toto*. On the whole, as

. . .

the historian Roger Chartier has pointed out in a discussion of *L'An 2440*, Mercier was a moderate; other men of letters of eighteenth-century France had advanced much more drastic expurgatory proposals: "Mercier was less radical than the wise old man of Morelly's *Basiliade* (1765), who argues in favor of allowing only one book, which condenses all useful knowledge and is possessed by all citizens" (*The Cultural Uses of Print*, pp. 216–17). How sinister is this utopian project when considered from the perspective of our own century's totalitarian experiments: did not Morelly's dream come close to being realized in our time, for instance in the Chinese Cultural Revolution of the 1960s, when the one book that condensed all knowledge was Chairman Mao's *Little Red Book*, reread in grotesque daily rituals by hundreds of millions of people?

It is clear that Mercier opposes reading, at least in an extensive sense: reading for pleasure, for variety and novelty, or for satisfying one's idle curiosity. Instead, he favors a stern, moralistic, political, and sentimentalist version of intensive reading—reading and rereading just the few books that are compatible with the strict principles of truth and the needs of reason and good taste. Along the lines of Rousseau's anti-intellectualism[14] and general opposition to civilization, Mercier occasionally goes so far as to adopt an openly militant attitude toward both reading and writing. In such a polemical mood he evokes the figure of Socrates, the symbolic philosophical antireader and antiwriter. Deploring the fondness of his contemporaries for new books and new fashions—specifically that inclination that makes the French into a nation possessed by an "idolatry of the pretty" (*idolâtrie du joli*)—Mercier draws an entirely negative image of reading as a solitary, silent, asocial activity when he asks rhetorically and polemically, "O Socrates! Did you read a lot? Was it in solitude that you studied men? Did you flee them in order to know them? Did you speak to them through writing?" (*Dictionnaire d'un polygraphe*, p. 263.)

Under attack here are some of the central social implications of reading: its private character (which in Mercier's vision partakes of the larger evil of privacy, itself deriving, in good Rousseauist logic, from the "original sin" of private property); its necessary association with writing, which represents a falling away from the communal sharing of the spoken word; and its flight from the vital truth about man, a truth that can only be uttered in live public speech in a transparent social space. The paradox that such conclusions about Socrates could be reached only through reading Plato (presumably privately and silently) seems to have eluded Mercier. Nor did he appear to be conscious of the fact that writing against

. . .

reading did not bring him any closer to the utopian live voice—the voice of truth—he was dreaming of but that he was actually proposing an ideal of extremely intensive (re)reading, understood in a narrow, dogmatic, moralistic-political way.

Classics and Romantics

Some of the hidden implications of the conflict between reading and rereading are amusingly brought out in the following literary anecdote. In 1842, the French romantic poet, playwright, and novelist Alfred de Vigny decided to become a candidate for the Académie Française and, as required by custom, started paying visits to its members to request their vote. This turned out to be a frustrating experience for him. Particularly humiliating was his visit to the octogenarian Pierre-Paul Royer-Collard, with whom he had the following conversation, as noted in his diary:

V: I would appreciate having your opinion regarding my candidacy.

R-C: My opinion is that you have no chance. . . . And, by the way, I would need to learn from you about your works.

V: You will never learn anything about my works from me, Sir, if you have not already learned from the voice of the people. Do you ever read the newspapers?

R-C: Never.

V: And, as you never go to the theatre, my plays performed at the Français for one or two years in a row, and my books printed in six or seven editions are also unknown to you?

R-C: Yes, Sir; I haven't read anything of what has been written for the last *thirty years.* . . .

V: The Académie must be surprised to see someone vote on works he has not read.

R-C: Oh! the Académie . . . I have already said it to others, I am at an age when one doesn't read any more, but only rereads the ancient works.

V: Since you don't read, you surely write a lot, don't you?

R-C: Not at all, I reread. . . .

V: But you don't know whether there are modern works worth rereading, since you have taken this habit of never reading anything.

R-C, rather ill at ease: Oh! it's possible, Sir, it's really very possible.
    (*Journal d'un poète*, pp. 183–87; my translation)

. . .

This is obviously an attack—albeit an ambivalent one—on rereading. In Vigny's little comedy of generational conflict and misunderstanding, rereading is embodied by a cantankerous and stuffy old man who resists new reading as if it were a threat to his intellectual integrity. Rereading would appear as the diehard classicist's last line of defense against change and novelty, represented by the romantics. In principle, of course, reading contemporary (romantic) literature should not be incompatible with re-reading the ancients. One might even read the new authors, as Vigny suggests to Royer-Collard, in the expectation that some will turn out to be rereadable. In fact, the most ambitious of the romantics aspire to nothing less than to produce fully rereadable works—works that will sooner or later gain the status of classics.

But the romantics will never be read—or read adequately—by the dogmatic classicists of their time. These, like Royer-Collard, will usually take it for granted that rereading the ancients implies staying away from the moderns. To such traditionalists modernity is always suspect. It should come as no surprise, then, that within the broader context of modern culture the question of rereading has been posed in such exclusionary terms. As we shall see in the next chapter, the intensive reading of religious works at the time of the Reformation and after often implied not reading contemporary secular books (on a popular level chapbooks, romances, broadsides, and ballads; on a more sophisticated level novels, poems, plays and other works for entertainment). The alternative—to read or to reread—also kept emerging in the periodically renewed outbursts of the old Quarrel between the Ancients and the Moderns, from the late seventeenth-century literary polemics around Charles Perrault's defense of the moderns in France, through the Battle of the Books in eighteenth-century England, to the late eighteenth- and early nineteenth-century clashes between the neoclassicists and the romantics. The aesthetic movement of the second half of the nineteenth century reformulates the issue in its own elegantly paradoxical terms (Oscar Wilde), and the major figures of high modernism in the twentieth century (Joyce, Pound, T. S. Eliot, Virginia Woolf) are clearly committed to an ideal of rereadability: their search for the new is in a more profound sense *a search for new forms of rereadability*.

What is most striking in the case of the ill-humored Royer-Collard in the Vigny anecdote is not so much that he rereads (for as one advances in age one may naturally tend to reread more and more) as that he adamantly refuses to read. His resistance to new reading is plainly not that of an

. . .

ordinary aged reader, but that of an embattled member of the old generation of intellectuals, whose values, beliefs, structures of feeling, and codes
are contested by a new generation. This points to a larger dynamics of
literary change (including methods and patterns of reading), which results
from an open and often bitter generational struggle between the defenders
of tradition and the proponents of innovation. It is a truism of modern
literary history that since romanticism virtually all the artistic movements
that had some lasting impact on the cultural scene (including natural-
ism, symbolism, futurism, expressionism, dadaism, and surrealism) have
begun at the initiative of young and sometimes extremely young writers, usually members of small, tightly knit, vocally iconoclastic literary
groups. One cannot sufficiently emphasize the degree to which such young
writers have felt a generational urge to oppose their literary elders, seen as
symbols of stagnation and stifling immobility, as defenders of the status
quo, as practitioners of unimaginative imitation and reactionary rereading. Vigny's portrait of Royer-Collard conforms to this pattern.

But the literary insurgency of youth against old age—like the stubborn, ultimately pathetic rejection of the new by certain embittered old-
timers—is only part of the story. The young rebels, in proportion to their
talent, will fairly quickly find their own way to the books of the classics,
from which they have much to learn if only by way of criticism or
antithesis. Proust, who wisely stayed away from the literary polemics of
his time, has called attention to the profound reasons for which an intelligent reader is bound to (re)discover the classics. With his extraordinary
sense of the subtleties of social conventions (and of how analogously
subtle conventions operate in the world of reading), Proust notes: "It is
from this contact with other minds, which reading is, that the education of
the 'manners' of the mind is gotten. In spite of everything, literary men are
still like the people of quality of the intelligence, and not to know a certain
book, a certain particularity of literary science, will always remain, even
in a man of genius, a mark of intellectual commonness. Distinction and
nobility consist, in the order of thought also, in a kind of freemasonry
of customs, and in an inheritance of traditions" (*On Reading Ruskin*,
p. 125).

That is why, as Proust adds, "in this taste for and this entertainment
in reading, very quickly the preference of great writers is for the classics [*livres des anciens*]. Even those writers who to their contemporaries
appeared to be the most 'romantic' (or more broadly rebellious) read
scarcely anything but the classics. In Victor Hugo's conversation, when he

. . .

speaks of his reading, it is the names of Molière, Horace, Ovid, Regnard that come up most often" (p. 126). If in Proust's statement we replace "romantic" with "modernist" or even "avant-garde" (consider such writers as Pound, Eliot, Joyce, or, closer to us in time, Samuel Beckett), his view appears to be as valid for the experience of the twentieth century as it was for that of the nineteenth. The texts that a Beckett reads and alludes to in his works (whether in an admiring, ironic, mock-serious, or nihilistically serious mode) are almost exclusively classical—including of course such modern classics as Joyce or, for that matter, Proust.

A related paradox is that, as Proust remarks, "the classicists have no better commentators than the 'romantics.' In fact, the romantics alone know how to read the classical works, because they read them as they have been written, romantically, because in order to read a poet or a prose writer well, one has to be oneself not a scholar, but a poet or a prose writer" (p. 138). Proust's theory of reading recalls Stendhal's famous distinction between classicism and romanticism. For Stendhal, romanticism was the kind of art that afforded the contemporary public the utmost possible pleasure, whereas classicism offered its readers a "literature that used to give the utmost pleasure to their great-great-grandfathers." "To imitate Sophocles and Euripides today," Stendhal went on to say in his 1823 essay *Racine and Shakespeare,* "and to pretend that these imitations will not cause nineteenth-century Frenchmen to yawn, is to be a classicist."[15] According to this relativistic definition, as Stendhal himself did not hesitate to make clear, Sophocles and Euripides were romantic in their day, and so was Racine.

What is new in Proust's revival of the Stendhalian dichotomy is the idea that the classics—the real classics, not their unimaginative imitators—can always be read romantically, that is, creatively. Proust seems to imply that the scholars' historical erudition and their "objective criteria" and "impersonality" lead to a reading that cannot compare in vitality and richness of insight to that of truly creative writers. If this is so, one might say that even scholars read best when they try to imitate or emulate not the "classical" readings of classical texts but the readings proposed by contemporary creative writers (Proust's "romantics"). It follows that those who ensure the literary survival of the classics are not the staunch traditionalists or the diehard neoclassicists and antiquarians, but precisely their presumed enemies, the most active and genuinely creative "romantics" (or, we might add, their direct successors, the modernists and the avant-gardists).

Proust's theory of creative reading recalls the views on reading ad-

. . .

vanced by the American romantic Ralph Waldo Emerson, whose work Proust knew well and held in high esteem. (Reading Emerson had been an "intoxicating" experience for him.)[16] In fact, the notion of creative reading was a constant of Emerson's thought. It received its perhaps most famous formulation in the address "The American Scholar": "One must be an inventor to read well. . . . There's then creative reading as well as creative writing. When the mind is braced by labor and invention, the page of whatever book becomes luminous with manifold allusion. Every sentence is doubly significant, and the sense of our author is as broad as the world."

Emerson also called attention to another, indirectly creative dimension of reading, namely, its role in "the mechanics of inspiration." In "Uses of Great Men" he explained "the secret of the reader's joy in literary genius" through the contagious character of felicitous expression and, again, through "contagious wisdom." In "Nominalist and Realist" he confessed to using books "for a mechanical help to the fancy and the imagination." Thus, he wrote, "I find the most pleasure in reading a book in a manner least flattering to the author. I read Proclus, and sometimes Plato, as I might read a dictionary, for a mechanical help to the fancy and the imagination, I read for the lustres, as if one should use a fine picture in a chromatic experiment, for its rich colors." In short, reading great texts may induce an independently creative state of mind in the reader, a sort of overflowing enthusiasm, a desire to write.

Proust's idea that writers read better than scholars has a more direct source in Proust's great model, John Ruskin. Ruskin maintained, for instance, that one "may obtain a more truthful idea of the nature of Greek religion and legend from the poems of Keats and . . . the recent work of Morris, than from frigid scholarship, however extensive. Not that a poet's impressions and renderings are wholly true, but their truth is vital, not formal" (*The Queen of the Air,* p. 309).

The characteristic features of Proust's creative reading may also bring to mind another, less romantic and more narrowly "practical" (and almost "artisanal") perspective: the one suggested by Henry James's disclosures about his habit of reading as a form of mental (re)writing. James pointed out on several occasions that he simply could not read a novel without "rewriting" it in his mind—in other words, without looking at the creative problems the novel tried to solve and then imagining the ways in which he would have dealt with these problems within the same structure of constraints. In a letter to Mrs. Humphry Ward (July 26, 1899),

. . .

Henry James thus explained that his criticisms of an early, fragmentary version of her novel *Eleanor* resulted from "giving way to my irresistible need of wondering how, *given* a subject, one could best work one's self into the presence of it. And, lo and behold, the subject isn't (of course, in so scant a show and brief a piece) 'given' at all—I have doubtless simply, with violence and mutilation, *stolen* it. It is of the nature of that violence that I'm a wretched person to *read* a novel—I begin so quickly and concomitantly, *for myself*, to write it rather—even before I know clearly what it's about! The novel I can *only* read, I can't read at all!" (*Letters*, vol. 4, p. 111). This method of reading can of course be used not only with contemporary authors but also with classical texts; not only with texts that can be improved or profitably changed but also with texts whose perfection (given the set of constraints within which their authors have composed them) can thus be tested, assessed from new perspectives, and effectively admired. Maybe Proust did not envisage such a vantage point when he spoke of romantic poets or prose writers, but decidedly *not* scholars, as capable of reading the classics fruitfully. Nonetheless, James's creative reading is in no way incompatible with Proust's larger insight.

In terms of the distinction between reading and rereading, one could say that it is precisely by rereading and renewing the classics, by challenging the "readability" they have acquired and a predictable, increasingly banalized, and minimally rewarding "scholarly" interpretation (which then becomes the standard didactic interpretation disseminated by schools), that the romantics themselves learn the art of writing truly rereadable texts. If they succeed, they become classics whose works will be renewed by future romantic readers; if they fail, they are forgotten. What is involved here is a literary equivalent of the concept of paradigm shift as defined in Thomas Kuhn's theory of scientific revolutions: the "readability" of the classics at a given time is a function of "normal" scholarship; their genuine rediscovery is made possible by the appearance of a new "paradigm," an unpredictable creative event—their rereading and actual rewriting by a major new author and the appearance of completely unforeseeable intertextualities[17]—whose strength and significance is measured, among other things, by the breathtaking quality it may give to the (re)reading of long-established classics.

One should note that the dialectic of reading and rereading suggested here is double, in the sense that it occurs on two distinct levels: on the level of "high literature," that is, the level on which the major stylistic battles from romanticism to modernism and postmodernism have been fought or,

. . .

should we say, the level of "rereadable" literature; and on the level of what is commonly called "popular literature" (a label to be taken without any demeaning or patronizing connotations) or, should we say, the level of "purely readable" literature. As its name suggests, the latter offers itself to immediate pleasurable reading by a potentially vast public, but is in no way precluded from developing its own forms of rereadability and, on occasion, from reaching the status of full classic rereadability outlined above.

That no precise answer to the question "To read or to reread?" has emerged from our zigzagging through several centuries of cultural history should not be surprising. My purpose has been simply to see how this question was posed, explicitly or implicitly, at some key junctures in the formation of modern cultural consciousness. What values, positive or negative, were associated with reading and rereading? The limited axiological history I have been able to sketch is one of ambivalences and paradoxes rather than clear-cut attitudes. Or, more appropriately, it is a history in which the ambivalences and paradoxes of Cervantes's critique of reading (as Quixotic misreading and misrereading) or those of the romantic and postromantic critique of rereading (leading to the eventual aestheticist canonization of the same, as in the case of Wilde) have balanced the more dogmatic and simplistic rejections of reading (whether religious or ethical or, as in the case illustrated by Sébastien Mercier, ideological). The historical flashbacks and flashforwards of this chapter have prepared the ground, I hope, for using the dichotomy between reading and rereading as a frame for a more comprehensive history of reading in modern times.

. . .

· · · · · · ·

Modernity and Reading:
An Overview

I am no despiser of profane literature. . . . But it was from the Bible
that I learned the symbols of Homer, and the faith of Horace: the
duty enforced upon me in early youth of reading every word of the
gospels and prophecies as if written by the hand of God, gave me
the habit of awed attention which afterwards made many passages
of the profane writers, frivolous to an irreligious reader, deeply
grave to me.
JOHN RUSKIN
The Bible of Amiens

· · · · · · ·

There are circumstances in which reading and rereading conflict in that
they demand different modes of attention, motivation, and goals of the
reader.[1] Switching from one to the other, while not unnatural, may give
rise to tricky problems of intellectual adjustment or tuning. Sacred texts,
which are paradigmatically repeatable (rereadable), create the "habit of
awed attention" of which Ruskin speaks so suggestively, but this habit
can only be misapplied to what should normally be the quick linear
reading of lighter entertaining texts. One can of course read the Bible as
literature, no less than one can read literature—literature that we cherish
and revere deeply—as the Bible. Still, one does not read a light adventure

· · ·

novel or a fantasy as one would read the Bible, "as if written by the hand of God," to quote Ruskin again. Or if one does, one may commit a sacrilege of sorts, for which the ironic punishment is likely to be some version of Quixotism.

A related problem stemming from the habit of reverential reading is that, paradoxically, the Bible itself has become almost impossible to read in the "normal," linear, naive fashion in which we read typical fictional works. Too much routinized "awed attention"—as a contemporary of Ruskin noted—has made many readers systematically miss the more humane aspects and concerns of biblical narratives. In the essay "Books Which Have Influenced Me," Robert Louis Stevenson lists, among other books (mostly fiction), the Gospel according to Matthew. Since such a claim might seem strange, Stevenson feels the need to explain that Matthew's story "would startle and move any one if they could make a certain effort of imagination and read it freshly like a book, not droningly and dully like a portion of the Bible" (*Essays,* p. 64). What Stevenson has in mind is precisely an (ideally) uninterrupted, linear reading at constant speed along the lines of the "classical" paradigm of readability.

The Reformation: The Bible for All

To understand the sources of potential tension between reading and rereading, some perspective on the broader history of literacy and reading may be useful. The rise of mass literacy has been essential to the very idea of modernity: modern man, we may say, enters the stage of history as a reader. To grasp fully how this new kind of person emerged one must go back to the fifteenth century and specifically to Gutenberg's epoch-making invention of movable type, followed by the rapid spread of printing and the dramatic growth in the circulation of books during and after the sixteenth-century Protestant Reformation in Europe.

The actual turning point in the history of reading in the West was without doubt the Reformation, nearly a century after Gutenberg: it was then that the obligation to read and thus to gain access to the Book and to the word of God, for purposes of one's salvation, became virtually universal in a large part of the Protestant world, the one dominated by Calvinism (Bible reading in Lutheran and other Protestant areas was less sweepingly encouraged). While medieval Christianity could function with a "tiny ecclesiastical and urban elite which enjoyed the monopoly of written culture . . . [coexisting] side by side with a multitude that clung to its

· · ·

images, rites and incantations," as François Furet and Jacques Ozouf point out in their classic study of post-Reformation literacy in France,

> the Reformation . . . confronted everyone, even the ignorant, with the problem of doctrine. Everybody was henceforth obliged to turn to the Book in place of oral tradition: each individual's relationship with God ceased to be taken for granted, or undergone passively: it now became a citizenship to which access was gained through reading, just at the very moment when the advent of printing was democratizing the book. Luther made necessary what Gutenberg had made possible: by placing the Scriptures at the center of Christian eschatology, the Reformation turned a technical invention into a spiritual obligation. (*Reading and Writing*, p. 59)

This new spiritual obligation engendered a new sense of individual responsibility and freedom in direct personal interpretation of the Bible, without the mediation of any higher interpretive authorities. In an essay on the revolutionary significance of reading, Michel de Certeau reminds us that the Roman Catholic Church traditionally gave the power to determine the "literal" or uniquely true meaning of the Scriptures to members of the clergy, that is, to a small group of institutionally authorized professionals of interpretation. As long as the Church was strong socially and politically, it "ensured the Scriptures the status of a 'Letter' that was supposed to be independent of its readers and, in fact, possessed by its exegetes." But, starting with the Reformation, "the reciprocity between the text and its readers (which the institution hid) appeared, as if by withdrawing the Church had opened to view the indefinite plurality of the 'writings' produced by readings. The creativity of the reader grows as the institution that controlled it declines" (*The Practice of Everyday Life*, p. 172).

The long and complex process of making the sacred texts accessible to ordinary readers actually began in the Middle Ages, with various translations of the Bible (based mostly on the Latin Vulgate) into the vernacular languages. But a qualitatively new phase, crucial in the history of mass reading, commenced only with the Reformation and the dissemination in print of such landmarks as Luther's New Testament (1522) and German Bible (1534), translated respectively from the Greek and the Hebrew, rather than from the Latin of the Vulgate, or William Tyndale's translations of the 1520s and 1530s (using Luther's Bible as their main source). Tyndale was to serve as the basis for several English versions, including the Coverdale Bible (1535), the Great Bible (published in 1539 at the demand

. . .

of Henry VIII), and the Authorized King James Version (1611). A special place in the Renaissance sequence of English Bibles was occupied by the Geneva Bible, the work of English Protestant exiles in Geneva during the reign of Bloody Mary (1553–58), which was offered to Queen Elizabeth soon after her accession to the throne (1560) and was read by the great Elizabethans, including Shakespeare.

Responding to the challenge of the Reformation, and particularly to the Protestant democratization of access to the Bible, the Roman Catholic Church reversed its long-standing earlier policy of tolerance in this regard. At the Council of Trent (1545–63), which marked the beginning of the Counter-Reformation, Catholicism proscribed all "heretical" editions of the Bible (in Hebrew, Greek, or Latin) as well as all unauthorized vernacular translations (the various Protestant Bibles that did not support the dogmatic claims of the Catholic Church). The Council strongly reaffirmed the "authenticity" of the Latin Vulgate, in spite of the egregious errors of translation it contained, errors that had been discovered through the patient philological and critical work of a host of humanist scholars, the best known of whom was Erasmus.

The precise sense of the word *authenticum* as applied to the text of the Vulgate has long been debated, but its broader political meaning left little room for doubt. Whereas the Reformation recognized only one source of authority in matters of religious life, namely, the word of God in the Bible, the Council of Trent reaffirmed the old position of Catholicism, the doctrine of the *triple* authority: the Church as an institution, the Tradition, and the Bible. From the orthodox Catholic point of view, to single out the Bible as the unique source of religious authority was tantamount to heresy. The Vulgate, then, was "authentic" simply because it had been used by the Church in accordance with Tradition for centuries. Since the Church was infallible in its God-given institutional wisdom, and again infallible in its understanding of Tradition, it was out of the question that it could have used an unauthentic text.

The result of Trent was that, in the Catholic world, a serious attempt was made to withdraw the Scriptures from the access of ordinary believers, even those who knew how to read but had no Latin, the language of scholarship and theology. The word of God, easily misinterpreted, was supposed to remain out of their reach, mysteriously sealed in the intellectual catholicity or universality of Latin. It was to be kept away even from those deeply committed religious people who were ignorant of Latin, such as many monks and the vast majority of nuns. Nuns were also affected by

. . .

the Council of Trent's newly proclaimed rules of "holy ignorance" for women.

It still comes as a surprise to learn that a religious figure of the prominence of Teresa of Avila, who was to be canonized in 1622, forty years after her death, had never read the Bible except in the form of quotations contained in devotional works in Spanish that she found so important to read as a help to meditation and prayer. At one point, in fulfillment of the provisions of Trent, even these books, or most of them, were formally prohibited in Spain. One can imagine how profoundly troubled Teresa was when she learned that such favorites of hers as Osuna's *Third Spiritual Alphabet* had been placed on the Index compiled by none other than Fernando de Valdés, the Inquisitor General of Spain. In her autobiography Teresa recalls the interdiction of her cherished books: "When they forbade the reading of many books in the vernacular, I felt the prohibition very much because reading some of them was an enjoyment for me, and I could no longer do so since only the Latin editions were allowed. The Lord said to me: 'Don't be sad, for I shall give you a living book.' . . . The Lord showed so much love for me by teaching me in many ways, that I had very little or almost no need for books" (*Collected Works,* vol. 1, p. 172). Needless to say, not all those affected by the inquisitorial prohibition were favored by the Lord with access to a mystical "living book."

Vernacular Bibles (labeled "mothers of heresy" by Cardinal Pacheco at Trent) could not be realistically withdrawn from circulation or forbidden in all Catholic countries and regions. Even Cardinal Pacheco recognized that conditions in Spain, where the Reformation had not penetrated, were different from and better than those in countries like Germany or France, where Protestantism was strong. He accordingly agreed that "where the habit had taken root of having vernacular Bibles, only portions of the Bible should be allowed, such as the Psalms and Acts, while on no account should the Epistles or Apocalypse be put in the hands of all and sundry."[2]

In France, where Calvinism was gaining ground rapidly, the official Catholic reaction against popular Bible reading went back to the early 1520s. One notes that between 1525 and 1566 "nobody in Paris had the courage to print the New Testament in French" (although copies printed in Calvinist Geneva were smuggled in constantly at some risk) and that, during the 1530s and 1540s, according to Henri Dolet (writing in 1566), "one had to hide to read a Bible in the vernacular as one hides to counterfeit money."[3] Reading as such was suspect, and reading the Scriptures was a deeply illicit activity. By the middle of the sixteenth century, however,

. . .

the Reformation had been so successful in disseminating Protestant Bibles in France, Germany, and other parts of Europe that the Catholic Church would have "lost what remained of its prestige had it simply forbidden the reading of the Bible in the vernacular" (Baroni, *La Contre-Reforme*, p. 301).

This explains the continued appearance of Catholic Bibles in the vernacular in certain countries, whose texts were consistent with the Vulgate and thus gave support to the dogmatic and institutional claims of the Church of Rome. Such Bibles appeared early on in German, to counter Luther's (Emser's New Testament of 1527, Eck's Bible of 1537), English (the Reims-Douai Bible, starting with the New Testament in 1582 and ending with the Old Testament in 1610), French (The Bible of Louvain), and other languages. The tactical motives behind the publication of such Catholic Bibles are not hard to guess. The fact is, however, that they were widely read and that they effectively contributed to the Reformation-initiated movement toward mass reading.

That the Catholic Church fought for its monopoly on biblical interpretation (the Bible being one of the most powerful weapons against its power) is perfectly understandable in the historical circumstances. But even beyond the Catholic world, one should not underrate the reluctance of any official church establishment or ruling religious body to let ordinary readers freely make sense of its sacred texts. Thus in non-Calvinist Protestant regions, at least early on, certain categories of people were explicitly prohibited from reading the Bible. In England, for example, under Henry VIII, an act of 1543 " 'for the advancement of true religion and for the abolishment of the contrarie', forbade reading of any English Bible by artificers, journeymen, serving-men under the rank of yeoman, husbandmen, labourers, and all women other than those of noble or gentle rank."[4] Possible misreading of Scripture by the lower classes was construed as both sacrilegious and socially dangerous. Moreover, in England as well as elsewhere in the Protestant world, there were other means (from authoritarian manipulation and peer pressure to persecution and ostracization of dissenters) by which the leaders of various churches or sects continued to control or shape the reading of the Bible by ordinary individuals. Calvin himself was no less intolerant of apostates than the harshest Catholic inquisitors (in his *Defensio* of 1554 he legitimized the execution by burning of Michel Servet with arguments that any Catholic inquisitor could have used). But the inner logic of the Reformation— as illustrated by Luther's condemnation of inquisitorial practices—went

· · ·

against Calvin's brand of fanaticism, and his view that apostates should be burned was soon to be abandoned by the bulk of his followers. In fact, in spite of occasional lapses into fanaticism (persecution, witch hunts, and the like), Protestantism occupies a central place in the history of modern religious toleration.

Catholicism had its own approaches to the question of reading, including Bible reading (in Latin or, where and when permitted, in the vernacular). Aside from the scholarly-theological way of reading and interpreting, Catholicism preserved the traditions of ritualistic or liturgical reading (*lectio divina*), which go back to early medieval monasticism. Of course, as techniques of extreme attention in the (re)reading of sacred texts, these traditions go even further back, to ancient Judaism. Over the centuries, and particularly at the time of troubles represented by the Reformation, liturgical reading developed more personalized versions of spiritual reading (*lectio spiritualis*) as techniques of meditation, prayer, or contemplation. Spiritual reading was increasingly a characteristic of postmedieval monasticism, but was not necessarily confined to monastic life and could be seen largely as an elitist Counter-Reformation response to the Reformation drive toward mass reading and the democratization of the Bible. Significantly, it was Jesuits (the religious order that exemplified best the spirit of the Counter-Reformation) who first used the phrase *lectio spiritualis*,[5] a phrase which has an obvious relation to the term and the concept of spiritual exercises: Ignatius Loyola, the founder of the Society of Jesus, wrote his *Spiritual Exercises,* the most influential devotional tract of the period of the Counter-Reformation, in 1548, during the Council of Trent).

From Intensive to Extensive Reading?

The significance of the Bible as the most powerful incentive to reading and rereading in Protestant Europe and America cannot be exaggerated. Recent historians of reading have proposed an interesting distinction between intensive reading, characteristic of "traditional literacy," and a more modern and secular kind of extensive reading. Intensive reading was practiced, according to the proponents of this distinction, in Protestant communities, roughly from the sixteenth to the late eighteenth century, when the typical literate person read and (re)read a small number of books (the Bible first and foremost and then mostly devotional works). Such intensive reading habits highlight the personal dimension of Protestant

. . .

reading. Reading was for the individual an opportunity to inspect and constantly reinspect his or her self in search of the mysterious "signs" of salvation.[6]

The biblical model of intensive reading had another important consequence: the eventual internalization of interpretive authority. This internalization must be taken in a double sense—textual and psychological. Textually, the Bible was to be seen as a self-contained entity: it was an enormously difficult and demanding text but also, on condition of repeated attentive rereading over long periods of time, a completely self-interpreting one. Certainly, the self-interpreting nature of the biblical text was not a novelty, but its forceful reaffirmation in the context of Protestantism played a new polemical role: it became a way of rejecting the two extratextual sources of interpretive authority invoked by the Catholic Church—the institution of the Church and the Tradition (the latter was supposed to have been transmitted orally and continuously from Jesus through Peter to the reigning pope). The hermeneutical insight on which the model of the Bible as a self-interpreting text was based went all the way back to the ancient midrashic tradition in Judaism, a tradition that had been variously reasserted at key moments in the history of Christianity.[7] Thus, at least on a theoretical plane, the view of a self-interpreting Scripture was not incompatible with the tenets of Catholicism. It was the second aspect of the internalization of interpretive authority, the moral-psychological one, that was dramatically new. The novelty consisted of the fact that the ultimate interpretive responsibility devolved on the ordinary individual reader, who was now both free and obliged to understand the Bible according to its internal logic as this logic disclosed itself in the process of repeated reading in the state that Ruskin described as "awed attention."

According to some historians (such as Rolf Engelsing in his *Der Bürger als Leser*), a drastic change in reading patterns, a veritable revolution in reading, occurred with the subsequent coming of modernity and secularization. Toward the end of the eighteenth century, a new kind of extensive reading became increasingly widespread: readers would typically be exposed to a larger number of often secular, often diversionary texts which they would peruse in an order decided entirely by themselves, as free individuals, independently of the religious calendar (which used to regulate the order of reading or rereading in the traditional model) or from other external constraints. The relationship of these new readers to the book would be less respectful; their general attitude would be more

· · ·

casual, superficial, and consumer-like. In other words, the new model of extensive reading would favor a linear single reading (and even reading in haste to satisfy one's more or less frivolous curiosity) over rereading.

Although this model of historical change from an intensive to an extensive type of reading does have certain heuristic merits, it is not free from the danger of oversimplification. The main criticism of the intensive/extensive reading scheme is that it does not sufficiently take into account the obvious possibility of individuals and even groups practicing both types of reading. Indeed, what would prevent one from switching from intensive to extensive reading according to circumstance, interest, or purpose? Furthermore, a person could adopt one attitude or the other in response to the suggestions or demands of the text itself or, to be more precise, in response to the promptings of such internal textual functions as those represented by, say, the "implied reader" (Wolfgang Iser), the "model reader" (Umberto Eco), or, more broadly, what might be called the "textual reader." Texts, as we shall see, have many ways to instruct the reader about the adequate pace of reading: ways of slowing down the reading (by such devices as the use of deliberate obscurity or ambiguity, recondite allusion, cryptic symbols, certain types of repetition) or, on the contrary, of speeding it up (by the use of suspense or the "cliff-hanger" style, by resort to certain kinds of redundancy or formulaic language and situations).

Faced with the claim that extensive reading supplanted intensive reading, one wonders why the historically documented diversification of the choices and purposes of reading would result in a generalized abandonment of intensive reading in favor of superficial, quick, disengaged reading? Why would individual readers, once in a position to pick from a larger diversity of available reading materials and freer to decide what, when, and how to read, be supposed to give up their deeper engagements with certain subjects and books (be these religious, philosophical, political, or literary) when occasionally indulging, as a recreation, in certain types of more relaxing reading? Studies of individual cases of "average" or "ordinary" bourgeois eighteenth-century readers, such as Robert Darnton's article on the merchant Jean Ranson of La Rochelle, who was a passionate reader of Rousseau, tend to cast doubt on the view that the broad social model of an eighteenth-century revolution in reading patterns could explain individual reading habits. Furthermore, such studies demonstrate that the very distinction between intensive and extensive reading is neither as neutral (or "scientific") nor as new as one might

· · ·

think. In regard to novelty, for instance, a comparable distinction, used polemically, is found in Rousseau himself.

For Rousseau, as one might expect, the distinction reflects the writer's "romantic" criticism of modern civilization, in contrast with the uncorrupted natural ways of human sensibility. In his epistolary novel *La nouvelle Héloïse,* Rousseau thus condemns extensive reading (of course not in these terms) as a typical vice of the French reader of his time, a reader who "reads much; but who reads only new books, or rather hurries through them, for his purpose is not to read them but only to say he has read them; [whereas] the Genevan reader reads only good books; he reads them, and he digests them; he doesn't judge them, but knows them."[8] A similar distinction, in which extensive reading was condemned even more drastically, was developed, as we saw in chapter 5, by Rousseau's disciple, Sébastien Mercier.

But such ideas were not confined to France. In England, readers of novels—a new and increasingly popular genre in the eighteenth century— were often perceived to be naive, easily duped extensive readers, and were described (by Samuel Johnson) as "the young, the ignorant, the idle."[9] The renewed attacks on reading for immediate gratification (as opposed to instruction or edification or even certain kinds of higher intellectual pleasure) have received various explanations. One of the most interesting of these, suggested by Ian Watt in his classic *The Rise of the Novel,* looks at the question in terms of the sociology of intellectual life: "The fact that literature . . . was addressed to an ever-widening audience must have weakened the relative importance of those readers with enough education and leisure to take a professional or semi-professional interest in classical and modern letters" (p. 48). According to Watt, the two new literary forms introduced by the eighteenth century, the newspaper and the novel, "both obviously encourage a rapid, inattentive, almost unconscious kind of reading habit. . . . It is certain that this change of emphasis was an essential permissive factor for the achievements of Defoe and Richardson" (p. 49). In his history of the mass reading public in nineteenth-century England, Richard D. Altick arrives at a similar conclusion with regard to the role played by the novel as it evolved during the eighteenth and nineteenth centuries, observing that "the popular audience owed its birth in large part to the novel" (*The English Common Reader,* p. 65).

But it would not be difficult to push the origins of the dichotomy between intensive and extensive reading (including popular reading "for transient satisfaction") even farther back in time, by showing, for in-

· · ·

stance, that many of the puritanical sixteenth- and seventeenth-century condemnations of reading for pleasure or entertainment (as opposed to reading for edification) already contain the basic ingredients of the intensive/extensive reading distinction.[10] Of these ingredients the most important is probably the puritanical distrust of pleasure and the tendency to associate any kind of pleasure with guilt. But reading for pleasure had been suspect in the Catholic world as well. Thus, in sixteenth-century Spain the moralistic condemnation of novels of chivalry (which did not prevent the spectacular growth of the genre) participated essentially in the same logic as that of the puritanical and, later, neopuritanical (Rousseauistic or otherwise ideological) censure of reading for pleasure, pleasure being equated with escape and irresponsibility.

Cultural Homogeneity, Cultural Diversity, and Patterns of Reading

If we admit that there has indeed been a historical passage from a time of intensive reading of few (culturally homogeneous) books to one of extensive exposure to many (culturally heterogeneous) books, it seems useful to reformulate the distinction in terms of reading and rereading. In speaking of reading and rereading we must be ready to acknowledge from the outset the paradox that the two can be at once complementary and divergent. In a culturally homogeneous situation, they tend to be continuous and complementary. Of course, cultural homogeneity is of many kinds and may have many causes. For a long time during the Middle Ages the scarcity of reading material (tied to its expensiveness but also to control by the Church) was an important factor in creating a homogeneous cultural environment for a small intellectual elite working in monastic institutions, with their libraries and scriptoria, which later gave birth to the first European universities. Once the democratizing effects of print were felt, cultural homogeneity tended to become more fluid. By and large, we may see it as a continuum between two ideal extremes: homogeneity deriving from a freely arrived-at consensus (in contemporary religious, political, cultural, or professional associations, for instance) and homogeneity imposed from above by a source of authority (a dominant church or religious establishment, an ideological apparatus or party).

The first case, that of homogeneity achieved by consensus, could be illustrated in the area of literary reading by the way in which (ideally) generation after generation of readers seem to have agreed to give certain

· · ·

authors the status of classics. But one should not forget that, practically, the classics are also imposed on often immature or reluctant readers by the school system, not to speak of other kinds of less obvious impositions denounced by various fashionable conspiracy theories of canon formation. The needs of education point to the fact that a certain degree of cultural homogeneity or community of knowledge is indispensable for purposes of articulate communication and intellectual creation. Such needs have been at the heart of recent debates about "cultural literacy" in this country and, on a more specialized level, at the center of ongoing discussions about the humanistic curriculum in higher education or the question of the literary canon.

The second case, that of imposed homogeneity, also gives rise to many forms and possibilities. The limits of what one can or ought to read may be set by self-imposed standards or may be directly controlled by an external authority, such as the leaders of the dominant church, the moral arbiters, or the censors beholden to the political leaders of closed, totalitarian societies. In the latter instance, intensive reading should be viewed more properly as forced reading, a coercive extension of propaganda that is part of a larger process of indoctrination. Forced reading may of course have an effect opposite to the one that is intended: it may, and often does, discourage rather than encourage belief and may foster tacit or outspoken dissent.

In a culturally heterogeneous model, which is essentially democratic, competitive, and pluralistic, reading and rereading are potentially more discontinuous and conflictive than in conditions of homogeneity: the passion for reading is in principle insatiable in regard to quantity, extension, curiosity, variety, pleasure, and quasi-hypnotic involvement with texts capable of captivating an average reader. Rereading, which often springs from a deeper personal commitment, religious or otherwise, but which can also be motivated by a reflective attitude and a strong desire to understand how a text works, represents the side of dedication, sustained attention, and sophisticated absorption.

. . .

SEVEN

Ages, Places, and Situations

No sooner has a word been said, somewhere, about the pleasure of
the text, than two policemen are ready to jump on you: the political
policeman and the psychoanalytical policeman: futility and/or guilt,
pleasure is either idle or vain, a class notion or an illusion. An old,
very old tradition: hedonism has been repressed by
nearly every philosophy.
ROLAND BARTHES
The Pleasure of the Text

· · · · · · ·

Reading for Pleasure and the Reader's Age

That the great variable in the reader's making sense of texts is history is
accepted by virtually all critical schools. Even the most conservative
believers in authorial intention or meaning and the reader's obligation to
recover it in its purest form agree that different generations will read the
same work differently, that aside from its strict linguistic meaning the
work will always acquire a new, unsuspected significance in a new historical context. But the responses of contemporary readers and rereaders—
irrespective of what conservative, normative critics may wish or require—
will also vary greatly, as a function of diverse psychosocial factors that

· · ·

have a direct bearing on the process of reading. I shall deal here only with three major variables: the age of the reader, the place or situation in which the reading occurs, and gender.

Of these three the most obvious is age. The awareness of different reading needs according to the age of the reader is reflected in the existence of specialized types of literary discourse, such as children's literature, with its diversity of narrative genres and subgenres (fairy tales, fantasies à la Tolkien or C. S. Lewis) or literature for young adults (adventure stories, science fiction). The broad questions I want to address here are: How and what do children read for pleasure? How and what do adolescents read? How do adults or older people read, not as individuals but as members of their age group? And, most important, how does the distinction between reading and rereading apply to the patterns of reading of different age groups?

Many psychologists of reading have addressed the question of reading and age from a limited perspective, focusing mainly on the teaching of reading. This line of study has been spurred by the crucial formative importance of reading—in the sense of the acquisition and development of reading skills—from early childhood to young adulthood. Literary reading in this context has tended to be regarded as one means toward acquiring "cultural literacy," an enabling condition for using reading in later life for various purposes, including recreation. This is certainly a highly desirable goal of reading education.

My primary interest here, however, is in reading as a self-motivated activity or reading for pleasure. This kind of reading is certainly not incompatible with what one reads (or is supposed to read) in school, since in many cases assigned reading can and does become reading for fun. Put in more technical psychological language: telic reading (reading for a goal external to itself—to satisfy a requirement, to obtain useful information, to improve one's reading comprehension, to deal with certain developmental or emotional problems, and so on) can always become paratelic or autotelic, that is, acquire an independent, originally unforeseen goal or become a goal in itself, an intrinsically motivated process. What is more, schools may encourage reading for pleasure, as when teachers, instructors, or school librarians recommend specific books to their students to read for fun, trying to match their assumed needs or desires with the content of particular books. Nonetheless, I shall focus on reading that is done outside the school system, unguided if not completely uninfluenced by it.

· · ·

In dealing with the question of reading and age, I shall avail myself of any pertinent results of the existing psychological studies of reading for pleasure, but for the most part I shall have to improvise, to make guesses and hypotheses which I cannot scientifically verify but which still seem to me worth offering for informal, introspective validation by the reader of this essay. Perhaps one day professional psychologists and sociologists of reading will consider the problems touched upon in this chapter with the proper scientific instruments, including questionnaires, statistical analyses of test results, and individual case histories.

Such inquiries might adopt a broad developmental approach similar to the one proposed by J. A. Appleyard in his book *Becoming a Reader*. Appleyard applies to the question of reading and age a model of unfolding cognitive schemes derived from the genetic epistemology of Jean Piaget, but significantly complemented by elements borrowed from psychoanalysis (mostly from Erik Erikson's views about childhood and society and the adolescent's search for an identity) and from the analytical psychology of C. G. Jung (mostly from Jung's insights into the archetypal patterns of human imagination). In his study, Appleyard defines five typical roles of the reader according to age: (1) the reader as player or, more precisely, *symbolic* player—corresponding to a child's preschool years when the experiences of being read to, of fantasizing, and of participating in various kinds of pretend play are often continuous and mutually reinforcing; (2) the reader as hero or heroine—corresponding to later childhood (ages 7–11), when the child voluntarily reads mostly adventure stories and tends to identify with fictional heroes; (3) the reader as thinker—corresponding to adolescence, when the young reader starts to reflect on fictional characters, motives, and feelings that differ from his or her own in an attempt to establish a stronger sense of personal identity; (4) the reader as interpreter—corresponding to the college years and later, when the educated reader becomes aware of the interpretability of a literary text and strives to understand the text and articulate a valid interpretation among many possible ones; and (5) the adult, "pragmatic" reader, that is, the fully mature person who can distinguish among the various purposes of reading for information, for intellectual or aesthetic satisfaction, for relaxation, and who, as a rule, tends to prefer nonfiction (history, biography) to fiction and, within fiction, character-dominated rather than plot-dominated texts. Appleyard's developmental typology is flexible enough to allow mature readers to synthesize the major characteristics of the previous ages of reading:

. . .

An important point to be made about adult reading is that it combines and reconstellates all the ways of reading that have mattered to an individual across a lifetime of responding to stories. The child is here as well as the juvenile and adolescent and student of literature, their special experiences available for recycling and refiguring as part of the complex responses adults have to what they read . . . But it is not simply a matter of addition [as C. S. Lewis remarks]: "I now enjoy fairy tales better than I did in childhood: being now able to put more in, of course I get more out." (p. 164)

In general terms, one cannot but agree with Appleyard that earlier phases in the development of a reader are not definitely left behind but are continuously and diversely subsumed under the new modes of reading characteristic of later phases. I shall try to deal with this important question from a somewhat different perspective—a perspective to which the phenomenon of rereading is as central as the phenomenon of reading itself.

"Charming Childhood Readings"

The Vigny anecdote recounted at the end of chapter 5 suggests that there may be a link—and a somewhat perverse one at that—between rereading and old age. The contrast between reading and rereading implied in Vigny's presentation of Royer-Collard could be rendered explicit, as one commentator proposes, by pointing out that the old academician regarded "rereading as an activity . . . of an age when one is naturally reasonable; reading being assimilated to some sort of debauch, inappropriate at an advanced age" (Bernard Abraham, "A propos de la relecture," p. 83). It goes without saying that such a comical counterposition has more to do with the polemical intent of Vigny's portrayal of Royer-Collard than with the complex question of how age may influence or shape modes of reading. The fact is, however, that other students of reading have associated rereading with old age. Thus, Emile Faguet—an academic French critic famous at the turn of the century but now almost completely forgotten—mentions Royer-Collard and concludes that "rereading is indeed an old man's pleasure" (*L'Art de lire,* p. 151). His argument is that rereading is a form of remembering and that, consequently, it could be seen as "reading one's own memoirs without having made the effort to write them down." And he suggests the intriguing idea of a reader's, or rather a rereader's, autobiography: "One could very well

· · ·

compose an autobiography," he notes, "by comparing reading impressions at various ages, an autobiography that could be entitled *Rereading* [*En relisant*]" (p. 159). Closer to us in time, Charles Grivel has drawn a portrait of the rereader not only as an old man, but also as a rather grouchy one: "le reliseur est un personnage amer" ("Les premières lectures," p. 134).

But can it be true that rereading is primarily a characteristic of old age? Hardly so. Just as young children like to be told their favorite story over and over (even when they know it by heart), it is a fact that young readers like to read their favorite books over and over, in order to repeat (both excitingly and reassuringly) an experience of involvement bordering on self-hypnosis. This youthful rereading is both phenomenologically and structurally different from the mature rediscovery of texts that one might have perused in one's youth, perhaps reluctantly, for some boring school assignment, as well as from other types of adult reflective rereading. In a general sense, we may say, the true classics—including many classics of children's literature such as Lewis Carroll's *Alice in Wonderland,* not to mention books enjoyed by children but not addressed to them such as Swift's *Gulliver's Travels* or Defoe's *Robinson Crusoe*—are more properly (re)read and (re)discovered at a mature age. (But of course such maturity need not be tied to one's chronological age: there are precocious maturities and late-blooming ones.) "Every reading of a classic is in fact a rereading," Italo Calvino observes in "Why Read the Classics?" (*The Uses of Literature,* p. 128), and he adds that "reading in youth can be rather unfruitful, owing to impatience, distraction, inexperience." The likelihood of young people reading the classics as they should be read ("not . . . out of duty or respect, but only out of love") is small. Young readers will certainly encounter the classics at school but, with rare exceptions, they will be able to establish that essential "personal rapport" with some of them only later. "School should enable you to know, either well or badly, a certain number of classics among which—or in reference to which—you can then choose *your* classics. School is obliged to give the instruments to make a choice, but the choices that count are those that occur outside and after school" (p. 129).

Focusing on the relationship between reading and age almost inevitably brings up the memory, vivid in most of us, of our "charming childhood readings," of those books which Proust so poetically evokes in the first part of his early seminal essay "Sur la lecture" (one of the first anticipa-

· · ·

tions of the tone and theme of *A la recherche du temps perdu,* a novel as much about reading as about time). Most of these are books that we do not reread in the reflective sense of the word (that is, because they promise us renewed pleasures and unexpected insights on rereading)[1] but that we still may occasionally leaf through, as Proust puts it, "for no other reason than that they are the only calendars we have kept of days that have vanished, and we hope to see reflected on their pages the dwellings and the ponds which no longer exist" (*On Reading Ruskin,* pp. 99–100). These are, we might say, not so much remembered texts as pretexts for remembering, occasions for attempting to reexplore certain spaces of memory and to relive certain events and impressions of our personal past which coincided in time with their reading.

Our early readings, whether our memory preserves or not the names of the authors or the titles of the books, may take on a disproportionate significance in our retrospective fantasies—disproportionate at least in regard to the intrinsic value of most of the books involved, if our mature self were to reassess it. It remains a fact, however, that our sense of personal identity and self-consciousness is often closely linked with our ability to read and with our first childhood readings, as Jean-Jacques Rousseau, the inventor of modern autobiography, suggests in a text often quoted by historians of reading: "I do not know what I did until I was five or six years old. I do not know how I learned to write; I only remember my earliest readings and the effect they had upon me; it is from that time that I date my uninterrupted consciousness of myself."[2]

Could we go so far as to say that childhood itself is essentially a "concept" of reading?[3] Yes, we could, I think, particularly if childhood, insofar as it is a romantic literary invention or myth, depends as much on reading *in* childhood as on reading *about* childhood. Moreover, reading about reading in childhood helps us to remember, and perhaps even to re-create, the sense of enchantment produced in us by certain involved, quasi-hypnotic reading experiences we had long ago. And even if we did not really have them, we can imagine them, particularly if what we are reading about reading in childhood is a text by Proust—the one I have just quoted or any relevant extended passage from *A la recherche du temps perdu* (such as the evocation of George Sand's *François le Champi* as read by the child Marcel or read to him by his mother) or from *Jean Santeuil.*[4] To use a key Proustian metaphor, such texts are like lenses through which a whole horizon of experience, real or possible, becomes magically recoverable: they represent reading as self-discovery.

. . .

The Reader as a Child

The notion of self-hypnosis is a good starting point for drawing a more complete portrait of the reader in childhood. For the child, including the older child or the teenager, involved reading appears to be an extension of play (mostly symbolic) and fantasy—an extension that raises these mental activities to high levels of complexity and sophistication. Since reading is always also work (perhaps invisible work, perhaps "work for play," but still work, and often hard work), many children today prefer to watch television, which performs some of the functions of reading at a fraction of the effort but also leaves out some of the essential ingredients of one's intellectual well-being (reading stimulates creativity much more than passive television watching, as most psychologists and cultural critics agree).

Be that as it may, the typical child or adolescent reader for pleasure (as opposed to the reluctant or lazy if not unskilled reader) is likely to have certain characteristics. Children who read tend to possess a good imagination and a healthy inclination for daydreaming. Reading, I would say, is a way for the child or adolescent to enrich his or her fantasy life and to develop what J. L. Singer calls "skill in daydreaming" (*Daydreaming*, p. 189). Materials derived from books (formulas, expressions, characters, imaginary adventures with cliff-hanging situations, hair's-breadth escapes, extremities of danger and success) can become immediate food for daydreaming. Also relevant here is Gaston Bachelard's concept of reverie and his *rêveur* or daydreamer, as portrayed in his *Poétique de la rêverie* and other essays on the phenomenology of the imaginary. Particularly significant for grasping the needs of the child or adolescent reader is Bachelard's theory of "the function of the unreal." Bachelard does not limit this function to a specific age and suggests that it may well be a lifelong phenomenon: significantly, he goes on to explain his own "hunger" in old age for reading and his deep enjoyment of a "reading life" (*une vie de lecture*) by reference to it (p. 23). But in fact the function of the unreal—the need of the mind for unreal, imaginary projections and idealizations, without which it might risk losing its balance and fall prey to anxiety, boredom, or even neurosis—is of greatest importance in children and adolescents, for reasons I shall make clear in Part III. Of course the need for unreality can be satisfied by means other than books (let alone books of poetry, which the old Bachelard relished): movies, television, cartoons, or even unguided, free modes of reverie or castle building. But reading remains, I think, the most deeply stimulating and constructive

. . .

way of satisfying the function of the unreal, by striking a delicate, almost magical balance between mental activity and mental rest.

A major characteristic of childhood and adolescent reading for pleasure is that it is likely to be unconnected with school. In fact, readers in this age group will seek, often in proportion to their intelligence and initiative, precisely those books that they are *not* encouraged to read at their age: "trashy" books that are usually gobbled up (pulp fiction, science fiction, mysteries, vaguely or not-so-vaguely pornographic books), but also, at the other extreme, more difficult or challenging books that it is thought they would not like or would not understand properly (which may include certain classics that will be recommended by the school at a later stage). A typically avid or voracious adolescent reader (note the prevalence of eating metaphors commonly applied to reading) will therefore thrive on a heterogeneous fare, with certain preferred genres—usually formulaic, popular, highly readable books of fiction, but not without surprising exceptions.

Linked to the "voraciousness" of adolescent readers is their tendency to read—or reread—quickly. One of the cardinal rules in their informal code of reading for pleasure seems to be speed: the right speed for being transported, for achieving what might be called a "reading trance." Hence, with rare exceptions, young readers tend to be fast readers who remorselessly skip minor textual difficulties for the sake of the total effect of the act of reading, of that quasi-hypnotic involvement which would not be possible with too many interruptions, delays, detours, and lengthy investigations to clear up obscure details.

Adolescent readers also display what I would call "methodical naivete," their willingness not only to suspend disbelief but actually to believe all that they are asked (or think they are asked) to believe for the duration of a pleasurable, engrossing reading. This naivete is methodical in the sense that it does not come naturally but is induced by the text itself and occasionally by the reactions of other readers (peers or friends who may have recommended a book by describing its effects). Being "played," performed as a role, or pretended, methodical naivete possesses a special and often quite subtle logic of its own. Not everything is permitted; certain huge incompatibilities with everyday experience and accepted definitions of reality will be all right, such as the positing of fantastic beings or situations as fictionally true, or the invocation of extraordinary coincidences, while smaller inconsistencies or barely noticeable wrong details will be censured. In other words, young readers of stories learn

· · ·

without difficulty both the psychological and the generic rules of fictional truth: flying horses and talking animals will be fictionally true in fairy tales or fantasies but not in science fiction; wizards and giants will be fictionally true in fantasies but not in mysteries. A young reader will accept without a problem that someone might sell his shadow for the purse of Fortunatus (the legendary purse containing an inexhaustible supply of gold coins), but will be bothered, say, by an unexplained change in the color of the hero's eyes. (This large question of fictional truth and the reader's credulousness will be discussed at greater length in Part III).

Ideal Age Types of Readers and Rereaders

The conflict between diverse types of reading and rereading can be elaborated in terms of ideal (metaphorical) age types. The model of the involved reader is a child or an adolescent—the child or adolescent who survives in us, in our fantasies, in our curiosity, and in our capacity for wonder, whether as a Freudian daydreamer, a version of the Jungian *puer aeternus,* or an avatar of Bachelard's confidently naive *rêveur.* By contrast, the model of the reflective rereader is a mature persona, although one whose actual age cannot and should not be specified. What I am trying to suggest here for the typical adult readers is an overall mental attitude, a way of seeing, a propensity toward revisiting places they have visited and reexperiencing things they have experienced not for the sake of repetition (which the child or adolescent reader appreciates so much) but for the sake of that subtle, paradoxical, puzzling difference which reveals itself only to a riper, more reflective mind. Last, we may posit an elderly persona who reads and often rereads for purposes of retrospective fantasizing, for hallucinating regained mastery over fictional worlds threatened by oblivion. Since this typology is metaphorical, real chronological age is irrelevant.

Assuming that the apprenticeship of literacy is over, the child reader or the older (re)readers as *roles* can appear successively or simultaneously, earlier or later in one's reading life. It is also possible that one may not appear at all or may disappear at a certain point—aging readers may lose their ability to play games of make-believe. But the typology of readers and rereaders I am proposing here in no way excludes the possible coexistence of types in the same individual, probably a fairly common case. Less frequent seem to be the "pure" cases, that is, those who on principle refuse to read (Royer-Collard) or, at the opposite extreme, to reread. An example

. . .

of the latter is those readers who will stubbornly refrain from rereading a book that might otherwise attract them (a mystery good for killing a few idle hours) if they suspect they have already read it. It seems to matter little to such people that they have forgotten everything about the first reading of a book except that it took place: for them a previously read book is like yesterday's newspaper.[5] They hate the idea of rereading. But such opponents of rereading are never children; they are rather over-age children, who occasionally read to kill time, in whom the inner child has long withered and lost all imaginative vitality, freshness of feeling, and capacity for getting engrossed in the reading of fiction.

As has already been pointed out, children do often reread favorite books and continue to be excited by them even when they know them almost by heart. One should distinguish, however, between reading the same book several times over, as children may, for the purpose of repeating what is basically the same favorite fantasy (the reassuring sameness of the experience being of the essence) and reflective rereading, which involves certain critical abilities and a fairly high degree of self-consciousness. In rereading of this kind, the repetition of a specific reading process has as its purpose not the sameness of the experience but precisely its opposite, the discovery of possibilities unsuspected the first time around, which may prove crucial to the mind bent on playing an interpretive game of absorption.

In reality, the child or adolescent reader is of course more complex than the simplified type sketched here. On the one hand, there is the younger child who may like to listen to the same story again and again, repeated word for word every night. This child will protest at the smallest change of content or variation in form—a typical occurrence in which Freud identified an instance of the "compulsion to repeat." This might be better explained, however, by analogy with Winnicott's "transitional object," an object that the child clings to in order to protect itself from the fear of separation from the parent or the fantasy of abandonment. (But this child will not necessarily refuse to listen to new stories.) On the other hand, there is the early adolescent, always "hungry" for books of adventure of all kinds, reading in a great hurry, possessed by a huge, inexhaustible curiosity and the most intense desire to experience (on the level of fantasy) new situations and travel in imagination through unknown, exotic worlds. In between the young child and the adolescent is the child reader who does not yet perceive the existence of a conflict between the magic of repetition and the passionate curiosity for new fictional adventures and reading experiences. This child reader will then read his favorite

· · ·

books over and over again while also eagerly and hurriedly exploring new fictional territories.[6]

Places: A Prisoner Rereading Proust

Differences of age among readers and the correspondingly different concepts of reality and unreality, imaginative needs, and patterns of expectations constitute only one of the major variables that a theory of literary (re)reading must take into account. An equally important variable is related to the place where the act of reading occurs and the personal situation of the reader. By "place" here I mean at once *physical* space or environment—bedroom or living room or den at home, library, airport or airplane, railway station or train, doctor's waiting room, hospital, prison, and so on—and *social* space, since physical spaces do all have a social definition that colors their connotations. In addition, the places of reading and rereading suggest more or less typical personal situations and corresponding moods, aside from the unpredictable and unchartable diversity of purely individual moods that always affect a reader's response. Thus one is likely to read or reread the same book quite differently according to whether the reading takes place in the comfort of one's home, a public space (whether a library or a beach during a vacation), a hospital room, or a prison cell.

The difficulty and complexity of the questions generated by the places and situations of reading should not deter us from paying attention to them. But how? Even if there are written testimonies about specific responses to specific books read under specific circumstances—say, Proust read in a Soviet political prison at the beginning of World War II—how is a student of Proust's reception to bring them all into the same focus, particularly when they appear to be exceedingly singular, uncommon, even literally outlandish? Literary criticism, including most reader-based criticism, tends to give us not only conveniently achronic (timeless, in a phenomenological sense) but also atopic (placeless) readings of literary works. Needless to say, sensibility to historical context of both literary production and reception has long been a widely accepted requirement of critical-reflective reading, but this has rarely involved taking into consideration such blatantly extratextual concerns as the age or place or personal situation of real readers. There is little doubt that the bracketing of these complicating factors is justified if not necessary in discussing a literary work. To take into account even the implied or "textual" reader—

. . .

the reader whose profile is inscribed, more or less precisely, in the text itself—slows down the critical act considerably, perhaps unbearably. Reception studies, with their close attention to historical detail, introduce even slower, more cumbersome reading protocols and procedures of critical exposition. An attempt to add to the reception record improbable, remote, exotic readings might result in sheer critical paralysis.

But still, I think, the "where" of reading—whatever the difficulties of mapping it—deserves to be pondered if what we want to understand is not the fate of a particular work or group of works but the process of reading itself, including the major influences that shape the construction of meaning by the reader. There has been scant interest in this area except from writers. In a very intelligent and witty essay on the "socio-physiological" aspects of reading ("Lire: Esquisse socio-physiologique" in *Penser/Classer*), Georges Perec has suggested an informal typology that uses classifying rubrics such as "time slots" (reading while waiting—at a hairdresser's, at a dentist's, in a ticket line at a box office), "corporeal" postures or activities (reading in a standing position, reading at table while eating, in bed while trying to fall asleep, on the toilet as Joyce's Leopold Bloom in the famous outhouse episode in *Ulysses*), and what he calls rather sweepingly "social space." This last category includes such subdivisions as "public transportation" (commuters reading in the bus or subway), "trips" (reading in airplanes or trains—*littérature de gare*), and "other" (reading while on vacation or "reading when one is ill, at home, at the hospital, during convalescence, etc."). "These are questions," Perec concludes, "which I ask, and I feel it would not be useless for a writer to give them some thought" (pp. 127–28).

Since it would be impossible here to do justice to the complexities of an issue that has been little studied by psychologists, reading specialists, or literary theorists, one example will suffice to indicate the dramatic significance that the place-factor may have in the overall process of (re)reading. (One notes in passing that, unlike age, the reader's place or situation is not particularly well suited for the techniques of contemporary psychological research. The studies that have been done in this area have looked mostly at the therapeutic or rehabilitative virtues of reading for school children with developmental problems or for people confined to such places as mental hospitals and prisons—hence the emerging field of "bibliotherapy,"[7] a branch of library science.) My example (I have chosen it also because Perec ignores this situation in his rather extensive typology) is doubly untypical: first, it concerns reading under circumstances of ex-

· · ·

treme physical and moral deprivation in a brutal political prison system (that of Stalinist Russia); second, it comes from an extraordinary witness, a writer and connoisseur of literature in several languages, not a common reader by any means. But spectacular untypicalness of this sort has the advantage of lending liveliness and drama to its opposite, the typical, by revealing deep, unsuspected analogies between the two. Aleksander Wat recounts key moments of his life—including his experiences in the Soviet Gulag—in *My Century,* a posthumously published memoir based on taped conversations with Czeslaw Milosz (the conversations between the two émigrés took place in Berkeley, California, in 1964–65). Wat's reflections on reading in prison are part of the description of his detention, in 1940–41, in the Lubyanka prison in Moscow. Arrested in Lwow soon after the occupation of eastern Poland by the Red Army, he spent some time in a jail where "it was a crime to possess a scrap of paper," before being moved to the Lubyanka where, at the time, and quite surprisingly, the prisoners were allowed to read. The prison librarian would come once every ten days with a supply of miscellaneous books for the inmates to choose from—works of philosophy, literature, even theology, but, again surprisingly, not Marxism. About the absence of Marxist literature Wat comments, "My fellow prisoners had a very intelligent explanation: it was only to keep the investigators, who were not terribly intelligent, from being nailed to the wall by Marxist arguments" (p. 203).

Reading in prison accounted for what the writer did not hesitate to characterize in exalted, quasi-religious terms as "one of the greatest experiences of my life. Not because [the books] allowed me an escape but because . . . they transformed me, influenced me and shaped me greatly. It was the way I read those books; I came at them from a completely new angle. And from then on I had a completely new understanding, not only of literature, but of everything" (p. 203). It is perhaps not fortuitous that the first inkling of what was to be such a profound change in Wat's existential outlook was occasioned by an act of rereading. His first book in a long time was *Du côté de chez Swann,* the first part of Proust's *A la recherche du temps perdu,* in a so-so Russian translation. Rereading the book in this mediocre translation accomplished what a first reading could not have done: it magically brought back the memory of Proust in the original French, with the verbatim memory of its first page, with the musical "cascade of Proustian sentences," to such a degree that from the beginning the "cadence of French replaced the Russian and was with me to the last word in the volume" (p. 193). Rereading, Wat also could realize how

. . .

far he had moved from his old self (oversophisticated, pretentious, irritatingly snobbish), which had made him sensitive to one aspect of Proust, namely the evocation of Parisian social life, aristocratic (*le côté des Guermantes*) or upper middle-class (the salon of Madame Verdurin), with its rituals, habits, manners, and codes. Now, reread in prison, the text disclosed its more profound tragic dimensions, its powerfully poetic "inward vibration," its peculiar sense of memory suspended between life and death. The rediscovered Proust offered Wat "a model for the agony I was suffering in prison." What was important now "was that, in its experience of time past, the book was, first and foremost, a state of constant agony in which nothing had yet died but everything was dying. . . . Proust's long sentences and time periods recaptured their original power for me. An exchange of form and power—the archetypal relationship between author and reader" (p. 204).

Thinking of "the power and the glory of reading," and specifically of reading in prison, Wat notes the paradox that the outwardly most pessimistic books may be the most helpful when help is needed most: they turn out to contain the richest underlying resources of vital energy and deep existential poetry: "The more pessimistic the book, the more pulsating energy, life energy, I felt beneath its surface. . . . I came across books that I had read before prison and that had sapped me of my will. For example [Dostoevsky's] *Notes from the Underground*. But there in my cell even those books sang hosannas" (p. 208). There are many more penetrating insights into prison reading, and reading in general, in Wat's memoir. Caught in prison time—a time that swings like a "pendulum . . . between agony and nothingness" (p. 206)—he is, as a reader, at once a singular "I" and a collective "us," an expression of unreflective, spontaneous solidarity with other political detainees. If we were to use the age typology sketched above, we might say that "us" is the locus of the child reader, the naive but powerful fantasizer. Under the harsh conditions of prison life, fantasy—fulfilling the function of the unreal—plays the vital role of renewing the sense of the suspended free life in the outside world: "Books brought us back to life, immersed us in the life of free people in the great and free world. We took fictional reality naively, like children listening to fairy tales" (p. 207). But a more mature, lucid, suspicious self cannot avoid the question: were not the same books ("in that laboratory of prison existence, where every detail had been thought out, quite possibly even by Stalin himself") perversely designed to produce confusion, "schizophrenic dissociation," and thus render the prisoner "defenseless against the inves-

· · ·

tigation"? Be that as it may, reading at the Lubyanka restored Wat's sense of the integrity of the literary work ("the whole that 'precedes' the parts and is their soul," p. 210), a sense that in the years before the war he thought he had definitively lost; and, more importantly, it helped him to recover his own sense of personal integrity in the degrading conditions of a cruel political prison system.

Gender and the Politics of (Re)Reading

Do women read differently from men? Attempts to answer this question have generated a huge bibliography, to which one cannot hope to do justice in a few pages. Feminism, however, and specifically feminist theories of reading, are of great relevance to the subject of rereading. Indeed, feminism proposes a whole program of rereading the literary canon from a political point of view, one which can serve to dramatize certain key aspects of rereading in general. So, do women read differently—or should they read differently? For most feminists, reading as an *intellectual* activity is clearly less influenced by gender per se than by other factors, such as social and cultural background, or the age and even the mood of the reader. In fact, it is precisely because reading could be seen as an indisputable locus of equality between the sexes that early feminists made full educational equality for women into one their major goals: if women were able to read what men read, a great step forward on the way to their emancipation would be taken. Women's access to literacy and reading had been historically proscribed or limited, often severely (as in the Council of Trent's proclamation of the principle of "holy ignorance" for women); but the advent of modernity, including the eighteenth-century "revolution in reading," has had important emancipatory consequences for women. One of these has been, in literature, the spectacular growth and diversification of writing by women since the mid-eighteenth century, as well as the constant expansion of an increasingly sophisticated female reading public.

In the individualistic and egalitarian logic of nineteenth- and early twentieth-century classical feminism the work of a woman author was to be judged strictly on its merits, like that of a male author, irrespective of considerations of gender or, for that matter, social class, ethnic background, religious creed, or political affiliation. Such considerations were seen as intolerably discriminatory in their very principle. Applied to reading, the same individualistic logic of classical feminism would lead to the conclusion that a reader's maleness or femaleness is accidental and ul-

. . .

timately secondary: a reader is a reader is a reader, as Gertrude Stein might have put it.

On the other hand, women as a group do have certain common characteristics, inclinations, and tastes, which cannot but play a role in their reception of texts, particularly when these are selected and read or reread primarily for pleasure. Such characteristics have not been ignored by psychologists and sociologists. In psychoanalysis, sexual differences in patterns of daydreaming have long been regarded as significant factors in literary production and reception. In his essay "Creative Writers and Day-Dreaming" (1907), for example, Freud saw fiction as an opportunity for one to indulge one's daydreams without feeling shame or guilt; and he noted that wishes may be "easily divided . . . into two principal groups. Either they are ambitious wishes . . . or they are erotic. In young women erotic wishes dominate the phantasies almost exclusively . . . ; in young men egoistic and ambitious wishes assert themselves plainly enough alongside their erotic desires." But since it focused on the broad phenomenon of wish-fulfilling literature, Freud's essay did not contain further elaborations on the two distinct modes of fantasizing and on their specific literary effects.

However, as publishers and booksellers know very well, there are popular genres that appeal mostly to a male readership (Westerns, stories of war and adventure), while others attract an overwhelmingly female audience (romances, gothic tales). Such choices have not been ignored by post-Freudian psychologists. Using new versions of psychoanalytic methodology (including feminist-revisionist viewpoints), Norman Holland and Leona F. Sherman have reflected on the appeal of the gothic to certain women in American society (women in their thirties and forties and belonging to the middle class), in contrast with its lack of attractiveness to other categories of readers (adolescent boys of any social background, most adult males). Some of the facts brought up by Holland and Sherman, in their essay included in the anthology of feminist criticism *Gender and Reading,* are of potentially great interest for literary production/reception studies: thus the observation that not only are gothic fictions preferred by women but "the writers are almost all women. One or two men write gothics, but they write under women's names" (p. 218). The strategic use of female pseudonymy illustrates graphically one of the generic requirements of the gothic, namely, that the implied or postulated or textually constructed author as well as the inscribed reader be female. Like the occasional male author of a gothic story who must pretend to be a female, the male reader must, in a perhaps less self-conscious sense, be able to

. . .

assume an imaginary female identity, however diffuse, in order to enjoy the reading. At any rate, reading fiction is enjoyable also because it can become the scene of many imaginary shifts in identity, including gender, gender-derived roles, social projections, and masks. If we see reading fiction, at least on one level, as playing a game of make-believe, we may assume that male readers can assume female personas and vice versa.

The issues of gender and reading tend to be addressed from a special perspective in contemporary feminist criticism or, at least, in its more radical versions. For classical (individualistic) feminism, as we saw, reading was a locus of intellectual equality between men and women. But this equality, contemporary feminists argue, is an illusion, a sham, an ideological ploy. It is a false equality, entirely on male terms, obtained at the price of repressing the woman's sense of being different, as well as of her being the persecuted *other* of a male-controlled society. This is the gist, for instance, of another essay in *Gender and Reading,* "The Reader's Construction of Meaning: Cognitive Research on Gender and Comprehension," by Mary Crawford and Roger Chaffin. The authors' conclusion is that the differences between male and female perceptions of texts are not readily apparent because "women learn to read and understand from a male point of view" (p. 21). This is so because females in our society are a "muted group": the male-controlled institutions (including language itself) make it difficult for them to articulate their real sensibilities, needs, and experiences. The standard point of view being the male one, it follows that "neither men nor women can readily step in and out of it as they attempt to apprehend their experiences."

Under these circumstances, "the development of a uniquely female viewpoint has been a major part of the work of the women's movement" (p. 25). In other words, a female viewpoint cannot be expressed except in a feminist mode: "It is to feminist literature that we should turn first in our search for gender differences in reading" (Ibid.). Such differences are erased or repressed or glossed over in the standard (male) perspective.[8] This is actually an older theme of feminist criticism, summarized by Jonathan Culler in his overview of feminist theories of reading in *On Deconstruction*: women, he writes, "have been constituted as subjects by discourses that have not identified or promoted the possibility of reading 'as a woman' . . . Feminist criticism undertakes, through the postulate of a woman reader, to bring about a new experience of reading and to make readers—men and women—question the literary and political assumptions on which their reading has been based" (p. 51).

· · ·

If this is indeed the case, the very issue of gender (including the perception of differences between male and female modes of reading) is primarily a political issue. The mere fact of asserting and describing otherwise inapparent gender differences in reading is possible only from the vantage point of a "raised consciousness" and of an unambiguous engagement with feminism. This is the position emphatically expressed in "Reading Ourselves: Toward a Feminist Theory of Reading," by Patrocinio Schweickart, who believes that a "feminist inquiry into the activity of reading begins with the realization that the canon is androcentric, and that this has a profoundly damaging effect on women readers" (*Gender and Reading*, p. 40). The main points of a feminist theory of reading are, according to Schweickart: attending to the issue of gender (gender blindness, by implication, can only be a male ploy), "giving a privileged status to the experience and interests of women readers," and being fully "conscious of the political dimensions of reading and writing" (p. xiii).

In summary, insofar as reading theory is concerned, the contemporary feminists have promoted a relentless revisionist orientation, sharply critical of the (male) canon and demanding its severe reassessment on the basis of an integral rereading of the literary tradition from a feminist political point of view. Incidentally, the terminology of rereading (often in the sense of an attentive demystifying *re*interpretation) abounds in feminist reader-oriented criticism. The act of rereading—of looking at the classics with new critical eyes—is central to the feminist project, which is certainly the major influence behind today's academic flourishing of theories of committed or militant writing/reading.

As an illustration of the feminist method of (re)reading I have chosen one of the shrewdest essays of practical criticism included in *Gender and Reading*, Susan Suleiman's "Malraux's Women: A Re-Vision." The piece belongs to a tradition in feminist criticism that goes back to the late 1940s and, more specifically, to a chapter in Simone de Beauvoir's pioneering study *The Second Sex* (1949), which analyzes "The Myth of Woman in Five Authors" (Montherlant, Lawrence, Claudel, Breton, and Stendhal). In English, this tradition has produced Kate Millet's *Sexual Politics* (1970) and her polemical readings of apparently sexually revolutionary—but, in fact, she claims, perniciously "counterrevolutionary" and deeply misogynist—male authors such as D. H. Lawrence, Henry Miller, or Norman Mailer. Suleiman, on her part, is careful to avoid the denunciatory style and the sometimes crude, or crudely applied, critical-political categories that have been in various degrees characteristic of this tradition. Thus,

· · ·

while on the whole she explicitly endorses the strategies of reading proposed by feminist theorists such as Judith Fetterley, in her widely read *The Resisting Reader: A Feminist Approach to American Fiction,* Suleiman is critical of Fetterley's tendency to automatically identify canonic male authors as "the enemy" (p. 143).

At the end of her sensitive analysis of the conspicuously few female characters in Malraux novels (there are only three women in his entire fictional corpus if we exclude the *figurantes* or "extras"), Suleiman pauses to ask herself:

> What is the usefulness of rereadings such as the one I have been practicing, given that they only confirm what might seem by now an all-too-familiar fact: the literature of adventure and heroism, whether in the past or in our own time, has been overwhelmingly male—written by men, about men, for men, embodying male fantasies and founded on the most enduring male fantasy of all: the fantasy of a world without women. Is there really a point in demonstrating . . . that Malraux's novels are exclusively "masculine" fictions? (p. 142)

Her answer is yes, because "it is one thing to notice something and leave it unexpressed, or cover it up like a guilty secret; it is quite another to examine it and attempt to state its significance." A feminist analysis of Malraux is therefore in order. But "does this mean that, from now on, every time I teach Malraux, I will insist on the 'macho' or antifeminine aspect of his work? Not at all. Shortly after I finished writing the bulk of this essay, I lectured to an advanced undergraduate literature class at Harvard on *La Condition humaine.* With only two lectures scheduled for this complex novel, I could hardly devote more than a few minutes to the question of women" (p. 143).

A committed feminist (re)reading of *La Condition humaine* or of Malraux's entire fictional corpus is both legitimate and necessary but it does not exhaust the possibilities of (re)reading Malraux. Furthermore, the feminist questioning of Malraux's text is not, or should not be, confined to exclusively political issues. As Suleiman pointedly remarks:

> I would not wish to see such . . . rereadings become territorialized as an exclusively feminist—or feminine—concern. . . . Why is misogyny a transcultural and transhistorical phenomenon, apparently as universal as the incest taboo? Is the need to negate woman—which is always, in the last instance, the need to negate one's mother—a permanent feature of male psychology? Questions such as these, which are prompted by, but go far

· · ·

109

beyond, the rereading of writers like Malraux, are being raised today increasingly not only by women or feminists or students of literature, but also by anthropologists, sociologists, psychologists, and cultural historians, male and female, who seek to understand our past and the directions of our future. (pp. 143–44)

A political rereading, in other words, is intellectually fruitful when it raises questions that go beyond politics and partisanship. I fully agree. But for such an intellectually fruitful political rereading to occur, I would argue, certain elementary requirements must be met by the reader, on the one hand, and by the text, on the other. For the reader, the test is how actively and broadly curious and open-minded he or she is, and ultimately how able he or she is to honestly entertain questions that might lead to disturbing answers, answers that might well end up challenging deep-seated political convictions and commitments. For the text, the major test is how it can withstand a searching, adversary, intensely critical reading without becoming a mere blend of "ideological" symptoms and a ready source of illustrations for the reader's anticipations, biases, or projections. Put differently, the text should preserve its capacity to be stimulating, intriguing, and rewarding even when read or reread with a maximum of intelligent hostility.

What I appreciate in "Malraux's Women" is a sense that the strongly focused, politically thematized rereading of a modern classic like Malraux need not be a merely prosecutorial affair—however accurate the charges—but that it can acquire a personally dramatic quality: as a feminist rereader, Suleiman feels called upon to revise an older attachment, to submit a formerly cherished text to tough, potentially destructive questioning; but, as her questioning progresses, she realizes that her newly found polemical urge cannot be satisfied in a simple manner, that the text refuses to collapse, as a mere "ideological" construct would, under the weight of critical scrutiny, that her older admiration for the text had not been baseless. Our relationship to texts that have acquired a personal significance for us—texts that have once occasioned moments of self-revelation or otherwise memorable reading experiences—cannot be erased in one act of one-dimensional political rereading. This relationship is too complex, too subtle, too rich in its play of ambivalences and ambiguities—in a word, too precious—to be easily given up. The paradox, at least in the area of critical-political rereadings or revisions, is that we can be intelligently hostile only to texts that we feel impelled to go on admiring.

. . .

. . . .

EIGHT

Notes for a Poetics of Reading

Is a Poetics of Reading Possible?

We have reached a point where we should ask ourselves: is there really such a thing as *literary* reading? And if so, how is it to be described? To the first question, my tentative answer is yes, if we define literary reading not in terms of what is read (a text that is inherently literary, that embodies certain definable qualities of literariness) but in terms of the mode of reading, namely, reading primarily for pleasure—that is, not for information, edification, self-improvement, saving one's soul, advancing one's career, or a myriad other worthwhile purposes. To make things more complicated, however, all of these extrinsic goals may be involved in the process of literary reading without changing its literary nature—its overall goal of pleasure. As for the pleasure sought after in the process of literary reading, it comprises what has been traditionally identified as aesthetic pleasure; but other kinds of gratification, from the more naive forms of emotional involvement with fictional situations to more cerebral types of intellectual absorption, are not excluded.

To the second question, I would reply that the pleasure of reading should be described in as many manners, and from as many disciplinary perspectives, as can contribute to rendering it more comprehensible. Such heterogeneous disciplines as cultural anthropology, linguistics, the history of religions, the history of books and reading, philosophy (including

. . .

epistemology), hermeneutics, psychology, aesthetics, literary criticism and theory, to name the principal ones, have interesting and sometimes crucially enlightening things to say on the question of (literary) reading. Literary reading is not an autonomous, but a profoundly heteronomous, phenomenon.

Having stressed the enormous complexity, relativity, and heteronomy of literary reading, does it make sense to search for a poetics of reading? Or, to put the question differently, is a poetics of reading at all possible without sacrificing crucial nuances or oversimplifying the intricate network of signifying processes that make up reading? And if so, have there been attempts to establish one? Over the years there has been some talk of a *rhetoric* of reading—focusing on what the explicitly, emphatically poetic text instructs its readers to do or not to do, on what persuasive means it uses to that effect, on what it tells them, directly or indirectly, they should be prepared to expect or not to expect, including the ironies and aporias brought about by such instructions (Michel Charles's *Rhétorique de la lecture*)—and, more recently, of a *poetics* of reading, with special application to the novel (Inge Crosman Wimmers's *Poetics of Reading*). Thus far, however, the theoretical status of either such a rhetoric or such a poetics has remained rather nebulous.

Virtually unnoticed has been the fact that the very possibility of a poetics of reading is premised on the perspective of rereading, more precisely on the paradoxical situation that the most enjoyable ways in which a text can be read (the best speed of reading, the kind of attention to be devoted to it, the conventions to be taken into account, the range of legitimate interpretations) can be fully determined only once the first reading is over. In other words, a poetics of reading cannot exist, on a self-conscious theoretical level, except on the basis of a concept of rereading. One might ask: is not rereading, as conceptualized here, more or less the same thing as the "close reading" advocated by the New Critics? There are at least two reasons why this question must be answered in the negative. First, even though the pedagogy of close reading certainly involves rereading (since it takes the ideal point of view of the whole work in order to assess the functions, tensions, and ambiguities of its various parts), this rereading is not aware of itself, nor of its relationship to a first linear reading in which one gets acquainted with the work. Second, and perhaps more important, the New Critical recommendation of close reading ignores the temporality of (re)reading, for which succession, sequence, and linear/circular models of time are essential.

. . .

More broadly, of course, no criticism—new or old, structuralist or poststructuralist—can exist outside the experience and perspective of rereading, although full awareness of this is not a necessary precondition of any critical act. In fact, it is only through rereading that a poetician may determine in what sense reading is or should be a "construction" or, more appropriately, a "performance," and therefore the possible object of a poetics, a system of procedures, protocols, or arrangements for happily making sense of texts.[1]

But the same notion of rereading seems to cast serious doubt on the possibility of a coherent poetics of reading. Is it not through rereading that one becomes aware of the openness of the text, of its degree of indeterminacy, of its irreducible plurality and of one's own crucially important role in shaping and articulating its meanings? Is it not through the practice of rereading that we discover that the same book is not only many things to many people but also many things to the same reader at different times and in different situations of his or her life? This point has been made again and again, most emphatically and memorably in romanticism. A reader, says Emerson, "may read what he writes" (mentally): "What can we see or acquire, but what we are? You have observed a skillful man reading Virgil. Well, that author is a thousand books to a thousand persons. Take the book into your two hands, and read your eyes out; you will never find what I find" (*Collected Works*, vol. 2, pp. 86–87).

Emerson speaks of reading, but the essential openness of the text is experienced even more directly in the act of rereading. This has not escaped the attention of reading theorists. Wolfgang Iser, for example, notes in *The Implied Reader*: "With all literary texts, then, we may say that the reading process is selective, and that the potential text is infinitely richer than any of its individual realizations. This is borne out by the fact that a second reading of a piece of literature often produces a different impression from the first. The reasons for this may lie in the reader's own change of circumstances, still, they must be such as to allow this variation. On a second reading familiar occurrences now tend to appear in a new light and seem to be at times corrected, at times enriched" (p. 280).

The always individual character of the concretization of the text—the unpredictable shapes it can take in the mind of the reader according to his or her background, age, place, situation and mood—clearly poses a great difficulty in the path of a proper poetics of reading, insofar as a poetics presupposes specifiable, observable regularities, as well as clear-cut goals and one's ability to achieve them. The awareness of such an unavoidable

. . .

difficulty should explain why a poetics of reading will be of necessity weaker and more fluid than a poetics of composition or text production. Still a poetics of reading may have its valuable heuristic uses. What is more, it seems likely that renewed efforts toward elaborating a poetics of reading will become more frequent, because it might offer a suitable frame for a more systematic reflection on the results of recent decades of very active reader-based criticism and theory.

The Rule of Pleasure

A poetics of (re)reading will deal with the basic rules, conventions, constraints, precepts, frames of reference and strategies (on various levels of the reading process) that are characteristic of good reading. What do I mean by *good reading?* For all practical purposes, the simplest definition of good (literary) reading happens to be the most hedonistic one. Good reading is reading that produces a maximum of pleasure and, one could emphasize, a maximum of pleasure of the kind—ranging from the "mindful" to the "mindless"—that an individual reader may be seeking. W. H. Auden once remarked on the subject of reading: "Pleasure is by no means an infallible guide, but it is the least fallible" (*The Dyer's Hand,* p. 5).

A poetics of (re)reading should not ignore the less complex types of pleasurable reading, including bad literature. (A poetician knows that there is such a thing as good bad literature, and consequently good bad reading, which may be a fascinating object of study and which, moreover, may well coexist with higher, more complex, demanding, and intellectually enriching forms of reading.) But even in the case of reading for pure entertainment, or for what critics with moralistic inclinations might regard as "mindless" pleasure, the poetics I have in mind cannot help but be based on rereading: the poetician must reread a bad book (a good bad book, hopefully: a really captivating cheap thriller, a wonderfully formulaic Western or gothic romance, or a rare genuine masterpiece of bad taste) in order to see how it is made and what the secrets of its success may be. The perspective obtained through rereading will also confirm the elementary, almost spontaneously followed rules of good bad reading: read fast, be naive, be curious (if your curiosity is not excited and satisfied, stop reading), and, above all, don't inhibit your impulses to fantasize. By the way, these are impulses that a highly intelligent and sophisticated reader will never disdain and might well decide to follow and even cultivate without any remorse or shame. The real problem for the literary critic and

· · ·

poetician of reading is how to include, not how to exclude, varieties and types of pleasurable reading. Hence one of the critic's tasks is to become fully aware of the continued influence of cultural puritanism, which is suspicious of pleasure in any form or shape. This hidden, resilient puritanism has survived in alliance with various utopian-revolutionary doctrines of the modern age, but its effects are still surprisingly widespread even in non-utopian societies.

More generally, as in the case of the traditional poetics of composition or "good writing," the paramount rule of a poetics of good reading should be simply to please. Racine knew very well this rule of pleasure when, in the preface to *Bérénice,* addressing those spectators who had liked his play but thought it was not composed according to the Aristotelian rules of tragedy, he wrote: "I beg them to have a high enough opinion of themselves not to believe that a play which moves them and which affords them pleasure could in any way go against the rules. The principal rule is to please and to move: all the others are made to get to this first one" (p. 468). Naturally, with the historical diversification of reading publics and the relativization of taste, the kinds of pleasure offered by reading have become more varied—almost unmanageably varied. At the same time, pleasure itself has been censored by a diffuse puritanical mentality that has persisted in modernist aesthetics (an aesthetics of the devaluation of pleasure, as Lionel Trilling once observed).[2]

A short review of the concept of poetics and its modern uses might be helpful. When Paul Valéry undertook to resurrect the word *poetics* in the 1930s he felt obliged first to dismiss its lingering old-fashioned neoclassical connotations of rules, prescriptions, and guidelines. Such connotations were the natural result of the prolonged neoclassical use of the term *poétique* in France (with Aristotle's *Poetics* the great model), coupled with its adoption by the French school system, in which the exemplary value of the *auteurs classiques* was routinely linked to the strict, unquestioning observance of the rules of good writing. To free the term from such unpleasantly didactic associations, Valéry brought up its forgotten etymological meaning of "making" (*poetics* derives from the Greek verb *poiein,* "to make").

So the task of poetics, according to Valéry, consists of examining and describing the way literary works *are* made, not the way they *should be* made so as to fit certain narrowly and dogmatically defined criteria (in the event, neoclassical and didactic requirements of taste and decorum). In other words, poetics is a general theory of literary forms and of their inner

. . .

logic. Such a definition seemed to correspond to a larger critical zeitgeist (if such a thing exists), since it was synchronous with the theories of literary form advanced by the Russian Formalists of the 1920s and 1930s and with the "intrinsic" approach to literature proposed by the Anglo-American New Critics.

Yet despite Valéry's attempt to free poetics of its prescriptive element, the problem of rules has remained central to any comprehensive poetics, including the possible poetics of (re)reading which concerns us here. The making of a literary work (or the construction of a reading) is not an anonymous process occurring in a historical vacuum. By whatever name we call them, rules are unavoidable: composition or reading will always proceed according to certain rules or conventions, some of a more general nature, others more clearly time-bound. Valéry and the more systematic French structuralist poeticians who have recognized in Valéry a great precursor actually deal with rules all the time (even though they clearly prefer to call them "conventions," "constraints," "structural demands," and so forth). What is different from the old neoclassical conception of the rules is the shift from an authoritative or normative or blatantly dogmatic tone in the formulation of the rules to the more "neutral" tone in which we describe, for instance, the rules of a game. Even so, I would say, the neoclassical poeticians were not essentially wrong as long as they recognized (as most of them did, if only implicitly) the primacy of the rule of pleasure. One is nonetheless entitled to reject their narrow, overly rigid understanding of the rules of the *literary* game, an understanding in which observance of the rules sometimes seemed to became an end in itself and the game and its fun (a broad notion including the tragic sentiments, terror and pity, as well as the comic sentiments) was all but forgotten.

How to Read

The central question of a poetics of (re)reading is *how to read,* how to construct or perform or execute (as one executes a piece of music) a fully satisfying and valid reading of a literary text (since satisfaction may depend on the performer's sense of the validity of the performance). It may be pursued in three directions. The first and most obvious, and the one in which most work has been done, sets out to describe and classify the various instructions about how to read that are contained in literary texts and that are thus directly available to the kind of textual analysis and theorizing practiced by poeticians. Each book, we might say, comes with

· · ·

its own user's manual, in which the instructions may be fully or clearly spelled out (as in the case of didactic literature) or only tantalizingly suggested (as in the case of more difficult playful-enigmatic texts), with any number of possibilities in between these two extremes. This line of research has given us a number of valuable studies about what might be called in a generic sense the "inscribed reader" or, with a perhaps more familiar label, the "reader in the text."[3] Such studies may consider, for instance, the "fictive reader" as a role or a script for the real reader to perform.[4] What we could call "rhetorical readers"—the "dear reader" or "idle reader" (Cervantes) or Baudelaire's "hypocrite lecteur, mon semblable, mon frère")—have also been studied both in general and in specific authors from Dante to Proust.

Readers can also become full-fledged characters, and reading itself can be the originator of the fictional drama that offers itself for what is in effect a metareading (reading about reading). Famous examples are Dante's Paolo and Francesca (as readers of the story of Lancialotto's illicit love in *Inferno*, V), Cervantes's Don Quixote, and Flaubert's Emma Bovary. Such characters are tragic or comic or ironic antimodels for the fictive reader.

A more precisely defined area of poetics (and a place where the poetics of composition encounters its more elusive twin, the poetics of reading) is the function of the "narratee"—the addressee of a narrative discourse, an addressee whose figure can be reconstructed from the text of the narrative itself. A poetics of reading would also deal with the validity, heuristic if not otherwise, of such constructs as the "ideal reader," the "informed reader" (Stanley Fish), the "implied" reader (Wolfgang Iser), the "model" reader (Umberto Eco), the "encoded" reader (Christine Brooke-Rose), the "competent" reader (Jonathan Culler in *Structuralist Poetics*), and so on. I do not intend to discuss this well-investigated area of literary studies in more detail at this time. Its relevance to a future poetics of reading is clear. What I feel tempted to add, though, is that if we want to ascertain and articulate the role played by the "textual reader" in a work (as opposed to merely responding more or less subliminally to that reader's indirect hints or urgings), we must reread and start from an acknowledgement of rereading. It should also be noted that many of the studies falling within this category use the word *reader* as little more than another name for the text itself.[5] This is a limitation. Other, metatextual or paratextual hypotheses (anthropological, psychological, sociological) can illuminate the process of (re)reading from angles that should not remain foreign to a poetics of

. . .

reading. A cluster of such hypotheses, originating in the notion of play, will be examined in Part III.

The second, more paradoxical, direction in which a poetics of (re)reading could be pursued starts with the examination of two extremely different categories of texts: personal diaries (such as those, say, of Stendhal, Amiel, Gide, or Anaïs Nin), on the one hand, and prefaces (of the kind Henry James wrote for the New York Edition of his works), on the other. What is common to these two otherwise unrelated literary "genres" is a strong tie to the idea of rereading. The diarist keeps his or her diary, that is, tries to record the fleeting details of daily occurrences, encounters, and experiences (including reading experiences) so that he or she may reread the entries at later dates. The diary is obviously a way of "saving" time, of snatching significant or epiphanic moments from the inescapable flow of linear time and conserving them for future remembrance, reinspection, revival—in a word, rereading. As Jean Rousset notes in his considerations of this "ambiguous genre" (a genre in which, at least theoretically, writing is supposed to be secret and thus not to have an addressee or reader in the usual sense but only one single rereader: the author), a personal diary of the kind Amiel wrote becomes not only an occasion for frequent self-rereading but also, more interestingly from the point of view of a poetician, an elaborate written record of such acts of rereading.[6] (Amiel, for instance, was a systematic rereader of his own journal, made extensive use of the terminology of *relecture,* and created a special type of endlessly sprawling, self-mirroring text for the benefit of a single reader, himself.)

Some of the rules of the game of writing, and therefore reading, diaries were modified in the first decades of the twentieth century when André Gide began publishing parts of his personal diary (until then diaries were supposed to be published, if at all, posthumously). The genre got closer to autobiography, although it preserved its distinguishing features: the aleatory structure, the special inner logic imposed by the requirement of dated entries or day-by-day notations, as well as its heterogeneous content (a diary can be a record of such diverse things as states of mind, personal events, instances of self-analysis, dreams, conversations, readings, impressions, memories, projects, rumors, gossip, and so on). Stylistically, if not in any other sense, the diary has also continued to be—and this is important—a species of secret writing. Diarists may choose to let other people in on their secrets, they may even use their secrets (or pseudo-secrets) for purposes of public self-flagellation or of self-advertising (or both): the

. . .

connection between the idea of a diary and the idea of secrecy remains unaffected, a structural feature of the genre.

This explains the two types of interest a journal may evoke in a reader. The first is the reader's eagerness to become privy to the secrets of the writer. Here the reader must be a fan, a devotee, or at least someone fairly well acquainted with the writer's work; otherwise the diarists's secrets wouldn't mean anything to him or her and the text of the diary would become unattractive, unreadable. Such interest in journals is increased by, and usually leads to, rereading a writer's *other* works. The diary gives potentially precious hints for constructing the reading or rereading of the author's other books. The second type of interest is that of the reader who is himself or herself a diarist or potential diarist. The reader, then, is curious to see, and ready to appropriate, the published diarist's ways of solving problems and his or her techniques for creating a diarist's persona.[7] Since the number of potential diarists among the general reading public is not large, the main criterion for a publisher, when deciding whether to publish someone's diary, remains the fame of the author (we are bored by the secrets of obscure people but very excited by those of the famous).

The importance of authorial prefaces for a theory of reading (which would include an "ethics of reading" and rereading, as J. Hillis Miller has pointed out) becomes abundantly clear if we consider James's prefaces as an exemplary case of critical self-reflection by a major writer and of a "prodigious act of re-reading" (Miller, *The Ethics of Reading*, p. 187). The diarist's act of rereading remains *in principle* a personal matter: even though a journal may in fact be written exclusively for future publication, its constitutive rule is and will always be that it cannot have an addressee other than its writer or, at the most, a few close friends, those "happy few" with whom Stendhal was ready to share his secrets. The general reader is stylistically excluded (no "dear reader" in a personal diary), even though this exclusion may stand in fact for an invitation. By contrast, the author who writes a preface to an earlier published work, as did James, involves himself or herself in an act of rereading which is doubly public, since it is a public reexamination of a work already in the public domain and as such gives us, in Miller's words, "a formulation of the ethics of writing as an ethics of reading and re-reading." The sense in which this ethics is also part of a poetics is obvious, for what else does a preface tell us except how to read?

One of the reasons for which people read diaries, as I have suggested, is

· · ·

curiosity about the extratextual secrets they may disclose. These secrets, however, may bear directly on the way we understand other texts—self-contained literary works—by the same author. It is in this respect that one may speak of certain analogies between writers' diaries and prefaces. These are most visible in the case of that subgenre of the diary that is "the journal of a novel" (for example Thomas Mann's journal of *Doktor Faustus*). Both diaries of this kind and prefaces (particularly retrospective prefaces like Henry James's) initiate new protocols of (re)reading the literary works to which they specifically refer or are appended. Another characteristic that diaries of this type and prefaces share is that they themselves are not, or at least do not aspire to be, rereadable.

If we follow the third direction, in which a poetics of (re)reading might be conceived as a set of rules for constructing a good, effective, pleasurable reading of a literary work, we will soon be confronted by the larger and more complex issue of literature, reading, rereading, and play. More precisely, we will soon come across an intriguing convergence of two issues: first, the sense of a playful text, of a text that invites us or challenges us to play a game (the game being sometimes perceived as internal to, and even constitutive of, the text); and second, the sense that in order to play the game well we will be forced to do a lot of rereading. Fortunately, these playful texts are designed in such a fashion as to specifically reward rereading. The broader relationship between play and literature, as well as the more specific topic of literature and games (going all the way from simple games, such as anagrams, rebuses, logographs, and other word puzzles to complex ones, such as extended textual ciphers, cryptic sets of allusions, and hidden numerological structuring), has been the object of scholarly investigation, and I shall consider these matters from closer range in Part III. What I would like to note at this point is that, strangely enough, the consequences of game-like textual structures for the theory of reading, not to speak of rereading, have received scant attention in literary criticism. It seems obvious, however, that books play games, or can be seen as playing games, and that readers, even without knowing it, engage in various types of complex ludic activities, among which rereading occupies a place of honor.

. . .

PART THREE

. . . .

Play

. . . .

Preliminaries

Rereading as Game: Nabokov's Pale Fire

Nabokov's metaphysical-parodic mystery novel *Pale Fire* is structured like an intricate and lunatic game of hide-and-seek and rereading. It consists of a foreword, an autobiographical poem of 999 lines by Professor John Shade, an apparently rambling commentary, and an index. The commentary, deliberately and delightfully ambiguous, is written by the poem's fictional editor—the former king Charles of Zembla or Charles Kinbote, a visiting professor of Zemblan at Wordsmith College in New Wye, who claims to be the former king of Zembla, or maybe by an émigré Russian, the paranoic professor V. Botkin (Kinbote being an anagram of Botkin or Botkine, as we are told at page 179).[1] The way the novel is constructed immediately suggests a nonlinear reading or rather (re)-reading of the kind that critical, abundantly annotated editions of classics (such as Nabokov's own translation and commentary of *Eugene Onegin*) require. Already on page 3 of the foreword the reader is referred to the note to line 991 of the poem, and halfway through this note Kinbote mentions an earlier note to lines 47–48 of the poem which, in a sequential order of reading, has not yet started! A sequential first reading of the book—that is, the normal way of reading a fictional text—is plainly impossible. Kinbote himself recommends, toward the end of the foreword, methods of parallel reading and rereading:

. . .

Although those notes, in conformity with custom, come after the poem, the reader is advised to consult them first and study the poem with their help, rereading them of course as he goes through the text, and perhaps, after having done with the poem, consulting them a third time so as to complete the picture. I find it wise in such cases as this to eliminate the bother of back-and-forth leafings by either cutting out and clipping together the pages with the text of the thing, or, even more simply, purchasing two copies of the same work which can then be placed in adjacent positions on a comfortable table. (p. 12)

In fact, *Pale Fire* offers itself for (nonsequential) rereading from the outset. Its implied reader, who is supposed to solve a large number of correlated onomastic, verbal, and intertextual literary puzzles, is actually a rereader.

Already in the title, *Pale Fire,* Vladimir Nabokov betrays his fondness for intricate playfulness in reading and rereading. How do readers learn that "pale fire" (a metaphor of stealth in its original occurence in Shakespeare) is a phrase lifted by Nabokov from a key poetic passage in one of Shakespeare's most obscure plays, *Timon of Athens?* Most likely they learn it (perhaps even before reading the novel) from critical commentaries of Nabokov's work. But let us suppose a reader who figures out the meaning of "pale fire" by reading the text carefully and by following up the intertextual leads it contains.

The note to line 962 of the poem says that the title is taken from Shakespeare but remains unspecific: "My readers," writes Kinbote/Botkin, the self-obsessed narrator-commentator, "must make their own search. All I have with me is a tiny vest pocket edition of *Timon of Athens*—in Zemblan! It certainly contains nothing that could be regarded as an equivalent of 'pale fire' (if it had, my luck would have been a statistical monster)" (pp. 191–92). Discussing this passage Peter Hutchinson, in *Games Authors Play,* notes: "These words give us the (false) impression that *Timon of Athens* is *not* the source for the title. Only the reader conversant with Nabokov's methods of working will . . . linger on the peculiar "statistical monster" in search for a clue. . . . Once we have recognized that *Timon* is the source, the play can act as a parallel to the novel, thereby giving us a different perspective on character and plot, and also helping us to predict developments" (p. 39).

My claim is that this kind of sophisticated literary game—which consists of strewing the text of a work with recondite allusions and clues (sometimes subtly misleading) to the work's sources, parodic parallels, and, more inclusively, key intertexts—aims at persuading the reader to

. . .

constantly reread and playfully reconsider the text from a variety of new perspectives suggested by the text itself. Literary reading becomes a sort of unpredictable (inter)textual game of chess; or, perhaps more accurately, it resembles repeated attempts to solve a difficult and brilliantly deceptive chess problem or the absorbing effort at deciphering a complicated cryptogram. Here I should note that Nabokov's novel could as well serve to introduce Part IV of this book, "Rereading for the Secret," as his games often consist of deliberately concealing information (the essential part of secrecy). The purpose, however, of hiding meaning, of conveying it stealthily, of delightfully misleading the innocent reader and trying to change him or her into a sophisticated rereader, remains essentially ludic. Let me simply observe, at this point, the partial overlapping of certain types of secrecy (hiding information as a game) and certain types of play (games with rules in which information is hidden).

How is the erudite hypothetical first-time reader of Nabokov's *Pale Fire,* having unhesitatingly assessed the true importance of the citation of *Timon of Athens,* to make use of this newly gained perspective? Its effects are mostly retroactive, and they can be fully enjoyed (but only if the first nonlinear reading has been enjoyed too) on a second reading, a reading that becomes the equivalent of playing the game once more, with a new attentiveness to its subtle possibilities and to the tiny details of its strategic moves, as well as with a greater awareness of its complexities and surprising turns.

But our highly intelligent and literate hypothetical reader will also make many exciting discoveries the second time around, and some of these will overturn or strongly modify the conclusions reached in a first reading and the expectations generated by them. Limiting our focus to the title of the book, it will thus turn out that the "pale fire"–*Timon* connection was itself meant to hide another deeper, more important Shakespearean intertext, namely, *Hamlet.* As Priscilla Meyer has shown in her extremely careful intertextual analysis of *Pale Fire,* "Nabokov embeds hints in Kinbote's commentary that point to *Timon of Athens* as the source for the title of Shade's poem. But just as Kinbote's Zemblan etymologies conceal Nabokov's, Nabokov's clues lead to a false bottom that conceals his own purposes. Shade's 'Pale Fire' may come from *Timon,* but Nabokov's *Pale Fire* comes from *Hamlet*" (Meyer, *Find What the Sailor Has Hidden,* p. 113).

It is indeed fascinating to realize that "pale fire" could come not only from the now obvious source, *Timon,* but also from a more obscure one, the lines uttered by the ghost of Hamlet's father taking leave of his son:

. . .

The glow-worm shows the matin to be near
And 'gins to pale his uneffectual fire. (*Hamlet*, I.v.89–90)

This doubly hidden intertextuality gives support to Meyer's claim that Nabokov's novel has a secret but essential autobiographical dimension—that it revolves, on a fictional level, around the writer's painful memory of the accidental killing of his father in Berlin in 1922 (the intended victim of the extreme right-wing assassin had been the liberal émigré politician Pavel Milyukov, the former foreign affairs minister in the Kerensky government in 1917, who was addressing a public meeting of the Russian emigration). The accidental killing of Shade (shot by mistake instead of Judge Goldworth by the lunatic murderer Jack Grey; shot by mistake instead of Kinbote/Charles of Zembla/Botkin by the monstrous assassin Jakob Gradus) would be the fictional projection of the traumatic autobiographical event. This would explain, among other things, Nabokov's close identification with Shade, an unmistakable father-figure.

The connection between "pale fire" and King Hamlet's ghost reinforces the sense of another possible Shakespearean intertextual relationship: that between the name of Kinbote and the famous lines in Hamlet's soliloquy in which he wonders about a man's willing acceptance of suffering

When he himself might his quietus make
With a bare bodkin? (III.i.75–76)

Bodkin (a "Danish stiletto," as the index to *Pale Fire* indicates) should also be seen as one of the sources of the name of Kinbote, obtained by a reversal of the order of the word's two syllables and a slight change in spelling (but this is only one of many allusions hidden in Kinbote's name, which in the first place is, as we already saw, an anagram and thus a disguise of the mad Russian professor Botkin, the "real" author of the commentary). Meyer comments: "Hamlet's soliloquy in which he contemplates suicide relates to Kinbote, who finally makes his own quietus" (p. 114). Seen in this light, Kinbote is an ambivalent (grotesque as well as empathic) portrayal of a Hamlet type, with whom Nabokov can identify himself in certain respects, either self-parodically or seriously (Meyer, p. 108). This sounds rather farfetched to me. An intellectually more satisfying hypothesis concerning Kinbote is, I think, the one that some older Nabokov critics (such as Andrew Field) have suggested and that Brian Boyd has recently developed, with new arguments, in his major critical biography of Nabokov. According to this view, Kinbote is a perfect antithesis of Shade,

. . .

a symmetrical reversal, a negative image created by Shade himself, since "Nabokov had Shade in mind as the author of the foreword, poem, commentary, and index. . . . In the final version of his foreword to *Speak, Memory,* Nabokov decided not to divulge *Pale Fire*'s secret, to leave it for the readers to discover quite unaided, but this draft leaves no doubt that he saw Shade as the compiler of the index, months after Jack Grey or Jakob Gradus supposedly shoots him through the heart" (Boyd, vol. 2, p. 445).[2]

Why, then, would Shade (or Nabokov himself, for that matter) be interested in creating a character—a homosexual, a madman, a suicide, an imaginary ex-king—so different from himself? Of course, in the present context, I am tempted to suggest a (dramatistically) playful motive similar to the one that makes certain actors want to perform roles of great villains, tyrants, or murderers (Iago, Richard III, Macbeth) or comically grotesque parallels of such villains (as Alfred Jarry's Ubu, an absurdly parodic reincarnation of Macbeth as king of a fictitious Poland). But one can imagine other motives. Indeed, one must imagine other motives in order to bring to life the hypothesizing vocation of reading that Nabokov manipulates with such consummate skill. All this is not intended to detract from the importance of the *Hamlet* intertext and from the real possibility that Nabokov might, among other things, have thought of the absurd death of his father at the hands of a political assassin who might also have been a revengeful madman—that is, both a Jakob Gradus and a Jack Grey.

We have now reached a point where we can formulate some preliminary theses, based on the example of *Pale Fire,* about the relation between literary play and (re)reading (including the play of rereading and rereading as play) as a step toward constructing a poetics of ludic (re)reading. First, the literary text, when it is (as in Nabokov's case) a calculated, rule-governed, and self-reflexive playful artifact, calls for rereading. The emphasis here should be on *playful* because there are games between authors and readers, such as in the case of detective fiction, in which the artifact itself (the text) is hardly playful—at least on the surface—and mainly serves as a means to play a one-time linear game of make-believe, suspicion, suspense, and guessing. In the next three chapters I shall have more to say about the distinction between games of make-believe and games with rules, and the ways in which it is relevant to (re)reading.

Second, the self-evidently playful text reveals what I would call the centrifugal force of any serious (seriously playful), attentive, inquisitively dedicated reading. Any reading that participates, even if only as a project

. . .

(the project to go over the text once more), in the nature of rereading makes the reader also search outside the text and (re)read other material. To confront this paradoxical centrifugal force more lucidly, one might try to comprehend it on an intuitive level first. Let us return to *Pale Fire* and *Timon of Athens* and to the highly intelligent and unusually literate reader we have posited. This reader is unlikely to realize from the outset that the title of the book is borrowed from the passage of *Timon* that reads:

> The sun's a thief, and with his great attraction
> Robs the vast sea; the moon's an arrant thief,
> And her pale fire she snatches from the sun . . . (IV.iii.439–41)

What do we imagine that our hypothetical reader will do when he or she deciphers the true import of the clue in Kinbote's commentary to line 962 of the poem "Pale Fire" by John Francis Shade? I for one imagine this reader doing the following things: (1) taking the decision to go ahead and finish reading the novel; (2) forming at the same time the project to (re)read *Timon* (a parenthesis here: given the parodic-intertextual and ludically erudite character of the novel, the reader's list of "things to read" has reached, by now, monstrous proportions; but *Timon* should rank high on that list, given its "privileged" connection with the title of the book); (3) carrying out the projected (re)reading of *Timon* while thinking of *Pale Fire* and rereading (or at least mentally reviewing) passages or scenes from the novel in light of the Shakespearean intertext; (4) discovering the partial deceptiveness of the *Timon* connection and the greater importance of the *Hamlet* intertext; (5) developing an independent interest in *Timon*, but also increasingly in *Hamlet*—in learning about their sources, models, philosophy, and imagery, as well as what Shakespeare critics and commentators have said about them (why does one of them occupy perhaps the most peripheral place in the Shakespearean canon, while the other holds perhaps the most central one?); (6) returning to Nabokov and speculating about what made him select these specific plays by Shakespeare as intertexts and about the relative weight and structuring roles (serious? comic? serio-comic?) of these specific intertexts in relation to the numerous others; and (7) focusing attention, for purposes of comparison, on other more or less important intertexts (say, Pope's *Essay on Man* and *Rape of the Lock* or Sterne's *Tristram Shandy*), developing an independent interest in them, and so on and so forth.

Of course, the hypothetical procedure just described is totally utopian, in the sense that it posits a reader (not necessarily an "ideal reader") with

. . .

an infinity of available time to explore an infinite text or textual network. But if our reader at least makes it to point 3 and (re)reads *Timon,* he or she will now interpret Kinbote's commentary to lines 39–40 of John Shade's poem differently from before. The commentary reads:

> One cannot help recalling a passage in *Timon of Athens* (Act IV, Scene 3) where the misanthrope talks to the three marauders. Having no library in the desolate log cabin where I live like Timon in his cave, I am compelled for the purpose of quick citation to retranslate this into English prose from a Zemblan poetical version of *Timon* . . . :

> > The sun is a thief: she lures the sea
> > and robs it. The moon is a thief:
> > he steals his silvery light from the sun. (p. 50)

The imaginary Zemblan translation of *Timon* retranslated into English (as a result of which the personification of the sun becomes feminine, and that of the moon masculine, alluding perhaps to Kinbote's sexual inversion and transvestite fantasies) raises yet another problem of reading: the unavoidable creation by the first-time reader or the rereader of a "virtual text," which can only be, in a large sense, a translation, a recasting of an elusive original (in our specific example, the unavailable text of Shakespeare's *Timon*). In the case of translation, the virtual text and its implications can be judged against the original. The precise types of (re)reading involved in translation, with their specific rules and the decisions or choices these rules allow, are studied within the separate domain of comparative poetics or translation theory and cannot be dealt with here. In a broader hermeneutical sense, however, the question of translation is central to any theory of reading, and if Priscilla Meyer is right in saying that pale fire is finally "a metaphor for translation," it may also be seen as a metaphor for that ceaseless unself-conscious translation that is the act of (re)reading.

The Library in the Book

Adequate (satisfyingly playful) reading or rereading of literary works like Nabokov's *Pale Fire* always requires more reading and rereading. Its logic is inexorably expansive. But one might say that from the point of view of the reader *any* literary text (not only one that teases so learnedly as *Pale Fire*) is infinite, for such a text indeed contains an infinite virtual library which it would take an infinite time to peruse.

· · ·

This infinity of the literary text, as progressively revealed in the process of attentive reading and rereading, has been sometimes cited as an argument against the possibility of a doctrine or consistent theory of reading or a proper poetics. Roland Barthes, for instance, noting the difficulty in "finding a *pertinence* from which to establish a coherent analysis of reading," linked it to the lack of a structural obligation to close a reading. In "On Reading" (1976), he writes:

> Of course, there is an *origin* of graphic reading: this is the apprenticeship to letters, to written words; but . . . once this *technè* is acquired, we do not know where to halt the depth and the dispersion of reading: at the apprehension of meaning? Which meaning? Denoted? Connoted? . . . But how far? To infinity: there is no *structural* obligation to close my reading. . . . Our knowing *how to read* can be determined, verified at its inaugural stage, but it very quickly becomes a knowledge without basis, without rules, without degrees, and without end. (*The Rustle of Language*, p. 35)

Still, I think, we can talk meaningfully about reading as a process, as a structuring activity that observes certain general rules, and not just about "a reader (you or myself)," as Barthes puts it, or about an always purely idiosyncratic individual reader. We can talk, I would insist, about "trans-individual forms," about "codes" (be they merely lists of cultural stereotypes), and even about "rules" that make the game of (re)reading possible, as Barthes himself seemed ready to admit in an essay written shortly after the publication of *S/Z*, his important contribution to the analysis of reading (and more precisely rereading). In the post-*S/Z* essay, playfully entitled "Writing Reading" (1970), Barthes delineates some of the areas of reading as a broadly conceived process that could lend itself to fruitful investigation, even though such investigation might not satisfy the criteria of structuralist (scientific) rigor that Barthes had dreamed of bringing to literary studies at an earlier stage in his career. In the 1970 essay, Barthes recognizes that

> every reading derives from trans-individual forms: the associations engendered by the letter . . . are never . . . anarchic; they are always caught up (sampled and inserted) by certain codes. . . . The most subjective reading imaginable is never anything but a game played according to certain rules. Where do these rules come from? . . . . [They] come from an age-old logic of narrative, from a symbolic form which constitutes us even before we are born—in a word, from the vast cultural space through which our person (whether author or reader) is only one passage. To open the text, to posit the

. . .

system of its reading . . . is . . . to gain acknowledgement that there is no objective or subjective truth of reading, but only a *ludic* truth; again, "game" must not be understood here as a distraction, but as a piece of work—from which, however, all labor has evaporated. (*The Rustle of Language*, p. 31)

It is precisely as a form of play, as a ludic activity, that a poetics of (re)reading should approach its object. Such a poetics would be historical and cultural and fundamentally intertextual. Its theoretical starting point could be, as Michel Picard has suggested in his *La Lecture comme jeu,* the "assimilation of language [*langue*] to a gigantic game [*jeu*] within which certain speech sequences [*paroles*] would constitute particular 'games' [*parties*]," a model that would be applicable to well-organized "cultural ensembles, however diversified these may be in their systems of forms and rules." This may sound quite forbidding, but the literary-critical consequences of such an approach are far from earth-shattering:

One is almost embarrassed to recall the truism that every text, and therefore its reading, can be understood only as *part* of a specific culture and at the same time *against* it; just as every individual constructs himself after and against his parental models; just as a great chess player invents his strategy in relation to all the preceding ones—and is followed all over the world by chess players who are able to appreciate the new combinations which stand out as innovations. *Don Quixote* is obviously understood against the background of chivalric novels and *Jacques le fataliste* against the background of sentimental journeys. (p. 243)

These may indeed look like embarrassing platitudes, but reading and (quite often) rereading are such mysteriously unself-conscious activities that one needs to be constantly reminded of them. Once this is done, one can proceed to consider the more interesting problems of a ludic poetics of (re)reading. This will involve not only understanding *Don Quixote* against the background of chivalric novels, but also understanding chivalric novels themselves as extensions of such mental activities as fantasy and (egotistic) daydreaming in a certain historical-cultural context. It will also require understanding *Don Quixote* against the background of what chivalric novels decidedly are *not* (but still can be construed as being, with whatever benefits or risks): texts for recollected rereading, religiously oriented texts meant to be read spiritually, meditatively, symbolically, or allegorically, and therefore with extreme attention. It will, in short, involve comparisons and contrasts between types of texts and types of

. . .

reading and rereading, including various possibilities of misreading and, more dangerously, misrereading.

But such a ludic poetics of (re)reading will also try to account for a definite centripetal, text-oriented dimension of reading. In *Pale Fire* there is, as Nina Berberova intelligently observes, "a structural surprise: the symbolic level, the fantastic, the poetic lies on the surface and is obvious, while the factual, the realistic is only slightly hinted at and may be approached as a riddle. The realistic level is hidden by the symbolic one which has nothing enigmatic in it and is immediately clear to the reader" ("The Mechanics of *Pale Fire*," pp. 147–48). This structural device calls for a very attentive (re)reading—but a (re)reading in an *intra*textual as opposed to an *inter*textual sense. In this case, the text plays at hiding its own elements of fictional truth, that is, those elements of plot that allow us to engage mentally, as we read the story, in a basically naive game of make-believe.[3] Fictional truth is always established intratextually. In a realistic novel, say, by Stendhal, it is self-evident: the reader has no difficulty in recognizing the fictional truth of Julien Sorel's affair with Madame de Rénal, of his later calculated seduction of Mathilde de la Mole, of his passionate desire to resume his relationship with Madame de Rénal and, once rebuffed, of his trying to kill her. Nabokov, in playing with his reader, obliges him or her to search for a fictional truth that is, paradoxically, important to find but in itself quite uninteresting. Nina Berberova gives us the following outline:

> Two men were living in the United States near a university campus. One of them, John Shade, was a famous poet; the other, Professor Charles Kinbote, had recently arrived from Europe. Kinbote had rented a house in the poet's neighborhood; his landlord happened to be Judge Goldsworth. Some time ago, Judge Goldsworth had put an assassin in a lunatic asylum; this man had recently escaped and was searching for the judge to avenge himself. On one summer evening Kinbote and Shade were walking between their houses. The killer appeared, mistook Shade in the darkness for the judge (they were slightly alike) and shot him. (p. 148)

The interest of reading and particularly of rereading Nabokov's text could not be derived from such a simple plot of fictionally true events—whatever complications and surprising turns we might imagine. Yet without it, or something close to it, the rich fantastic-symbolic-parodic-intertextual planes of the novel might become chaotic and fail to acquire the suggestive power they exert on us as intricate fantasies with their own

. . .

compelling if elusive inner truth. Of course, Kinbote is not—in terms of mimetic fictional truth—the exiled king Charles the Beloved of Zembla trying to escape the dogged pursuit of the hired assassin Jakob Gradus. (He may not even be Kinbote, but only a projection or delusion of the mad Russian professor Botkin as imagined by John Francis Shade.) In a sense, however, Kinbote *is* the king of Zembla forced into exile by a revolution: his commentary to Shade's poem, ramblingly solipsistic as it is, establishes a certain consistency, with its own points of fictional truth even on the level of (delusional) images.

Intratextual or centripetal reading for solving internal puzzles and clarifying confusions remains, however, dependent on our sense of the symbolic intertextuality of the book. In other words, the more conscious we are of the "library in the book," of the intended or even unintended wealth of intertextual material it contains, the more we are going to pay attention to tiny, easily overlooked textual details, and the more we are going to search for clues that allow us to establish its internal fictional truth. For the joys of reading intertextually dissolve in the absence of a principle of internal coherence. To be sure, a narrative text with a less apparent symbolic-intertextual dimension can offer us more direct access to its fictional world and make it more attractive for us to engage in playing—and perhaps even replaying—an essentially simple game of make-believe. But even such a text, if we look for its hidden rules and sources, ends up revealing a hidden library: a book is not only a thousand things to a thousand people, it is also a thousand books to the same unhurried, attentive, inquisitive reader.

Three Perspectives on Reading and Play

In spite of its notorious fluidity, which has inspired devastating critiques, the concept of play continues to be used by distinguished representatives of many disciplines and subdisciplines: cultural anthropology, game theory, communication theory, psychology, sociology, aesthetics, philosophy, and the philosophy of science or epistemology are only some of them.[4] The three broad perspectives from which I look at (re)reading and play are determined, somewhat arbitrarily, by what I see as three interdisciplinary semantic areas covered by the notion of play and relevant to the problematic of reading.

The first area refers to varied manifestations of play as an expression of imagination or creativity, from its simplest, most spontaneous, and unre-

· · ·

flective forms to the highest and most intricate. Students of play have often pointed to the close relationship between playing and creativity. Even at the most elementary preverbal or nonverbal level, the play of the young child with its mother or with its first toys clearly involves such creative functions of the mind as the ability to imagine (to form and manipulate images of things outside the immediate perceptual field), to symbolize, and more generally to engage in exploratory activity. Certain theorists of play have insisted on the intimate connection, and sometimes even the identity, of playful behavior and exploratory behavior, emphasizing among the latter's components such impulses or faculties as curiosity, initiative, desire for novelty and new experiences, openness to surroundings, alertness, inquisitiveness, self-confidence, and, in the fully developed human being, thirst for knowledge for its own sake, inventiveness, and what might be called the heuristic impulse, the impulse toward discovery.

My discussion of (re)reading and play starts by focusing on the intellectual end-results of such playful behavior in the creative human adult. In other words, I have seen fit to deal first not with the elementary but with the most sophisticated and apparently cerebral kinds of (re)reading as play, including highly specialized, professional, or even purely scientific or mathematical reading. This reversal is justified, if not (chrono)logically, at least rhetorically: it allows me to dramatize certain game-like aspects of reading, show them in their spectacular intellectual complexity, and then move toward their more simple components, like viewing an intricately woven fabric before unraveling its strands.

An observation made by the ethologist Konrad Lorenz might serve to show the essential continuity that exists between play of the most spontaneous, unreflective kind and highly theoretical knowledge. Speaking about curiosity, Lorenz points out:

> All purely material research conducted by a human scientist [but also, I would add, all reading bearing on such research] is pure inquisitive behavior—appetitive behavior *in free operation*. In this sense, it is *play behavior*. All scientific knowledge . . . arose from playful activities conducted in a free field entirely for their own sake. When Benjamin Franklin drew sparks from the leash of his kite, he thought no more about the possibility of a lightning conductor than Hertz thought about the possibilities of radio when investigating electric waves. Anybody who has seen in his own activity the smooth transition from childhood play to the life-work of a scientist could never doubt the fundamental identity of play and research. ("Psychology and Phylogeny," p. 95)

. . .

From a radically different philosophical perspective, the psychoanalyst D. W. Winnicott makes a similar statement when he equates playing with "living fully, creatively," irrespective of whether the experience is physical or intellectual. In *Playing and Reality,* he notes: "The creative impulse is . . . something that can be looked at as a thing in itself, something that of course is necessary if an artist is to produce a work of art, but also as something that is present when *anyone*—baby, child, adolescent, adult, old man or woman—looks in a healthy way at anything. . . . It is present as much in the moment-by-moment living of a backward child who is enjoying breathing as it is in the inspiration of an architect who suddenly knows what it is that he wishes to construct" (p. 69). The central concept here is that of enjoyment in the achievement, unconscious or conscious, be it of breathing, looking, discovering or, I should add, reading and rereading.

From the perspective of play as creativity, and more specifically *intellectual* creativity, chapter 10, "The Ludic Dimension," raises such diverse questions as: What constitutes the playful-creative dimension of (re)reading, including the aesthetic dimension, as opposed to what might be called "work reading" (reading to fulfill a duty, to learn or gain information necessary for achieving longer-term projects of a pragmatic order)? Are there any clear-cut distinctions between play and work and how do they apply to reading? When and how can reading be seen as a game? Is there any relationship between the games analyzed by game theory and the possible games of reading? In what sense can one speak of "correctness" or "correct play" in regard to reading?

The second broad area of application of the concept of play is psychology in a stricter, more technical sense. In agreement with other students of play (social and cultural anthropologists, such as Roger Caillois), some psychologists distinguish between a more spontaneous and markedly imaginative "symbolic play" and "games with rules" (Piaget's terms). The psychologists' explanations of the diverse forms and functions of symbolic-imitative play in children and their survivals in adults differ greatly, but there are significant areas of consensus in regard to the functional description of symbolic play, and these are the source of important analogies with certain aspects of literary reading and rereading. The category of symbolic play includes children's play with symbolic-imitative toys (from simple pieces of cloth or other early "fetish objects," teddy bears, dolls, or stuffed animals, to more complicated imitative toys like electric trains, ships, airplanes, and building or construction games); it also includes—and this is more obviously related to the enjoyment of stories and, later, reading—

. . .

135

all sorts of pretend play, role playing, impersonation, playing with imaginary companions, and conceiving whole worlds of make-believe without any apparent difficulty.

Chapter 11, "Psychological Approaches," concentrates on the psychological relationships between symbolic play (in its various manifestations) and reading, within the larger network of related phenomena such as play, daydreaming, fantasy, dreaming, and imagining. Is reading, particularly popular literary reading, merely a way of legitimizing processes of egotistic daydreaming, or of satisfying "His Majesty the Ego" (Freud)? What are the possible psychological explanations for the reader's often passionate interest in what happens to obviously fictional characters in fictional situations? What are the implications of using the concept of play as a model of reading? How is one to understand the phenomenon of reading involvement or hypnotic-like trance? Does involvement differ from absorption and if so, how? The discussion of the phenomenon of absorption as distinct from involvement anticipates some problems encountered in the next section (particularly in chapter 13).

The third semantic area in which I use the concept of play refers to games with rules. Games with rules, which gain in importance in later developmental stages in the life of the individual (they are directly linked to the processes of socialization of the older child), are more openly competitive and, if we leave aside the special case of games of chance, fall into two groups (which may of course overlap): games of physical ability ("sports"—ball games, races) and games of mental ability, involving such faculties as memory, attention, intelligence, inferential or hypothetical thought, and inventiveness (chess, certain card games, such as bridge, in which chance plays a limited role).

Chapter 12 ("Fictionality") naturally excludes games of physical ability and sports, which present only incidental analogies with reading (although writers may occasionally use sporting events, with their characteristic suspense so relished by spectators, as a structuring device and as a way of creating reader interest). This chapter attempts to establish the ways in which games with rules provide valid models of reflective reading and particularly rereading. I discuss the general problem of reading rules versus specified zones of textual indeterminacy and the kinds of constraints as well as choice-situations they create for the player/reader who is conscious of the fictionality of what he or she reads. In this chapter I return to some of the questions previously examined from a psychological standpoint, but look at them from a new, *structural,* philosophical, and

. . .

communicational perspective. Belief or pseudo-belief in fictions is now seen not as an egocentrical impulse but *as a rule of the game* of (re)reading and the whole category of fictionality is accounted for in terms of a communicational and, more specifically, a *metacommunicational* frame—a frame which instructs us to react nonpragmatically to the messages it contains; a frame which tells us "This is play! This is fiction! This is *not* real!" The two final chapters of Part III focus on rereading as such and offer examples of literary works that not only can sustain but *demand rereading*, works such as Henry James's *The Turn of the Screw*, which is the object of an extended analysis from the point of view of an implied logic of rereading, or some modernist/postmodernist pseudodetective experimental texts, such as Alain Robbe-Grillet's *The Erasers* and *The Voyeur*. These two analytical chapters are "interludes"—they hark back to the book's Borgesian "prelude"—and are meant not only to illustrate but also to refine some of the concepts and distinctions elaborated in the theoretical discussion of play and (re)reading, as well as of (re)reading in general, including questions that will be taken up in more detail in Part IV, which deals with secrecy or hidden meaning from the reader's point of view.

. . .

TEN

The Ludic Dimension

Games of Reading

Any reading of a worthwhile text, be it undertaken for purposes of entertainment or knowledge, can acquire a ludic dimension. In other words, any reading of a text that is perceived as valuable or interesting can take on, in addition to its more obvious features and explicit goals, the characteristics of a game. In certain cases this game may be intended by the author as a challenge to the reader's ingenuity, for instance by proposing a mystery or puzzle, as in detective fiction. On a higher level of sophistication, as we saw in the case of Nabokov's *Pale Fire,* the author may propose more complicated kinds of inter- and intratextual puzzles, parodic allusions, and games of concealment. Other texts propose games of make-believe and participation in imaginary situations, from blatant wish-fulfilling fantasies to complex and highly ambiguous psychological dramas. But the ludic element in reading often has its origin in the reader and in his or her attitude toward the text—any text that is deemed worth reading.

My assumed reader, X, is a scholar or a scientist who reads a text pertaining to his or her field for professional reasons. Evidently, there is nothing immediately playful about this reading. That X will bring to the text in question certain more or less well-defined expectations and even anticipations (X may know the author from other publications and may

· · ·

think highly, indifferently, or poorly of him or her), as well as a fairly high degree of familiarity with the general subject, and even with the specific topic treated in the text, goes almost without saying. Now, depending on a variety of other factors that can influence the reading process but must be put aside for the time being, my claim is that X may at one point in the reading of the text develop a ludic attitude toward it.[1] This attitude will not prevent him or her from attending intellectually to the way the text articulates the issues (and from determining how clearly, elegantly, and persuasively it handles them), nor from lucidly appreciating whatever claims to truth it may make. Actually, the reader's concentration, attention, and alertness to the details of the text, including mere hints and connotative minutiae, will often be increased by the adoption of a ludic perspective.

What do I mean here by ludic perspective or attitude? No more than that at a certain point in the perusal of the text the reader X may decide to play an imaginary game with its author, or perhaps only with himself or herself as a (self-conscious) reader. This may in part be a guessing game in the form of anticipations containing an element of wager: a good guess brings a small psychological reward in terms of self-esteem. It may also be a polemical game of controverting, refuting, second-guessing, searching for the weak spots in the author's argumentation or presentation. But the kind of reading I have in mind can also develop as a half-cooperative, half-competitive game, in which the reader essentially accepts the problem posed by the author but tries to find better, finer, and more convincing angles from which to attack it.

Another significant component of such a game of reading, and certainly a contributor to its intellectual excitement, consists of the lively, informal, and playful switching of the reader's mind from the one text/game to other texts/games of the same kind held in his or her memory: the frequency and quality of such comparisons, which often bear on minute but fascinating details, are a measure of the stimulating value of the text under (ludic) scrutiny. Poor or mediocre texts do not inspire such comparisons and generally are not conducive to a ludic attitude on the part of the reader.

A final element that contributes directly to the excitement of playing the game of reading (especially when the player/reader is not only highly intelligent and skilled but also in an independently good, curious, expectant, generous, and creative mood) I shall call "heuristic hope" or the hope of making a discovery. Readers may hope that something in a particular act of reading—a reading that takes place under the happy conditions just

· · ·

mentioned—might lead them to an independent discovery in their field of interest or research, that some unforeseen detail or association might turn out to hold the key to some problem only indirectly related to the subject addressed in the text. This heuristic hope is of course more than the idle expectation of a serendipitous find; it is a state of *creative readiness,* and even if X does not make any specific independent discovery as a result of reading a particular text, this state, enhanced by the high quality of the game proposed by that text, is of great value in that it strengthens his or her self-confidence and "will to creation." This kind of creative self-consciousness naturally leads to writing.

The heuristic possibilities of reading are by no means limited to reading within one's profession. From the point of view of an intelligent, inquisitive, and alert reader the heuristics of reading is indeed cross-disciplinary: one might find an answer to a question encountered in one's professional research by reading a poem, a novel, a biography, or virtually any stimulating text. The explanation of this phenomenon must be sought in the fact that we, as readers, always carry in our mind—most of the time unconsciously—hundreds of not-yet-answered questions and hypotheses. Reading may at any time, often completely unexpectedly, activate any of these by way of suggesting a possible answer to an old nagging question, an argument in support of an incomplete hypothesis, an interesting consequence of a long-held and half-forgotten assumption.

The creative impulse triggered in the active reader by a seminal text explains the use of (re)reading as a preparation for original writing. In this case the heuristic hope begins to shade into a goal, albeit a vague, indeterminate, unspecified one. Proust, quoting Emerson and recalling Dante's tribute to Virgil, gives us an eloquent account of (re)reading as a writer's pre-creative ritual, as a sort of propitiatory practice before setting out to compose and explore unknown regions of thought and imagination: Emerson "would rarely begin to write without rereading some pages of Plato," and Dante "is not the only poet whom Virgil led to the threshold of paradise" (*On Reading Ruskin,* p. 118). Which is to say that reading or rather rereading—the way Dante read Virgil, not imitating him but entrusting him with the role of heuristic master and guide—may be an essential part of the creative act.

But when and how does play come into the equation of certain kinds of reading and creative writing? Creative *reading*—deep, meditative reading—is after all a recognizable form of "production," as Roland Barthes has noted in "On Reading" (1976):

. . .

Reading is a conductor of the Desire to write . . . ; not that we necessarily want to write *like* the author we enjoy reading. . . . This has been very clearly put by the writer Roger Laporte: "A *pure* reading which does not call for *another writing* is incomprehensible to me. . . . Reading Proust, Blanchot, Kafka, Artaud gave me no desire to write on these authors (not even, I might add, *like* them), but to *write*." In this perspective, reading is a veritable production: no longer of interior images, of projections, of hallucinations, but literally of *work* (*The Rustle of Language*, pp. 40–41).

But is there any link between this kind of work—a form of mental writing or rewriting—and play? Barthes himself, in an earlier paper, pointed to such a connection by characterizing reading as a purposeful, serious activity, structurally analogous to playing a game and as such diametrically opposed to labor: " 'Game' must not be understood here as a distraction," Barthes observed in "Writing Reading" (1970), "but as a piece of work—from which, however, all labor has evaporated" (*The Rustle of Language*, p. 31). This formulation is memorable even though the idea it expresses is not all that new. Barthes joins here a long line of thinkers, starting with Friedrich Schiller, who variously saw in play a paradigm for a liberated (nonalienated and nonalienating) kind of work—work raised to the level of an aesthetic, autotelic, or intrinsically motivated activity.

Let me provisionally sum up my thoughts on the ludic attitude in reading. A highly skilled reader *may* adopt a ludic attitude toward a text, whether the text is within or without his or her area of expertise. The ability to approach a text ludically is an expression of a state of overall well-being, self-confidence, and creativeness. The ludic attitude may prompt the reader to construct his or her reading as a game (competitive, cooperative, or mixed). The same basic attitude may also give rise in the reader to a vague but vital, healthy (in Winnicott's sense) "heuristic hope." A heuristic theory of ludic reading is justified both in disciplinary and, more importantly, interdisciplinary terms given the hypothesizing nature and vocation of reading. Finally, a certain kind of ludic or quasi-ludic reading, and particularly the *rereading* of certain classic texts (Emerson rereading Plato) may enhance the creativity and originality of the reader and inspire genuinely new work.

Play or Work?

Certainly the most complicated issue that has been raised thus far is the relationship between work and play. Virtually all the major modern

· · ·

attempts to define play in a broad cultural-anthropological perspective (from Johan Huizinga's 1938 classic, *Homo ludens,* through the brilliant 1947 essay on play as structure by Emile Benveniste, to the studies on play and games by Roger Caillois) establish an opposition between play (an essentially gratuitous or disinterested activity) and work (a useful, productive activity, clearly interested in its pragmatic result). In his *Man, Play, and Games,* for instance, Roger Caillois defines play as an activity that is

1. *Free*: in which playing is not obligatory; if it were, it would at once lose its attractive and joyous quality as diversion;
2. *Separate*: circumscribed within limits of space and time, defined and fixed in advance;
3. *Uncertain*: the course of which cannot be determined, nor the result attained beforehand, and some latitude for innovation being left to the player's initiative;
4. *Unproductive*: creating neither goods, nor wealth, nor new elements of any kind . . . ;
5. *Governed by rules*: under conventions that suspend ordinary laws, and for the moment establish new legislation, which alone counts;
6. *Make-believe*: accompanied by a special awareness of a second reality or of a free unreality, as against real life. (pp. 10–11)

No less than five of these six points are relevant to the opposition between work and play: the first point suggests that, unlike play, work is often perceived as an obligation; the third that the results of work are determined beforehand, while those of play are not; the fourth that work, unlike play, is always supposed to be productive; the fifth that the rules governing work do not suspend ordinary legislation (the commonly accepted rules, regulations, conventions of everyday social living); and the sixth that work does not aim at creating a "second reality" but remains confined to the shared reality of the ordinarily accepted world.

These points of contrast between play and work present obvious difficulties. The most significant one is that play may also be perceived as an obligation or even an ordeal. An individual or team in a competition may feel under the obligation to win and thus experience all the anxiety that such an obligation usually creates. In a different sense, serious, dedicated chess players are obliged to study (that is, to work) no less than good pianists are obliged to practice daily—often a boring routine—in order to keep up their ability to play well. On a social level, the general sordidness

. . .

of the lives of hundreds of aspiring professional chess players—to stay with the example of chess—who participate again and again in low-level or middle-level tournament circuits to qualify for an elusive promotion to a higher category, who experience more often than the joys of play the bitter feelings of rivalry, resentment, and failure, may in some ways remind one of the messy world of addiction, by comparison with which life in the world of a disciplined workplace would appear to be almost pastoral.[2] And is it true that the results of play can never be determined beforehand? Is it not the case that a trained player will display more predictable skills and will obtain more predictable results than an untrained one? More importantly, is training itself not work? What is the difference between training for play and training for work or just working? Also, one cannot simply state that play suspends "ordinary legislation" while work does not. What is "ordinary legislation" anyway? Why would the rules governing a workplace be more ordinary than the rules governing, say, a championship game in an Olympics competition? Are not both sets of rules different from the more ordinary and informal conventions of everyday social life? Nor is the notion that play establishes a "second reality" definitive. This is always a matter of perspective: work can also establish a second reality in relation to a primary reality one wishes to flee or forget, whatever that may be. "Second reality" is just a synonym for any sphere of activity one values for intrinsic motives, and it would be counterintuitive to deny that work, under certain circumstances, can be intrinsically motivated.

Aside from such impromptu questions, the definition of play proposed by Caillois has generated a good deal of more systematic criticism. Some of his most articulate critics have found fault with the very distinction between work and play that concerns us here. Jacques Ehrmann, in his "*Homo ludens* Revisited," thinks that the antithesis *work/play* as used by Caillois reflects some of the most pervasive biases of the Western cultural consciousness, biases that ultimately favor an ethic of work and seriousness and are dismissive of play. It can hardly be fortuitous, or a result of a value-free judgment, that the Huizinga-Benveniste-Caillois approach ranges work together with such honorific notions as seriousness, usefulness, fecundity, and science, while it characterizes play by more dubious qualities such as gratuitousness, sterility, leisure, art, and unreality (p. 41). Personally, I doubt that in Western discourse such characteristics as seriousness and usefulness are always honorific; it all depends on context and usage. Seriousness is not all that honorific, for instance, when used as

. . .

a synonym for humorlessness, ponderousness, or dullness; seriousness may also imply rigidity and stubborn fixation rather than flexibility and doubt, which can be perceived as highly desirable intellectual qualities. Ehrmann may be building a theoretical straw man here.

At any rate, Ehrmann makes a number of shrewd remarks with regard to the logical difficulties of the positions taken by Huizinga, Benveniste, and Caillois, and his critique of the tacit, unexamined assumptions that underlie their philosophical position is at times quite convincing. According to Ehrmann, these unexamined assumptions in the main derive from an ethnocentric conception of history as a progression from primitive man—infantile, savage, playful, and visionary—to civilized Western man—serious, productive, logical, and realistic. Unfortunately, after Ehrmann's critique of the framework within which these three authors developed their radical distinction between play and reality (including work), his own theoretical conclusion comes as something of a letdown: "The distinguishing characteristic of reality is that it is played. Play, reality, culture are synonymous and interchangeable. Nature does not exist prior to culture" (p. 56). But how, and from what, is reality distinguished by being played? And who, or what, plays it? And how? These questions are particularly puzzling in view of the sweeping synonymity (play = reality = culture) that Ehrmann proposes at the end of his essay. If play is one and the same thing as reality, how can the "distinguishing characteristic" of reality be that it is played? Collapsing the traditional distinctions between play and reality, gratuitousness and work, Ehrmann ends up with a huge tautology.

Leaving aside this non-conclusion, one can accept the tenor of the criticism Ehrmann makes of Huizinga, Benveniste, and Caillois and still go on (re)reading them, bracketing the metaphysical implications of their concepts and treating such concepts as mere operational constructs. In such a reading, the oppositions work/play, seriousness/gratuitousness, etc., would have a limited and strictly local heuristic function. Ehrmann's deconstructive argumentation is interesting in itself, but his final string of identities (play = reality = culture) does not allow any local heuristic usage of his insights. And this criticism leaves out his exorbitant last injunction: "All of our critical methods must be reconsidered according to these new norms" (p. 57). Such sweeping and inapplicable "new norms" are little more than vacuous language, language that, one might say, neither plays nor works.

But where does the foregoing discussion of Ehrmann leave us with

· · ·

respect to the question of work and play? By now, I think, it should be apparent that positing an absolute gap between work and play (the position criticized by Ehrmann) is neither right nor wrong in and of itself. It all depends on how productive—in terms of analytical insight and general perception—the resulting dichotomy turns out to be. In spite of the limitations it imposes, the antithesis between work and play functions reasonably well for Huizinga and Caillois, in the sense that it allows them to make some intelligent, penetrating observations on their subject: play and games in a cultural-anthropological context. And intelligent observations, even when fragmentary or imperfectly integrated in an overall theory, have a cutting edge that may stimulate exciting thinking.

But it is also clear that positing a gap between work and play would *not* be helpful in an investigation of the play element in (re)reading. For in an important sense, all reading is work, even when such work remains invisible. And attentive, close reading—the kind of reading that might lead to an absorption akin to that achieved in playing certain very complex games—is extremely hard work. It is, metaphorically, as Ruskin suggests in *Sesame and Lilies,* very much like a miner's work:

> When you come to a good book, you must ask yourself, "Am I inclined to work as an Australian miner would? Are my pickaxes and shovels in good order, and am I in good trim myself, my sleeves well up the elbow, and my breath good, and my temper?" And, keeping the figure a little longer, . . . the metal you are in search of being the author's mind and meaning, his words are as the rock you have to crush and smelt in order to get at it. And your pickaxes are your own care, wit, and learning; your smelting furnace is your own thoughtful soul. Do not hope to get at any good author's meaning without those tools and that fire. (p. 64)

That may be why readers, when they plan to read or reread for pleasure, may hesitate before undertaking a particular act of reading: will their effort of concentration, no smaller for usually being unself-conscious, be repaid? On the other hand, under favorable circumstances, reading and rereading can and do become play—and the reader gains access to a highly desirable and sought-after condition, a condition in which his or her mind is happily immersed in an engrossing and intrinsically motivated activity. The miner analogy is no longer applicable here.

Roland Barthes's characterization of the work of reading as "work from which labor has evaporated" proves helpful in describing such an apparently paradoxical situation. Another way of approaching the same

· · ·

phenomenon is the concept of "work for play and play for work." I borrow this striking formula (altering it slightly) from the Polish writer Witold Gombrowicz. Speaking in his *Diary* about "the art of discussion," Gombrowicz makes the following remarks, which, I think, can be justifiably applied to the art of reading—an art that clearly incorporates elements of mental discussion or dialogue: "People who forget about other people and concentrate exclusively on striving for the Truth speak heavily and falsely. . . . But those who know how to liberate pleasure, who treat discussion as both work and play, play for work and work for play, they will not allow themselves to be crushed and then the exchange of opinions will sprout wings, flash grace, passion, poetry. . . . Even absolute idiocy or lies will not be able to knock you flat on your back if your are able to play with them" (pp. 73–74). In agreeing that reading can be both work and play, we neither reject nor accept the customary antinomy between work and play, but we do in a certain sense acknowledge it. For this antinomy, as it exists in ordinary language, provides the necessary background against which such notions as "laborless work" or "work for play and play for work" become, in spite of their apparently paradoxical character, useful models for understanding the complexities of (re)reading.

But we must not forget that there is "work for work" even in the midst of what we would consider intrinsically playful activities. Take once again the example of chess: a good player will have to bear with many boring, unenlightening, irritatingly banal games to experience the thrill of a truly great game. Students of play usually ignore this phenomenon of boredom in the midst of a playful activity. Let me briefly recall as an example of such ignorance the general argument of the behavioral scientist Mihaly Csikszentmihalyi in his book *Beyond Boredom and Anxiety*. Csikszentmihalyi's study of playful ("autotelic") behavior is based on two assumptions, one that I believe is correct ("there is no unbridgeable gap between 'work' and 'leisure' ") and another that I consider fallacious ("by studying play one can learn how work can be made more enjoyable," p. 4). It is quite true that what the author calls *flow* (a "peculiar dynamic state—the holistic sensation that people feel when they act with total involvement") may be experienced in any activity, and "even in some activities that seem least designed to give enjoyment—on the battlefront, on a factory assembly line, or in a concentration camp" (p. 36). On the other hand, I would suggest, it is equally true that both boredom and anxiety can occur in activities that have been specifically designed to give enjoyment. A prime example is the world of literary reading: passionate readers (readers who

. . .

work for play and play for work) will recognize immediately that, in order to be able to indulge their passion, they have to put up with numerous tedious and sometimes frustrating or at least disappointing reading experiences—the bad books of a loved author, the tedious but informative books about a loved author, the uninspiring books of one's colleagues. What Csikszentmihalyi calls flow is, as I see it, extraordinarily elusive and rare—a moment of grace that comes as unexpectedly and blissfully as what poets call inspiration.

Game Theory and Reading: Analogies and Paradoxes

The notion of work for play and play for work can help us to understand the intricacies and ambiguities of ludic reading. On the one hand, what is obviously work—the reading of a professional text for professional purposes—can lead to forms of intellectual play, including the introduction of a larger strategy of game playing: for example, one can read the text along the lines of an assumed game-like structure; or one can search for the undeclared rules of an author's game within the structural rules of the genre of discourse to which the text belongs; or one can evaluate the author's assumed game (in terms of other possible strategies, as more or less effective, economical, elegant, etc.). On the other hand, this kind of conceptual play can, and indeed should, lead to work: producing original research and writing.

The view of reading as playing a game requires us to consider more closely the problem of reader motivation. For now I shall limit myself to speaking of motivation only on the abstract level of game theory. My assumption is that reading can be regarded as an intricate game, in which case the question of motivation can be answered quite simply in terms of the game-theoretical notion of payoff. But at least two complicating qualifications need to be introduced: (1) reading a text of any length is never one continuous game but many simultaneous and successive, intertwined, often fragmentary games, each with its own potential payoff matrix; (2) reading has little if anything to do with the kinds of games that can be formalized and treated mathematically (clear-cut games with clear-cut winners and losers, or zero-sum games).

With these qualifications and caveats in mind, one can point to certain parallelisms between reading and games. In both, the purpose is to "win"; and in the case of reading, a good payoff could be simply a forceful, incisive, superior understanding of the issues raised by a text. In this context,

. . .

147

the principle of romantic hermeneutics, as formulated by Schleiermacher, comes to mind: namely, the task of the interpreter of a text is to *understand it better than its own author*. That this principle, as far as I know, has not been approached from a broad game-theoretical perspective does not preclude the possibility of accounting for it in such terms: in a certain sense, the notion that interpreters could or should interpret works more insightfully than their own authors argues in favor of a competitive strategic model of hermeneutics, even though the questions involved are not only unmanageably complex but often undecidable and paradoxical.

Undecidability, however, does not disqualify the strategic model suggested here or lessen the importance of *correct play*. This means playing by the rules; and if the rules, or certain rules, are not immediately visible or recognizable, then one must search for these rules. Such rules may or may not exclude cheating or deception. There are games in which the possibility of cheating must be taken into account as part of playing the game correctly (as in certain bargaining or negotiating games, in which bluffing, dissembling, and outright lying are assumed to occur and strategies are shaped accordingly).

A literary analogy to such games immediately suggests itself: reading a story told by an "unreliable narrator" (a confirmed or suspected liar, an unbalanced or insane witness, an interested party). In some of the first-person fantastic tales of Edgar Allan Poe, the author—or rather the implied author (to borrow this useful notion from Wayne Booth's *Rhetoric of Fiction*)—engages the reader in a complicated game of false expectations, surprises and reversals, and inferential constructions from distorted testimony or puzzling symptoms. This kind of "symptomatic" reading and rereading also presents analogies with the mental operations performed by someone involved in a game of "strategic interaction," as conceived by the sociologist Erving Goffman: for example, an intelligence officer may receive a message that could come from a friend in enemy territory, but could as well come from the enemy counterintelligence service or from a friend captured by the enemy and acting under duress, in which cases its purpose would be to disinform. What is true (within the fictional paradigm) and what is false (attributable to willful deception or perhaps to the hallucinations of a madman) in such stories as "The Black Cat" or "The Tell-Tale Heart"? What is sincere and what insincere?

The game of reading such tales must tackle problems that are, on the level of literary fiction, the equivalent of problems posed by a game of negotiations with an opponent one cannot and must not trust. Second-

· · ·

guessing the narrator, building a consistent scenario out of loose, contradictory, deliberately or unintentionally misleading statements, and attempting to guess what the implied author guessed that the implied reader's reaction would be are among the strategies available to the ludic reader when trying to come to terms with ambiguous narratives. In certain modernist, ironically self-reflexive prose works, such as Nabokov's novel *Despair,* the author teasingly and brazenly plays with the reader by manipulating the figure of a pathetically unreliable but at the same time masterfully suspenseful narrator. The implied author himself enacts the role of a ventriloquist magician who constantly challenges the reader to discover his tricks as well as the tricks of his main character. This brings about the excitement of a special kind of game of detection in which readers become detectives whose task is to sort out what the narrator, Hermann, "really" does, and what he believes he does, and why he does it. Hermann, a chocolate factory owner who devises a wild scheme to collect an extravagant life insurance premium by killing his presumed perfect double, Felix, is a self-confessed liar (hence the brilliant fictional exploitation of the classic Epimenides paradox, "I am a liar—is this true?") and a methodically inventive madman.

Games of Mutual Guessing

The sense in which game-theoretical concepts, such as the concept of correct play, can be relevant to reading shall become clearer once we have considered examples of possible games. An excellent source is Thomas C. Schelling's *The Strategy of Conflict,* a classic of game theory dealing with questions of international strategy, bargaining, and negotiations. The games he considers in chapter 4, "Toward a Theory of Interdependent Decision," typically involve *mutual knowledge* and *mutual guessing* on the part of the players (that is, one's way of playing the game is shaped by what one guesses the other will guess one's self to guess). One of Schelling's examples is a hypothetical game of chess whose payoff matrix is changed so as to make it a non-zero-sum game, and more specifically a game "that rewards the players not only for the pieces they capture but for the pieces they have left over at the end, as well as the squares they occupy, in such fashion that both players have some interest in minimizing the 'gross' mutual capture of pieces with its mutual destruction of value" (p. 107).[3]

In this example, all the known rules of the game of chess, that is, the way the pieces are to be moved, the comparative worth of each chessman,

. . .

and so on, remain unchanged; only the payoff matrix or the desired outcome is affected. This variation, however, dramatically modifies the way each player should play the game. Whereas in standard chess it does not make any difference to the players what the game is called and what the pieces look like or whether the squares are blank or have decorative overlays on them, "Now," Schelling writes, "it may make a difference to the players . . . whether the pieces look like horses, soldiers, explorers, or children on an Easter egg hunt; what map or picture is superimposed on the playing board . . . or what background story the players are told before they begin." The new significance of shapes, colors, images, visual patterns, background stories, and the like is because now

> the players must *bargain* their way to the outcome. . . . They must find ways of regulating their behavior, communicating their intentions, letting themselves be lead to some meeting of the minds, tacit or explicit, to avoid the destruction of potential gains. The "incidental details" may facilitate the players' discovery of expressive behavior patterns; and the extent to which the *symbolic* contents of the game—the suggestions and connotations— suggest compromises, limits, and regulations should be expected to make a difference. It should, because it can be a help to both players not to limit themselves to the abstract structure of the game in their search for stable, mutually nondestructive, recognizable patterns of movement. The fundamental psychic and intellectual process is that of participating in the creation of *traditions*; and the ingredients out of which traditions can be created, or the materials in which potential traditions can be perceived and jointly recognized, are not at all coincident with the mathematical contents of the game. (pp. 106–07)

In the new situation, then, it is "rational" for each player to take into account, for possible strategic use, symbolic contents and connotative values, potential "traditions" and patterns of reaction that could lead to a tacit joint recognition of intentions by the players. I think that all the elements that make it possible for the players in this example to coordinate their moves (expressive details, patterns, connotations, symbols, the kinds of materials on which and from which traditions can be built) are also important in the world of (re)reading. The critical understanding of a literary work participates in a tradition of reading, which it attempts to both confirm and renew. In such an undertaking the joint recognition of relevant features by the implied author and the implied reader, but also by two or more actual readers of the work who share their views with one another, is paramount.

· · ·

A case in point is that of a critic who is to review a new novel about which nobody else has written yet. The critic's reading of the novel will operate simultaneously on several levels, ranging from the most "naive" involvement with the subject matter or plot to the reflective appreciation of its merits and defects from the perspective of a would-be connoisseur to a game of competition/coordination with an implied or invented "author." On the level of "naive" involvement, the critic will probably try to play a game of make-believe. The word "naive" needs quotation marks because this can be a methodical and in fact quite sophisticated naivete: the critic puts himself or herself in the mind of a hypothetical credulous reader in an attempt to guess what the latter's reactions would be; and in guessing the credulous reader's reactions, the critic also tries to establish what kind of reader the author had in mind in the process of writing the book and what kind of readership the book might actually reach.

What is at stake in playing the game of reading on the level of connoisseurship? From the vantage point of mutual knowledge and guessing, a literary critic will naturally try to guess what other important critics might write about a new novel, what these other critics might expect one's self to write about it, and so forth. A mixed-motive game model describes the situation conveniently: up to a certain point, this critic tries to coordinate his or her game with that of other critics (one does not want one's reading to be considered off the wall) and seeks to identify the areas where "some meeting of the minds, tacit or explicit," might occur; on the other hand, the critic is also involved in a competitive game in which he or she wants to be the first to have made certain interesting, subtle, compelling, and quotable observations.

There is, however, a sense in which the relevance of Schelling's games of "precarious partnership" to reading and rereading may not be immediately clear, since reading is such an obviously solitary activity. One might even argue that, if we want to seek parallels to reading in the world of games, we should look in the direction of the so-called singular games (like solitaire or crossword puzzles). Such games do not involve either conflict or cooperation/coordination. The single player's plans, whatever the difficulties of choosing the right course, are not checked or thwarted by an opponent; and there is no play of reciprocal expectations (one player guessing what the other guesses that one's self guesses, etc.) or involvement of mutual knowledge. But as soon as we look more closely at what happens when (to return to an earlier example) an accomplished reader, X, reads a text within his or her unspecified professional field, we

· · ·

realize that the play element in his or her reading, if there is such an element, cannot be fully explained through a singular game model. X will quite likely play against the author of the text, or perhaps in (precarious) partnership with the author. Another possible game will oppose the reader to, or bring him or her in a more or less precarious partnership with, an imagined community of readers of comparable skills. If for some reason the author is not apparent, the sophisticated playful reader will invent an authorial figure on the basis of promptings and clues found in the text. Likewise, if such a reader has no knowledge of other readers' responses (in the form of published reviews or simply orally expressed opinions), he or she will imagine or invent these other readers.

This need to invent an author and other readers is strongest in the case of literary reading, in spite of the fact that singular game forms—riddles, enigmas, and other such puzzles—seem to be major devices in literature. But these puzzles are seen by the ludic reader as emanating from an author who has thereby issued a "personal" invitation for him or her to participate in a two-person game rather than an abstract, anonymous, purely combinatorial challenge.[4] This may be so because a book involves a reader differently—more personally and also more inventively—than a Rubik's cube or an electronic video game. Further, in dealing with literary enigmas or puzzles, a sophisticated ludic reader cannot help thinking of how other readers would handle these—how ingeniously, how effectively, how satisfyingly.

More generally, the notion of convention (as a principle of mutually expected behavior among the members of a community) can serve as a basis for conceiving various social activities—among them writing and reading—in terms of coordination games. Thomas Pavel has proposed such a view in his *Fictional Worlds*. Referring to the definition of convention formulated by the philosopher David K. Lewis (a convention is a regularity in behavior based on a system of mutual expectations), Pavel emphasizes the frequent absence of any *explicit* linguistic understanding or "contract" in the establishment and observance of such conventions, an absence that allows us to look at them as basic coordination games. He then goes on to suggest that "the horizon of expectations within which writers and their public operate can be seen as the background of various coordination games involving tacit cooperation between the members of the literary community" (p. 120). In the literary situation, the achievement of an equilibrium of coordination does not require the actual presence of the other participants: "One can imagine a coordination game—finding a

. . .

hidden object, a letter or a treasure—in which the participants are not allowed to come in touch with one another and must decipher signs left behind by the coplayers. Is the absence of the other participants an insuperable obstacle to finding the letter or the treasure and, consequently, to the obtaining of equilibrium? To further dramatize the question, is the death of one participant an obstacle? In Poe's 'The Gold-Bug' the treasure is found in spite of Kidd's death" (p. 121).

From the perspective of (re)reading, the real issue seems not so much the finding of the "treasure" as the process by which the coordination game proposed by the text can be played successfully and satisfyingly, particularly under conditions in which, as Pavel notes in regard to literature, conventions are in a state of incessant change and therefore have a "weak obligatoriness" (p. 122). Such a regime of weak conventionality, which allows for both ambiguity and innovation, naturally leads to what I shall discuss later as games of rereading. For the time being, it suffices to say that the reader's uncertainty as to whether the right coordination equilibrium has been reached may engender *the need to reread*. This is true especially of modernist literature, which tries to make obvious the usually hidden conventionality of the literary game by the technique of the "foregrounding of the device," as the Russian Formalists called it, but also by the opposite technique of teasingly hiding it again right away, in a literary equivalent of a magician's game, of which Nabokov's prose is an outstanding example.

One of the most interesting views advanced by Pavel concerns the parallel between the gradual training and self-improvement in the reading of literature and the process of becoming a better, more sophisticated player of a game by consistent practice: "In a game-theory perspective, literary texts are assumed to be built around a few basic rules that give access to the text; while a naive reader knows these and only these rules, more advanced strategies can gradually become available through training and practice. Just as good chess players master not only the elementary rules of the game but are capable of applying such strategic laws as the principle of intermediary goals, or the principle of controlling the central squares, good readers know how to detect regularities that are invisible to less-trained readers" (p. 126). What is missing in this account is only the explicit recognition that a good reader is an inveterate rereader and that texts containing regularities (regularities worth discovering) and strategic possibilities invisible to the eye of the naive reader are rereadable texts.

. . .

Imagining the Author and the Importance of Correct Play

In order to account for the element of play in a scientist's or scholar's reading of a professional text (say, a mathematician's reading of a new mathematical work by a respected colleague),[5] we need a dual game model of the kind presented by Schelling in his hypothetical game of chess with an unconventional payoff matrix. The game of reading—to the extent to which reading can be made into a game—is in an important sense played between the reader and the author. Imagining or inventing the author is actually one of the most complicated and interesting aspects of the game. To support this general claim I shall refer again to that quintessentially playful author, Vladimir Nabokov. It is intriguing that the typically Nabokovian statement I wish to quote is about chess problems (which would normally fall under the category of singular games) and not about the openly competitive, strategic game of chess itself. Nonetheless, Nabokov—like Perec—does not hesitate to speak about competition where few people would look for it. Here is what he has to say about chess problems (a subject on which he was something of an expert) and about the analogy between these and works of fiction: "It should be understood that competition in chess problems is not really between Black and White but between the composer and the hypothetical solver (just as in a first rate work of fiction the real clash is not between the characters but between the author and the world), so that a great part of a problem's value is due to the number of 'tries'—delusive opening moves, false scents, specious lines of play, astutely and lovingly prepared to lead the would-be solver astray" (*Speak Memory*, p. 290).[6]

As Nabokov later made clear, he intended "the world" in this sentence to be understood as the world of readers: "[The author] clashes with readerdom because he is his own ideal reader and those other readers are so often mere lip-moving ghosts and amnesiacs. On the other hand, a good reader is bound to make fierce efforts when wrestling with a difficult author, but those efforts can be most rewarding after the bright dust has settled" (*Strong Opinions*, p. 183).

This is very nicely put. For my own purposes, however, I would modify Nabokov's statement to convey, alongside the notion of conflict or clash, the sense of a possible collaboration between the reader and the author he or she imagines. This collaboration would be justified by the reader's intention to play the game correctly for a reward that may include creating new games (or, in other words, the exciting chance for the reader to

. . .

become an author). In playing the game correctly, the reader has a sense of participating in the creation of a tradition. Thus in the world of (re)reading, correct play is *creative* play (a tradition is being created) in the very precise, unmysterious, unmystical, and purely logical sense that Schelling conveys.

Every reading that reaches the level of play and involves the reader in a competitive/cooperative game with the author will pay attention, among other things, to those "incidental details" noted by Schelling. For the reader, expressive patterns (of linguistic-textual "behavior") and the interrelations of various suggestions, connotations, and symbolisms gain in significance in direct ratio to the overall importance of the play element in a specific act of reading. The case of mathematics is telling in this context since the language of mathematics is (or aims to be) purely denotative, in contrast to poetic language, which tends toward pure connotation.[7] It remains true, though, that suggestive-connotative elements are constantly and consistently involved in the process of mathematical reading and creation. Calling attention to this does not imply that the goal of the mathematician is not pure denotation, although its achievement by economic and beautiful means is of great importance. Connotation may be— and in effect often is—helpful in finding the most elegant solution to a complex problem.

In the game between the reader and the imagined author of a literary work, denotation, to reverse the terms, can be made to serve the goal of connotation; that is, precision (concreteness, "realistic" detail, literalness) can enhance suggestiveness and symbolism. This complex interplay and interdependence of the literal and the symbolic endows the allegorical with an effect of reality while giving an emblematic or allegorical value to the most common concrete figures of reality. More important, however, than the relationship between denotation and connotation is the strategic question of correct play in literary reading. Dealing with it, however briefly, may help us to detach ourselves from the vexed issue of whether there is such a thing as a single correct interpretation of an artistic or literary work and, if not, whether it is possible to avoid interpretive anarchy. This is simply not an issue. Correct play is correct not as measured against an absolute (fixed, eternal) standard but as a function of the specific game being played, its rules, its traditions, its pace, its structures of expectation, the backgrounds and strengths of the players, and the quality of enjoyment that is derived from playing it. Hence a correct move may be spontaneous and almost aleatory or, on the contrary, carefully calculated;

. . .

it may involve forgoing or deferring an interpretive decision or making such a decision and feeling bound by it, even at the price of recognizing the incorrectness (including the dullness) of previous decisions and doing all the retrospective mental work of revision and reassessment; finally, it may include questions about its own correctness (was it a good move? an advantageous move? an intelligent move?). From this last point of view, correct play does not exclude but actually requires the kind of imagination by which the interpreter asserts his or her individual skill and creativity within the rules of the game by playing the game as excitingly as possible. Correctness of play is by no means synonymous with dullness, and the interpreter is not only a follower of generally accepted rules but also a creator of new, subtle, strategic rules which he or she then puts to use in producing insight.

. . .

ELEVEN

Psychological Approaches

Freud and Play

So far I have delayed consideration of the various psychological factors that form an integral part of both playing and reading. Looking at reading as play from an almost purely cerebral standpoint was, among other things, a deliberate attempt to desentimentalize the concept of play, to free it from the web of romantic-affective associations (spontaneity, fancy, emotivity) with which a certain "naive" ideology of play, still widespread in Western culture, tends to surround it. But the psychological components of reading as play cannot and should not be ignored.

One route to understanding reading as play is through examining the relationship between reading and fantasy (to be taken in its broadest sense as a synonym of the Greek *phantasia*) or even fantasizing. I shall first consider the views on fantasy and literature articulated by Sigmund Freud and some of his direct followers. The main reason for giving priority to Freudian psychoanalysis is that, aside from the phenomenology of aesthetic experience, including reading (from Roman Ingarden to Georges Poulet to Wolfgang Iser), psychoanalysis has always shown a keen interest in the broad area of response (the response of the analysand to the analyst in the phenomenon of transference; the response of the analyst to the analysand's transference in the form of countertransference) and, more

· · ·

recently, has dealt with questions of literary response (Norman Holland, for instance) and even of reading as play (Michel Picard).

In his 1907 paper "Creative Writers and Daydreaming" Freud tied the problems of writing, reading, play, and fantasy in an elegant and bold hypothesis:

> You will say that, although I have put the creative writer first in the title of my paper, I have told you far less about him than about phantasies. I am aware of that. . . . As for the other problem—by what means the creative writer achieves the emotional effects in us that are aroused by his creations . . . I should like . . . to point to you the path that leads from our discussion of phantasies to the problems of poetical effects. . . . The daydreamer carefully conceals his phantasies . . . [and] even if he were to communicate them to us he could give us no pleasure by his disclosures. . . . But when a creative writer presents his plays to us or tells what we are inclined to take to be his personal daydreams, we experience great pleasure . . . How the writer accomplishes this is his innermost secret; the essential *ars poetica* lies in the technique of overcoming the feeling of repulsion in us which is undoubtedly connected with the barriers that rise between each single ego and the others. We can guess two methods used by this technique. The writer softens the character of his egoistic daydreams by altering and disguising it, and he bribes us by the purely formal—that is, aesthetic—yield of pleasure which he offers in the presentation of his phantasies. We give the name of an *incentive bonus*, or a fore-pleasure, to a yield of pleasure such as this, which is offered to us so as to make possible the release of still greater pleasure arising from deeper psychical sources. In my opinion, all the aesthetic pleasure which a creative writer affords us has the character of a fore-pleasure of this kind, and our actual enjoyment of an imaginative work proceeds from a liberation of tension in our minds. It may even be that not a little of this effect is due to the writer's enabling us thenceforward to enjoy our own daydreams without self-reproach or shame. (*Standard Edition*, vol. 9, pp. 152–53)

This passage is remarkable from several points of view. First, it is one of the earliest psychoanalytical attempts to explain our attraction to literary fictions. Second, even though Freud remains concerned with the creative artist and not with the reader, the final part of the article suggests that writing and reading could be seen as psychologically symmetrical activities, at least insofar as they enable those who undertake them to indulge their cherished fantasies without the feelings of shame that usually accompany such fantasies in the adult. Freud's article may thus be seen as laying the basis of a psychoanalytical theory of reading. Third, and most

. . .

important, the mediating instance, in both writing and reading, appears to be a special kind of play, namely, *artistic* play, which consists of the elaboration of credible imaginary worlds and brings with it a characteristic formal yield of pleasure and a "liberation of tension in our minds."

Like childhood play, for which it is an adult substitute, artistic play enables one to turn painful or otherwise overpowering experiences into games and thus gain mastery over them. Crucial for understanding subsequent psychoanalytical theories of play, including the artistic play of writing (and its counterpart in reading), is Freud's famous description and analysis of the Fort/Da game in *Beyond the Pleasure Principle*. The child who played the game was observed by Freud at the age of one and a half. A boy greatly attached to his mother, he used to throw objects or toys away from himself, uttering an "o-o-o-o" sound that, according to Freud,

> represented the German word "*fort*" ["gone"]. . . . It was a game and the only use he made of any of his toys was to play "gone" with them. One day . . . the child had a wooden reel with a piece of string tied round it. . . . What he did was to hold the reel by the string and very skillfully throw it over the edge of his curtained cot, so that it disappeared into it, at the same time uttering his expressive "o-o-o-o." He then pulled the reel out of the cot again by the string and hailed its reappearance with a joyful "*da*" ["there"]. This, then, was the complete game—disappearance and return. (*SE*, vol. 18, pp. 14–15)

In Freud's interpretation the game was "related to the child's great cultural achievement—the . . . renunciation of instinctual satisfaction . . . he had made in allowing his mother to go away without protesting." The game was then a compensation for a distressing experience (the separation from the mother, an occurrence over which he had no control) by means of symbolically "staging the disappearance and return of the objects within his reach." In this way, the child moved from a *passive* role in reality to an *active* role on the level of the fictionality of play, obtaining mastery over an unpleasant emotion and the special kind of pleasure that accompanies the sense of mastery; in addition, the game allowed the child "to revenge himself on his mother for going away," that is, to discharge symbolically a negative emotion by deflecting it through play.

The Freudian theory of play can be adapted to account for both creative writing and literary reading if these activities are construed as having essentially the same functions as play (that is, as legitimizing daydreaming, providing loosely structured scripts for fantasying, afford-

. . .

ing symbolic mastery over negative emotions and dealing with them through deflection or displacement). In speaking of the imaginative writer as a "dreamer in broad daylight," Freud had in mind not authors highly esteemed by critics but the "less pretentious authors of novels, romances, and short stories, who . . . have the widest and most eager circle of readers of both sexes." It is in such stories—where the hero, realizing the author's erotic or ambitious daydreams, triumphs over the most incredible perils and obstacles—that Freud identifies most directly what he calls "His Majesty the Ego, the hero alike of every day-dream and of every story."

If every story is an expression of the royal ego, some stories are less transparently and directly so. Not only the writing but also the reading of great literature are activities in which higher ("secondary") processes of consciousness and acts of intellection are substantially involved. Thus Freud's own fictional model becomes more complicated and indirect in the case of the psychological novel, in which, as he points out, the modern writer shows an inclination "to split up his ego, by self-observation, into many part-egos, and, in consequence, to personify the conflicting currents of his mental life." The formula becomes even more "alarmingly complex" when the work itself—as a form of elaborate artistic play—is seen as the fulfillment of a wish. The writer in this case is typically prompted by a strong experience, "which awakens . . . a memory of an earlier experience . . . from which there . . . proceeds a wish which finds its fulfillment in the creative work. . . . Creative writing, like a day-dream, is a continuation of, and a substitute for, what was once the play of childhood" ("Creative Writers and Daydreaming," *Standard Edition*, vol. 9, p. 150). Substitutes for play may of course differ a great deal: some are more immediately recognizable and therefore of greater immediate appeal to a wide audience; others are more subtle and intricate, indicating a higher degree of sublimation.

But Freud regards childhood play itself as distinct from simple fantasying. First, play is aware of its difference from reality; in other words, it is self-consciously fictional—the "opposite of play is not what is serious but what is real," and "the child distinguishes it [play] quite well from reality." Second, and also unlike pure fantasying, play is always related in a certain way to "tangible and visible things of the real world" (toys or objects used as props for playing are real, although they are charged with meanings shaped by fantasy). Two important additional elements are involved in the adult substitute for play in literature: (1) the disguising not only of fantasy through play but also of play itself (this operation, when the intended

. . .

reader is more sophisticated, can become quite elaborate, complex, and fascinating) and (2) the growing importance (again depending on the degree of sophistication of the intended reader) of the formal or aesthetic aspect of the disguising operation, a result of the process of sublimation.

Freud's theory of play remained embryonic, and it was later to be developed in a variety of not always congruent directions by such psycho analysts as Melanie Klein, D. W. Winnicott, and Erik Erikson. Neither did Freud carry his tantalizing insight into literature and art as play beyond brilliant but summary aperçus. The crucial distinction between "pure" fantasy, which directly reflects unconscious processes, and play, which produces a different, more indirect, more mediated kind of fantasy (an example of which would be the text-bound fantasy of reading) is there in his essays, but again its farther-reaching consequences are not yet fully visible.

Even so, Freud's concepts of disguise and formal elaboration contain interesting implications from the perspective of the reading/rereading dichotomy. If we grant that a work of fiction is in some sense a disguise of an author's fantasies, reading appears as an acceptance at face value of the disguises (lofty symbols, heroic roles, incredible adventures) by a reader anxious to indulge vicariously his or her own similar fantasies. Rereading, or at least rereading of the reflective, critical variety, would on the contrary be an attempt to penetrate such disguises, to pierce the veils of secrecy and reveal the hidden. Rereading of this sort would be akin to psychoanalysis itself.

As for the formal elaboration of literary play, psychoanalysis is not really equipped to illuminate it. The study of this aspect is the province of literary criticism and poetics. I shall briefly add here that formal elaboration, insofar as it demands a structural rather than a sequential attention, tends to give even the first reading of a work a certain dimension of rereading. Obviously, the more complex the form of a work, the more it will be unreadable and only rereadable (see chapter 2). I might add here, in the new framework of play, that this latter kind of rereading is keenly interested in the trade secrets of the work, in its craftsmanship within the rules of the game—the game itself being, this time, less of a simple (egotistic) game of make-believe and more of a second-degree game of playing at playing games of make-believe for the purpose of understanding their inner logic and analyzing them. But before getting into such questions we need to consider other psychological components of the play of reading.

. . .

Psychoanalysis of Reader Response

Norman Holland is among the leading exponents of a psychoanalytical theory of reading and literary response. Although he makes a limited use of the concept of play, Holland develops the basic Freudian model of literature as a "transformation" of fantasy (that is, as both a disguise and a formal elaboration of fantasy) in his book *The Dynamics of Literary Response* (1968). Subsequently, in *5 Readers Reading* (1975) and more recent writings, he has revised and refined his original formulations of the theory so as better to account for the irreducible individuality of each reader's response. Literature (or reading literature) is for Holland a transformation of "our primitive wishes and fears into significance and coherence, and this transformation gives us pleasure. . . . Fantasy gives force to conscious meaning, but conscious meaning mollifies and manages our deepest fears and drives" (*Dynamics,* p. 30).

Discussing the reasons why the reader may feel transported by literature, and specifically why he or she may become deeply involved in fictional matters (such as the destinies of purely fictional beings), Holland proposes a reinterpretation, along psychoanalytic lines, of the famous Coleridgean notion of the willing suspension of disbelief. Reading, he argues, presents striking analogies with hypnosis, in the sense that the reader "introjects" the work and accepts it as a "subsystem" within the overall ego, not unlike the subject of hypnosis, who willingly internalizes and executes the instructions given by the hypnotist. The reader, in allowing himself or herself to be hypnotized by the text, or in willingly suspending disbelief in what the text is suggesting, does not abandon other ego functions (including reality testing or the ability to distinguish between reality and fiction).

Holland does not develop further this model of involved reading as hypnotic trance. His working analogy for reading remains the more comprehensive but also more abstract and less graspable notion of a passage from unconscious, or preconscious, primary processes to consciously articulated, higher-level secondary processes. Certain popular texts, he goes on to say, create in the reader a mood that is close to subliminal unconscious reverie; whereas the more complex and demanding texts of literary masterpieces require the reader to engage secondary, conscious processes of elaboration of meaning. The dynamics of response is predictably different in the two cases: "We can simply indicate the two processes, conscious and unconscious, as a line of higher and lower. . . . Being

· · ·

engrossed in an entertainment, we are involved primarily at the deeper levels. . . . Conversely, confronted with 'great' literature, we think and feel more and introject less" (pp. 92–93). In other words, in the case of a masterpiece there is less direct stimulation toward primitive fantasying. To understand Holland's point adequately, one must take into account the factor of form, which he sees—rather simplistically—as analogous to a defensive strategy, one that ultimately shapes the reader's response. As Holland puts it, "Very loosely, then, we can say that form in literary work corresponds to defense; content, to fantasy or impulse. . . . [But] just as in life impulse and defense interact and shape each other" (p. 131). This is not only loose but, as an application of psychoanalytical concepts for different purposes, too mechanical.

In *5 Readers Reading* Holland introduces the notion of the reader's "individual style" and asserts, within the reading process, that each reader develops a unique identity theme involving both the lower and the higher ego functions. The central principle of this reformulation is that "character transforms characteristically. . . . The reader creates a fantasy within his individual style. Then he transforms that fantasy . . . into a synthesis and unity that he finds consciously integrative and satisfying" (p. 125). As for fantasy, it is no longer seen as existing "in" the work (to be simply "introjected" by the reader); the individual fantasy theme now appears in "the creative relation between reader and work" (p. 117), a relation that becomes the focus of a new kind of psychoanalytical criticism called "transactive." Clearly, Holland has moved from an early model of reading that emphasized the mechanical introjective aspect of the relation between the reader and the text to a more complicated, transactive model.

As for the concept of play, Holland uses it in *The Dynamics of Literary Response,* but very crudely. In the chapter "Evaluation," for example, he tries to pinpoint the difference between aesthetic pleasure and "the mere sensuous pleasure of a well-mixed martini," in other words, to answer the fundamental question of literary aesthetics: What is value? What constitutes a "good" literary work? Quoting Erik Erikson's view of play (to play is "to hallucinate ego mastery"), Holland notes that "both play and literature can be understood in this sense as first, letting a disturbing influence happen to us, then, second, mastering that disturbance. . . . Saying a literary work is 'good,' then, . . . is predicting it will pass the test of time; that it 'can please many and please long'; that it is a widely satisfying form of play; or, more formally, that it embodies a fantasy with the power to disturb many readers over a long period of time and, built in,

. . .

163

a defensive maneuver that will enable those readers to master the poem's disturbance" (*Dynamics*, pp. 202–03).

The comparison between involved reading and hypnosis, which Holland does not develop fully, has occasioned insights among other psychologists of the imagination and specifically of reading. Starting from their work I propose to elaborate a full-fledged and reading-adequate distinction between involvement and absorption: involvement is the effect of reading as playing a game of make-believe; absorption is the state in which we reread a text and is conceived as an invitation to play a game with rules.

Involvement and Absorption

Let us look more closely at two mainstream psychological accounts of involvement in reading, the first proposed by Josephine Hilgard in *Personality and Hypnosis* (1970) and the second put forward by Victor Nell in *Lost in a Book: The Psychology of Reading for Pleasure* (1988).

Hilgard, summarizing the results and reflections of a long-term study she conducted at the Laboratory of Hypnosis Research at Stanford University, examines the possibility of establishing a correlation between certain types of imaginative involvement (in reading fiction, in music, in the enjoyment of nature, in religion) and degrees of susceptibility to hypnosis. But beyond her ostensible goal of devising methods for accurately testing hypnotic susceptibility, Hilgard has offered a fine psychological study of imagination in its relationship to personality and involvement. Central to her argument is the distinction between two superficially similar but in fact very different states of mind: involvement and absorption. Being involved implies a definite if not always evident emotional commitment, as a result of which one is transported to another world. An involved reader thus participates in the experience of fictive people through some sort of fantasy and may identify with them or empathize with them or, at the least, be there and watch them (always taking sides, favoring some, opposing others). Absorption, on the other hand, is a state of high concentration of attention; and though it may display some of the appearances of involvement (such as obliviousness to the immediate surroundings), it lacks the sense of personal immersion so characteristic of involvement. Absorption, then, would be more imaginatively detached and more intellectual (the reader of a scientific work could become absorbed but not, in Hilgard's view, involved).

· · ·

The most typical example of noninvolved absorption among the interviewees of the Stanford study was that of Richard, who, we are told,

> gets quite absorbed, but does not meet our picture of involvement. . . . He reads "quite a bit," mostly novels. If he has a good book and has time he becomes so absorbed that he cannot hear himself being called. While he is close to involvement through his concentration of attention, there is a kind of detachment that distinguishes him from the truly involved. He has a deep interest in the plot, likes to predict how it will end, and is a little aloof from what is going on. He does not identify with the characters and never takes part in the action himself. He might feel sympathy for a character, but he is not deeply empathic. Sometimes he theorizes about the book. . . . It comes as no surprise that he was not a responsive hypnotic subject. (p. 41)

Although Hilgard's dichotomy between involvement and absorption can aid the study of reading versus rereading (linear reading of a narrative being more likely to produce involvement, reflective rereading being more likely to lead to absorption), I also believe that the line between the two is much less precise than she suggests. The concept of play, which Hilgard does not use, can help bring this out. Involvement occurs most often in the various forms of symbolic-mimetic play (like pretend play, games of make-believe, impersonation, role-playing, and imitation) whereas absorption is more characteristic of games with rules (such as chess). The reading of fiction, as we shall see, most resembles games of make-believe; but a complex novel, with an ingeniously constructed plot—a rereadable novel—will, like a strategic game with rules, command intense attention and generate absorption, even on a first reading.

Childhood games of make-believe obviously draw on the resources of the imagination to produce the involvement sought by the player, but no play is possible without rules and hence without some potential for absorption. Games with rules also derive at least some of their excitement from the imaginary situations—the parallel, "secondary" worlds—they end up creating or evoking. Hence the possibility of becoming partially involved in them. Chess fans closely following a chess match, for instance, will be absorbed in the analysis of the successive games, move by move, but as they will probably favor one player or one style of play over the other they will also become (vicariously, symbolically, personally) involved. Various spectator sports, which are a combination of games with rules and contests of physical skills, have an uncanny ability to symbolize personal and social conflicts and to lead to involvement for both players

. . .

and watchers. So the line between involvement and absorption may not be as clear-cut as Hilgard believes.[1]

A rundown of the common points Hilgard finds between involved reading and hypnosis will help us to get a better grasp of the concept of involvement: (1) both the reader and the subject of hypnosis are influenced by the power of words; (2) both are highly receptive; (3) both enjoy the experience of the moment; (4) both engage in vivid imagery (to the point that images may take on a hallucinatory quality); (5) both suspend the critical (reality-testing) processes; and (6) both retain the ability to distinguish their experience of the moment from the "normal routines" of "real life."

The power of words in both hypnosis and reading forms the basis for distinguishing between stimulus-incited, directed fantasy (a fantasy triggered by the words of the hypnotist or the words in the book) and an impulse-incited fantasy, a more autistic kind expressive of internal, unconscious conflicts. In regard to reading, the degree to which the reader's fantasy is controlled by the text is widely debated by literary theorists and critics. Some radical skeptics point to the unresolvable indeterminacy of textual meaning and affirm the virtually unlimited liberty of the reader to create that meaning. At the opposite extreme, staunch traditionalists believe that meaning is wholly determinate and that the reader must retrieve precisely the intended meaning. But even the traditionalists distinguish, as does E. D. Hirsch, Jr., between the fixed "meaning" of a text and the variability of its "significance" (the latter being dependent on the specific context, historical or personal, in which the act of reading takes place) and thus admit the existence of a vast area of indeterminacy. What seems important to the present discussion, however, is that the words of the hypnotist ("there's a rabbit on your lap") or the infinitely more complicated, and more interpretable, combinations of words in a fictional text spark and shape a fantasy process under conditions in which the involved subject (reader), to repeat Hilgard's points, is receptive, enjoys the experience (enjoyment is crucial), images vividly, and suspends critical processes without losing the distinction between the engrossing imaginary situation and everyday reality.

Of course the verbal directions given by a literary text for constructing mental pictures and situations are subject to various legitimate interpretations and imaginings. Because of the necessarily sketchy nature of even the most detailed and elaborate descriptions in a novel, the reader enjoys the liberty to match his or her own images to the schemata offered by the text.

. . .

For example, we often match the faces of people we know, or alterations and combinations of features from such faces, to the names of characters in a novel; and in the process of reading, in light of more specific information obtained later (about their hair and eye color, age, temperament, deportment, way of dressing) we change these images and may even replace them with completely new ones. In a film narrative, where this kind of indeterminacy does not exist (there are others, however), viewers of a movie based on a novel they have previously read may be bothered by the discrepancy between their mental images of the characters and the faces of the actors who enact their roles.

In reading there are also various types and degrees of misinterpretation. Ignorance may be responsible for some, as in the case of an unknown word or phrase whose improperly guessed meaning may give rise to an inappropriate or incongruous image. There are mistakes, as when a key word is simply misread for another, that cause the wrong image to appear on the mental screen. There are, unavoidably, moments of inattention or weakened attention to the text, as when misreadings result from obsessive preoccupations. And the very fact of involvement may be responsible for some misreadings: a reader who is deeply involved may be led to neglect certain parts of the text or certain nuances (which seem to sidetrack the attention), as when one gets carried away by the action of a novel and skips an apparently less significant passage, say a description, which may however contain essential information. Such accidents are always possible in reading, particularly in involved reading. Many are sooner or later corrected (a degree of redundancy in classical or realistic literary texts may contribute to this), but many are bound to remain uncorrected, and even these count for little as long as they do not break the spell of reading. When it comes to rereading, such accidents are naturally less tolerable and the absorbed (re)reader is better at avoiding them, or spotting them and correcting them, even at the price of interrupting the flow of reading to consult, for instance, dictionaries or encyclopedias.

The absorbed reader, I would say, does not mind interruption, backtracking, ascertaining the precise meaning of a word or phrase, or constructing and reconstructing detailed mental images with the lucid and dedicated patience of someone fitting together a jigsaw puzzle. Also, the problem of validity in interpretation poses itself differently in the case of rereading, with a new stress on intersubjective acceptability. I have noted that the domain of rereading is the domain of games with rules and, consequently, of a certain ludic competitiveness, which is largely if not

· · ·

totally absent in involved subjective reading. Rereading, then, is more interested in correct play even in the case of a text that is reread not for purposes of critical communication or publication but for strictly personal reasons. In other words, rereading and the characteristic absorption that accompanies it strive for an interpretation of the text in terms of a complete hermeneutic system in which the significance of each part is seen in the light of the whole and that of the whole in the light of each part.

The fundamental openness or ambiguity of any literary text (particularly when it is revealed in an act of rereading) makes it possible for critics to propose competing global interpretations of the same text. This is actually the goal of all interpretive criticism: to offer *new* interpretations of the same work. In this regard, and excluding from consideration all the global interpretations that are demonstrably false (because they ignore or contradict textual clues, because they use extratextual, arbitrary inferences, because, in short, they do not observe the rules of the game), one must admit that the number of competing but valid global interpretations, or of different but valid critical rereadings of the same text, is theoretically infinite. This obviously does not mean that all criticism is subjective, capricious, and based on irrational choices. In fact, speaking of an infinite number of competing interpretations, I should perhaps stress the notion of *ludic competition.*

It is this competition, based on commonly recognized rules, that founds the critical-institutional game of (re)reading. A more openly ludic equivalent is the history and theory of chess, including the analysis and discussion of famous actual games. But of course the games of criticism and interpretation are infinitely more complex, flexible, and diverse, in part because they allow for frequent innovative changes in the rules; and in part because the richer imaginary situations such games propose reflect social, ideological, ethical, and psychological concerns that are less relevant to a purely strategic game like chess than to criticism (although it would be wrong to ignore the physical and psychological elements that are so subtly involved in the playing of a real championship chess match, as well as the social, ideological, and ethical concerns that may accompany the watching of such a match).

Victor Nell's *Lost in a Book* is one of the best psychological studies of "reading for pleasure," or what the author alternatively calls "ludic reading." His concept of ludic reading differs from mine in that it excludes more difficult or rereadable texts—virtually all the acknowledged classics of ancient or modern literature. Refreshingly, Nell defines ludic reading in

. . .

opposition to the conventional view of *literary* reading, which reflects what he calls "the elitist fallacy" and leads to an arrogant dismissal of popular literature as trash, subliterature, or kitsch. On the basis of numerous interviews and other experimental and statistical data, he draws a highly interesting psychological profile of the ludic reader (defined as one who reads for pleasure at least one book a week, but usually several), a profile that seriously calls into question the clichés of the critics of mass culture (namely, that mass culture destroys the intelligence and the sensitivity of its consumers, that it is a sort of deadly ideological drug, and so on).

Actually, Nell's ludic reader rates highly on reading-comprehension speed tests, is very articulate, and displays great sensitivity to the "witchery of a story," to the "trance potential" of narrative (whether fictional or not). One can agree with all these points without endorsing, as Nell appears to do, what I would call his antielitist fallacy. One form this fallacy takes is the equation of the pleasure of reading and effortlessness, an equation that our high culture supposedly would refuse to acknowledge. According to Nell, the triumph in the West of the Protestant work ethic, with its strictures against idleness, leisure, sloth, unreal pleasures, and daydreaming, has resulted in our unquestioning acceptance of the pessimistic dogma that "good reading demands an effort of will—that Saul Bellow is therefore 'better' than Ian Fleming" and that "true pleasure is consequent on suffering" (p. 46). High culture, in this view, enshrines an essentially perverse cult of difficulty, complexity, and displeasure and is in total opposition to our naturally hedonistic impulses. In other words, our high culture—the culture that informs our entire system of education—is based on a "merciless critical asceticism" (p. 27) and typically punishes the ludic reader with a bad conscience for reading "trash."

Nell proposes his own antielitist version of the desert island game, in which he imagines a highbrow reader marooned "on a desert island with a vast store of fiction, both Harlequin romances and classics, all carefully stripped of their original covers and served up anonymously in brown paper wrappers" (pp. 45–46). Under such circumstances, would not "the highbrow reader turn for pleasure, relaxation, and reading trance to exactly the same books as the lowbrow on the adjacent island?" My own answer would be considerably less clear-cut than the one Nell suggests: depending on the amount of time spent on the island, and also on the sense of personal tragedy coming from the experience of isolation and oppressive solitude, the lowbrow reader might well end up dis-

· · ·

covering and cherishing the classics, and prefer rereading them reflectively to reading the ultimately monotonous Harlequin books. On the other hand, highbrow readers need not despise the romances, although they will end up rereading the classics, which may have better answers for their tormenting existential questions. My own position looks for a middle ground between Nell's virtual rejection of high culture as a source of pleasure and the arrogant and simplistic condemnation of mass culture by cultural critics on both the right and the left of the political spectrum.

This brings me to my philosophical disagreement with Nell on the question of effort and effortlessness in reading. I do not think that only effortlessness is pleasurable and that reading the classics is a form of asceticism or, worse, cultural masochism. I regard ludic reading (in my own more comprehensive sense of the adjective) as a choice among a variety of reading protocols offering a variety of potential rewards: from intellectual stimulation and "the mechanics of inspiration" (as in Emerson's reading a page from Plato before setting out to write) to relaxation (as in reading a mystery or a spy story after one has done one's share of work). Nell's most intriguing views about effortlessness occur in his discussion of absorption and entrancement in relation to attention.

On the basis of recent psychological research on attention, Nell proposes that the characteristic trance induced by ludic reading is made possible mainly by effortless attention or concentration. It is this kind of free attention (which, like fantasy, "is not subject to feedback control from the real world," p. 75) that becomes, when summoned by arousal, intensely focused without any perceptible effort. According to this theory, effort, on the contrary, would diminish the attention and involvement of the reader, or at least disrupt its continuity, without which there can be no "reading trance." To illustrate the apparent paradox, Nell compares the experience of reading James Joyce and Wilbur Smith:

> This full commitment of conscious attention gives rise to the ludic reader's absorption. . . . The simpler passages fill cognitive capacity more completely than the difficult ones. Indeed, the richness of the structure the ludic reader creates in his head may be inversely proportional to the literary power and originality of the reading matter. . . . The processing demands made by James Joyce may require frequent pauses and regressions, whereas the even pace of Wilbur Smith, and the well-practiced ease with which the reader can image his stereotyped characters and settings, may impose a heavier continuous load on attention. (p. 77)

. . .

What seems to differ here, beyond the quantity (load) is the quality of attention demanded by Joyce and Smith: the continuity of attention in the case of reading Smith is predicated on the banality and high predictability of the text ("stereotyped characters and settings"). Reading Joyce requires a completely different quality of attention, which is impossible to sustain continuously on a first reading or even on rereading. But does this mean that one can never be transported to the Joycean fictional universe? Or that, however rare and difficult to achieve, there may be no such thing as a Joycean trance, that sudden flash of insight which Joyce himself called epiphany? But Joyce—the Joyce of *Ulysses* or *Finnegans Wake*—is an extreme example.

Here again I would like to suggest a middle ground by observing that various kinds of games of reading and rereading require various levels of attention (and effort), and that deep involvement need not be totally effortless. For example, the involved readers in Hilgard's study, all Stanford University undergraduates, achieved their states of trance by reading books that, in Nell's judgment, would have been much too difficult for ludic reading: Dostoevsky's *The Brothers Karamazov*, T. S. Eliot's *Murder in the Cathedral*, Emile Zola's *L'Assomoir*, and William Golding's *Lord of the Flies*, as well as works by Conrad, Faulkner, and Nabokov. In addition, the Stanford readers read rather slowly by Nell's standards and did not seem to be averse to detailed imaging—that is, constructing mental images for the situations described in the text, a process that, by contrast with the more abstract propositional comprehension, is not only taxing but also reduces the speed of reading. And reading speed is essential to Nell's ludic reading: "fast readers enjoy books more than slow readers" (p. 92); "ludic readers are proud of the rapidity of their reading" (p. 93). This rapidity seems to be maintained even in the case of ludic readers rereading favorite books.

Nell's paradigm of involvement implies that "intensely focused attention" or "totally committed attention" is, in its subjective effortlessness, comparable not only to hypnotic trance but also to "the drug user's altered state of consciousness" (pp. 214–15). I would expand his list to include the states of inspiration that artists, creative or re-creative (like musicians and actors), occasionally experience, and the effortless concentration achieved after long periods of meditative practice in religious communities.

Aside from the similarities, we should also focus on the distinguishing features of the kinds of involuntary attention that characterize involve-

. . .

ment and absorption. On the lowest level is the changed consciousness produced by psychotropic drugs: subjective effortlessness here is attained in an objectively effortless manner. Other states of momentary total concentration, more spontaneous and mysterious at the same time, may be achieved by serendipity. An example of an extraordinarily vivid image or impression in whose unexplainable spell one becomes blissfully caught is the sense of overpowering intoxication produced in childhood in Proust's narrator, Marcel, by the sight of the steeples of Martinville.[2] Other forms of effortless attention and entrancement may be the result of personal interaction, as in the case of the hypnotic subject's acceptance of the instructions of the hypnotist. But still others may be the result of long periods of intense preparation or practice (artistic, meditative).

Reading, even in the sense of Nell's ludic reading, is always based on significant preparatory effort (unlike drugs) and is always objectively if invisibly effortful (unlike hypnosis), even at its subjectively most effortless and involved. In the case of literary rereading, or reading by inveterate rereaders, the effort to conquer difficulty may become more pronounced at times (it still remains subordinate to the principle of "work for play"); but when the mind attains a state of full absorption it partakes in a reading that is equivalent in grace and creative effortlessness to artistic inspiration. One can legitimately speak, then, of inspired readers and even more so of inspired rereaders.

A Theory of Reading as Play

Starting, like Norman Holland, from psychoanalysis, Michel Picard proposes in *La Lecture comme jeu* a comprehensive theory of literary reading which stresses the notion of play throughout the reading process. Picard has the merit of having reflected on all the major approaches to the phenomenon of play in both children and adults, including the classic cultural anthropological studies of Huizinga, Benveniste, and Caillois, the crucial nonpsychoanalytic studies of Jean Piaget (*La Formation du symbole chez l'enfant*) and Jean Chateau (*L'Enfant et le jeu*), and the Freudian and post-Freudian psychoanalytic contributions dealing specifically with play, such as D. W. Winnicott's *Playing and Reality* (1971) and Philippe Gutton's *Le Jeu chez l'enfant: Essai psychanalytique* (1973). Picard is also conversant with the insights into the reading process obtained from such diverse methodological perspectives as the reception theory of the Konstanz school (Wolfgang Iser, Hans Robert Jauss), structuralist poetics and

. . .

literary semiotics (Gérard Genette, Yuri Lotman), the sociology of literature as practiced by the Bordeaux school (R. Escarpit), the Marxist-
oriented sociology of reading of Jacques Leenhardt, the history of reading
(Roger Chartier), and the psychoanalysis of literary response (Norman
Holland).

Perhaps the best way to get a grasp of Picard's own position on literary
reading is to look at his reaction to the work of his most direct precursor,
Norman Holland. While recognizing the pioneering quality of Holland's
psychoanalytic account of literary response and following Holland's
model in several key respects, Picard criticizes the overall views Holland
advances as "primitive" and dangerously "subjectivist." Thus, in *The
Dynamics of Literary Response* Holland posits, according to Picard, a
much too simple and unsophisticated equation between reading and the
"primitive mechanism of introjection," a criticism with which I concur
(*La Lecture comme jeu,* p. 139). This model, even as subsequently revised
in *5 Readers Reading* (with its new insistence that the reader's responses
are purely individual "variations on an identity theme"), renders any
"scientific" approach to reading impossible, insofar as there can be no
science of that which is purely individual. Here Picard explicitly endorses
the severe Marxian-sociological critique of Holland—coming close to a
rejection out of hand—formulated by Jacques Leenhardt and Pierre Jozsa
in *Lire la lecture* (a critique that, in my view, simply replaces one kind of
reductionism with another). Picard's own approach, however, remains
predominantly psychoanalytic: his isolated attempts to use Marxian instruments of analysis (in dealing, for instance, with Flaubert) are elementary and quite banal.

The two main goals that *La Lecture comme jeu* sets itself and achieves
with rather mixed results are, first, to offer a ludic (as opposed to a merely
"communicative") theory of reading and, second, to offer practical examples of ludic-psychoanalytic readings, in the form of a series of critical
essays, called "interludes," devoted to individual works of fiction by
Colette (*La Maison de Claudine*), Alexandre Dumas (*Les Trois Mousque-
taires*), Roger Vailland (*La Fête*), Jules Verne (*L'Ile mystérieuse*), Stendhal
(*Le Rouge et le noir*), and Flaubert (*Madame Bovary*). This list includes
both acknowledged literary classics and such old favorites of literature for
young adults as Dumas's *Three Musketeers* and Jules Verne's *Mysterious
Island*. The main frame of reference of Picard's book is an ultimately
eclectic concept of play, of which he offers the following "functional" and
"formal" definition:

. . .

Insofar as its functions are concerned, play ["le jeu"], which is directly re-lated to *symbolization,* would be both *defensive* and *constructive;* providing a peculiar form of *mastery* . . . it would fulfill a capital *integrative* role. . . . Insofar as its forms are concerned, it would involve an *activity, absorbing* and *uncertain,* having ties both to *fantasying* ["la fantasmatique"] and to the *real,* an activity which would be experienced as *fictive* but which would also be bound by *rules.* Its range would extend . . . from *playing* (with the exclusion of *fooling*) to *games* (with the exclusion of *gambling*). (p. 30; italicized words are used in English in the original French text)

Central to Picard's argument throughout the book is the distinction and indeed the tension between *playing* and *games.* His theory of reading as play actually follows a wavering course between these two poles, always in search of an elusive middle ground, but attracted more to playing, a topic more congenial to psychoanalytic elaboration. Playing refers to those ludic activities that are primarily symbolic, fictional, and freely imaginative, involving "illusion" and abundant "fantasying." By contrast, the notion of games would cover those ludic activities based on rules, conventions, codes, contracts, pacts, or compacts. Here is how Picard sees the *playing/games* relation in the process of reading:

> *Game* disciplines *playing* . . . and the association of the two constitutes one of the fundamental characteristics of reading. . . . But it is only very rarely that either *playing* does not gain the upper hand or, conversely, *game.* . . . Hui-zinga warns that "as soon as the rules are broken, the universe of play col-lapses": if *playing* gains the upper hand, the reading protocol remains child-ish, partial, fragile, risking to be undone at any moment and to slide toward fantasying. If, on the other hand, *game* comes out on top the reading proto-col remains equally partial, but in a different manner: this time the reading is executed at the heights of irony, of formalist taking-apart, and of rationaliz-ing cerebrality—and the danger is for the whole process to be of reduced psychic efficacy and to veer into work, to slide toward reality. (p. 168)

This polarity of reading protocols (one infantile and irrational, the other adult and cerebral) has its source in a distinction used by most theorists of play irrespective of the doctrines, creeds, or ideologies to which they may subscribe, as we shall see momentarily. The principal merit of Picard is to have shown that this distinction, when applied to reading, produces highly interesting results. But since his own com-mitment to psychoanalysis (particularly Winnicott's view of play as the source of all creativity) is stronger than his commitment to the study of games on their own terms, including the more reflective protocols of adult

. . .

reading, Picard's most penetrating observations bear largely on the "infantile" pole of reading and fantasy, dream images, symbolization, narcissism, illusion, and the book as toy. Moreover, even the little that he has to say about games is also fundamentally psychoanalytical and as such hardly conducive to understanding the internal logic of games with rules as it applies to reading, and more precisely to rereading. Thus, on the subject of absorption Picard keeps bringing up the notion of the "anal character," which may make sense in the framework of a psychoanalytical theory of reading but tells us little about the nature of absorption in (re)reading (as opposed, for instance, to the more directly emotive involvement) or about the preconditions and consequences of absorption (a consideration of which might have made him aware of the problem of rereading, which he hardly addresses). Sometimes his remarks seem farfetched, as when he compares the gaze of the reader to the "famous string" in Freud's description of the Fort/Da game (p. 154), or suggest rather cockeyed and even psychoanalytically unjustified analogies: "The concentration of the reader," Picard writes, "which gives his face an expression so serious, so austere, so absent and at the same time passionate, resembles quite closely that of a child sitting on the pot" (p. 63). In the chapter on "Literary Games and Ludic Dialectics," Picard goes on insisting on the "anal overdetermination" essential to any intellectual game, including reading (p. 211). Such reductions are typical of the psychoanalytic attitude and are perhaps justified in terms of its own goals (theoretical or practical), but they are beside the point when our concern is to grasp the specificity of the games of literary reading. As for the more elaborate games of rereading, Picard does not take them into account beyond one or two almost ritual references to the "compulsion to repeat." Picard's own literary analyses are predictably more interesting when he discusses works by Alexandre Dumas or Jules Verne, that is, classics of adolescent daydream fiction, than when he focuses on a novel like Flaubert's *Madame Bovary*. In regard to the latter, he himself feels a need to resort to instruments other than those offered by psychoanalysis, but the half-baked Marxist notions he manages to bring in about class differences in bourgeois society do not produce enlightening results.

Piaget: Between Symbolic Play and Games with Rules

Outside the area of reading, the distinction between playing and games with rules is neither new nor in any way tied to psychoanalysis. Roger

. . .

Caillois, for instance, from his broad cultural anthropological perspective, articulates a perfectly analogous dichotomy between the joyful, tumultuous, turbulent, improvisational, potentially chaotic world of *paidia* (the Greek word for child's play, by which he designates a whole category of spontaneous games of fantasy and vertigo) and the intellectual, regulated, disciplined world of *ludus* (the Latin word for game), in which calculation, contrivance, and ingenuity are among the main qualities of a good player. *Paidia,* which may lead to loss of self-control and to various forms of intoxication, fatigue, or even panic if its exuberance is not checked, is "disciplined" and indeed "domesticated" by *ludus,* the game with rules. *Paidia* is thus turned into a source of "cultural creativity" (*Man, Play and Games,* p. 33).

The distinction between playing and games is also commonly made by child psychologists. It occupies a prominent place, for example, in the work of Jean Piaget, who elaborates it in great detail and with numerous carefully analyzed observations in his classic study of the formation of the symbolic function in children, first published in 1945 and translated into English as *Play, Dreams, and Imitation in Childhood.* There are, according to him, three major categories of play corresponding roughly to the three developmental stages (ages 0–4, 4–7, 7–11) through which the child progresses from total dependence to fully adapted activity (work). The first form of playful activity is what Piaget calls "practice play," a sensorimotor phase of ludic experimentation that appears in the first months of life and can extend itself throughout childhood (as rough-and-tumble fights, jumping, climbing, and so on) but is usually completely replaced during the third period (7–11) by an important class of games with rules: namely, races, ball games, and other competitive sports.

The crucial distinction involved in the Piagetian concept of play remains, however, the one between what he calls "symbolic play" and "games with rules." In symbolic play, which is characteristic of the 4–7 age group, symbols (objects, mental images, imaginary constructions, fictions) are used as tools for egocentric assimilation. Symbolic play is thus akin to dreaming or other types of fantasy, in which the forms of the external world are used merely for projecting internal impressions (wishes, conflicts) without any attempt at accommodation or adaptation to reality on the part of the subject. Games with rules, which may build on earlier symbolic games (by organizing their symbols in a more coherent fashion, by making them more closely imitative of reality, by giving them a competitive edge), are characteristic of the third period, that of the child's

. . .

socialization. These latter games, in their more evolved forms, continue to be played by the adult. Piaget writes, "In the adult stage, although examples of practice games . . . and symbolic games (e.g. telling oneself a story) are rare, games with rules remain, and even develop throughout life (sports, cards, chess, etc.). The explanation of this late appearance and protracted continuation of games with rules is very simple: they are the ludic activity of the socialized being" (p. 142). But games with rules do not abandon purely subjective assimilation to the ego (which remains "the principle of all play"), they only make it socially acceptable or legitimate. As Piaget notes, the satisfactions of playing (including now the chance of individual victory over opponents) are "made 'legitimate' by the rules of the game, through which competition is controlled by a collective discipline, with a code of honor and fair play. This third and last type of play is therefore not inconsistent with the idea of assimilation of reality to the ego, while at the same time it reconciles this ludic assimilation with the demands of social reciprocity" (p. 168). This reconciliation of egotism with social demands could easily be extended to reading for pleasure (at least the kind of reading that unlike reading pornographic literature, for example, is a socially approved, even recommended activity).

The Piagetian explanation of symbolic make-believe in children and of dream symbolism in general differs from Freud's but, interestingly, the functional description he gives of these phenomena corresponds quite closely to the observations made by the founder of psychoanalysis. Thus, for Piaget ludic symbolism, both conscious and unconscious, is rooted in the ego, in the total egocentrism of the young child (a notion that brings to mind Freud's concept of narcissism). What this symbolism accomplishes, as Piaget puts it, is the pleasurable "assimilation of reality to the ego and intensification of this same pleasure through fictitious control of the whole natural and social world" (p. 146). Piaget's functions of play also are compatible with Freud's less elaborate and more incidental insights. Symbolic play, Piaget demonstrates, offers the pleasure of (1) "compensation" or fulfillment of wishes ("correcting reality" by means of make-believe); (2) catharsis (as illustrated by one of his daughters, age 4 years and 2 months, "who did not dare to go alone to a neighboring barn where some children were making a theatre. She then organized with her dolls a big theatre game, both as compensation and to 'purge' her fear," pp. 132–33); (3) assimilation or integration of a difficult, unpleasant situation by reliving it in a symbolic transposition (as illustrated in the following story about his daughter Jacqueline, age 4 years and 6 months: "I knocked

. . .

against J.'s hands with a rake and made her cry. I said how sorry I was, and blamed my clumsiness. At first she didn't believe me. . . . Then she suddenly said, half-appeased: 'You are Jacqueline and I am daddy. There! (she hit my fingers). Now say: 'You've hurt me. (I said it.) I'm sorry, darling. I didn't do it on purpose. You know how clumsy I am,' etc. In short, she merely reversed the parts and repeated my exact words," p. 133); (4) anticipatory symbolic combinations (a way of accepting advice or orders by symbolically anticipating what would happen should they not be followed).

The major philosophical difference between Piaget and Freud consists of Piaget's preference for a stricter dynamic-evolutionary approach to the human mind, as opposed to Freud's firm belief, in spite of his well-known developmentalism, that deep mental structures are permanent and that change affects only their appearance ("We can never give anything up; we only exchange one thing for another"). For Piaget, developmental phases are essentially transitory, in the sense that most early developmental acquisitions are subject to a law of involution once their functions are performed on a higher (operational, fully socialized) level by the acquisitions of a later phase. Thus, the symbolic play of children is gradually replaced by socialized games with rules, with few and insignificant survivals. From the point of view of Freud and the psychoanalysts, nothing could be farther from the deep, hidden truth. The mind never gives anything up; it will resort to all sorts of stratagems, disguises, substitutions, and charades in order not to relinquish the "yield of pleasure" it experienced in early childhood.

The difficulty of applying to reading a Piagetian model of symbolic play as distinct from regulated play (both kinds being equally relevant, and in fact indispensable, to a psychological theory of reading as play) is apparent: in Piaget's developmental model, symbolic play is gradually replaced by the higher, more operational games with rules. But the symbolic (imaginal, imaginative, make-believe) dimension of literary reading and rereading is too obvious to ignore. In fact, it is precisely this dimension that distinguishes reading from the two varieties of adult games with rules of which Piaget speaks: games offering, beyond the pleasurable chance of winning, sensorimotor satisfaction (sports) or intellectual satisfaction (board games). (The pleasures of watching games and the vicarious satisfactions such watching may produce do not attract his attention.) Involved literary reading, even if considered as a game with rules, would contain too much make-believe, too many puerile, immature,

. . .

symbolic-imaginative-imitative elements to fit the Piagetian definition of adulthood.

This may explain why many contemporary critics who are interested in the psychology of literary response, and specifically in the playful (fictive) element of literary response, show a clear preference for a psychoanalytic model in which the child in us, the symbolic player, continues to exist within our adult personality and to be active under different, often completely unexpected, (dis)guises. This model may be useful for understanding certain aspects or types of reading, but it tells us little if anything about our absorption in games with rules and about the ludic (rule-governed) pole of reading and rereading, which may exclude involvement but often coexists with it and sometimes even leads to it. Piaget helps us perceive the developmental differences between symbolic play and games with rules, but his analysis does not extend to varieties of literary playing or gaming, and he himself has little to say about the phenomenon of reading, literary or not. To grasp the complex relationship between play and literature, including literary (re)reading, we must look at both play and literature as structures within a communicational system and characterize the special place they occupy within it, a place, as we shall see, defined by the notion of fictionality.

. . .

. . . .

TWELVE

Fictionality

Fictionality and Reality

Philosophically, the difference between literary works and other kinds of texts has often been expressed in terms of a broad notion of poetry or "fictionality" as opposed to serious or pragmatic reference. The tradition of identifying poetry with fiction goes back to Plato, who regarded (and condemned) the poet as a creator and perpetrator of mere fictions or lies. But poetic fictions qua fictions (including fables, myths, heroic or comic stories, inventions, fantasies, and other kinds of beautiful lies) have also been traditionally defended, on a great variety of grounds, by both philosophers and poets. Aristotle, for instance, considered that poetic fictions, unlike historical accounts, which are restricted only to what has actually happened, express what *may* happen, that is, what is probable or possible. Poetry thus is more "universal" and "philosophical" than history (*Poetics* 9.3).

Reexamining the distinction between history and poetry at the time of the Renaissance in light of renewed moralistic (Platonic, Augustinian, and, closer to home, Puritan) accusations that poets are liars, Sir Philip Sidney completely turned the tables on the enemies of poetry and argued that it is in fact the historians who are very likely to be liars, whereas poets simply cannot lie since they do not affirm anything:

. . .

Now, for the poet, he nothing affirmeth, and therefore never lieth. For, as I take it, to lie is to affirm that to be true which is false; so as the other artists, and especially the historian, affirming many things, can, in the cloudy knowledge of mankind, hardly escape from many lies. But the poet (as I said before) never affirmeth. . . . And therefore, though he recount things not true, yet because he telleth them not for true, he lieth not. . . . What child is there that, coming to a play, and seeing *Thebes* written in great letters upon an old door, doth believe that it is Thebes? If a man can arrive to that child's age to know that the poets' persons and doings are but pictures of what should be, and not stories of what have been, they will never give the lie to things not affirmatively but allegorically and figuratively written. . . . So in poesy, looking but for fiction, they shall use the narration but as imaginative ground-plot of a profitable invention. (*A Defence of Poetry,* p. 53)

Modern philosophers in the linguistic-analytic tradition have dealt with fictionality as a case of "empty" reference (that is, reference to things that do not exist outside language). This notion, understood very broadly, is not all that far from Sidney's view of poetry as consisting of fictional statements that do not make any claims to truth and therefore cannot be judged as either true or false. Considered, however, from a modern logical-ontological point of view (including possible-world semantics, counterfactuals, and theories of worldmaking), the status of fictional entities leads to new complexities and paradoxes.

Let us think for a moment of the intriguing logical questions raised by fictional names, a subclass of the so-called empty singular terms—the most obvious and fascinating examples of which are the names of literary characters: Don Quixote, David Copperfield, Anna Karenina, Emma Bovary. Some of these questions, and particularly those related to singular existential statements (of the type: Don Quixote exists), or singular negative existential statements (of the type: Don Quixote does not exist) are insightfully examined by Gareth Evans in *The Varieties of Reference* (1982). Statements of this kind can be (fictionally) true within a framework of games of make-believe if we are willing to *pretend* that things are as they seem to be or as they are presented to us or, more precisely, "as the information we share presents them as being" (p. 359).[1] Evans notes that games of make-believe in general (including such sophisticated forms as theatrical performances, films, or novels) "exploit the fundamental characteristic of the informational system, that informational states are belief-independent" and adds that "a story-teller pretends to tell (inform) us

· · ·

about things. . . . We, hearing him, are prone to carry on the pretence . . . : we pretend to have been told of these things (to know them by testimony)" (p. 359). In other words, we are inclined to take narrated events (whether fictional or nonfictional) as if they were testified to by the narrator. (If the author is different from the narrator we have two distinct testimonies.) And we tend to judge such narrated events on the basis of the "reliability" of the narrator-witness as established in the process of storytelling itself (in terms of plausibility and internal consistency), since any form of outside verification would not only be impossible but, given the tacit rules of the narrative-fictional game, beside the point.

Semantically, then, a literary text is made up of sentences that are not intended to refer to the real (empirical) world, even when they seem to refer to it, and thus are neither true nor false. Fictionality is often designated semantically in the fictional text itself, in the form of specified or implied generic indications, such as "novel," "novella," "comedy," or "tragedy." And there are numerous other signals of fictionality—some quite unambiguous (like the inaugural formula "Once upon a time"), others more sophisticated, ambiguous, indirect, and playfully tricky (such as forms of fictional self-reflexivity, by which fictions comment on their own fictional nature, in modernist or postmodernist literature; or even denials of fictionality that are meant to function precisely as signals of fictionality). Pragmatically, a literary text is properly understood when its fictional character is recognized as such. When fiction is taken for reality, the response is usually perceived as comically inadequate, as in the famous episode in which Don Quixote interferes in Master Pedro's puppet show to protect the two fugitives, Don Gaiferos and Señora Melisendra, from their Moorish pursuers. "Don Quixote thought that it would be a good thing for him to aid the fugitives. . . . 'Halt, lowborn rabble; cease your pursuit and persecution, or otherwise ye shall do battle with me!' With these words he drew his sword, and in one bound was beside the stage; and then with accelerated and unheard-of fury he began slashing at the Moorish puppets" (p. 683).

The opposite situation, in which a reality is framed fictionally or a referential text—a historical evocation, a geographical description, a piece of testimony, a news item, a letter—is read as if it were fiction appears to be less inadequate, unless it has immediately undesirable practical consequences. An example would be a fictional or "as-if" reading of a letter as a result of which one would fail to take practical measures

. . .

regarding a threat, a warning, or a request for help contained therein. But a letter written, say, in the eighteenth or nineteenth century—a letter whose writer and addressee have long been dead—may well be read fictionally or for its story content as opposed to its value as a historical document, a value determined by using the instruments and methods of critical historicism.

As a rule, if a referential (nonfictional) text has a strong narrative quality, and if it does not involve the reader personally, a fictional reading and a nonfictional one become almost indistinguishable. It is the sheer narrative quality, as exploited by the gifted storyteller (who makes the tale suspenseful and engrossing) that gives urgency to the reading of a text and increases its claims to our interest, attention, and emotional involvement. In other words, a nonfictional narrative (a news story or a biography, for instance) may become as legitimate a starting point for a game of make-believe or imaginary reenactment as an openly fictional one. As a matter of fact, the fictional and the nonfictional often coincide in the "as-if" of the act of imaginative understanding, which may require in various degrees and combinations the fictionalization of the nonfictional and the (mental) realization, or treatment as a reality, of the fictional.

The Fictionality of Play

Many contemporary theorists (formalists, structuralists, textualists) tend to ignore the play element in both the production and the reception of fiction, including the case I have just discussed of the blurring of the distinction between fiction and nonfiction in the reading of gripping narratives. The reason for this theoretical blindness to the playful dimension of fictional texts (as well as the potentially playful or make-believe dimension of any narrative text) may have something to do with the formalist-structuralist preference for a purely communicational model of the literary process, a model that cannot properly account for the metacommunicative signals which frame playful behavior or modes of expression.

There should be little surprise, then, that a connection between the metacommunicative and the fictional has been suggested and elaborated mainly outside the area of literary studies. A first, truly seminal contribution to defining the status of play as fiction is Gregory Bateson's 1955 essay "A Theory of Play and Fantasy," reprinted in *Steps to an Ecology of*

. . .

Mind (1972). Bateson arrived at his view of play as an activity framed by metacommunicative messages (of the type "this is play") as a result of observations he made in the Fleischhacker Zoo in San Francisco:

> What I encountered at the zoo was a phenomenon well known to every-body: I saw two young monkeys *playing*, *i.e.*, engaged in an interactive sequence of which the unit actions or signals were similar to but not the same as those of combat. It was evident, even to the human observer, that to the participant monkeys this was 'not combat.' Now, this phenomenon, play, could only occur if the participant organisms were capable of some degree of metacommunication, *i.e.*, of exchanging signals which would carry the message, "This is play." (p. 179)

Human verbal communication, which is of course infinitely more com-plex, operates at various levels of abstraction and could be schematically represented as ranging between a metalinguistic pole, in which the subject of discourse is language itself (Bateson's example: "The verbal sound 'cat' stands for any member of such and such a class of objects") and a metacommunicative pole, in which the subject of discourse is the given communicative situation, "the relationship between the speakers," and the way the message should be taken (for example: "My telling you where to find the cat was friendly," or "This is play"). Midway between the metalinguistic and the metacommunicative is "the seemingly simple de-notative level" ("The cat is on the mat") (p. 178). The roots of denotative, as well as of metalinguistic and metacommunicative communication, go back to a prehuman and preverbal evolutionary stage. Play (and other structurally related types of behavior, such as histrionics or deceit or threats) seems to have constituted a crucial step in the biological evolution of communication. Animal play provides us with a first clear-cut elemen-tary model of fictionality. In a famous passage, Bateson writes about playfighting dogs (whose play "imitates" or simulates combat): "Not only does the playful nip not denote what would be denoted by the bite for which it stands, but, in addition, *the bite itself is fictional*. Not only do the playing animals not quite mean what they are saying but, also, they are usually communicating about something which does not exist. At the human level, this leads to the vast variety of complications and inversions in the fields of play, fantasy, and art" (p. 182; italics mine).

Central to Bateson's concept of play, as well as to related concepts like ritualistic behavior and deceptive behavior, is the distinction between literalness (seriousness, doing something in earnest, "meaning what one is

. . .

saying") and nonliteralness (unseriousness, pretense, fictionality, "saying one thing and meaning something else"). The dichotomy implied here between reality and fictionality is of course purely functional and does not involve any metaphysical assumptions. We must consider "real" or "literal" what is seriously meant when something is done or said in a specific situation or framework (a real bite is a real bite; a real insult is a real insult). We must consider "playful" or "nonliteral" or "fictional" what mimics or imitates or simulates or bears resemblance to a potentially serious message, nonverbal or verbal, without actually meaning it (a playful nip is a fictional bite; a playful insult is a fictional insult that means no harm).

Frames, Roles, and the Limits of Play

Drawing on Bateson's article (particularly on his notion of frame as a metacommunicative message) as well as on insights found in William James (the chapter "The Perception of Reality" in *Principles of Psychology*), in phenomenology (Alfred Schutz's "On Multiple Realities"), in logic and speech-act theory (R. Carnap, W. Quine, J. L. Austin, John Searle), in sociolinguistics, and in other areas of research on communication, Erving Goffman offers a comprehensive sociology of the "organization of experience" in terms of "frames" and "keys," including the crucial frame of play. This frame applies to an array of activities and attitudes ranging from pretending and joking, to role playing, to playing dangerous games of suspicion and strategic interaction, such as the games of deception and unmasking involved in secret operations or spying, in which false clues are consistently used and consistently assumed.[2]

In the introduction to his *Frame Analysis* (1974) Goffman explains that by "frames" he means the basic frames of reference that society makes available to us "for making sense out of events" or, more precisely, out of strings or "strips" of events, or "sequences of happenings, real or fictive, as seen from the perspective of those subjectively involved in sustaining an interest in them" (p. 10). These frames obviously have a "metacommunicative" value. Metaphorically speaking, they allow us to "read" and "reread" strips of events according to both the communicative and the metacommunicative values and modulations they may contain or be thought to contain—an interpreter being always in a position to decide whether and when to trust or to doubt a message or simply not to take it seriously.

. . .

One such frame is the "theatrical frame," whose particular importance derives from the fact that, as Goffman writes, "the language of the theater has become deeply embedded in the sociology from which [*Frame Analysis*] derives" (p. 124). The theatrical frame comprises the vast variety of performances, from formal stage performances to rehearsals, from sporting matches to various other contests (game shows, professional wrestling), and from personal ceremonies (weddings, funerals) to any social activities that display dramatic elements and that typically require or at least permit watchers (like job interviews, in which the interviewers are also the watchers). Goffman's sociology from early on (*The Presentation of Self in Everyday Life,* 1959) used a dramatistic model and suggested that, in the diverse kinds of social interactions in which we are daily involved, we all play roles all the time—at home (spouse, parent, child), school (teacher, student), and work (employer, worker, consultant).

In his discussion of play Goffman naturally refers to Bateson but also to more recent work on play, specifically animal play (P. A. Jewel and Caroline Loizos, Konrad Lorenz, W. H. Thorpe). Speaking of the "rules" observed by animals for transforming serious action into something playful, Goffman highlights some of the most general characteristics of play. One basic rule is that "the playful act is so performed that its ordinary function is not realized" (p. 41), as in the case of mock fighting, in which to ensure the maintenance of play and its requirements "the stronger and more competent participant restrains himself sufficiently to be a match for the weaker and less competent." Other fundamental rules derive from the principle of "role switching . . . resulting in a mixing up of the dominance order found among players during occasions of literal activity" (p. 43).

Psychologists of play have found similar patterns of nonliteralness and role playing and role switching in children, including infants and very young children playing at home with their parents. Thus the psychologist David Cohen, in *The Development of Play* (1987), a book based in part on observations on his own children, notes the extraordinary variety and complexity of what appear to be the most simple pretend games, from peekaboo to imitation and role playing (p. 117).

Both Goffman and Cohen, from their different perspectives, are interested in the limits of play. Mock fights can degenerate into real fights and provoke real pain and anguish. On the other hand, certain real sequences of action can be presented as games or jokes and thus remain unanswered. As Cohen notes, children can "get away with some naughtiness by turning it into a game. If you 'played' at being a brat, you were less likely to be

. . .

186

punished for it" (p. 117). There are always nuances and countless possibilities for deceit (including self-deception). The various troubles that arise in framing can be due to a range of causes, from the inherent ambiguity of certain messages (whether intended or unintended) to errors on the part of the framer or the "reader."

Within the central category of playfulness—namely, make believe—there are always certain unstated but precise conditions that must be observed to avoid frame breakups and the intrusion of practical considerations and serious (possibly violent) reactions. Goffman analyzes some suggestive cases from social life, such as those represented by jokes and joking. Jokes and jests, of course, are to be taken playfully (or fictionally), but there are limits beyond which jokes become offensive and insulting. Goffman writes: "Among familiars, there will be appeals to 'taste'; it is not nice to make light of certain aspects of the lives of friends. In the game of 'dozens' played by black urban youths, statements made about a player's parent are seen as displaying the wit of the insulter, not the features of the parent, and so can be wonderfully obscene. A mild-sounding insult that happened to refer to known features of the particular parent would be given a different relevance and cease to be unserious" (pp. 49–50).[3] The game of "dozens," in which the players exchange insults in a ludic contest of obscene inventiveness, offers an interesting social parallel to some of the uses of fictionality in literature. Fictionality, insofar as it constitutes a ritualistic and playful imaginary space, has traditionally allowed poets to deal openly with otherwise forbidden topics, themes, and images.

The case of parody or comic fictionality can provide a multitude of examples. In the Middle Ages and the Renaissance, mock-heroic, burlesque, and broadly carnivalesque traditions authorized, within the Christian culture of European society, forms of impious or even directly blasphemous humor that at the time would have been inconceivable outside the protected domain of play/fiction. In his book on Rabelais, Mikhail Bakhtin refers to numerous examples of the popular medieval culture of carnival and the carnivalesque, at whose center is the phenomenon of laughter. Laughter, Bakhtin writes, "was as universal as seriousness. . . . It was, as it were, . . . the second revelation of the world in play" (*Rabelais and His World,* p. 84). Everything was subject to parody, including the most respected and sacred symbols of the official church. "Parody played a completely unbridled game. . . . Especially in the eleventh [century], parody drew into its game all the themes of the official teaching and cult" (p. 85). There were thus parodies of prayers, including the Lord's Prayer

. . .

and the Ave Maria, and even the liturgy and the gospels were not spared (as in "The Liturgy of the Drunkards," "The Liturgy of the Gamblers," and "The Money Gospel of the Paris Student").

Such instances of licensed disorder, authorized (fictional) transgression, or permitted reversal of social conventions occur within specified time limits (on festive occasions like Mardi Gras preceding Lent), in specified places (carnivalesque processions have their assigned public spaces; theatrical performances take place on a stage), and are subject to the implicit rules of play. Even so, playfulness and fictionality are not without their risks, which are in proportion to the serious suspicions they may provoke. Owing to their unavoidable ambiguity, to the precariousness of pretending, to the deliberate or undeliberate confusions they can produce, and to their ability to deceive, fictional statements may always be taken seriously either for what they purportedly reveal or for what they hide. What is more, under the cover of play they are sometimes used—resourcefully, ingeniously, duplicitously—for serious secret purposes: this is the case, for instance, in oblique political criticism of a totalitarian regime through the medium of fiction.

Reading, Rereading, and Games of Make-Believe

I have sketched some of the ways in which play and fiction imply each other and, more important, are framed similarly, in contrast with "real" actions or communications referring to states of affairs in the "real" world. I have also tried to show that play and fiction, precisely on account of their being recognized as nonserious or nonliteral, enjoy within their limits (temporal, spatial, situational, generic, and stylistic) certain privileges that would not normally be granted to their "serious" or "real" analogues. These privileges (let us disregard for now that play and fiction can also be contemptuously dismissed as "mere" play and "mere" fiction) also point to a special cultural significance we attribute to such "as-if" modes of acting or communicating.

I have briefly mentioned Gareth Evans's views on fictional reference and truth and on their role in making possible the games of make-believe we play when we read fiction. Over the last three decades, much interesting work has been done by analytic philosophers (Kendall Walton, David K. Lewis, Gareth Evans) and literary theorists (Thomas Pavel) regarding the question of fictionality and forms of truth in fictional worlds. For present purposes (namely, to determine the play element in reading and

. . .

rereading) it will suffice to focus on the answer that the analytic approach can give to what Kendall Walton has described as "the fundamental question of why and how fiction is important" ("Fearing Fictions," p. 24).[4]

Walton's article "Fearing Fictions" is of particular relevance here. It deals convincingly not only with the broad implications of our capacity to enter fictional worlds and be make-believedly present within them, but also with our desire and ability to reread certain fictions, or to replay certain games of reading and rereading, with unabated excitement, even though we know how they will end. The main point of Walton's theory of fictional worlds is that these are worlds in which we are attracted to play games of make-believe because they afford us the opportunity to experience a wide range of emotions that are *make-believedly true.*

"Charles," the player made up by Walton to exemplify his theory, watches a "a horror movie about a terrible green slime. He cringes in his seat as the slime oozes slowly but relentlessly over the earth. . . . [He] emits a shriek and clutches desperately at his chair. Afterwards, still shaken, Charles confesses that he was 'terrified' of the slime. *Was* he?" (p. 5). The answer, supported by several other examples (coming from children's games, theatrical situations, and literature) is that Charles is make-believedly afraid; that is, he "is playing a game of make-believe in which he uses the images on the screen as props" (p. 13). In short, he is an actor impersonating himself in the imaginary situation presented in the movie.

What this means is that, insofar as we recognize ourselves in such examples, we must be endowed with the ability to portray ourselves as actors of our own selves—but also of other selves—and thus be able to become inhabitants of fictional worlds, where all sorts of things may make-believedly happen and directly affect us. Walton's approach brings, from the unexpected quarter of analytical philosophy, a confirmation of the view I have propounded throughout, mostly on psychological grounds, that reading involves mental mechanisms that are also active in daydreaming and in various forms, simpler or more developed, of symbolic play (including role playing). Walton's theory, refreshingly, takes us all the way back to Aristotle's concepts of *mimesis,* reinterpreted as imitative make-believe, and *catharsis,* or the purgation of the soul from pent-up affects by experiencing the typically tragic emotions of fear and pity. The Aristotelian connection is emphasized from the very beginning, in the epigraph (taken from chapter 14 of the *Poetics*), which suggests the way or "key" in which we should read the whole article, and is reinforced toward the end by the direct allusion to the purging of emotional tensions

. . .

as a result of participating in games of make-believe. As Walton writes, "Much of the value of dreaming, fantasizing, and making-believe depends crucially on one's thinking of oneself as belonging to a fictional world. It is chiefly by fictionally facing certain situations, engaging in certain activities, and having or expressing certain feelings, I think, that a dreamer, a fantasizer, or game player comes to terms with his actual feelings—that he discovers them, learns to accept them, purges himself of them, or whatever exactly it is that he does" (p. 24).

Walton's theory provides an elegant explanation for how certain literary or artistic works are able to survive multiple readings, viewings, or hearings. To use one of his examples, a rereader of *The Adventures of Tom Sawyer* may be as concerned about Tom and Becky being lost in the cave as someone who reads Twain's novel for the first time. The rereader of course knows the outcome but, being engaged once again in the same game of make-believe, may pretend for the sake of playing it effectively and satisfyingly that he or she does not know more about Tom and Becky in the cave episode now than on reading the book for the first time. Tom and Becky's uncertainty is contagious and spreads to the reader's own self once he or she has truly managed to be present to the fictional situation. The rereader of a gripping narrative is able, in other words, to produce a make-believe uncertainty, distinct from any actual uncertainty, which helps him or her to feel excitement and suspense as the story unfolds episode by episode.

At the same time, the rereader replaying a game of make-believe that has once been intensely enjoyed (be it "realistic" or "fantastic" or both) experiences a subtly satisfying feeling of certainty, which has been aptly described by Georges Perec in his *W or The Memory of Childhood*. Perec's testimony on this matter is all the more compelling since, as a writer, he is known as a fan of games with rules, games imposing strict compositional-stylistic constraints (such as, for instance, not using the most frequent letter in the French language, "e," in the lipogrammatic novel *La disparition*). Speaking of rereading the historical novels of Dumas, Perec reflects more broadly:

> The words were where they should be, and the books told a story you could follow; you could re-read, and on re-reading, re-encounter, enhanced by the certainty that you would encounter those words again, the impression you had felt for the first time. This pleasure has never ceased for me; I do not read much, but I never stopped re-reading Flaubert and Jules Verne, Roussel and Kafka, Leiris and Queneau; I re-read the books I love and I love the

. . .

books I re-read, and each time it is the same enjoyment, whether I re-read twenty pages, three chapters, or the whole book: an enjoyment of complicity, of collusion, or more especially, and in addition, of having in the end found kin again. (pp. 142–43)

Taking the case of a child listening to *Jack and the Beanstalk* for the umpteenth time, Walton observes that the "point of hearing the story is not, or not merely, to learn about Jack's confrontation with the giant, but to play a game of make-believe. One cannot learn, each time one hears the story, what make-believedly Jack and the giant do. . . . But one can and does participate each time in a game of make-believe." The same game? There may be differences each time around, but, according to Walton, "one's emotional needs may require the therapy of several or many repetitions" (p. 27).

My own explanation of why a child would listen to the same story over and over is slightly different. I see two elements in the desire to hear again a favorite story: the expectation of an emotionally satisfying game of make-believe one knows how to play skillfully (because of previous training); and the anticipation of a sense of reassurance, derived mainly from the fact that the make-believe uncertainty necessary for the story to be exciting is independent from the more real and undoubtedly more anxious uncertainty the first time around. Especially for young children, such a real uncertainty as to how a new story will turn out may be exciting but also somewhat disturbing and even frightening.

A third explanation, then, of the phenomenon of rereading lies in what C. S. Lewis calls "ideal surprisingness" as opposed to "the shock of actual surprise":

The re-reader is looking not for actual surprises (which come only once) but for a certain ideal surprisingness. The point has been often misunderstood. . . . In the only sense that matters the surprise works as well the twentieth time than the first. It is the *quality* of unexpectedness not the *fact* that delights us. It is even better the second time. . . . We do not enjoy a story fully at the first reading. Not till the curiosity, the sheer narrative lust, has been given its sop and laid asleep, are we at leisure to savor the real beauties. . . . The children understand this well when they ask for the same story over and over again, and in the same words. They want to have again the "surprise" of discovering that what seemed Little-Red-Riding-Hood's grandmother is really the wolf. It is better when you know it's coming: free from one shock of actual surprise you can better attend to the intrinsic surprisingness of the *peripeteia*. ("On Stories," p. 87)

. . .

As for the mature rereader, his motives and goals become almost inextricably complex as a manifold model of intricate games with rules, games of strategic cooperation or conflict, and games of interpretation and detection is superimposed on the elementary model of make-believe games. Such intricate games determine different kinds of rereading, in which repeated make-believe may still play a role, but in which the center stage of mental activities is often taken over by distinctly reflective operations and forms of attention. The involvement that typically sustains games of make-believe may itself become the focus of a game of absorption in which the rereader tries to understand and specify the conditions of involvement the first time around, and perhaps the general rules of composition that insure simple, linear readability. But this is only one of the numerous possible themes of the games of absorption that can be played in the process of rereading. To illustrate some of these complex games, the next two chapters will take up specific literary examples in which the theoretical concepts of rereading elaborated thus far will be put to a practical test.

. . .

THIRTEEN

A *"Christmas-tide Toy"*:
Henry James's The Turn of the Screw

The games of rereading I want to examine in this chapter are typically inspired by rereadable fictional works that can also be read straightforwardly by a reader who is more interested in a gripping story than in the subtle epistemological ambiguities that may subtend it. In other words, the works I have in mind lend themselves to (re)reading close to the ludic pole represented by games with rules, although the symbolic or make-believe element remains strong in them and they can be read and even reread in that mode as well.

But on the whole such works end up confronting the attentive reader with such questions as: What is really the make-believe game I am supposed to play in reading this text? What precisely am I to pretend to believe? How am I to determine this? How do I know that the game I played the first time around was not the wrong game? How do I make sure that the second time around I am not duped by false appearances, misinterpreted clues, and inappropriate hypotheses ("abductions," to borrow C. S. Peirce's term)? Of course there are texts—difficult modernist texts— whose narrative and other codes seem to have been deliberately scrambled so as to bring up questions of that kind early on in a first reading. In such works a plausible make-believe scenario (consisting of the fictionally true elements of the story) is not immediately available: the reader must put it together from ambiguous textual hints or blurred images, and he or she

· · ·

may end up with two or more quite doubtful scenarios for the imaginary reenactment of a single narrative text. The discovery of a plausible make-believe scenario is then itself the goal of a complicated game with rules. (The ways in which such texts are (re)read will be discussed in chapter 14.)

Henry James's famous "nouvelle" *The Turn of the Screw* bears examining here because it is deliberately constructed as a game, it uses devices of structural ambiguity that call for highly attentive rereading and reinterpretation (even though the story is compellingly readable on the elementary level of make-believe of a ghost story), and it has been the object of a masterful act of rereading by the author himself (in his preface to the New York Edition). An added advantage is that the almost unmanageably rich critical literature on *The Turn of the Screw,* which I see as a record of the interpretive games actually played by a large number of critics stimulated by the ambiguities of the text, has been periodically surveyed and assessed over the last several decades. This will simplify my task of dealing briefly and, I hope, clearly with a text of great complexity, to which it would be otherwise impossible to do analytical justice in the present context of a largely theoretical discussion of rereading and its possible game-like strategies.

Let me start by recalling a few fictional facts that contribute to making *The Turn of the Screw* a rereadable text. Remarkably, these very facts tend to be easily forgotten in a single linear reading: they might even be designed so as to be easily forgotten by a first-time, one-time reader once they have done the job they were supposed to do. The facts in question are related to us in the prologue and constitute the narrative frame for the main story. The opening sentence is crucially, if invisibly, important because it provides basic information as to how the rest of the text is to be construed: "The story had held us, round the fire, sufficiently breathless, but except the obvious remark that it was gruesome, as, on Christmas eve in an old house, a strange tale should essentially be, I remember no comment uttered till somebody happened to say that it was the only case he had met in which such a visitation had fallen on a child."

The first-person narrator of the prologue, "I," who remains unnamed, is with a group of friends ("us") in an old house in front of a fireplace, where one of them has just finished telling a ghost story about a supernatural visitation suffered by a child. A little later (in the second paragraph) another member of the group, Douglas, mentions a story in which not just one but two children are involved in a strange visitation episode. Douglas is of course asked to tell his tantalizing story of "uncanny ugliness

. . .

and horror and pain" (his own words). He explains that it had been written a long time before, by a woman he had known as a young man (she was his sister's governess and he may have been vaguely in love with her); the woman had been dead for twenty years. Douglas is prevailed upon to send for the manuscript (which turns out to be "a thin old-fashioned gilt-edged album") and to read it out loud over several nights. The prologue ends with an intriguing comparison: "Douglas . . . had begun to read with a fine clearness that was like a rendering to the ear of the beauty of the author's hand."

The text of the main story that follows, the memoir of the unnamed governess—or rather, an "exact transcript" made by the narrator—is thus presented to us as the quoted testimony of a long-dead witness. We fictionally assume that the first-person narrator of the prologue, perhaps "Henry James" (that is, the name on the cover of the book), has published the text without any intervention except that he has given it a title. At the beginning of the last paragraph of the prologue, the narrator exclaims, before hearing the story, that he has found a title (again we fictionally assume that it is *The Turn of the Screw,* but we note that this very phrase had been uttered, in the prologue, by Douglas; it had been part of his first quoted remark).

Looked at under the magnifying glass of attention characteristic of rereading, the prologue, a simple and rather banal pretextual framing device, becomes a very complex affair indeed. But from the perspective of a first reading, the prologue's job is no more than to promise the reader a powerful, sinister, extremely gruesome ghost story with two children. To put it differently, the reader is invited to prepare for a specific kind of literary game of make-believe—a game of the uncanny and the terrifying. The main story of demonic ghosts and demonized children, told in the first person by the young governess, fully satisfies such expectations, including the generic expectations of suspense and a steady build-up of tension toward a final climax—which is reached, elegantly from the point of view of literary art, in the last sentence of the text, in which the sudden death of the boy, Miles, in the arms of the terrified governess is announced: "We were alone with the quiet day, and his little heart, dispossessed, had stopped." But since the ending is so abrupt and open—we do not learn what happened to the governess and must be content with the few vague things we already know from the prologue, if we have not forgotten them by now—we may be inclined to ponder the text over again, recheck it for clues that might have escaped us the first time around, and in fact reread it

· · ·

to squeeze out more information about the hidden elements of what has struck us as its obvious but incomplete fictional truth. Significantly, in the process of rereading, many aspects of what on a first reading appeared as obvious fictional truth will become more indeterminate, obscure, impossible to decide with certainty. *The Turn of the Screw* thus becomes a uniquely rereadable exemplar of an otherwise purely readable genre, the ghost story.

A rereading of *The Turn of the Screw* (1898) alongside the preface (1908), in which James recounts his own experience of rereading his tale, yields rich insights into the ludic concept of (re)reading. In the preface, in looking back at the story, James insists on its characteristics as an ingenious modern-day version of a "time-honored Christmas-tide toy" (note the intriguing equation of ghost stories and toys; *The Art of the Novel*, p. 170). He then goes on to characterize this "sinister romance" and its intended effects on the reader in clearly ludic terms: "I find here a perfect example of an exercise of the imagination unassisted, unassociated— playing the game, making the score, in the phrase of our sporting day, off its own bat. To what degree the game was worth playing, I needn't attempt to say: the exercise I have noted strikes me now, I confess, as the interesting thing, the imaginative faculty acting with the whole of the case on its hands" (p. 171).

James stresses quite convincingly the quality of "high fancy" of *The Turn of the Screw* and that it is a variation on a basic fairy-tale model, "save indeed as to its springing not from an artless and measureless, but from a conscious and cultivated credulity." Criticism seems to have had little use for this fascinating idea of *The Turn of the Screw* as a lurid and sinister variation on the fairy tale. Even more fascinating, however, is the notion of "conscious and cultivated credulity" on which the story is built. This ties in nicely with the view of games of make-believe and fictionality developed in the previous chapter. James's *conscious* credulity also makes us aware of the high degree of sophistication that may be required for achieving belief in certain kinds of fiction. To the concept of methodical naivete, advanced earlier in relation to the youthful passion for reading adventure stories, we may now add the equally paradoxical concept of a highly sophisticated naivete. This notion may help us to understand the desire to reread a tale such as *The Turn of the Screw*. As we shall soon see, the main problem of the attentive reflective rereader of James's tale is that it contains two mutually exclusive but almost equally plausible stories: a ghost story and the story of a mental breakdown. Either one of these

. . .

stories, to be effective as make-believe, demands credulity on the part of the reader, but not of a particularly sophisticated kind: actually the ghost story demands a simple-minded, superstitious credulity comparable to that demanded by a fairy tale.

Sophistication enters the picture only when the reader realizes the existence of the two stories in one. It takes sophistication to become aware of ambiguous structures and possible alternative interpretations of the same text. Paradoxically, this sophistication leads to a special form of naivete on the level of rereading, which consists mainly in the urge to choose between the two stories, as if one fiction were better, more appropriate, more "genuine" than the other. It is this naive urge that maintains the interpretive tension, the state of indecision that calls for even more careful rereading and reinterpretation. So we may say, again paradoxically, that naivete results in a renewed, heightened sophistication: it stimulates further thinking and rethinking of hermeneutical strategies and attempts to assess the reliability of this piece of fictional testimony. It is in this convoluted sense that we may use a phrase like "sophisticated naivete," which at first sight is nothing but a contradiction in terms. The only candid answer to the fundamental question, Why is it important to reinterpret *The Turn of the Screw* so as to establish the fictional truth of one story over the other? would be, Because it is difficult, because it is challenging, because it is in fact impossible.

Returning now to the preface, James is fully aware that the central imaginative principle of his work is that of an "improvisation" in which extreme freedom, on the one hand, and extreme intellectual calculation and control, on the other, are mutually dependent—the way they are, I would add, in such complex games with rules as chess or bridge when such games are inventively played by experienced players. The metaphor of the work as toy or game is evocatively summed up when James proposes that it is fundamentally "an *amusette* to catch those not easily caught . . . , the jaded, the disillusioned, the fastidious" (p. 172).

How are we to take this notion of the tale as a playful trap for capturing the refined skeptical reader? There are two major interpretations of the ghosts (Peter Quint, Miss Jessel) in the story: (1) they are "real revenants," ominous irruptions of the supernatural into the otherwise peaceful everyday world of Bly, and the young governess reacts "normally" throughout her valiant but losing battle against the demonic seducer-persecutors of the two children in her care, Flora and Miles; and (2) the ghosts are mere "hallucinations" of the governess herself who, in the words of Edmund

. . .

197

Wilson, is nothing but "a neurotic case of sex repression" and who, consequently, must be seen as the "unreliable narrator" of a chain of events that happen as much in her imagination as in reality, and for which she must be held accountable.[1] But beyond these two simple games of make-believe (the governess sees real ghosts, the governess is crazy), James's text proposes two other distinct, though not unrelated, games.

First is the game of the fantastic as a genre of fiction whose distinctive feature is, according to Tzvetan Todorov, the "hesitation" of the reader (more specifically the textually implied reader) between two equally plausible explanations of certain bizarre and troubling events. In a fantastic story about the devil, for example, the reader may be manipulated into considering that the devil as presented is either "an illusion, an imaginary being; or else he really exists, precisely like other living beings—with this reservation, that we encounter him infrequently. The fantastic occupies the duration of this uncertainty. Once we choose one answer over the other, we leave the fantastic for a neighboring genre, the uncanny or the marvelous" (*The Fantastic,* p. 25). As we shall see, some of the most interesting recent commentaries on *The Turn of the Screw* consider it among the most elaborate and successful examples of the pure fantastic as defined by Todorov. In the ludic terms I am proposing, the game would be one of dramatizing undecidability and uncertainty, of making the reader proceed through a labyrinth of interpretations and counterinterpretations. The real fun of (re)reading would come from the sustained and intricate stimulation of the reader's hermeneutical imagination.

The second subsidiary game is a peculiar form of the game played by readers of fiction who like to second-guess the author or the narrator or a key character. In the James tale, if we think that the governess is indeed a case of quasi-pathological self-delusion, the need for second-guessing (as well as for rereading and thus double-checking) is naturally increased since the only version of the strange, shocking happenings at Bly is the governess's own. The first-person account being the only evidence that is offered us as a basis for judging the case, we are implicitly invited to play a fourth and quite interesting legal-epistemological game: How to construct "realistic" interpretive scenarios on the basis of an obviously fragmentary, consciously or unconsciously distorted, and implicitly self-serving narrative testimony?

Returning to the two traditional rival theories about what "really" happens in *The Turn of the Screw,* it is clear that from the perspective of the fantastic neither is true or tenable, though both are equally necessary

. . .

to the special effect of the story on our imagination and to the tantalizingly renewed desire to reread. To understand how this is possible, the concept of ambiguity, as elaborated by Shlomith Rimmon in her book *The Concept of Ambiguity: The Example of Henry James* (1977), may be useful. Rimmon articulates a general theory of ambiguity, which she then tests analytically against several works by James, *The Turn of the Screw* among them. For Rimmon the two competing and mutually exclusive hypotheses (real ghosts/hallucinations) are supported in equal measure by two systems of conflicting clues distributed with great skill throughout the text. In other words, if we want to apply the widely used narratological distinction between story (*fabula* in the terminology of the Russian Formalists, which Rimmon seems to prefer, or simply the raw facts arranged in chronological order, to which the narrative may be reduced) and discourse (or *sjuzet,* or plot, the actual arrangement and presentation of the raw facts), *The Turn of the Screw* would appear to be a perfect example of narrative ambiguity, for the work contains two perfectly distinct stories in one discourse. Rimmon helps us to form a clearer representation of this puzzling situation by citing the suggestive analogue of visual ambiguity as defined by E. H. Gombrich in his *Art and Illusion*. Commenting on a humorously tricky drawing that can be "read" either as a rabbit or a duck, Gombrich notes:

> Clearly we do not have the illusion that we are confronted with a "real" duck or rabbit. The shape on the paper resembles neither animal very closely. And yet there is no doubt that the shape transforms itself in some subtle way when the duck's beak becomes the rabbit's ears and brings an otherwise neglected spot into prominence as the rabbit's mouth. I say "neglected," but does it enter our experience at all when we switch back to reading "duck"? To answer this question, we are compelled to look for what is "really there," to see the shape apart from its interpretation, and this, we discover, is not really possible. (*Art and Illusion*, p. 5)

The various clues that the reader of *The Turn of the Screw* is given by the text, Rimmon points out, are either "singly directed" (that is, support only one hypothesis but are "balanced somewhere else in the narrative by another scene, conversation, or verbal expression which supports exclusively the opposite hypothesis") or "doubly directed" ("open to a double interpretation and support simultaneously the two alternatives," pp. 51–52). These clues function as directions for filling in both the "central permanent gap" in narrative information, which lies at the core of the

. . .

story (certain essential facts the governess fails to mention), and the numerous "ancillary, local gaps" the reader encounters at every important turn in the narrative. The power of the story comes in part from the fact that none of these gaps is arbitrary but, on the contrary, carefully and subtly motivated. Thus, the gap at the center of the story (concerning the sketchiness of the governess's testimony)

> is realistically "motivated" in various ways. The isolation of Bly explains both why the governess has hardly anyone to talk to in order to ascertain the facts and why nobody detects her madness (if madness it is). . . . As for the children, the governess is often tempted to ask them whether they see, or rather to prove to them that she knows they do, but she is deterred "by the very chance that such an injury might prove greater than the injury to be averted." It is her own uncertainty, horror of the facts, and lack of experience . . . that makes silence the best solution. (p. 127)

Rimmon's detailed discussion of *The Turn of the Screw* in terms of patterns of conflicting clues is a product of repeated critical rereading. It comes as no surprise therefore that some of her shrewdest observations bear on the question of rereading itself, and specifically on that of "retrospective ambiguity," a technique by which the reader is made to discover the ambiguity of what on a first reading had appeared straightforward and unambiguous. Rimmon's main example is the retrospective "ambiguization" of the prologue of the tale, which is the only external source of information about the governess and the fate of the manuscript of her story. The bulk of Rimmon's discussion is devoted, however, to what she calls "prospective ambiguity," the kind of ambiguity that appears in the forward movement of reading as we encounter things that lend themselves to double interpretation because of what we have learned up to that point in the story.

My view is that even such prospective ambiguity is largely a result of retrospective critical reconstruction, that its prospective dimension is rooted in hindsight and that, anyway, it generates an urge and a need to reread. But, on the other hand, I do not think that there is much to be gained, at least by way of analytical precision, from the recognition of the paradox that in reading such a text we need to look backwards in order to advance—to move into the future backwards, with our eyes riveted on an increasingly ambiguous past.

Retrospective or prospective, the systematic ambiguity so characteristic of much of James's fiction (including, aside from *The Turn of the Screw,*

. . .

shorter pieces like "The Lesson and the Master" or "The Figure in the Carpet" and the novel *The Sacred Fount*) would be impossible without the skillful use of silences and narrative gaps. As such gaps turn out to be unfillable, the either/or tension of the older theories about *The Turn of the Screw* (either ghosts or hallucinations) is replaced by the simultaneous both/and and neither/nor of strictly unresolvable ambiguity. If we accept this position, the question arises: Why would one be interested in reading, and rereading, such a rigorously ambiguous work? My answer is that our absorption in a short novel like *The Turn of the Screw* is, or eventually becomes, ludic: we are willing to play the critical game so intelligently devised by the author, an important part of which consists of searching precisely for the textual gaps and attempting to define their strategic role in manipulating reader interest and in creating a desire to reread. It is by identifying and circumscribing these gaps through rereading that we are enabled to discover not the "truth" of the story but the more subtle, hidden, tacit rules by which the hermeneutical game it proposes can be played and replayed, as well as the incidental loopholes that may allow for new, unsuspected interpretive possibilities. The secret hope of solving the puzzle definitively, of triumphing where all other readers have failed, must not be discounted either: this "let-*me*-have-a-look-at-it" attitude under-lies much of the competitive rereading that forms the basis of literary criticism.

The more cerebral ludic approach I have suggested does not exclude, but actually implies, the emotional involvement of playing games of make-believe that we experience when reading dramatic, powerful narra-tives. For *The Turn of the Screw* would not have become a "puzzle" (as Wayne Booth calls it in *The Rhetoric of Fiction*)[2] if it had not been an effective ghost story in the first place. Incidentally, as the friend and correspondent of Horace Walpole, Madame du Deffand, pointed out so wittily, we need not believe in ghosts to be scared of them. This awareness seems to have been part of James's "cold artistic calculation" with respect to the effect of the tale on the "jaded" and "disillusioned" reader he had in mind when writing. If this is so, Booth's notion that the story exemplifies an "unintentional ambiguity of effect" becomes groundless. To use again the visual analogy of the ambiguous duck-or-rabbit figure, it is very hard to imagine, and at any rate impossible to demonstrate, that the draftsman who produced the image intended it to look like only a duck or a rabbit and that the ambiguity was unintended. In terms of its effects, James's text is a literary illustration of such double intentionality: it is at once a ghost

. . .

story, a gripping story of supernatural horror, and a powerful account of an elusive psychopathological case to be inferred by the reader.

That ultimately neither of these readings holds and that, as we saw, they are mutually exclusive mysteriously strengthens certain images: the strange erect male, later identified as Peter Quint, looking at once fixedly and blankly at the governess from atop the tower; the same intruder staring chillingly at her through the window; the ghost of Miss Jessel at the lakeside. Such sharply focused images take on an independent haunting quality of their own. This would seem to confirm Roger Caillois's intuition that the fantastic may hinge on the privileged relationship between images and the unreal.[3] If this is so, the ability of *The Turn of the Screw* to scare the (re)reader is tied largely to these images as such and to the way they might be explained and then visualized in a fantastic game of make-believe peopled by demonic revenants or in a realistic-psychological game of make-believe in which the governess is losing her mind and frightens little Miles literally to death. An explanation through natural causes, as in the hallucinationist theory, does not diminish the anxiety-producing potential of these images: the specters of madness can be every bit as frightening as any revenant, gruesome spirit, or walking dead man.

The most important consequence of James's clearly ludic conception of *The Turn of the Screw* is the active involvement of the reader in the narrative game on an equal footing with the author. This is one of the central themes of an occasionally interesting if uneven book on Henry James by Susanne Kappeler (1980). Leaving aside her addiction to jargon and her clumsy, sometimes flatly contradictory theoretical formulations (the reader "produces" the text but the author can still refuse to grant him "the Realist guarantee of Truth"), Kappeler is one of the few Jamesian critics who interprets the preface to *The Turn of the Screw* along ludic lines similar to those proposed here. She is right to suggest that the Jamesian game is a way of reflecting on the communicative function of language while suspending it in any pragmatic sense. Of course, other theorists of reading as play, such as Michel Picard, have also insisted, in different contexts, on the essential inadequacy of the communicational model of literary writing or reading as just another form of informational coding and decoding: in writing and reading we are not simply using codes but playing with them as well (*La Lecture comme jeu*, pp. 9–11, 22). Hence, in the specific case of the Jamesian game, " 'the events' . . . are suspended in the structural ambiguity of their presentation" (Kappeler, *Writing and Reading in Henry James*, p. 74).

. . .

In *A Rhetoric of the Unreal* (1981) Christine Brooke-Rose gives us, together with her lucid critique of previous interpretations of *The Turn of the Screw,* two extremely elaborate readings of the Jamesian short novel, the first in terms of what she calls "basic structures," the second in terms of "surface structures." I shall start with the second, which I find more congenial: it is a formalist or textualist reading, using concepts derived from Genette (macrotext/microtext), Todorov (the fantastic as hesitation), and the Russian Formalists, and it leads to a new version of Rimmon's concept of ambiguity. What is exemplary in this reading is the way it unfolds from a close consideration of the relationship between the "text" (*The Turn of the Screw* understood structurally, or synchronically, down to the tiniest, finest, most easily overlooked detail) and the "metatext," defined as the ensemble of possible or permissible inferences about the various gaps of narrative information, as opposed to the purely extratextual and thus impermissible inferences or loose speculations to which so many earlier critics have resorted. Such speculations have to do with what the characters might have felt or done in circumstances never suggested by the text, nor directly imaginable within the fictional world created by the text, but assumed to be plausible in a broad human sense (speculations, for instance, on the love life of the governess, about which the text itself tells us nothing).

As for Brooke-Rose's reading of *The Turn of the Screw* on the deeper but much more opaque level of "basic structures"—or on the even deeper level of the "bare structure," where the fundamental transgression at the origin of every narrative is supposed to occur—I would say that it is so sweepingly speculative and aggressively abstract as not to be "testable" by the standards of Brooke-Rose's own distinction between metatextually permissible and metatextually impermissible inferences. Her inferences here are broadly metaphorical: symmetries of mirrorings, double movements, the figure *four*—four apparitions of each sex, four scenes with a child of each sex, four main living characters at Bly, all linked to the "normally four-sided" frame of a mirror! True, such metaphoric associations are extracted from the text, but many of them could have been extracted from almost any narrative text of similar length. Their significance, as the critic conceives it, remains elusive until Brooke-Rose explicitly endorses the conclusions reached by Shoshana Felman in "Turning the Screw of Interpretation," namely, that James's story could be understood as a fictional analogue of the basic conflicts of the psyche in the drama of psychoanalysis. At least in certain quarters, psychoanalytically

. . .

allegorical readings of fiction—that is, readings in which characters and situations in fictional works are seen as allegories of such processes as repression, the return of the repressed, or typical conflicts among functions of the psychic apparatus, the id, ego, and superego—seem to be as widespread today as allegorical readings of the Bible and of the pagan poets were in the Middle Ages.

Perhaps the most influential example of such modern psychoanalytical allegorizing—whatever its expository justifications and far-reaching aims—is Jacques Lacan's reading of Edgar Allan Poe's story "The Purloined Letter" as a dramatization or even a fictional "double" or "parody" of his own version of psychoanalysis.[4] Symptomatically, this reading has generated, by way of reaction and counterreaction, a whole body of intricate theoretical, often "pretextual" commentaries on Poe's classic tale of detection and ratiocination.[5] Allegorical readings of this type, even though they can be extremely detailed and penetrating, tend to transform the work under scrutiny into a "pretext" for exploring a radically different "text"—in the case of Lacan, his structuralist version of Freudian psychoanalysis; in the case of Lacanians, their particular version of Lacan's quasi-hermetic neo-Freudian doctrines; in the case of critics of Lacan (like Jacques Derrida), their view of the irreconcilable contradictions and aporias found in Lacan's discourse.

The Felman/Brooke-Rose approach to *The Turn of the Screw* does call attention to certain moments or aspects of James's tale that other interpretations leave out, for instance, the symbolic importance of the Master who hires the governess and strangely forbids her to bother him under any circumstances. (The Master, we are told toward the end of the prologue, hired the governess on condition "that she never trouble him—but never, never: neither appeal nor complain nor write about anything; only meet all questions herself, receive all moneys from his solicitor, take the whole thing over and let him alone.") But the role of the Master need not have anything to do with the "law as a form of censorship" or "the supreme instance of power" or the "unconscious." It may simply be that of imposing a limiting condition or an exclusionary rule (which precludes the reader from asking such questions as "Why does not the governess inform her employer about the crisis situation at Bly sooner?") for the sake of enhancing the interest of the game by narrowing the range of certain strategic choices. The interpretation of James's short novel in terms of different levels of play—a double game of make-believe on one level, a "fantastic" game of hesitation between mutually exclusive hypotheses on another, and an intricate legal-

. . .

epistemological game on a third level of more cerebral games with rules—clearly has the greater explanatory power. Furthermore, such an approach in no way rules out a psychological (Freudian or, in the case of Felman/Brooke-Rose, neo-Freudian) attempt to account for the fascination the James story exerts on many of its readers. But psychological hypotheses and explanations (including the highly speculative and metaphorical ones characteristic of neo-Freudianism) should be refocused from the text, with its open-ended allegorical (re)readability, onto its reception and more specifically onto the types of play involved in reading and rereading it. The text's haunting ambiguities, its ability to suggest scripts for anxious daydreams, its additional ability to challenge the mind with puzzles of a fictive epistemological-legal nature, do certainly have a psychological significance, but one that cannot be seized directly from the text. To grasp it properly we need to take into consideration the mediating categories of the play of reading, from the games of make-believe and involvement characteristic of linear reading to the games of absorption and structural attention characteristic of rereading.

. . .

· · · · · · ·

FOURTEEN

Mysteries for Rereading

The *gnosis* of a concrete crime and the *gnosis* of abstract ideas
nicely parallel and parody each other.
W. H. AUDEN
The Dyer's Hand

· · · · · · ·

A mystery tale displays an astute narrative strategy in order to
produce a naive Model Reader eager to fall into the traps of the
narrator (to feel fear and to suspect the innocent one) but usually
wants to produce also a critical Model Reader able to enjoy, at a
second reading, the brilliant narrative strategy by which the first-
level naive reader was designed.
UMBERTO ECO
The Limits of Interpretation

· · · · · · ·

The interpreter must go back and forth among provisionally
acceptable fictional truths until he finds a convincing combination.
KENDALL WALTON
Mimesis as Make-Believe

· · · · · · ·

· · ·

Linear Reading: A Generic Rule of the Mystery

There are numerous studies of contemporary (modernist or postmodernist) variations on the basic narrative model of the popular genre of detective fiction.[1] Virtually all acknowledge that a significant category of modern works of fiction makes wide—if peculiar and often idiosyncratic—use of detective ways of plotting and narrative devices originally calculated to create suspense, bring about surprise, and stimulate reader interest. Among such devices are the manipulation of the order and manner in which clues, including false clues, are disclosed; the technique of omitting important information at strategic points (occasionally at the very center of the plot); and the opposite technique of bringing minute details and nearly insignificant particulars into the focus of intense reader attention, especially the details surrounding a mysterious crime or other crucial events in the story. Many distinguished twentieth-century authors have at one time or another played with detective narrative situations or procedures—from Vladimir Nabokov (*Despair, Pale Fire*) to Jorge Luis Borges ("Death and the Compass," "Emma Zunz"), from Alain Robbe-Grillet (*The Erasers, The Voyeur*) and Michel Butor (*Pastime*) to Italo Calvino (*If on a Winter's Night a Traveler*) and Umberto Eco (*The Name of the Rose*). Some of the characteristic fictional works of these authors could be regarded, perhaps oxymoronically, as mysteries for rereading (although a number of them are coded for both linear reading and non-linear rereading).

No matter how curious or excited they may be, the typical readers of detective fiction will hardly be tempted to "cheat," that is, to learn ahead of time the solution of the riddle, which they could easily do by looking at the last few pages: the book, a one-time game meant to occupy several hours intelligently and pleasurably, would suddenly become almost unreadable, its fun gone and the words on the page looking sadly futile. That is why revealing the ending of a detective story to someone who plans to read it ranks among the least forgivable offenses in the informal deontology of detective fiction fans. (There are, however, atypical readers for whom the sheer tension of waiting in uncertainty for the mystery to be solved may be unbearable; these readers will start with the ending, with the solution of the puzzle, and go through the story in the usual, linear fashion, only afterward; such reading contains at least one of the elements of rereading, namely, the psychological ingredients of foreknowledge and reassurance.)

. . .

The paramount importance of the ending (the last unexpected revelation, the mystery neatly solved, all the loose ends tied up) remains one of the structural features of the mystery, a genre of literature that prizes pure readability. The reader is of course allowed to go back, to recheck the accuracy with which he or she has retained certain pieces of information; but this will slow down the flow of reading, and excessive slowness in perusing a detective novel is subject to a law of diminishing returns. (There are additional "socially-determined" penalties for reading detective fiction too slowly: one may feel ashamed to give too much of one's time to a leisure activity that others perform, apparently with greater ease and fun, in a shorter interval.) Students of the genre have discussed at some length the mystery story as a "basic model of the readable text," pointing to the methods by which it entices and preserves reader interest. According to Dennis Porter these are the promise of intelligibility, the promise of a surprising denouement that will reveal the wholeness of an apparently fragmented picture, commitment to the principle of non-contradiction and nonreversibility, skillful manipulation of the traditional Manichean hero/villain narrative schemes, and wide use of stylistic redundancy in the form of synonyms and metaphors.[2] This basic readability has made some sophisticated commentators speak of the (classical) detective novel as paradoxically caught between a purely cerebral game of ingenuity—a mathematical puzzle, an exercise in which the mind tries to overcome a difficulty within a structure of fixed rules—and, as Roger Caillois puts it, "the most naive and most primitively novelistic of all forms of the novel."[3] One may quarrel with the last point, however; the readability of the detective novel is not at all primitive. Historically, the first novels had a loose episodic structure closer to the modes of oral narrative composition than to the well-constructed, tight plot of a good mystery.

The normal reading of detective fiction is thus emphatically linear, a forward-going one-time affair in which the reader's interest builds progressively to reach its climax right before the ending. But on closer consideration, it turns out that such "normal reading" need not preclude the possibility of rereading. In his "Casual Notes on the Mystery Novel" Raymond Chandler observes that the "mystery novel must have a sound story value apart from the mystery element. . . . All really good mysteries are reread, some of them many times. Obviously, this would not happen if the puzzle were the only motive for the reader's interest. The mysteries that survive over the years invariably have the qualities of good fiction."[4]

· · ·

Chandler is perfectly right. Good narrative fiction succeeds in providing the reader with convincing "props" (to use Kendall Walton's term) for playing a game of make-believe, for becoming involved in the fictional events of the story. Such props, when they are skillfully crafted, are reusable: what a first-time reader experiences as surprise can give place, the second time around, to an experience of that "ideal surprisingness" or "quality of unexpectedness" of which C. S. Lewis speaks in "On Stories." This does not, however, change the essential generic requirement that a detective story be readable in the sense of a "good read," and that it prove satisfying, as Chandler puts it, to a virtual "cross section of the entire reading public. . . . Semi-literates don't read Flaubert and intellectuals don't as a rule read the current fat slab of goosed history masquerading as an historical novel. But everyone reads mysteries from time to time" (p. 83). What is more, as W. H. Auden points out, reading detective fiction can become an addiction ("like tobacco and alcohol"), particularly for intellectuals: "The most curious fact about detective fiction," he writes, "is that it makes its greatest appeal precisely to those classes of people who are most immune to other forms of daydream literature. The typical detective story addict is a doctor or clergyman or scientist or artist, i.e. a fairly successful professional man" (*The Dyer's Hand,* p. 175). But Auden seems to be in disagreement with Chandler on the question of rereadability: "I forget the story as soon as I have finished it, and have no wish to read it again. If, as sometimes happens, I start reading one and find out after a few pages that I have read it before, I cannot go on" (p. 146).

Aside from replaying a game of make-believe, there are certainly other ways of rereading mysteries—not only the classics of the genre but also certain exemplars that are interestingly or instructively flawed. One thus may reread for purposes of study: how is the detective story made? What are, so to speak, the tricks of the trade? On rereading, the interest in the investigative enigma posed by the narrative fades; curiosity is now directed to the text itself—particularly the successful text—as a different kind of enigma devised by a craftsman, to be compared with other carefully crafted enigmas of the same kind.[5] Another mode of rereading, which is not necessarily divorced from the studious type and may even be conceived as its extension, is primarily reflective in a philosophical (ontological and epistemological) as well as aesthetic sense. That such a rereading of mystery stories can be intellectually rewarding is demonstrated by the essay *What Will Have Happened,* by Robert Champigny.

. . .

209

The broader view Champigny adopts is decidedly one of rereading, although the first-reading perspective is acknowledged as always paramount in dealing with detective fiction. Champigny explains:

> In one way, reading and rereading offer markedly different perspectives in the case of mystery stories, if one remembers the denouement. But in another way, mystery stories make the two perspectives more similar, because on the first reading they convey a more precise idea of the narrative goal than straight stories usually do. . . . A critical essay stems from a rereading experience. . . . One may enjoy watching a game and not be partial to televised replays. Similarly, some readers may prefer to read texts, mystery stories in particular, only once and dispense with commentaries. I have no objection to this kind of preference. But my outlook is based on a rereading experience. . . . Accordingly, some of my analyses will break a rule by which most reviewers abide: I shall disclose the denouement. (pp. 5–6)

Detective fiction privileges the first-reading perspective as a generic requirement. A mystery story is always primarily constructed, and all its main effects calculated, with the first-time reader in mind; that is, the implied reader it constructs in the process of constructing itself gets acquainted with the unfamiliar text progressively and in a strict sequential manner culminating in the ending. Porter concurs when he says that "the average detective story [is] more end-oriented than almost any other type of fiction" (p. 235).

Nothing appears to be more opposed to such a model of readability than certain kinds of modernist or postmodernist literature, which seem to thrive on difficulty and on their evident, self-advertising, snobbish "unreadability" (perceived as a challenge to the ingenuity of even the most highly literate readers). The phenomenon looks like a literary equivalent of the so-called perverse effects in economics, by which an increase in the price of a commodity, usually a luxury, raises the demand for it insofar as its acquisition is seen as conferring social prestige on the owner. But extending this market analogy would be unfair—as unfair as its elitist counterpart, that is, the rejection of popular literature (including detective fiction) simply because it is accessible or inexpensive, in both monetary and temporal terms.

Playing with Codes and Formal Constraints

What is fascinating in the contrast between "easy" and near-universally engrossing texts like detective mysteries and "difficult" texts, such as the

· · ·

"unreadable" *nouveaux romans* of Robbe-Grillet or Butor (which are sometimes ostensibly patterned like detective stories), is the degree to which they are faced with similar technical problems and challenged by equally rigorous formal constraints, and the way in which they use their imaginative findings for purposes of initiating widely different reading games. The "unreadable" texts also have a clear ludic structure, but the game they propose is non-linear, a game of "rereading from the outset" (Roland Barthes) or multiple reading and absorption, as opposed to the hybrid game of involvement and hypothesizing invited by a text conceived for an ideal single reading. A game of rereading may well start with knowledge of the ending (and even with knowledge that the ending does not count and that in fact there is no such thing as an ending or closure) and can be played as slowly and with as many interruptions as one wishes. In it, guessing who is responsible for the crime (if there is a crime) is far less interesting than guessing the rules of the game; and the solution is not really a solution but an invitation or challenge to replay the game differently.

The relationship between straight detective fiction and certain avant-garde self-conscious manipulations of the "hermeneutic code" or "the code of the enigma" has enjoyed significant critical attention. A witty and insightful discussion of some of its implications, in the wake of the publication of Roland Barthes's *S/Z* (1970), is in Frank Kermode's *Novel and Narrative* (1972). To illustrate the way we read detective stories, Kermode focuses on a (rather untypical) classic of the genre, *Trent's Last Case,* by E. C. Bentley, showing how the reader processes the complex information variously provided by a text that is meant to be "primarily a hermeneutic game" (p. 15). This processing involves a series of interpretive decisions as to which information is relevant to the solution of the enigma as opposed to information that turns out to be irrelevant, if not deceptive. But such interpretive decisions invariably entail the activation of other reading codes, such as the cultural and the symbolic.

Before proceeding further, let me clarify the question of the codes under which readers organize and memorize the bits and pieces of variegated information they gather as they move through the narrative text in time. Barthes proposes five codes, and Kermode in the main accepts them. For our limited purposes here Kermode's summary presentation of these codes is helpful: "Two [codes] have to do with what we think of as narrative, distinguished as the proairetic and the hermeneutic codes: that is, the sequence of actions (dependent on choices), and the proposing of enigmas

. . .

which are eventually, after delay, concealment, deception, and so on, solved. The other codes relate to information not processed sequentially: semantic, cultural and symbolic, they stand on the vertical rather than the horizontal axis of the work, and remain rather vague" (p. 22). To understand what is meant by the three "vertical" codes some additional information is needed.

For Barthes the "semic" (not "semantic") code is the one under which we process indirect, connotative information regarding the narrative identity or personality of characters: in moral terms (good, bad), psychological terms (calm, cool, eager, nervous, sensitive, jittery), and social terms (belonging to the upper, middle, or lower classes). The semic or character code is less important, or less extensively and subtly involved, in stories in which the action and hermeneutic codes are widely utilized. In tales of adventure, suspense, and detection character development is neither possible nor desirable. As for Barthes's "cultural" code, it is the one under which the reader files the connotations derived from ideological aspects or biases of the text—cultural prejudices, class, gender, and national-racial stereotypes, clichés, unquestioned epistemological assumptions, matters of "common knowledge," and so on. From the viewpoint of literary criticism this code is certainly the most helpful for defining the implied reader in terms of social class or group, status, gender, race, and religious or political allegiance.

The "symbolic" code is the one that deals—along idiosyncratically psychoanalytic lines for Barthes—with the symbolic meanings of the human body (in terms of sex differences). A reelaboration of this code in broader terms to account for the appeal of archetypal patterns and images—images that are capable of triggering reverie in the sense of Bachelard's poetics of the imaginary—would be welcome, although probably not in a discussion of reading mysteries, in which the symbolic dimension plays a minor role.

Kermode attempts to show in regard to Bentley's detective story that the hermeneutically relevant material we identify in it spawns material that is of cultural-ideological or even symbolic significance, and this contention is easy to accept. There is no point in arguing that, from the point of view of the reader, "plurisignificance" or plurality of meaning is the normal condition of any narrative text. The opposite argument would seem to be of more interest. It can be demonstrated that in a successful detective story information that would appear to be hermeneutically superfluous or completely neutral is made to play a *potential* (teasing,

. . .

occasionally tantalizing) hermeneutical role. The game proposed by the detective story would then be one in which information, including information of cultural, semic, and symbolic nature, would be made hermeneutically significant and thus become the focus of heightened attention. A failed detective story would be one in which most of the various types of information provided by the text turn out to be hermeneutically irrelevant, to have been used for no other reason than to make the book fatter, a not infrequent occurrence.

What Kermode does in his commentary is to look at Bentley's text not with the eyes of a normal (eager, curious, methodically naive) reader but with those of a professional and highly reflective rereader. This curiously blinds him to the built-in one-time character of the game, but helps him to establish a convincing connection between certain structures of detective fiction and the oversophisticated games of attention and rereading proposed by a Queneau, Robbe-Grillet, or Butor. Kermode argues that Robbe-Grillet's novel *The Erasers* (*Les Gommes*) or Butor's *Pastime* (*L'Emploi du temps*) are detective stories in a special sense, that is, they may be described as "narrative sequences of enigmas . . . and ambiguous clues . . . [which are] of great interest, especially if you give up the notion . . . that they ought to lock together with great exactness, and abandon the attempt at full hermeneutic closure" (p. 16). But, I should add, with the requirement of closure gone, and with the teleological sense of the ending removed, this "great interest" of which Kermode speaks is of a purely theoretical-critical nature and will be perceived only by dedicated rereaders, largely members of the literature departments of that institution of rereading, the university.

These bizarre inverse detective stories, in which the crime may be produced by its very investigation, are in fact complex parodies or other types of playful distortions of established literary conventions of the mystery narrative genre; thus they are implicit forms of literary criticism. The potential for innovation that comes of raising the procedures of a "low" genre to the level of new "high" literary norms has long been recognized by writers, although in criticism it was noticed first by the Russian Formalists. The main source as well as the objective of such experiments is the *process of reading*. That is why the avant-garde texts discussed by Kermode could be best described as experimental games of metareading: reading reading, as it were, and reading against reading, and exploring the largely unconscious ambiguities, puzzles, and complexities of reading, and the fascinating absurdities, accidents, and epiphanies of

. . .

knowingly and deliberately reading the wrong way—literally when one should read figuratively, antiteleologically when one should read teleologically, and so on. Such games of double reading and rereading are often based on removing one or some of the requirements of normal hermeneutical reading. The true hero of these games, the one who is repeatedly put to the test by the adventures of conceptualization and reconceptualization, who is tossed about by dramatic swerves and changes of context, is none other than the reader—the persistent, stubborn, and perhaps "hypocritical" reader (in the sense of Baudelaire's "hypocrite lecteur, mon semblable, mon frère"), the reader who is or becomes obsessed with rereading and, inescapably, rewriting.

Rereading as Rewriting: Reading in the Second Degree

There is little doubt that Baudelaire's "hypocritical reader" is first and foremost a poet or "maker" (*poietes* in Greek). This reader is a highly skilled and knowledgeable craftsman or, to paraphrase Henry James, a squeezer of the literary material, not so much for meaning as for new, unsuspected *possibilities* of meaning and creative literary play. Even when perusing a text for the first time, such a reader is also a mental rereader and rewriter. Not only do creative readers construct a "virtual text" (every reader does that) but they are fully conscious of doing so. What is more, given the rules of the game as well as the specific problems (of diction, plot, characterization, verisimilitude, surprise) that the text poses, they keep imagining different strategies and trying out richer, subtler, better solutions. Earlier (in chapter 5) I referred to Henry James's statement that he simply could not read a novel which did not tempt him to rewrite it. James makes a similar point about reading as a form of imaginary rewriting in a letter to Mrs. W. K. Clifford: "My only way of reading . . . is to imagine myself *writing* the thing before me, treating the subject. . . . I find G. W. [the initials stand for the title of Mrs. Clifford's recently published novel] very brisk and alive. . . . What I feel critically . . . is that you don't *squeeze* your material hard and tight enough. . . . *I* squeeze as I read you— but that, as I say, is rewriting!" (*Letters*, vol. 4, p. 617).

In a larger sense, all literary writing has its ultimate root in such mental rewriting. Certain modes and genres are of course more directly and recognizably derived from it. Consider parody. In its simplest but not necessarily crudest forms, parody is explicitly a case of rewriting, transposing, or recasting an original in a playfully mocking mode. In the more

· · ·

complex types of parody, often combined with noncomical forms of intertextuality such as imitation, adaptation, allusion, and re-creation in a different mode or genre, the mocking techniques of rewriting may themselves end up looking so subtly ambiguous that parody dissolves into a sort of gently ironical or joyously playful homage to the original. In its classical embodiments—consider the mock-heroic or seriocomic genres, an elegant example of which is Pope's *The Rape of the Lock*—parody remains the clearest example of ludic bitextuality. It is, however, by no means the only or even dominant mode of bitextuality.

The vast phenomenon of rewriting has been studied by numerous modern critics from a variety of perspectives. The Russian Formalists have insisted on "defamiliarization" and deviation from the norm. Mikhail Bakhtin proposed a more complex, dialectical theory of dialogism and "carnivalization." More recently, the structuralists and the poststructuralists have seen rewriting in terms intertextuality, some stressing the ludic element (Roland Barthes in the later part of his career, Jacques Derrida in his commentaries on Mallarmé, Joyce, or Celan), while others have preferred an agonistic or confrontational model derived from Freud's theory of repression. Perhaps the best illustration of this last position is Harold Bloom's view of poetic production as a result of "the anxiety of influence," with its central tenet that "the meaning of a poem is always another poem."

One of the most helpful general studies of rewriting, Gérard Genette's *Palimpsestes* (1982), bears directly, although only partially, on the problematic of literature and play. *Palimpsestes* is entirely devoted to "literature in the second degree," or literature derived through various kinds of transformation or "transtextualization" from earlier literature. Leaving aside its cumbersome technical terminology of "textuality" (transtextuality, paratextuality, hypertextuality, hypotextuality, architextuality) *Palimpsestes* is a learned essay, rich in lucid observations and well-chosen examples, on textual transformations ranging from comic reduction— parodies and other such games—to serious "transposition," as exemplified by such works as Joyce's *Ulysses,* Thomas Mann's *Doktor Faustus,* or Michel Tournier's *Vendredi* (a rewriting of *Robinson Crusoe*).[6]

There are two points in *Palimpsestes* with which I would take issue. The first concerns Genette's limited view of play or the ludic element in literature as applying only to nonserious textual transformations (obvious parodies, burlesques, Oulipo-type games).[7] But play, as I have maintained in this chapter, in both the sense of games of make-believe and games with

. . .

rules, cannot be confined to certain literary genres or modes: play is central to the category of fictionality as such, on which the very possibility of literature and therefore of literary (re)reading is founded.

The notion of reading brings me to my second critical point. Genette's overall perspective in *Palimpsestes,* even when he occasionally mentions reading (reading, however, seen only as a disembodied textual function), remains unshakably text-centered. This does not come as a surprise from an orthodox structuralist—a textual engineer, if I may say so—like Genette and, moreover, it is not without certain advantages: it makes a systematic, clearly outlined, almost technologically precise treatment of textual issues possible. On the other hand, such a perspective cannot but ignore the *creativity* of (re)reading.

I now want to examine some cases of modern or postmodern creative rewriting that are immediately related to the question of (re)reading and that find their ultimate aesthetic justification in making reading a fully self-conscious ludic process. Let us take a closer look at the first two published novels by Alain Robbe-Grillet, *The Erasers* (1953) and *The Voyeur* (1955), both of them rewritings of basic types of mystery stories.

Rereading Robbe-Grillet's The Erasers

The plot of *The Erasers* goes back to the archetypal mystery plot, the Oedipal situation. Sophocles' Oedipus is not only the first detective in world literature but also the first murderer to be discovered as a result of a successful investigation. Paradoxically, the investigation is conducted by the murderer himself, an idea that Robbe-Grillet preserves. But the plot of *The Erasers* is also anti-Oedipal in one important sense: whereas the Oedipal paradigm requires us to look for an *earlier* crime (the unsolved slaying of Laius) as an explanation of the present crisis (the plague that has hit Thebes and the ensuing turmoil), in Robbe-Grillet's story the clumsy detective, Wallas, investigates a murder that has not taken place (the botched attempt on the life of Professor Daniel Dupont by the hired killer Garinati), only to become himself the murderer, exactly twenty-four hours later, when he shoots Dupont, his symbolic father, in a scene of mistaken identities and roles. Wallas, the special investigator sent from the center to the unnamed provincial Flemish city where the action of *The Erasers* is set, is ostensibly the representative of the law but in fact becomes the unsuspecting instrument of the terrorist Bona, who for undisclosed reasons wants Professor Dupont killed, as the ninth victim in a

. . .

series of ten carefully planned murders (the tenth murder, mentioned in the epilogue, is that of a merchant named Albert Dupont, and its perpetrator is a certain Monsieur André who might be Wallas or someone using his name). One assumes that Bona wants to send a message—but to whom? And for what purpose? The murders are devised as a manner of writing—but writing what?

Such questions, which come up in a second, analytical reading of the novel, are never answered. That Bona's reasons remain unknown is a comment on the lack of importance of reasons (and more generally verisimilitude) in the second-degree detective story that Robbe-Grillet offers for a second-degree ludic reading. Important here is that instead of solving a crime, the investigation leads to one. But is the investigation real? The relationship between Wallas—named by paronomasia after the writer of detective fiction Edgar Wallace—and Garinati is at times so ambiguous that the reader may legitimately think that Wallas is not only a phony detective but even a stand-in or double of Garinati. And the ending (the accidental actual killing of Daniel Dupont) turns out not to be the real (textual) ending, since it is followed (as we are told in the epilogue) by another murder, that of the wood merchant Albert Dupont. Moreover, the linearity of the main plot is constantly challenged by instances of repetition (both duplication and recurrence), which is symbolized by the Boulevard Circulaire in the unnamed city of Wallas's endless wanderings in circles.

The great model of such metaphysical mysteries remains Borges's story "Death and the Compass," with which Robbe-Grillet was certainly familiar when he wrote *Les Gommes*.[8] Paradoxical in a precise logical sense and thus comparable to other cases of famous aporias (the Cretan liar declaring that he is a liar or Zeno's demonstrations of the impossibility of movement), Borges's tale has the murderer Red Scharlach trap the reasoner Lönnrot (an Auguste Dupin/Sherlock Holmes type of investigator) by means of a succession of three carefully thought-out murders. The first one, whose victim is a Talmudic scholar, Doctor Marcel Yarmolinsky, is accidental,[9] but it suggests to Scharlach the possibility of the Kabbalistically and geometrically devised next two. The three murders taken together represent, unmistakably if perversely, the first three letters of the Tetragrammaton (JHVH, the secret, unspeakable name of God) as well as three of the four cardinal points on the compass (North, West, East). Temporally, the murders are separated by exactly one month; spatially, they occur at the tips of an equilateral triangle (North, West, East),

. . .

suggesting that the fourth and final murder must take place in the south of Buenos Aires, at a point indicated by the symmetrical opposite of the northernmost point (the Hôtel du Nord) on the map. The perfect triangle thus becomes a perfect square (the two shapes accord with the numerology of threes and fours in the story). When Scharlach finally succeeds in making Lönnrot come to Triste-le-Roy, the place of the fourth murder, Lönnrot the sophisticated reasoner suddenly discovers that the intended victim this time is necessarily, inescapably, mathematically none other than himself. Like Robbe-Grillet's *The Erasers,* where the symbol of "erasers" is part of the larger paradigm of writing, Borges's story is ultimately about writing and rewriting and, implicitly, about reading and rereading: the pair *murderer/detective* subtly and ironically corresponds to the pair *author/reader.*

The background knowledge that the implied reader of *The Erasers* is expected to have is threefold: a certain familiarity with the "classics" of literature (especially the main episodes of the Oedipus myth and its treatment by Sophocles) as well as with the way the "moderns" have dealt with similar mythical scenarios (as for instance Joyce in his version of the *Odyssey*); an acquaintance with the narrative conventions of detective fiction itself; and, last, an awareness of the conventions and stylistic features of "realistic," Balzacian novel writing. These three backgrounds are necessary for the reader to make sense of the three planes on which Robbe-Grillet's novel evolves: the plane of literary allusions, particularly to *Oedipus Rex* and the place of Oedipus in the Western cultural heritage; the plane on which the text plays, both parodically and "seriously," with themes, techniques, strategies of storytelling, and stereotypes of mystery narratives; and the more polemical plane on which the novel rejects "realistic" literature, with its vaunted transparency to reality as well as its ideal of representation, introducing startlingly new, self-conscious, self-questioning, and often self-canceling conventions.

What I have said thus far may convey the idea that an actual reading of the novel is an enormously complex affair. This is doubtless so as long as we approach it as a traditional novel. Readers who come to the text with the wrong expectations will see them repeatedly thwarted and are likely to give up soon. They may well possess the necessary threefold knowledge and still feel so disoriented that they will fail to summon the relevant information at the right junctures, and will be unable to activate and alternate the appropriate reading codes in the order demanded by the text. As a consequence, they will be bored and possibly furious.

· · ·

On the other hand, read in a context that provides a general sense of orientation, *The Erasers* becomes not only readable but even entertaining. Such a context is, for example, a college course on literature, in which the process of literary reading tends to become more self-conscious and indeed closer to the nature of rereading. Used in a course, say, on the evolution of the novel as a genre, or on types of modern fiction, or on the relationship between popular literature and the avant-garde, Robbe-Grillet's novel will appear to be both easier to read and, from the instructor's viewpoint, easier to teach than some classics of modern fiction (infinitely simpler than Proust, Joyce, Faulkner, Musil, or Thomas Mann). The secret of a work like Robbe-Grillet's *The Erasers* is that, behind its forbidding but actually quite superficial difficulties, it is essentially an ingenious toy that lends itself to didactic usage: a verbal toy for self-conscious reading, rereading, and metareading, or reading in the second degree, to paraphrase Genette's notion of "literature in the second degree."

Unreadable under ordinary circumstances, Robbe-Grillet becomes a highly readable and rereadable author (and, what is more, readable with *fun,* as many of my undergraduate students in courses on contemporary fiction have been surprised to find out) under special, mostly didactic, circumstances: this would explain the academic success of such an otherwise difficult, artificial, quirky, often pretentious and sometimes absurdly contrived author. Analyzing *The Erasers* is like discovering how to play with a complicated, odd, and esoteric-looking toy: one comes to understand the meaning and function of each part within the whole.

To go through the two-hundred-odd pages of *The Erasers* one needs first and foremost the guidance of a reliable narrative thread of actions that could be taken as fictionally true. In other words, the text should provide the reader with some essential props, some minimally necessary elements of fictional truth, which should enable him or her to play, however sketchily, a game of make-believe of mystery and detection. But these elements are not offered immediately by the text, as they would be in a "normal" novel or even more emphatically in a mystery, the novelistic subgenre that Robbe-Grillet directly "imitates" and that is so heavily plot-dependent. This means that the reader—and here I have a hypothetical first-time reader in mind—has to search for such a narrative thread. In *The Erasers* this essential thread ends up appearing after the prologue, in which the implied author describes (in an obsessive present tense) the Kafkaesque roamings of the special investigator Wallas through the strange

. . .

unnamed city in which he is supposed to conduct his investigation. With the help of this thread the reader manages to connect, in sequential order, the fictionally true—or at least potentially true—scenes of *The Erasers,* selected from other scenes that are fictionally "fictitious." In the case of a traditional novel this selection is made for the reader by the text itself as a matter of course. But Robbe-Grillet refuses to demarcate clearly what is fictionally true (what a protagonist does or says, "what really happens" in the story) from what is fictionally fictitious (what a protagonist dreams, dreams up, fantasizes, vividly anticipates, imagines, hypothesizes, falsely remembers, projects, and so on). This refusal, whatever its motivation— ludic experimentalism seems to me more likely than the philosophical reasons adduced by some critics—has the consequence of showing how dramatically important the concept of fictional truth is in the reception of narrative works. *The Erasers* is perhaps not the best example in this respect, since the patient reader's expectation of a fictionally true detective plot with an element of suspense and a final surprise is eventually re- warded, if not without certain lingering ambiguities. In *The Voyeur,* how- ever, the reader's need for fictional truth is put to a much more severe test.

Rereading (The Voyeur) *for the Fictional Truth*

It is primarily in terms of fictional truth that readers of narrative texts conceive and pursue their games of make-believe. Once what is fictionally true in a story is clearly perceived, the various deviations from such truth as described in the text (as imaginings, lies, hallucinations, or whatever) may add important nuances and help to modulate the basic game of make- believe in unexpected, enriching ways. But in Robbe-Grillet the markers of *fiction within fiction* (expressed in traditional novels by means of such simple phrases as "he thought" or "remembered" or "imagined") are absent, whence the reader's difficulty in putting together a fictionally true, or even a fictionally-more-likely-than-others, narrative line. What the author is proposing here is not a game of make-believe but a game with rules—specifically, hidden rules—or perhaps a game consisting of a sys- tem of ingenious traps, snares, and textual ambushes for the reader, as Robbe-Grillet himself has maintained.[10] But this cannot change the funda- mental rule, without which one cannot speak of a fictional world (as opposed to meaningless, arbitrary fictional chaos), namely, the rule that within a fictional world one should in principle be able to separate be- tween fictional truth (or potential truth) and fictional types of fictitious-

. . .

ness—even when the latter perform as large a role as they do in many literary works from *Don Quixote* to Kafka's novels.

In the case of Cervantes the demarcation line between fictional truth and the hero's self-delusions is quite clear, although in the second part things tend to get more complicated. In the case of Kafka and other moderns (directly or indirectly influenced by Kafka) the separation becomes more problematic, but its possibility is always there, however teasingly elusive. This possibility of discerning fictional truth has nothing to do with "realism" or the "representation of reality": it is thus fictionally true that one morning Gregor Samsa, in "The Metamorphosis," wakes up as a giant bug or beetle, and it is fictionally true that one morning Joseph K. is arrested, in *The Trial,* and that at the end of the novel he is executed. Thus framed, the drama of Joseph K.'s mysterious and increasingly anguishing trial may consist of episodes whose fictional truth is undecidable; but even the most nightmarish scenes and the strangest occurrences contain a grain of fictional truth or potential fictional truth that makes them broadly believable and effective (in the make-believe mode) and thus gives them power over the imagination of the reader.

Without the dramatic ingredient of fictional truth the literary reading of works of any great length is simply impossible. If the fictional truth is not there, unambiguously provided by the text, one will always look for it, as one will always look for signs by which to orient oneself in unknown territory. Thus, even in Robbe-Grillet's polemically antirealistic novels there is actually more fictional truth (and quasi-realistic truth at that) than meets the eye. It is this element of fictional truth that allows us to summarize the plot of a novel like *The Voyeur.* Of course, we may not be interested in such a summary; but if we want one, we can put together a more or less convincing one, even though it may retain many "spots of indeterminacy" even after several careful readings. A structuralist analysis of Robbe-Grillet, like the one performed by Roland Barthes in "Littérature littérale" (originally published as a review of *The Voyeur* in 1955), can do without any references to plot or story, ignoring even the crucial fact that the novel is a mystery—a mystery of a special kind, not for reading (*against* reading would be perhaps a more appropriate description) but ultimately for rereading. In the 1950s, when he wrote this essay, Barthes was not yet interested in the process of either reading or rereading, as he would become in the 1960s. Among the early critics of Robbe-Grillet, the one who adopted a largely "spontaneous," nonsystematic, but sustained reader-response approach (derived from the tradition of close reading of the New

· · ·

Criticism) was the American Bruce Morrisette, the author of one of the analytically most helpful studies of Robbe-Grillet. Morrisette does not shun the critical task, usually looked down upon by avant-garde critics, of providing summaries or synopses of Robbe-Grillet's novels as starting points for more extensive critical discussions. In the course of putting together these plots, Morrisette cannot help using various equivalents of what I have called fictional truth, including potential fictional truth, a category relevant to modernist and postmodernist writing.

In the intricate plot of *The Voyeur* the event of central importance from the point of view of fictional truth—namely, the murder by the traveling salesman Mathias of the thirteen-year-old Jacqueline/Viola—is presented in the form of a gap at the very center of the novel, a gap that the reader must fill on the basis of clues or hints whose own fictional truth (or, by elimination, misleading character or falsehood) can be established only in relation to that central event. This raises serious difficulties, which might explain why some critics (Maurice Blanchot, Germaine Brée) have claimed that Mathias's crime happens only in his imagination. The difficulties, however, are not insurmountable, and the careful reader learns "to distinguish without intervention on the part of the author between reality, dream, memory, and, finally, paroxysmic vision," as Morrisette puts it (*The Novels of Robbe-Grillet,* p. 88). The narrative, alternating freely between present actions (fictionally true), memories (fictionally true but as part of a past that should be clearly distinguishable from the present), false memories, anticipations (fictionally possible), imaginary scenes and daydreams, inventions, lies, and alibis (all fictionally false), is constructed in such a way as to disorient readers as well as reveal to them, as a reward for their generous attention, a system of subtle criteria by which they can, if not really solve the narrative puzzle, at least see it for what it is: a puzzle that can be solved only in part. But even such a partial solution will help the patient reader put together a powerful story—or at least a frame for a possible game of make-believe—of obsession and crime. The text seems to hide a brutally sadistic fantasy. To get to its concealed meaning we need to reread for the secret (a question that I shall explore in Part IV).

The technique of hiding used by Robbe-Grillet is paradoxically one of verbally showing, of presenting cinematically. The possibilities, hypotheses, projections, and imaginings that go through Mathias's mind (the third-person narrative carries Mathias's point of view most of the time) are described in painstaking detail, dwelt upon as concrete-imagistic presences, scrutinized as if by a camera filming in slow motion. The verbal

. . .

result is lengthy and often repetitious-sounding descriptions, which the reader, to perceive the real differences among them, has to visualize. But visualizing—drawing mental images for words—slows down the process of reading and demands intense, unabated attention. In film, whose principal medium is the language of images (a language of much greater immediacy and simultancity than words), the effect of projecting parallel versions of the same event is more natural, as Robbe-Grillet himself once noted:

> Having granted memory, the spectator can also readily grant the imaginary, nor do we hear protests in neighborhood movie theaters, against those courtroom scenes in a detective story when we *see* a hypothesis concerning the circumstances of a crime, a hypothesis that can just as well be false as true, made mentally or verbally by the examining magistrate; and we then see, in the same way, during the testimony of various witnesses, some of whom are lying, other fragments of scenes that are more or less contradictory, more or less likely, but which are all presented with the same kind of image, the same realism, the same presentness, the same objectivity. And this is equally true if we are shown a scene in the future imagined by one of the characters, etc. (*Last Year at Marienbad*, p. 13)

This is quite so, but ordinary spectators have no trouble following the courtroom drama, first because they have a clear idea of the general context (a crime has taken place, there is a trial, witnesses, etc.) and second because the parallel versions presented on the screen are clearly attributed to specific characters, each character's version being self-consistent. Neither of these conditions is fulfilled in *The Voyeur*, in which the cinematic procedure is employed in another medium—literary fiction—experimentally and highly unconventionally.

The general premise suggested to the reader is that of a salesman of wristwatches taking a trip to a little island to ply his trade; that a heinous crime may have been committed is apparent only in the second half of the book. Moreover, the parallel versions of hypothetical scenes, memories, anticipations, and dramatized lies, with their blatant inconsistencies and mutually exclusive details, are all attributed (in the third-person narrative mode) to a single character, the salesman Mathias, whose point of view controls the center of the narrative field. This procedure violates both the principle of noncontradiction and the principle of nonreversibility, which a straight detective novel must always observe.

Thus, what in a typical detective story would be decoded automatically by a reader caught in a gripping narrative becomes in Robbe-Grillet's

. . .

mystery for rereading completely deautomatized through the insistent and repeated violation of an "ordinary" novel reader's expectations. Increasingly, described actions become strangely self-conscious, illogical, and outrageously self-contradictory. A tentative reading hypothesis in which these contradictions would become explainable, if not reconciled, can be reached only after a first attentive reading has been completed, and it can be tested only on rereading. Joseph Frank would say that Robbe-Grillet's narrative art is yet another modernist attempt at achieving fully "spatial form," or simultaneity, with the result that his literature is in fact unreadable and only rereadable. In the terms proposed here, a novel like *The Voyeur* is—and this constitutes its chief literary originality—an experiment in reading or the readable: the need for rereading would arise from the text's insistent deautomatization of the reading process. Deautomatized literary reading tends to become self-conscious and self-questioning, with attention focusing intensely on separate aspects of a reading act whose internal harmony can no longer be taken for granted. Such aspects, given the model of "pure" and therefore unself-conscious reading of mystery stories (visualizing as precisely as possible the scene of the crime, trying to memorize the details surrounding the crime for later use in solving the puzzle, making constant inferences and hypotheses), are torn from their conventional functional context and placed, as it were, under the magnifying glass of rereading.

The new rules of the game we are supposed to learn when we read and reread a novel like *Le Voyeur* are to a large extent deautomatized reversals of the old overlearned and routinized rules of reading detective fiction. Reading and rereading merge into an experience of second-degree reading—an experience for which students and teachers of literature are probably better prepared than ordinary readers or rereaders. This would explain the paradox of the academic popularity of an avant-garde author like Robbe-Grillet and, more generally, of the possibility of making good didactical use of certain kinds of unreadable texts intelligently, elegantly put together.

. . .

PART FOUR

Rereading for the Secret

· · · · · · ·

FIFTEEN

Introducing Secrecy:
Henry James's "The Private Life"

We were of the same general communion, chalk-marked for
recognition by signs from the same alphabet. . . . We were more or
less governed by the laws and the language, the traditions and
shibboleths of the same dense social state.

HENRY JAMES
"The Private Life"

· · · · · · ·

Few texts could provide a better informal introduction to the issues
raised by the notions of privacy and secrecy and by the roles that public
life imposes on us than Henry James's relatively little known novella "The
Private Life." In making this statement, of course, I have already framed
my rereading of the story, and this cannot but influence what I shall see
in it, what parts of it I shall be sensitive to and what parts I shall, willy-
nilly, leave unattended. Other frames would naturally lead to different
(re)readings.

A brief preliminary definition of the term *secrecy* will be helpful in
specifying the frame of my rereading. By *secrecy* I mean the calculated and
selective concealment of information. Several fundamental aspects of
secrecy are covered by this definition: (1) its deliberateness (someone
decides to hide knowledge of something); (2) its selectivity (the knowledge

· · ·

is hidden from some but not from all); (3) the double coding of the message: it may be publicly coded so as to convey spurious or deceptive or merely neutral information to the layman and at the same time secretly coded so as to convey the privileged information to the initiate only; (4) the implication that the concealed information can always be disclosed, made public, betrayed, guessed, or independently discovered by those whom it is designed to exclude; and (5) the additional implication that secrecy, not unlike play, activates a metacommunicational level or function: a secret message, whether doubly coded or not, always instructs its privileged addressee that it is secret and that it should be treated as such, kept in confidence and not be divulged.[1] Play, then, may have its secret dimensions and secrecy its playful ones, and many other reciprocal relationships between the two are possible. One of them is especially interesting to the student of (re)reading: our playful urge to crack codes that are meant to exclude us, our perception of someone else's secrets as challenges to our interpretive ingenuity. These matters shall be taken up in more detail in chapters 16 and 17.

Let us now consider the "The Private Life." The story cannot easily be summarized, but before going into how the text relates to the issues of secrecy we must recall the main elements of its plot. At the end of a holiday season around 1890 a group of English travelers, all of them artists ("all of us, even the ladies, 'did' something," the narrator recounts, and that "something" was of an artistic nature), are reunited in Switzerland by a happy coincidence. There are five fully drawn characters who are directly involved in the strange central events of the story. Lord and Lady Mellifont (he is a painter, her occupation remains unclear), the great novelist Clare Vawdrey, the celebrated comedienne Blanche Adney, and the unnamed first-person narrator (a young writer who, we understand, has been less than successful as a playwright: perhaps an alter ego of James himself). A sixth character, Mrs. Adney's husband, Vincent Adney, the "fond musician," is more effaced and seemingly unaware of what is going on around him.

But what happens in "The Private Life"? The reader is told about two startling discoveries. First is Mrs. Adney's discovery that Lord Mellifont, the charming public man, literally ceases to exist when he is without a public: when nobody pays attention to him he vanishes like a ghost. The second, made by the narrator, is that Clare Vawdrey is actually two people: one is an uninspiring, banal, gregarious socializer; the other, Vawdrey's mysterious creative double, uncannily seems to write his works

· · ·

for him at night, in the dark, in a state of total trance and self-oblivion. The two physically identical versions of Vawdrey can be in different places and do different things at the same time; they evidently stand for the two sides of an artist's self: the public and the private.

How are the contrasting "secrets" of Lord Mellifont's socially embarrassing invisibility (meaning private inexistence) and Clare Vawdrey's eerie doubleness uncovered? What renders them vulnerable? The answer is found at the very beginning of the story, from which the epigraph to this chapter is taken. All the characters knew each other from London, where they belonged to the same world or "general communion" or, might we say, informal secret society, with its exclusive laws, customs, passwords, and other tacitly shared signs of recognition. While in London—that is, under the usual circumstances of their social encounters—they interacted within the frame of a certain game of sociability or social conversation,[2] a game whose rules required them not to touch on personal matters and also to carefully avoid talking shop (a grave lapse of taste); in Switzerland, however, at the end of a holiday period, they somehow agree "to be different," to be more "human," that is, more direct and candid about themselves. In England, the narrator tells us, "all of us, even the ladies, 'did' something, though we pretended we didn't when it was mentioned. Such things aren't mentioned indeed in London, but it was our innocent pleasure to be different here" (p. 218).

It is in this more relaxed atmosphere of collegial intimacy that the personal secrets of Vawdrey and Lord Mellifont become more vulnerable. A reexamination of the text reveals that the characters with secrets are the first to be more extensively portrayed: first Vawdrey (always equal to himself, always banal in society, unable to "utter a paradox or express a shade or play with an idea," p. 220); then Lord Mellifont, whose presentation is anticipated by that of his wife, Lady Mellifont, strangely, mysteriously looking like a widow ("in perpetual mourning," p. 221). Lady Mellifont's dark appearance tells us more about her husband than we can possibly understand on a first reading, and it gives a second reading (once we know that Lord Mellifont is indeed a ghost of sorts) a strong symbolic dimension.

Significantly, it is in speaking of Lady Mellifont that the narrator uses the word *secret* for the first time. True, the intimation of a certain kind of secrecy, of a vague secret-society mentality characteristic of the "dense social state" to which the characters belonged, had occurred earlier in the story. But that diffuse atmosphere of secrecy suggested by the characters'

· · ·

sharing in exclusive habits and rituals was of a decidedly social, not a private kind: and the story, as its title shows, looks at people and situations from the perspective of privacy.

The distinction between social secrets and private ones is important, and I shall be saying more about it before long. For the time being, let us consider Lady Mellifont's portrait: "I had originally been rather afraid of her, thinking her, with her stiff silences and the extreme blackness of almost everything that made up her person, somewhat hard, even a little saturnine. . . . She was in perpetual mourning and wore numberless ornaments of jet and onyx, a thousand clicking chains and bugles and beads. I heard Mrs. Adney call her the Queen of Night. . . . She had a secret. . . . She was like a woman with a painless malady (pp. 221–22).

The secret, the painless but incurable disease from which Lady Mellifont suffers and which, as we learn later in the story, she prefers to keep hidden or half-hidden even from herself, is her consciousness of her husband's personal inexistence, of his lack of a private being, and of the fact that his very perfection and "finishedness" as a social persona or mask might hide not a face but the hollowness of death. To put it differently: the secret of Lady Mellifont, which is also the secret of Lord Mellifont, is that he has no personal secrets and no privacy, which in turn is a form of death. (A brief parenthesis here: secrecy can obviously exist without privacy— the case of the initiatory rituals of many secret societies as well as the signs of recognition and shibboleths of social groups—but privacy without an ability to have personal secrets, without an ability to withhold or conceal information about one's intimacy or one's deeper personal identity, is inconceivable.)

The subsequent portrait of Lord Mellifont suggests that his public image is disquietingly indistinguishable from the reputation of a dead man. James proposes a series of analogies that point to the idea of death with uncanny insistence. Thus, the mere mention of Lord Mellifont gave one a "sense of speaking of the dead," and his "reputation was a kind of gilded obelisk, as if he had been buried beneath it; the body of legend and reminiscence of which he was to be the subject had crystallized in advance" (p. 226).

The plot of "The Private Life" revolves in large part around the figure of the charming actress Blanche Adney, who has been promised a play by Clare Vawdrey, a play that, as the narrator discovers, Vawdrey's secret, private double is writing for him. Some of the paradoxes of theater, more particularly of acting, as an art of disclosing secrets that may not exist

· · ·

(both onstage and offstage), are subtly woven into the portrait of the actress. Blanche carries her acting into social life, where she consummately plays the role of an actress:

> It is difficult to be cursory over this charming woman, who was beautiful without beauty and complete with a dozen deficiencies. The perspective of the stage made her over, and in society she was like the model off the pedestal. She was a picture walking about, which to the artless social mind was a perpetual surprise—a miracle. People thought she told them secrets of the pictorial nature, in return for which they gave her relaxation and tea. She told them nothing and she drank the tea; but they had all the same the best of the bargain. (p. 229)

"Beautiful without beauty" is a memorable formula for conveying the mysterious power of theatrical illusion, whether that illusion is experienced in the theater proper, as it occurs in the "magic box" of the stage during a performance, or affects our perception of social situations in ordinary life, which is not without its theatrical dimension. It is hardly necessary to recall here the ancientness and pervasiveness of the vocabulary of theater in descriptions of social relations—from the fatalistic literary topoi of the world as theater and of life as a stage on which people are actors performing their preordained roles, to modern specialized approaches—rhetorical, psychological, sociological—which use a theatrical model for the analysis of communication in terms of roles and role expectations.

What is central to "The Private Life," insofar as it is a story not only about secrecy but also about theatricality, is the problem of fictionality or the as-if. Blanche Adney behaves as if she were beautiful and becomes indeed a woman who is beautiful without beauty; but we must not forget that she is a professional actress and that her achievement of beauty without beauty is a measure of her talent and of the particular kind of creativity involved in her métier, that of impersonating imaginary characters with imaginary qualities and making them appear compellingly "real" and convincing. Lord Mellifont, the social paragon, is also a past master at manipulating the as-if of pure sociability, almost in Georg Simmel's sense of sociability as a social version of a game played for its own sake. But, in the case of Mellifont, this comes into conflict with his professional and personal duty to his art, namely, painting. In other words, in letting himself be totally absorbed by the performance of his social role as the eternal host or patron or "moderator at every board"

· · ·

(p. 227), in overdoing the protean performance of tactfulness and external style, in bringing too much art to it, he has little if anything left to give to his painting. He is so used to pretending that rather than paint he pretends to be painting. But, as James seems to imply, this kind of theatricality cancels the privacy that fosters genuine art: Lord Mellifont socializes his private (and artistic) self out of existence. Blanche Adney's notion that in terms of "filling the stage" he easily beats her is quite correct. His stage may be anywhere: his theatrical presence transforms even the sublime landscape of a "great bristling primeval glacier" into a decorative stage set.

It is naturally only on rereading the story that we can grasp the more subtle and, as it were, tantalizing implications of the theatrical vocabulary used by the narrator to describe the "spectacle" of Lord Mellifont sketching in the mountains:

> He painted while he talked and he talked while he painted; and if the painting was as miscellaneous as the talk, the talk would equally have graced an album. We stayed while the exhibition went on. . . . All nature deferred to him and the very elements waited. Blanche Adney communed with me dumbly, and I could read the language of her eyes: "Oh if *we* could do it as well as that! He fills the stage in a way that beats us." We could no more have left him than we could have quitted the theater till the play was over. (pp. 257–58)

Lord Mellifont finally produces a watercolor which he gracefully offers to Blanche, but omits to sign it. This omission is narratively quite important because it determines the subsequent episode. Knowing from Blanche the strange story of Lord Mellifont's disappearances, the narrator volunteers to seek him in his apartments at the inn and to request his signature on the watercolor: this is obviously a pretext for the narrator to satisfy his curiosity, to verify if his lordship indeed ceases to exist in private circumstances. The narrator assumes that Lord Mellifont is alone and, in order to surprise him, plans to open the door quickly and without knocking in advance (breaking a rule of polite behavior in order to penetrate a secret): "If I were to knock I should spoil everything. . . . I had gone so far as to lay my hand on the knob when I became aware (having my wits so about me) that exactly in the manner I was thinking of—gently, gently, without a sound—another door had moved, and on the opposite side of the hall. At the same instant I found myself smiling rather constrainedly at Lady Mellifont" (p. 260).

· · ·

Lady Mellifont almost soundlessly implores the narrator, "Don't!" He reads in her eyes "the confession of her own curiosity and the dread of the consequences of mine. . . . From the moment my experiment could strike her as an act of violence I was ready to renounce it; yet I thought I caught from her frightened face a still deeper betrayal—a possibility of disappointment if I should give way. It was as if she had said: 'I'll let you do it if you take the responsibility. Yes, with someone else I'd surprise him. But it would never do for him to think it was I' " (p. 261). But at the last moment Lady Mellifont is able to resist her "temptation"—forcing the narrator to resist his—and thus misses her "great chance" to find out the full truth about her husband.

What is remarkable about this passage—and even more so on rereading and on trying to see the whole story from its perspective—is the way it brings out, discreetly but unmistakably, the entangled social and psychological consequences of secrecy. Once one identifies (rightly or wrongly) someone else's secret, one almost automatically posits an intention not simply to hide—to keep something private—but also to deceive or trick, which in turn seems to legitimize the use of deception or trickery to penetrate the secret. The narrator, when his curiosity is stimulated, starts acting like a peeping Tom and a spy. He is ready to circumvent or break the rules of civilized behavior—in secret, of course, when he is not seen— and gives up what he tellingly calls his "experiment" only when he becomes convinced that it might be perceived as an "act of violence"— which, by the way, it would certainly be, at least symbolically.

Interestingly, when Lady Mellifont catches the narrator in what appears to be an act of spying, she feels for a moment infected by his curiosity and tempted to go along with his experiment—a case of sheer fascination with both learning and betraying the secret of her husband. (The fascination of betrayal is one of major themes of Simmel's reflections on secrecy, which have in large part shaped my reading of James's story.) Lady Mellifont is, in other words, confronted by a dilemma: should she discover the half-guessed truth of her husband's lack of a private ego by letting the narrator proceed with his intrusion, or should she rather protect his secret, his spot of vulnerability, by choosing to remain herself ignorant or half-ignorant? In the story, of course, she chooses to carry on with her secret disease—the "painless malady" of her husband's undisclosed secret.

Although ostensibly "The Private Life" is a story of the supernatural, and more precisely a variety of ghost story, its abundant use of ambiguity

. . .

is not of the sort that makes the reader hesitate between two incompatible but equally plausible sets of explanations, as required by Todorov's definition of the fantastic which so suited *The Turn of the Screw*. In Todorovian terms the fantastic of "The Private Life" is no more than a mere hint that dissolves into the symbolic long before the first reading is completed. In other words, this apparent ghost story is in fact a parable. On rereading, its ambiguities turn out to be of a type perfectly in keeping with the genre of parable, whose mode of address is at once exoteric and esoteric, and thus premised on a distinction between outsiders and insiders among its listeners or readers. To put it differently, parabolic texts are by definition texts with secrets, texts that are doubly coded in order to hide their "true" meaning from some while revealing it to others. From that standpoint "The Private Life" is a parable twice over: not only does it have secrets but it also chooses secrecy—at least insofar as secrecy and privacy coincide— as its main theme.

That "The Private Life" is a parable or allegory affects particularly the nature of rereading. The first time around, the story will probably be read as a game of make-believe: the basic elements for playing such a game—a narrative, characters presented in some detail, the occurrence of certain strange, intriguing events—are clearly there. But on this level it appears to be not entirely satisfying. One feels increasingly that the story's strength lies elsewhere, and that to enjoy it better one has to decipher its secret allusions.

James himself fully disclosed in the preface to the New York Edition one of the two central hermeneutical clues to the story: that the doubleness of Vawdrey had been his own fictional (and admittedly "whimsical") solution to the "puzzle" that had "mystified" him for many years, the puzzle of the split personality of Robert Browning, "a rich proud genius one adored" and at the same time a totally "undistinguished" man. In order to dramatize this case of double personality, "to supply the 'drama,' . . . the precious element of contrast and antithesis," the author of "The Private Life" set it against the case of someone who does not even have a single personality, who seems to lack "any private and domestic *ego*" (p. xiv). Although James admitted that this second character—the second central hermeneutical clue—was also based on a personage from the same social "London world" of the time, for obvious reasons he did not mention the name of the real model, who was the painter Sir Frederic Leighton, the president of the Royal Academy.[3]

The question arises: what is the relationship between such allusions

. . .

(and more generally between narratives *à clef*) and secrecy? The immediate answer would be that, functionally, allusions are akin to secrecy insofar as their understanding justifies making a distinction between insiders and outsiders. If secrecy is a deliberate concealment of information for limited and privileged sharing, then James's conception of Vawdrey/Browning and Lord Mellifont/Lord Leighton participates somehow in the nature of secrecy. But how? In trying to answer that question, we come up against the social, historical, and, I would say, situational characteristics of secrecy.

In 1892, when "The Private Life" appeared in the *Atlantic Monthly*, the possibility of identifying Vawdrey as a fictionalization of Robert Browning was strictly limited to the circle of Henry James's intimates and close friends; even the most careful rereading of the story by an "outsider" would not have yielded that specific insight. If one does not have an inkling, or the right assumption based on privileged information, a secret of this kind simply cannot be decoded; since it remains totally invisible, it cannot even be identified as a secret. In 1909, when James disclosed in the preface to volume 17 of the New York Edition, *The Altar of the Dead*, the real identity of Vawdrey, the status of the secret allusion to Browning became that of an "open secret," at least for the devotees and critical readers of Henry James.

In a great writer, in a writer whose work comes alive both when we read and, more mysteriously, when we reread it, such an open secret does not lose its fascination by virtue of its being open. Its continued appeal derives in large part from its ability to suggest other similar, but not yet open or not entirely open, secret dimensions of the writer's work. Even today, when a first reading of "The Private Life" might well be done with a prior awareness of the Vawdrey-Browning connection, the character of Vawdrey may lead to further explorations of the world of Henry James in its enigmatic relation to the world of Robert Browning. Such explorations, if pursued, will confront one with a new kind of secrets, the *professional secrets* of a major artist, or what we might call metaphorically his creative laboratory, including his art of (re)reading the works of other writers. Indeed, nowhere is James's peculiar way of reading as rewriting more extensively illustrated than in his 1912 lecture, given on the occasion of the centenary of Browning's birth, "The Novel in *The Ring and the Book*," later published in *Notes on Novelists*.

But is all this still relevant to the question of secret allusions in "The Private Life"? The immediate answer is no—Vawdrey could not possibly

. . .

allude to a lecture on Browning that James was to deliver two decades later. But this negative answer becomes much less trenchant if we adopt the point of view of the reader and the particular logic generated by the circular time of reading. Secretly or not, "The Novel in *The Ring and the Book*" is in several ways relevant to a rereading of "The Private Life." First, it is the fullest statement by James on Browning as an artist and, what is more, as an artist at his best, that is, as the author of a universally acclaimed masterpiece; second, it refers back, however briefly and allusively, to "The Private Life";[4] third, it casts a new and revealing light on the Jamesian conception of Browning's creative privacy or intimacy. This last point deserves attention both for its intrinsic intellectual interest and for its clarifying value in regard to an easily overlooked but vital detail in "The Private Life"—namely, that Vawdrey/Browning is described as a *novelist* and not as a poet. Let us consider the following key passage from James's lecture, the paragraph that deals with the typically *poetic* urge for expression "at any cost," as James puts it:

> That, essentially, *is* the world of poetry—which in the cases known to our experience where it seems to us to differ from Browning's world does so but through this latter's having been, by the vigor and violence, the bold familiarity, of his grasp and pull at it, moved several degrees nearer us, so to speak, than any other of the same general sort with which we are acquainted; so that, intellectually, we back away from it a little, back down before it, again and again, as we try to get off from a picture or a group or a view which is too much *upon* us and thereby out of focus. Browning is "upon" us, straighter upon us always, somehow, than anyone else of his race . . . as if he came up against us, each time, on the same side of the street and not on the other side, across the way, where we mostly see the poets elegantly walk, and where we greet them without danger of concussion. It is on the same side, as I call it, on *our* side, on the other hand, that I rather see our encounter with the novelists taking place. (pp. 468–69)

This extraordinary sense of closeness and creative intimacy—which for James results from our inevitably personal involvement with great prose writing rather than from our "greeting" more formally the aloof and ceremoniously "elegant" figures of poetry—gives us a clue as to why Browning is portrayed as a novelist in James's fable. It also explains the peculiar meaning attached by him to the *privacy of genius*—privacy as a wellspring of creative imagination. And, finally, in speaking so memorably about the intimacy of the relationship achieved by the reader and the writer of fiction, he brings out one of the essential preconditions of what

· · ·

we might call the shared creativity of the act of reading, a notion that forms the theme of the whole lecture-essay. "The Novel in *The Ring and the Book*" is James's most complete, sophisticated, and clearly articulated statement on his method ("wretched" as he once qualified it with a characteristic touch of self-irony) of *reading as rewriting,* of which we find many accounts in his letters;[5] it certainly is his most comprehensive attempt to compare a real text, Browning's poem, with a "virtual text," which is the result of an act of both co-creation and, more boldly, re-creation.

The reader of James's 1909 preface to "The Private Life" is, as we have seen, kept in the dark about the real-life model for Lord Mellifont. His identification with Lord Leighton remained a secret shared probably only by James's intimate friends, perhaps as an article of private gossip, until it was revealed posthumously in biographical studies and comments on his *Notebooks* when these were published. This raises another aspect of secrecy as withholding of information: secrecy as a form of social reticence or discretion, the image of Lord Mellifont being more damaging to the reputation of its model, Lord Leighton, not only artistically but also personally, than the image of Vawdrey is to Browning. The relationship between secrecy and gossip—gossip as a blamable activity, but also gossip seen anthropologically as a kind of informal epistemological sharing of private information about others—is too complex to get into now. It will suffice here to briefly point to the triple interconnection between (personal) secrecy, gossip, and prose fiction: secrecy of a personal kind is invariably the subject of gossip, and gossip, as has been observed many times, is a loose paradigm of the novel, which could well be described as a fictional form of gossip.[6] "The Private Life" can serve as an apt example of artistic extension and fictional elaboration of gossip. At the same time, our own readerly interest in pursuing secretive or half-secretive biographical allusions (to Browning and Leighton, but also potentially to other characters: might not Blanche Adney also have a real-life model?) is clearly akin to that curiosity which gives gossip its particular flavor.

The secrets of Lady Mellifont, Clare Vawdrey, and Lord Mellifont remain ultimately elusive; they are accidentally "discovered" by outsiders (the narrator, Blanche) but never fully verified. But even if they were narratively elucidated in terms of indubitable fictional truth, they would continue to remain enigmatic and open to interpretation on the level on which the story is a parable or allegory about art and types of artists. Even the more precise extratextual secrets of this story *à clef* (the Vawdrey-

. . .

237

Browning or the Mellifont-Leighton connections) open directions of understanding that cannot be easily closed. The portrayal of Vawdrey points to a whole implicit Jamesian *philosophy of reading*—reading Browning as a novelist, reading poetry as prose, reading as writing or rewriting virtual texts. The portrayal of Leighton points to a more social-informal and apparently more frivolous use of secrecy as an object of gossip—gossip being itself nothing but stories about secrets. But is fiction essentially different? Is it not in some sense, in the mode of the as-if, also "stories about secrets"? And then is not "The Private Life" ultimately an allegory of fiction itself?

. . .

SIXTEEN

Understanding Texts with Secrets

The Role of Secrecy in Stimulating Reader Interest

The rereading of Henry James's "The Private Life" accomplished in the last chapter has barely begun to suggest the complexity of the problematic of secrecy in literature. Even so, it has offered us a few elementary coordinates for orienting a broader discussion of secrecy in relation to reading and rereading. One of these coordinates, which is directly relevant to the reading of narrative fiction, is the correlation between secrecy and curiosity, as revealed, for example, in the phenomenon of gossip. If we agree that, on a "naive" level, reading a piece of fiction is playing a game of make-believe, we implicitly recognize that the reader's interest in the game is at least in part akin to that of a recipient of gossip, of one who is made privy to the secrets of other people—imaginary people in the event. As D. W. Harding notes in "Psychological Processes in the Reading of Fiction": "Important aspects of fiction are illuminated if the reader of a novel is compared with the man who hears about other people and their doings in the course of ordinary gossip" (p. 59). By its very nature, a "normal" fictional text promises to make certain significant disclosures about certain interesting inhabitants of a fictional world. The logic of the novel is in a way analogous to the logic of disclosing secrets; but whereas in reality we know the people whose secrets excite us when they are revealed to us, in literature we must first get acquainted with them, since we usually are

. . .

not interested in the secrets of people whom we do not know. The writer's art consists to a large extent in making such imaginary beings and their world present to the reader's mind.

This art may include the skillful use of techniques of "enigmatization" of narrative information and plot construction. Enigma must be distinguished from secrecy: an enigma is a riddle, a puzzle, at the limit a purely mathematical puzzle, whereas secrets always involve human agency and people intentionally and selectively concealing information from other people. The techniques of enigma in literature (and particularly in fiction) involve the manipulation of narrative data to create suspense along the lines of what Barthes calls the hermeneutic code or, alternatively, "the code of the enigma"; but they are only indirectly related to the question of secrecy as such. From the point of view of poetics, the various uses of gaps—temporary gaps or retarding structures meant to create suspense, and permanent gaps that shape the plot and determine strategic ambiguities (these ambiguities may create a retrospective curiosity)—have been studied in some detail by, for example, Meir Sternberg in his *Expositional Modes and Temporal Ordering in Fiction* (1978). Such studies, however, rarely if ever deal with the question of secrecy in literature and, more specifically, in the reading and rereading of literary works. Aside from the calculated suppression or release of narrative information, a text may be perceived as containing secrets, as withholding or concealing important information under the guise of offering innocuous, unproblematic, smooth literary entertainment. The code of the enigma and various kinds of ostensible fictional secrets—disclosed in varieties of fictional gossip— can be used as diversionary maneuvers to hide other, deeper secrets ranging from the personal to the political. The kinds of secrets that can be concealed in a text, and the motivations for such concealment, are not only countless but also extremely heterogeneous. That is why (re)reading is so hard, if not plainly impossible, to study in any systematic fashion. On the other hand, one cannot simply ignore the attitudes toward reading and the methods of reading generated by the potential existence of meaning that may have been deliberately concealed in a text.

Taking the standard dichotomy between insiders and outsiders that is implied by the very idea of secrecy, we can—without making any claims to exhaustiveness or even to broad inclusiveness—enumerate some of the secrets found in literary texts in terms of the insiders to whom they are addressed. We may thus speak of secrets embedded in texts that are no more than mere secret signs of recognition—like the passwords of a secret soci-

. . .

ety—meant to reward the attentive, faithful reader of a specific writer's work. Many writers have such favors in store for their would-be devotees, in the form of otherwise cryptic allusions, recurrent names of marginal characters, or brief references to situations which only one who is familiar with earlier works by the same author can properly decode or recognize.

By extension, we may distinguish textual secrets that are addressed, as signs of recognition and invitations to communion, to special groups of initiates. The initiates may be believers in an esoteric doctrine: Yeats, for example, was associated for many years with the hermetic-traditional Order of the Golden Dawn, with interests in the Kabbalah and Rosicrucianism. Initiates may be members of a secret society, which may be either legal or illegal: Freemasonry, for instance, while legal in the West, became illegal in Fascist, National-Socialist, and Communist regimes in the twentieth century. When they belong to a forbidden, heretical, or persecuted group, secret communication may become dangerous. To make things more complicated, the secret communication, even in such cases, is not totally impenetrable to the intelligent and sensitive outsider, since it aims, however prudently and obscurely, at attracting new believers from among those readers who may be already intellectually and spiritually prepared to be instructed in the secret truth. The use of symbols and images in secret messages is often premised on the hope that their secret meaning might be spontaneously recognized by those who are ripe for initiation: secrecy here goes hand in hand with a certain didactic-initiatory intention, to which I shall return.

Another large category of secrets that may be embedded in texts is personal authorial secrets, and these often are the most paradoxical ones, as they can be indirectly confessed, hidden even in the act of their obstreperous, exaggerated declaration or betrayed in the act of their very repression. Such authorial secrets—particularly those of the skeleton-in-the-closet type—may generate interesting textual problems, insofar as the texts in which their indirect presence is identified can be seen as attempts at exorcising a shameful, unavowable past and at bringing about an amnesia that stubbornly refuses to come. Old "dirty secrets" may haunt an author's texts as revenants haunt certain places. This has been recently illustrated, in the unlikely area of literary theory, by the curious Paul de Man affair, which has polarized American critical opinion in academia and beyond. When the articles published by the young de Man in a pro-Nazi newspaper in German-occupied Belgium during World War II were discovered, his deconstructionist friends and disciples saw in his silence

· · ·

about his past an almost heroic refusal to be diverted from the creation of an important intellectual-critical work, which also was a secret deconstruction of an earlier intellectual and political mistake. De Man's adversaries took two main lines of attack: (1) his later work was essentially a disguised continuation, if not of his early ideas as such, then of the same nihilistic mode of thinking adapted to a new, radically changed ideological climate; and (2) his later work, with its central contentions that meaning is always indeterminate and that textual matters remain ultimately undecidable, was a secret attempt to relativize and indeed to deny any clear-cut significance to his earlier statements. The details of the debate need not concern us here. What is relevant to the present discussion is the dramatic effect of the sudden disclosure of an old skeleton in the closet. The sheer fascination of secrecy and revelation made an otherwise abstruse, often disagreeably technical critical debate so exciting that it spilled into large-circulation magazines—where its gossipy aspects were of course stressed and where personal-biographical matters, such as de Man's possible secret bigamy, were added to his youthful political sins.[1]

From Reading to Rereading for the Secret

In the case of texts with secrets, whether these belong to the first, second, or third category, the theoretically most interesting position is that of the reader who is an outsider. How will the outsider realize that the text in question—say, a novel that offers a perfectly satisfying experience of make-believe and of gossipy involvement with the superficial personal secrets of imaginary beings—may also contain other kinds of deeper secrets? Such a discovery is made possible by a certain suspicion, which grows toward the end of the first reading of an intriguing fictional text and prompts a more attentive and searching rereading. One might say that a trusting naivete, an easily excited curiosity, a desire to participate in the story and to "identify" with the characters or the situations (whether realistic or fantastic), an inclination to take things at face value, are elementary conditions of most reading. (Re)reading for the secret is just the opposite. The suspicion that the text is double, that it has a manifest content but also, like a suitcase with a false bottom, a hidden one, will direct the reader's attention to structural or strategic aspects of the work. As a good chess player will answer the opponent's unexpected move only after having weighed its secret intentions or hidden threats, so a good rereader will always also reread for the secret, that is, will always try to

. . .

discover what a read text may hold away, conceal, or veil, and for what reasons. Rereading, in other words, is always also reading between the lines, reading to uncover something hidden.

The suspicious outsider practices an attitude that is a distant cousin of Descartes' methodical doubt. There are many reasons for which we may reread, but piercing the secrets of a text, whatever these may be—or whatever the manner in which the rereader thinks he or she may use them—is certainly one of the major ones. It also is one of the most fascinating ones, given the endless fascination that surrounds the notions of secrecy and revelation. A writer's work both hides and reveals—or, perhaps more accurately, half reveals in the very process of hiding— something of potentially deep significance. The attitude of the serious reader, and all the more so of the rereader, regarding this subtle dialectic of hiding and revealing—a dialectic that clearly goes beyond the mere manipulation of narrative information—is likely to confirm André Gide's observation about Oscar Wilde's aestheticism. Gide saw it as a mask:

> I believe . . . that this affected aestheticism was for him merely an ingenious cloak to hide, while half revealing, what he could not let be seen openly; to excuse, provide a pretext, and even apparently motivate; but that the very motivation is but a pretense. Here, as almost always, and often without the artist's knowing it, it is the secret of the depths of his flesh that prompts, inspires, and decides. Lighted in this way and, as it were, from beneath, Wilde's plays reveal, beside the surface witticisms, sparkling like false jewels, many oddly revelatory sentences of great psychological interest. And it is for them that Wilde wrote the whole play—let there be no doubt about it. (*The Journals of André Gide,* vol. 2, p. 24)

The real problem is whether this hiding is conscious or not. The difficulty of a clear-cut answer is apparent when one considers the contradictory terms in which Gide deals with this very issue: "ingenious," "half revealing," and "pretense" seem to involve consciousness; but such an inference on the part of the reader is flatly contradicted by the notion of the artist veiling his speech "often without . . . knowing it." That Wilde's homosexuality ("the secret of the depth of his flesh") had to be hidden in the social atmosphere of at once diffuse and very severe Victorian sexual censorship needs little arguing. To reduce, however, Wilde's veiled "message" to an all-too-human desire to express his homosexuality would be simplifying and uninteresting. Wilde's insights come from his *consciousness* of the need to hide, dissemble, speak obliquely, allude, pretend, lie,

· · ·

play roles—all of which he can perform brilliantly—and such insights cannot be gained except by a combination of great intelligence and imaginative artistry. It is the originality of these insights and not the secrecy per se that counts. Rereading for the secret, in this case, is thus rereading for the quality of insight and for the construction of the circumstances under which such insight occurs. Secrets that do not lead to independent, non-secret insights are often boring.

But What Is Secrecy?

I have already offered, in discussing "The Private Life," a brief definition of secrecy: calculated or intentional concealment of information.[2] But secrecy is also *selective communication of concealed information,* even if it is communication to one's own self in an interior dialogue or a personal diary. Deliberateness is an essential feature of deciding to withhold something from open communication. A complicating psychological factor, however, is that such consciousness may be lost or "forgotten" in time as a result of a process of repression that may push unbearable secret knowledge—the skeleton in the closet—into the unconscious.[3] One may, for example, hide or keep to oneself certain thoughts that cross one's mind, thoughts that may be socially embarrassing or even dangerous to express. Such secret thoughts can be anything from self-gratifying daydreams to ill wishes, feelings of hatred, and criminal fantasies, the latter often accompanied by fears of the uncanny which have their origin in what Freud identified as the magical "omnipotence of thoughts."[4] Purely personal thoughts of this kind become secrets—as opposed to mere fleeting images or words or disjointed phrases in the stream of consciousness—only in light of the anxious fantasy that they could suddenly become public or, even more frighteningly, that they could come true, that a transitory ill wish, for instance, might result in the death of its object. All the things that one keeps to oneself in this manner participate, even when the withholding of information is incomplete or marginal, in the dialectics of secrecy.

Georg Simmel identifies the two crucial moments of the dialectics of secrecy as "the fascination of secrecy" and "the fascination of betrayal," including, I would add, self-betrayal.[5] What the intentional or conscious dimension of secrecy means, even on this elementary personal level, is that one's innermost secrets contain within themselves the *temptation* to disclose, whatever the consequences: one somehow perceives one's secrets as a burden of which one would wish to relieve one's conscience or mind. We

• • •

have, in other words, a sort of deep-seated, mysterious nostalgia for transparency. Such psychological and personal secrecy always toys with, and sometimes agonizes over, the idea of confession. The practice of confession in certain religions responds to this inclination.

Staying within the same broad psychological framework, it is clear that personal secrecy is frequently related to play—as an extension and re elaboration of daydreams, for instance, or as a special form of pretending, feigning, or otherwise manipulating the as-if dimension of the mental universe. But the play of secrecy is perceived to be, and often is, more immediately *dangerous*. Children sometimes use play to express secret wishes under the protective umbrella of the as-if. At other times, however, they use secrecy to enhance the pleasures of play: they will invent codes and secret languages, or hide away in order to play "forbidden" games— including reading unapproved books in secret places. The association with danger explains the protected/protective nature of secrecy: secrets are *protected* (kept, guarded) because they hide areas of vulnerability; but secrets are also *used to protect,* to shield or defend such vulnerable spots, whether they are located in the privacy of one's personal life or occur on an intersubjective and social level—as in the case of shared secret beliefs, esoteric allegiances or associations, and so on.

Its intentional-conscious nature now established, it remains to be stressed that secrecy belongs structurally to the area of human communication. Yes, it is indeed a form of communication—deliberately selective, exclusive, often elliptical, oblique, or indirect. Leaving aside such special cases as that of purely personal secrets that are never shared with anyone, secrets exist only socially and communicationally. (Secrets, we may say, are always kept *from someone.*) Hence the sustained interest of modern social scientists in the problem of secrecy and privacy, from Georg Simmel—who made his theory of secret societies into a cornerstone of his whole sociology—to Erving Goffman, Edward Shils, and many others.[6] Hence also the attention these social scientists devote to the specifically communicational implications of secrecy.

Goffman thus proposes a communicational typology of secrets from the point of view of their importance for the social image an individual or a team attempts to project. The purpose of such secrets is to prevent the disclosure of "destructive information," that is, information that would contradict or discredit the image to be fostered. Some of the (occasionally overlapping) categories Goffman distinguishes are relevant to literary production and reception. His first rubric, that of "dark secrets"—which

. . .

conceal "facts incompatible with the image of self" that is being projected (*The Presentation of Self in Everyday Life,* p. 141)—could easily be extended to comprise literary matters and specifically questions of authorial reputation or public standing. There is little doubt that "destructive information" about the political past of an author can affect his readership adversely—Paul de Man's wartime collaborationism, Heidegger's National Socialist past, Mircea Eliade's sympathy in the 1930s for the Romanian fascist organization the Iron Guard. Goffman's "strategic secrets"—secrets about possible moves and countermoves of teams in competition with one another—are less immediately relevant to literature; but his third category, that of "inside secrets"—secrets that "mark an individual as being a member of a group and help the group feel separate ... from those individuals who are not 'in the know' " (p. 142)—could be applied to a sociology of literary life, particularly of literary fashions and counterfashions. The notion of inside secrets would go a long way to explain phenomena like preciousness, snobbery, affectation, and the use of jargon. And if "entrusted secrets"—secrets one would be expected to keep—do not seem to have specifically literary correspondents, what Goffman calls "free secrets"—somebody else's secrets that one can disclose without discrediting oneself—constitute the common fare of major literary-critical genres such as biography.

There are many other communicational-social implications of secrecy that have literary parallels. As Hans Speier reminds us in an article devoted explicitly to "the communication of hidden meaning," the purpose of communication may not be to inform or to produce or obtain understanding: "It may be not to spread knowledge to a given ignoramus but to maintain his ignorance; not to profess feelings but to hide or feign them; to lead astray rather than guide the perplexed; . . . not to enlighten but to obscure, to explain inadequately, to oversimplify, to slant, to popularize, to tell only part of the truth, to mask it, or simply to lie" (p. 471). It may also be, as we saw in Part III, to play—to use types and modes of communication playfully (fictionally). Of course, the ultimate purposes of concealment may be as varied as human purposes: one may conceal information to be kind or to protect, when disclosure would be painful or harmful; one may remain silent, or speak misleadingly or deceptively in the face of an intrusive or oppressive authority to avoid persecution; one may withhold information to avoid misunderstanding; in fiction (and in good storytelling generally) information is concealed or disclosed at strategic points of the narrative to maintain the interest of the listener/reader

. . .

(but this kind of manipulation should be studied under the heading of enigma rather than secrecy, as I have already suggested); and one may pretend to conceal important information for the prestige the possession of secret knowledge seems to confer.

Textual Concealment from the Point of View of the Reader

Keeping in mind the always social-communicational context of secrecy, and considering the whole matter from the point of view of the literary-philosophical reader who is ready to accept the challenge of the text and become a rereader,[7] textual concealment may have the following kinds of purposes. First, meaning may be concealed in order to make it inaccessible to outsiders. The results of exclusionary secrets of this type are best discussed in terms of the old esoteric/exoteric distinction. The concealment of meaning is devised in such a manner as to deceive the noninitiates and make the secret knowledge available only to initiates. Given the vulnerability of writing—a piece of writing can always fall into the hands of a party deliberately excluded from the community of secret sharers and, if it is ciphered, may eventually be deciphered—the deceptive exoteric plausibility of the esoteric text is of great importance, particularly when the vehicle for secrecy is a literary work. In successful literary works the deceptive exoteric plausibility may be so delightful and full of charm that it makes them survive the ultimate meaninglessness of their hidden messages. The usual assumption is that the secret meaning can best be communicated by means of naturally ambiguous forms of speech, which abound in poetic discourse (metaphor, symbol, allegory). The danger here, for the interested, alert, inventive rereader, is to overinterpret, to discover esoteric communication where there is little or none, and to exaggerate the importance of perhaps some marginally plausible allusions, imagining that they imply a full-fledged secret doctrine. A classic example would be the views on Dante of many esoterically inclined interpreters, from Gabriele Rossetti to Luigi Valli to René Guénon.[8] But overinterpretation is not necessarily uninteresting. Always far from the exegetical mainstream, revisionist readings are so unusual, controversial, and hard to prove that they may begin by stimulating our hermeneutical imagination. But such stimulation is hard to sustain and in the end, when the overinterpreter's demonstrations appear flimsy, farfetched, cranky, or otherwise pathetically unconvincing, revisionism eventually disappoints and even bores.

. . .

In this first category of communication of hidden meaning by way of equivocation or amphibolic speech I also range the various strategies used by writers for circumventing censorship. Freedom of thought and expression, as they are enjoyed today in part of the Western world (although this enjoyment is not without its own problems),[9] is a comparatively recent invention, a consequence mainly of the Reformation and the rise of democracy, and is fully granted even today in only a limited geopolitical area of the world. In order to compensate for the strictures of ideological censorship, there are numerous ways of evading the censor to which correspond, on the reader's side, the various techniques of reading between the lines. The main problem that arises here is an ethical one: to evade the censor one must play, to a large extent (too large, perhaps) by the censor's rules; one must be duplicitous, pretend to accept what one rejects and to reject what one cherishes. "Secret critics" of a regime may end up doing propaganda for the very beliefs they secretly abhor and would like to subvert.[10] The opposite paradox is that of provocation, also a child of repressive rule and censorship: an authoritarian system may use provocation to make the hidden dissidents manifest themselves publicly. (The Chinese policy of the "One Hundred Flowers" in 1957, which encouraged criticism of the Communist party line in cultural life by dissenting intellectuals, was such a provocation, followed by a period of renewed repression in which those who had spoken out were severely persecuted.) Of course, provocation is not without dangers for its own promoters: it may well turn out that there are more hidden opponents than was estimated, and a provocation—as happened in Russia in 1905 or in Czechoslovakia in 1989—may trigger a true revolution. If the secret critic is forced to lie in the name of a hidden truth, which can be communicated only prudently and selectively by subtle allusion and double entendre, the provocateur is ironically forced to tell the truth, or at least part of the truth, in the name of lying and as a screen for the (political) trap he or she is setting.

A second type of textual concealment is that in which the purpose of hiding meaning is to make it available selectively only to the reader who meets certain more or less well defined conditions. This kind of concealment, which we might term didactic, is closely tied to the ways in which a text fictionalizes its reader, and more precisely to the implied demands it makes of the reader. A text may thus be said to withhold information, even essential information, from an immature reader, or from one who lacks a specific type of experience or background that he or she could,

· · ·

given the time and the opportunity, acquire. Admittedly, such secret meanings, which become transparent when one gains the necessary insight, or simply when one rereads the text repeatedly and with great attention, cannot be separated precisely from other kinds of unintended difficulties a text might present—such as originally transparent allusions in an older book, which the passage of time has rendered obscure.

At any rate, from the perspective of a reader sensitive to nuances of secrecy and hiddenness, virtually all of the great classic texts of literature, from Homer to Joyce, contain such secrets, whether intended by their authors or credibly attributed to them by generations of interpreters. Rereading the classics from this point of view may be a way, if not of directly improving ourselves (whatever sense we choose to give the notion of improvement), at least of measuring the degree to which we have changed and become capable of penetrating textual secrets that are likely to demand not only special training or learning but also a particular frame of mind or mode of understanding. Such secrets are of course exclusive, as all secrets are, but they differ from those in the first category, which are conceived to exclude all hostile outsiders and persecutors and to be shared only by the initiate. The didactic secrets, by contrast, can in principle be penetrated by anyone who undergoes a process of self-education or self-initiation. They come close to what John Ruskin had in mind when he argued that the concealment, the veiled speech, and the talking in enigmas characteristic of great poetry do not express contempt for "the many" but rather deep ethical concern for "the few" who are intent on "bettering" themselves. In this sense, all great works of art have always been, as Ruskin puts it in *The Queen of the Air* (1869),

> didactic in the purest way, indirectly and occultly, so that, first, you shall only be bettered by them if you are already hard at work in bettering yourself, and when you are bettered by them it shall be partly . . . by a gift of unexpected truth, which you shall only find by slow mining for it; which is withheld on purpose, and close-locked, that you not get it till you have forged the key of it in a furnace of your own heating. And this withholding of their meaning is continual, and confessed, in great poets . . . . And neither Pindar, nor Aeschylus, nor Hesiod, nor Homer, nor any of the greater poets or teachers of any nation or time, ever spoke but with intentional reservation. (p. 308)

A third category of purposes for concealing meaning belongs to the explicitly ludic dimension of literary writing and reading. What we may

. . .

call playful secrets cannot always be clearly distinguished from certain sophisticated manipulations of the code of the enigma: these include riddles used as structuring devices; riddles within riddles, stories within stories, or figures within figures meant to echo each other playfully, to initiate dizzying mirror games and *mises en abyme* and produce in the reader the need to figure out what is going on structurally and thus to reread; enigmas of various kinds—some solved within the text, some left unsolved and solvable only intertextually; hidden (serious or parodic) quotations, distortions, or allusions; and hidden "rules of the game."

An intriguing case of hidden rules is Georges Perec's *Life: A User's Manual*. These rules range from mathematical compositional procedures to an elaborate system of secret quotations which the reader is supposed to discover for the sheer pleasure of seeing how this ingenious and complex puzzle of a work was generated. With the order of its chapters determined by the solution of a classic chess conundrum in the case of an oversize board ten squares by ten squares (the solution shows how a knight can be maneuvered to alight on each of the hundred squares exactly once), Perec's novel, made up of numerous little strange stories, highly readable and tantalizingly elusive hybrids of Jules Verne, Kafka, and Raymond Roussel, contains no less than 203 passages copied from twenty authors including Borges, Flaubert, Joyce, Kafka, Proust, Queneau, Rabelais, Roussel, Stendhal, Sterne, and Verne.[11] These secret quotations are introduced, as David Bellos explains, according to a special program of combinations determined by the use of a ten-by-ten magic square in conjunction with two lists of ten authors each (pp. 186–87). What is more interesting is that these quotations—representing a small part of the borrowed textual material incorporated into *Life: A User's Manual,* which comes from sources as diverse as encyclopedias, dictionaries, cookbooks, and catalogues—are perfectly camouflaged. The secret quotations, like much else in this masterpiece of congeries and magic textual tricks, are an extraordinary *tour de force:* a quotation from Proust is made to look like a verse from Ibn Zaydun, a passage from Nabokov's *Lolita* appears as a description of a fictive painting by a certain "Organ Trapp" showing a gas station at Sheridan, Wyoming, and so on. As Bellos observes, "Perec sidesteps the reader's 'stylistic' reflexes and manages to insert whole chunks of (for example) Rabelais, without disturbing the register, vocabulary and syntax of his own prose" (p. 190).

Perec uses the most varied means of concealing or making the meaning of his quotations ludically unrecognizable, including "absence of camou-

· · ·

flage," which "best hides the material; even more, the presence of insistent narrative and typographic indications of the borrowed nature of the material systematically diverts recognition away from the true origin" (p. 191). Even a highly literate reader would never be able to spot such hidden "playgiarisms" (to use the amusing and enlightening pun by which Raymond Federman designates a specifically postmodern technique). Writing about Perec's novel before the deciphering work done by his translator, David Bellos, an enthusiastic and very knowledgeable reader such as Gabriel Josipovici could identify on his own only one of the 203 quotations, the description of the Victorian doll's house drawn from the end of the penultimate chapter of Joyce's *Ulysses*. But did not Joyce himself use such secret or quasi-secret references, allusions, and quotations, whose discovery constitutes one of the joys of Joyce scholarship and which are now accessible—via specialized dictionaries, commentaries, and glossaries—to the ordinary Joyce reader? Did not Raymond Roussel, in his own quirky manner, employ a similar riddling compositional technique for purposes of cryptical self-reference, as he explained in his *Comment j'ai écrit certains de mes livres*? Did not Nabokov—another great model for Perec—practice his own version of the art of ludically hiding his sources (as is the case with the dissolution of Edgar Allan Poe's poem "Annabel Lee" in the text of *Lolita,* even in the name Lo-*lee*-ta, so that the novel becomes in part a subtly perverse parody of the poem)?

Perec's work is just one more example of a procedure of concealing meaning for playful purposes and to enhance the pleasures of rereading. In this area, secrecy, enigma, and play come very close, so close indeed that they may become almost indistinguishable. Texts with ludic ciphers can be treated with equal justification under the heading of play (as I did with Nabokov's *Pale Fire* in chapter 9) or under the heading of secrecy (where I have placed Perec's *La Vie: mode d'emploi*). Such ludic concealment of meaning is made possible by the larger phenomenon of intertextuality. One could then suggest a tentative distinction between intertextual secrets, which challenge the reader's ability to recognize or uncover hidden meanings by reference to *other* texts, and mere textual gaps in narrative information, which may be filled later (for an ideal effect of surprise after suspense) or left unfilled for compositional or semantic purposes. Gaps of the latter kind are used to create ambiguity and even essential indeterminacy, as is the case with many parabolic stories from the Bible to Kafka and Borges.

A fourth kind of textual concealment is rather a pseudo-concealment

. . .

motivated primarily by the desire to participate in the prestige afforded by secrecy, by the wish to profit—in terms of gaining attention, serious consideration, or recognition—from the quasi-magic that surrounds secret rituals, languages, or modes of behavior. Our natural fascination with secrecy is often exploited in literary texts. This exploitation can take as many forms as elaborate obscurity, snobbery, or pretentiousness can— from the parroting of certain stylistic features of exclusive, aristocratic, highly mannered styles of literary discourse (such as Euphuism, *préciosité*, Gongorism, and Marinism, to limit ourselves to the age of the baroque, when the declared aim of poetry was, according to Giambattista Marino, *la meraviglia*, or the astonishment of the reader) to the more subtle simulation of allusive reference and suggestive obscurity. The problem of bogus secrecy in literature (how do you tell a bogus secret from a real one?) is theoretically as complex and practically leads to issues that are as undecidable as those belonging to the broader question of aesthetic falsification, dishonest imitation, plagiarism, forgery, and counterfeiting. That there is much fake secrecy in minor, epigonic, hermetic poetry, for instance, can hardly be doubted. The real question is to distinguish legitimate obscurity—and the high intellectual-moral drama of secrecy—from the mere mimicking of obscurity for purposes of showing off. There is really no method for doing this, and mere intuition or judgments of personal taste can be dangerously deceptive.

The question of distinguishing between "legitimate" types of poetic statement—from simple statement to complex "reinforced" or "embroidered statement"—and "disguised statement" or "statement masquerading as obliquity" or simply "false obliquity" was discussed some time ago by E. M. W. Tillyard (*Poetry Direct and Oblique,* pp. 32–35). The model Tillyard used is a simple one. There is, on the one hand, a direct poetry of statement that basically means what it says: for example, the description of the Auburn village green with its idyllic pleasures in Oliver Goldsmith's *The Deserted Village.* On the other hand, there is an oblique poetry that "implies without a word of statement" or gives "its meaning without any trace of statement" (pp. 68, 76). This poetry does say something, and can say it convincingly and skillfully, but means something else: for example, William Blake's description of a perfectly allegorical village green in "The Echoing Green" in his *Songs of Innocence.* In between these two poles is the poetry of "reinforced statement," in which statement is subtly enhanced and complicated by the use of imagery, hyperbole, and understatement, such as Yeats's "The Tower." This poetry is not only aesthetically

. . .

legitimate but actually better than the poetry of simple statement. But obliquity, which in Tillyard's view is always poetically superior to direct statement (he does not explain why), can be faked, so that a poem consisting essentially of statement can masquerade as oblique poetry. His examples of such "disguised statement" come from Ezra Pound, whose *Hugh Selwyn Mauberley* he declares to be full of disguised statement— that is, pretentiousness.

Tillyard singles out the following lines from the first poem of Pound's series *E. P. Ode pour l'élection de son sépulcre*:

> His true Penelope was Flaubert,
> He fished by obstinate isles;
> Observed the elegance of Circe's hair
> Rather than the mottoes on sundials.
>
> Unaffected by 'the march of events'
> He passed from men's memory in *l'an trentiesme*
> *De son eage*; the case presents
> No adjunct to the Muses' diadem.

Here are some excerpts from the commentary: "The metaphors are mere translations of statement. . . . The mottoes on sundials move us no more than the simpler 'flight of time'; and the phrase 'adjunct to the Muses' diadem,' is no more interesting than the common circumlocutions of the daily press. The reference to Villon in *l'an trentiesme de son eage* is more bogus obliquity. The poet is elaborately parading his pretended failure to achieve poetic distinction and slips in the quotation to make us contrast him with Villon, who, although an unregenerate café-loafer, did succeed in writing poetry: would be obliquity through allusion" (pp. 34–35). But for a reader who knows Pound well (Pound has become fully a modern classic since 1934, when the first version of Tillyard's book was published), the quoted lines do not have anything fake or spurious about them; they may be difficult and arrogantly elliptic, but each one of them hides and reveals identifiable references to other parts of the Pound corpus, whose mere recognition by the Pound devotee constitutes a special reward for sustained attention and allegiance. The line "His true Penelope was Flaubert," for instance, not only evokes the many Homeric allusions or quotations in Pound, particularly his fondness for the model of *The Odyssey,* but also daringly advances the allegorical image of the poet as a Ulysses of words who is married to a Penelope of *prose.* This may remind us of Pound's striking statements in *ABC of Reading* to the effect that the

. . .

modern poet has more to learn from great, sparse, unadorned, "hard" prose, for which Flaubert is the exemplary model, than from the "soft," flabby, ornamental language of most nineteenth-century poets, whether romantic or postromantic. Of course, there is affectation and *maniera* in Pound's lines, but the *maniera* is recognizably his own, whatever we might otherwise think of it. And the secrets contained in these lines are not bogus: they are there to reward the patient, faithful, and ingenious reader of Pound's work (poetry and criticism) and to reaffirm a certain original *ars poetica.*

The rule of thumb to distinguish between true and bogus secrecy is that texts that have achieved the status of classics—a status achieved through the ruthless selection executed by extremely careful (re)reading over generations—contain mostly legitimate secrets, often of the didactic kind. Unfortunately, false secrets are extremely hard to pinpoint, except in cases of egregiously bad ("beautiful") writing, that is, in cases of writing which, according to Hermann Broch, answers the command of kitsch ("Work beautifully!") rather than the command of art ("Work well!").[12] But in such cases the false secrets are often little more than an overindulgence in the language *about* secrecy used for rhetorical purposes—adjectives such as *mysterious, mystical, arcane, profound, enigmatic, baffling,* and *inextricable.*

Why Read Texts That Conceal Meaning?

An examination of the motives that underlie the concealment of meaning by the use of special codes, disguised ciphers, and invisible cryptographical techniques, as seen by the reader of a cryptic text, would remain incomplete if we ignored the possible motivations for rereading. Who are the rereaders of texts with secrets (or potential secrets) and why do they reread? Are such close rereaders censors, inquisitors, or judges? Are they, in other words, in a position to impede or stop the distribution of the texts they reread in order to make sure that they are not disseminating so-called harmful ideas, heretical views, or immoral, obscene representations? Or are these rereaders, on the contrary, opponents of the powers that be, intent on reading between the lines and on catching (and enjoying) critical allusions, Aesopian references, or even open challenges that may have escaped the censor's attention?

Questions like these indicate the political nature of rereading for the secret from the position one occupies in society in relation to the powers

. . .

that be. It is of course in repressive societies that this kind of censorial/ subversive reading is practiced most widely. But there is a place for it in open societies as well, where it is practiced on a more limited scale and mostly in the mode of a theoretical as-if: the motive is now to understand how communication in closed societies or situations works, how people write and read, how people hide, find, and use meaning that is officially controlled in such societies. It is in this as-if mode that a Western reader might wish to approach works produced under conditions of totalitarian censorship in the Soviet Union or Eastern Europe before the collapse of the main classical versions of communism between 1989 and 1991. I have in mind such diverse works of fiction as Mikhail Bulgakov's *The Master and Margarita* (written during the heyday of Stalinism, 1928–40, but published in a posthumous and censored edition only in the 1960s), Milan Kundera's *The Joke,* George Konrad's *The Case Worker,* or a host of other works with a similarly complicated publishing history in their original language.

This brings us to the more theoretical problem of rereading for the secret in order to understand a text—a text that seems itself to understand something that it does not communicate straightforwardly. When a text seems to understand something important, even the ways in which it was itself understood (or perhaps misunderstood) become important: hence the attempt at historical understanding. If books can be called "machines to think with" (as I. A. Richards famously put it), the elucidation of the secret devices meant to prevent their use by incompetents or people likely to misconstrue their function is even more important. The impulse of the reader in such cases is one of Ruskinian bettering of oneself, of learning to use powerful "machines to think with" with proper care, discretion, and intelligence. Traditionally, truth and the means of getting to truth were considered dangerous by the great philosophers before the modern era of democratic ideals of transparency. The major texts of philosophy from Plato to Spinoza, and the major literary classics, will continue to be reread for their secrets in this broad, didactic, self-improving sense, leaving aside the need to clarify historical or textual obscurities owing to accidents of transmission or changes in mentality.

But insofar as modernity has developed its own "hermeneutics of suspicion" and has come to regard "truth as lying" (according to Paul Ricoeur), the reader's desire to establish the secret truth of a text has not disappeared; it has only taken on new forms. To limit ourselves to just one example, from the domain of psychoanalysis, treating the text as at once a

. . .

defense and a symptom opens the way to endless rereading for the secret. Nicolas Abraham and Maria Torok, the authors of *The Wolf Man's Magic Word: A Cryptonymy,* have continually reread, over many years, Freud's famous case history of the Wolf Man, as well as the Wolf Man's auto-biographical account of his relationship with Freud and other analysts, before coming to the conclusion that the real secret, the Wolf Man's "cryptonym" or "magic word," had escaped Freud. The magic word itself (a bizarre, totally idiosyncratic Russian-German-English lexical hybrid reconstructed no less idiosyncratically and speculatively) is certainly less interesting from our point of view than the elaborate theory of cryptonyms devised by the authors, a theory of rereading for reconstructing an almost infinitely elusive secret from its faintest textual traces. The trouble with the theory (aside from its major logical-scientific flaw, which is its total irrefutability) is that it does not specify any criteria for deciding what may count as a verbal-textual trace of secrecy: anything seems to go so long as it serves the purposes—freely metaphorical and allegorical—of the analyst. One does not see how such a theory might "revolutionize" literary criticism, as has been claimed.[13]

Aside from the political, epistemological, and psychological motivations behind rereading for the secret, an equally important role (and decidedly more important in the case of literature) may be that of the pleasure of solving a complex puzzle, or of playing the game proposed by the text better, more elegantly, more intelligently, more satisfyingly, the second or third time around. Such a broadly ludic motivation, with its complex components and ramifications, has been discussed at some length in Part III. Here, from the vantage point of secrecy, one should perhaps emphasize just a few points. In a first involved reading of a work of fiction—a reading that takes the form of a game of make-believe—secrecy is relevant in two ways. First, the text may conceal and disclose information at strategic junctures to create interest in the resolution of a *linear enigma* (the ending is always perceived as important: it is the final disclosure of information, the final word). Second, secrecy is also relevant insofar as the text makes the reader a participant in a situation of imaginary gossip, in which he or she becomes privy to the characters' "secrets." Rereading for the secret, in the same ludic context, will also direct the attention toward the formal aspects of the work as a game with rules. Here I should perhaps stress that the term *form* and its cognates are not to be taken as designating merely external, superficial, "technical" procedures: literary forms always evoke contents, which they can express

· · ·

with more or less efficacy, adequacy, and inventiveness. After one has reread and mentally rewritten a work, depending on the quality of the rereading, that work will yield some of its innermost formal secrets—trade secrets, as it were—of literary craftsmanship and imagination. Rereading for the secret in this formal, almost artisanal sense is tantamount to fulfilling one of the basic requirements of literary criticism.

. . .

SEVENTEEN

The Language of Secrecy
and the Politics
of Interpretation

Communication about Hidden Communication

Since its remotest origins writing has entertained a complex, intriguing, and ever-changing relation to secrecy. Writing, like any system of coding thought, has always had the function of conveying information to those— and inevitably only to those—who know the code. But insofar as writing is a sophisticated, second-degree coding (a coding of thought that has already been coded as language), its potential for withholding the information it carries from those who ignore the code is greater than that of spoken and heard (or overheard) language. The intelligibility of spoken language benefits not only from the clues provided by the situational context and the presence of the speaker but also from the possibility of asking the speaker to rephrase, perhaps even recode or otherwise clarify his message. Writing decontextualizes communication, in the first place, by depriving the reader of situational and expressive clues (physical appearance, gestures, tone of voice, and so on); and, second, since the author of a written message is usually absent at the moment of its reading, the reader does not have a chance to get any extra help in understanding the message: the message is received in silence and what it states remains surrounded by silence.

To these difficulties of processing written communication must be added the sheer difficulty of mastering the technology of writing and the

. . .

art of reading. Before the great step made by the ancient Greeks in the direction of the democratization of the written word (via fully alphabetic writing), the ability to write (to store information in a textual memory) and to read (to retrieve that information) was rare; writing and reading were a truly secret art. Scribes in pre-alphabetic times were few, and their arcane craft kept them close to the centers of religious and political power, which controlled them and used them for safeguarding the secrets of their own power and the even deeper symbolic power that secrecy itself acquires in hierarchically organized societies. From this point of view, alphabetic writing and reading can be linked not only to democracy but also to the development of privacy.[1]

From the point of view of secrecy, the great paradox of writing—including the most sacred/secret kind of writing—derives from its permanence (*scripta manent*) as opposed to the transitoriness of oral speech (*verba volant*). From this permanence of the medium follows the possibility that writing, even writing that is doubly or triply coded to conceal its true meaning, may one day be deciphered by people who were purposely excluded from the information it stores. In other words, writing (in its capacity as textual memory) is not the most reliable repository of secret knowledge. Whatever the risks, which come with the very notion of secrecy and with "the fascination of betrayal" that accompanies it (to refer once again to Simmel's theory of secrecy), a secret is ultimately better kept by a person than by a text.[2] One also notes that the traditions of secrecy and keeping secrets are much older than writing and have survived to this day (as in the Mafia's "code of silence"). The historical roots of secrecy go back to the most archaic societies, where initiatory rites and various symbolic practices were invariably surrounded by secrecy and generated secret behavior.[3]

Students of secrecy have long recognized its social role. Secrets can be effectively used to bind the members of groups and even large, complex organizations. As in the case of the Poro rituals of West Africa (Poro is a secret society that cuts across tribal, linguistic, and national boundaries), secrets are methods for regulating and articulating the flow of knowledge in a community. In addition, the anthropologist Beryl Bellman notes, the devices used for controlling the flow of information can be "more important than the information that is concealed" (*The Language of Secrecy*, p. 49). Paradoxically, the language of secrecy is largely, if not exclusively, a "corpus of procedures" for selectively *revealing* concealed information to certain people under certain circumstances, and thus is a mode of social

· · ·

interaction: "The enactment of Poro rituals serves to establish the ways in which concealed information is communicated. It provides instruction in how to deal with concealed information. . . . It offers methods for mentioning the unmentionable" (p. 141). In archaic societies, then, the language of secrecy is often little more than a set of rules for sharing or protecting privileged information.

Writing has developed its own ways of dealing with secret matters, but it has never supplanted the parallel tradition of oral communication of secrets (or even half-secrets or nonsecrets, which may, however, participate in a diffuse atmosphere of social secrecy) within a group or in the relationship between groups or persons, such as that between master and disciple. Even if, say, a teacher-student relationship is not governed by well-defined rules of secrecy, a number of impromptu codes, recurrent metaphors and formulas, humorous cryptonyms to designate unwelcome outsiders, and signs of reciprocal recognition will emerge and bring about some of the characteristics of a secret society, often combined with the more obvious features of openly elitist, snobbish groups. Even today's more widespread intellectual fashions rely to a certain extent on quasi-secret or exclusive bits of knowledge (for instance, the special knowledge that can be tacitly assumed by its leading representatives), which are communicated personally and orally; it is this type of knowledge that constitutes the cherished privilege of the minority who are "in" by contrast with the majority of the less distinguished followers of the fashion, who are necessarily "out."

Careful Reading as a Way of Recovering Hidden Meaning

Totally different from the mild exclusivism of modern intellectual fashions is the secrecy and obliqueness of discourse practiced by potential victims of persecution. The question of persecution, in both a narrow and a philosophically extended sense, is dealt with interestingly if sometimes confusingly in Leo Strauss's *Persecution and the Art of Writing*. The confusion stems from Strauss's failure to distinguish clearly between, on the one hand, a certain obliquity or even a carefully observed public silence about one's true thoughts—Plato's esoteric doctrine, for example—for fear that the truth might be misunderstood by the vulgar and, on the other, the kind of oblique speech used by writers who have a well-founded fear of persecution by powerful authorities. In the latter case we are confronted with reactions to censorship established by religious

. . .

bodies or inquisitions, including those set up by modern totalitarian regimes. Strauss's views remain stimulating, however, for someone interested in the process of reading or rereading between the lines. In effect, they suggest a full-fledged method of reading the classics, specifically the classics of philosophy and political philosophy from Plato to Maimonides and Spinoza but also, if we purge it of its eccentricities, some of the great literary classics. But before looking more closely at this method, let us consider Strauss's larger argument, which emphasizes the old cleavage between an *esoteric* and predominantly oral tradition and a written *exoteric* tradition; for the great problem of reading is to keep constantly aware of this cleavage and to try to recover, from its exoteric expression, the true oral-esoteric meaning buried in a great premodern text. Even though the exoteric writing in the classics (which is what has survived and come down to us) is deliberately evasive and misleading, it is so, Strauss believes, only for the superficial and naive reader. This same writing will eventually disclose its hidden truth to those who deserve it by their reading extremely carefully and being highly intelligent as well as virtuous, in keeping with the fundamental Socratic equation of knowledge and virtue. Earlier philosophical writers, Strauss goes on to say,

> believed that the gulf separating "the wise" and "the vulgar" was a basic fact of human nature which could not be influenced by any progress of popular education: philosophy, or science, was essentially the privilege of "the few." . . . Even if they had nothing to fear from any particular political quarter . . . [they thought] that public communication of the philosophic or scientific truth was impossible or undesirable, not only for the time being but for all times. They must conceal their opinions from all but philosophers, either by limiting themselves to oral instruction of a carefully selected group of pupils, or by writing about the most important subject by means of "brief indication." (p. 35)

In times of political persecution and strict censorship, the means of hiding true or deeply believed statements become more diverse and elaborate. But essentially, for Strauss, whose own position is that of a highly sophisticated antimodernist, all the major premodern (that is, pre-eighteenth-century) philosophers chose the method of disclosing the truth only briefly and, as it were, in passing, amid a host of statements fit only for "exoteric consumption" by the vast "nonphilosophic majority" of readers. Such exoteric statements had the status of mere "opinions" which, moreover would be only accidentally "consonant with the truth":

· · ·

Being a philosopher, that is, hating "the lie in the soul" more than anything else, he would not deceive himself about the fact that such opinions are merely "likely tales," or "noble lies," or "probable opinions," and would leave it to his readers to disentangle the truth from its poetic or dialectic presentation. From the standpoint of the literary historian at least, there is no more noteworthy distinction between the typical premodern philosopher . . . and the typical modern philosopher than that of their attitudes toward "noble (or just) lies," "pious frauds," the "ductus obliquus" or "economy of truth" (p. 35).

Strauss also notes that "the decent modern reader" can only be shocked at the thought that "a great man might have deliberately deceived a large majority of his readers." The antimodernism of Strauss's stance could not be brought out more clearly.

The Hidden-Treasure Model of Reading

Strauss's model of reading—extremely careful reading and constant rereading of the classics—presumes a "hidden treasure" of meaning for which one must search patiently, indefatigably, almost heroically. This model need not be interpreted along politically conservative or socially aristocratic lines; what it presupposes is only an aristocracy of the mind, which is in fact the equivalent of an intellectual meritocracy of those who think well and read well. I have already touched on this issue in the discussion of what I called "didactic secrets" in the previous chapter, where I quoted John Ruskin. His testimony is as relevant in today's more political, or politically colored, context as it was in his own time. Ruskin, who was in many ways a political radical with clearly articulated ideals of liberal social justice, proposed a model of reading the classics that is hauntingly similar to that of Strauss: "It is a strange habit of wise humanity to speak in enigmas only, so that the highest truths and usefullest laws must be hunted through whole picture galleries of dreams, which to the vulgar seem dreams only. Thus Homer, the Greek tragedians, Plato, Dante, Chaucer, Shakespeare, and Goethe, have hidden all that is chiefly serviceable in their work; and in all the various literature they absorbed and re-embodied, under types which have rendered it quite useless to the multitude" (*Munera pulveris*, p. 208).

Presented in such terms, the model of reading under discussion here is hardly attractive not only to Strauss's "decent modern reader"—one who is assumed to long for transparency and thus expect straight meaning

. . .

from straight talk—but also to the much more sophisticated and suspicious contemporary theorist. The theorist will reject the hidden-treasure metaphor as inadequate not so much for political reasons (even though its would-be antidemocratic or elitist implications are quite unsavory) as because he or she sees the very distinction between an overt and a covert meaning as questionable in light of the impossibility to decide who is ultimately responsible for the meaning of any text. The meaning of a text, the argument goes, is not there to be uncovered, mined like a precious ore or found as a patient, well-trained treasure hunter will find a long-sought treasure; if we readers are involved creatively in the production of textual meaning—as we always are, according to various orientations in contemporary theory—how are we to tell the difference between what an author puts in a text, or "the author's intention," and what we put in it?

My answer is a pragmatic one: there is no universal method for telling the difference between the intention of the author, the intention of the text, and the intention of the reader, but individual texts will present us with individual versions of this problem. Such individual versions will lend themselves to individual solutions depending on the would-be solver's focus and interests. In other words, the question of textual meaning (overt or covert, authorial or lectorial, and so on) cannot be dealt with profitably unless a few additional questions, usually ignored by theorists, are considered: Why do we (re)read a specific text and why do we want to ascertain its meaning? What do we hope to accomplish in (re)reading the text and articulating its meaning? And—most important, at least to literary critics—why do we think that what we hope to accomplish is interesting and deserves to be communicated to others?

I think that in the context of rereading for the secret, the simile of the hidden treasure of meaning is apt, whatever the reasons for rejecting it in other contexts. At any rate, let us grant that an author who is worth anything "cannot say it all; and what is more strange, *will* not, but in a hidden way and in parables, in order that he may be sure you want it. I cannot quite see the reason of this, nor analyse that cruel reticence in the breasts of wise men which makes them always hide their deeper thought" (Ruskin, *Sesame and Lilies*, p. 63).

Beyond the sense of reading as self-reading and self-discovery (I see the metaphor of the treasure buried in the text as a way of referring to the treasure buried in the reader's own mind or psyche) there is the much older and larger tradition of Biblical exegesis, to which Ruskin is undoubtedly alluding. More specifically, in mentioning hidden ways and parables,

. . .

Ruskin indirectly cites passages from the Bible, such as the words Jesus utters in Mark (4:10–12) right after he tells the parable of the sower to the multitude gathered by the sea:

> And when he was alone, they that were about him with the twelve asked of him the parable.
>
> And he said unto them, Unto you it is given to know the mystery of the kingdom of God: but unto them that are without, all *these* things are done in parables:
>
> That seeing they may see, and not perceive; and hearing they may hear, and not understand; lest at any time they should be converted, and *their* sins should be forgiven them.

Jesus goes on to interpret the meaning of the parable, even though those to whom he speaks should have had immediate access to it since, as Jesus had indicated, they *knew* the mystery of the kingdom of God. Intriguingly, Jesus's explanatory allegories turn out to be other parables, ultimately more difficult to understand than the deceptively simple first parable of the sower, whose sense they were supposed to clarify. Speaking of all these allegories taken together, Mark (4:33–34) offers these comments: "And with many such parables spake he the word unto them, as they were able to hear *it*. But without a parable spake he not unto them: and when they were alone, he expounded all things to his disciples."

Mark, who like the other gospel writers worked in the rich Jewish tradition of midrash and rabbinical interpretation, alludes here to a passage in Ezekiel (17:1–2) where the prophet declares that God ordered him to "put forth a riddle [the parable of the two eagles and a vine] and speak a parable unto the house of Israel." Over its long canonic existence, Mark 4 and its parallels in the other gospels have been the object of a huge exegetical literature of ever-different and ever-unexpected (if often rapidly banalized) rereadings—from theological, historical, and secular-literary perspectives. The literary perspective is adopted, for example, in an elegant book by Frank Kermode, *The Genesis of Secrecy,* which starts by focusing on the parables in Mark and then compares them with those in other gospel writers and with symbolic literary narratives as diverse as those of Henry Green, Franz Kafka, or James Joyce. Kermode's thesis is that any narrative worth its while participates to some degree in the obliquity and secrecy of parabolic narration.

I have mentioned Ruskin and the Bible merely to suggest the importance and ancientness of the tradition of recognizing the essential obliq-

. . .

uity or doubleness of major writing. Even major modernist writing—as the works of a Kafka or Joyce or Faulkner or Pound testify—participates in that tradition and demands from its readers a kind of attention that is not unrelated to the extraordinary attention demanded by Scripture from its faithful rereaders.

The Modern Myth of Transparency

With the growth of "extensive reading," the growing prestige of science, and the rise of political democracy, modernity has fostered a powerful longing for transparency doubled by a hostility to those forms of secrecy that were traditionally claimed as a prerogative of power, whether supernatural or human. But the modern ideal of transparency does not apply to the personal secrets of individuals, which, again reversing a long-standing tradition, should from now on be protected by the modern "right to privacy." The democratic longing for transparency in public affairs has certainly been one of the factors that favored the writing and reading of clear, unmysterious, largely self-explanatory texts, be they for entertainment, as in the case of the modern popular genres and subgenres of fiction, or for instruction and intellectual enlightenment. This same longing for transparency explains the proliferation of explanatory texts—commentaries on more difficult primary classical texts and even commentaries on commentaries—which many students of literature prefer to read in place of the more difficult primary texts.

In describing this new situation, Frank Kermode speaks of a veritable modern "myth of transparency" and underscores the corrective purpose of a book like his *The Genesis of Secrecy,* which attempts to make a persuasive case for reading the original texts and not only what has been written *about* them:

> We are so habituated to the myth of transparency that we continue, as Jean Starobinski neatly puts it, to ignore *what is written* in favor of *what is written about.* One purpose of this book is to reverse that priority. . . . The scholarly tradition that cultivated seriously this form of attention was Jewish; and from our point of view its most important representative was Spinoza. When he drew his rules of scriptural interpretation . . . he distinguished strictly between meaning and truth (what is written and what is written about): in exegesis "we are at work," he said, "not on the truth of passages but on their meaning." . . . Five centuries of Jewish interpretative rationalism stood behind Spinoza; but he was addressing the problems of

· · ·

265

his own day, and saw that the confusion of meaning and truth might result in the suppression of religious liberty. His pious book seemed blasphemous in 1670; so powerful is the atavistic preference for truth over meaning. (p. 119)

The fact is, however, that Spinoza's *Tractatus Theologico-Politicus,* a landmark in the history of modern liberal democracy and, more specifically, in the history of the concept of freedom of thought, has remained highly controversial to this day. The *Tractatus* indeed raises delicate and still explosive issues: How are we to read sacred texts or texts that are held sacred by large numbers of people? And how are we to communicate the true conclusions we reach in reading such texts, if these conclusions are unorthodox and we live in an orthodox, more or less intolerant or inquisitorial, milieu? Spinoza's defense of religious tolerance and freedom of thought is an example of how extreme theoretical courage (a courage, it has sometimes been said, of being a full-fledged atheist at a time of fanatical religious commitments) can ally itself to subtle obliquity, apparent inconsistency, and unapparent subversion.

Spinoza, the Bible, and the Fictionalization of the Sacred

The rationalistic hermeneutic rules established by Spinoza, mostly in chapter 7 of the *Tractatus,* are meant to help the interpreter of the Bible distinguish between the "true meaning"—or the meaning *believed to be true* by the author of the text—and truth itself insofar as we can have access to it by way of our rational faculty. Of course the Bible makes claims to truth all the time, but these we are in no position to judge since the truth involved is revealed, suprarational, and therefore inaccessible to human reason. The true meaning of the stories in the Bible is another matter, however: we can, through rational analysis in the context of the Bible as a whole, determine, for instance, whether a certain passage should be understood literally or metaphorically. Likewise we can decide, on the basis of the frequency with which certain clear and distinct moral ideas occur, what the major teachings of the Bible are. These teachings, according to Spinoza, are simple and indeed accessible to everybody. Nonetheless, many passages will remain unclear, and to establish their true meaning one would have first to establish when the text was written, by whom, and for what purpose, without neglecting possible linguistic ambiguities or indeterminacies resulting from the Hebrew writing system.

· · ·

Historical research of this kind is unnecessary when we read simple and clear texts, such as the principles of Euclid.

But interpreting Scripture from its own history, as Spinoza notes, will not remove all the obscurities. Actually, so many obscurities remain that he does not "hesitate to say that the true meaning of Scripture is in many places inexplicable, or at best mere subject for guesswork" (*A Theologico-Political Treatise,* p. 112). Still, Spinoza points out, we will judge a story in the Bible, however incomprehensible, differently from a similar story told in order to amuse (a fictitious narrative such as Ariosto's *Orlando Furioso*) or from one that has a political purpose. The style as well as the intent of the following passage is characteristic of Spinoza's way of writing in the *Tractatus,* which touched on such extremely delicate matters that it had to be published, in even relatively tolerant Amsterdam, anonymously and with the name of a fictitious Hamburg publisher:

> It often happens that in different books we read histories in themselves similar, but which we judge very differently, according to the opinions we have formed of the authors. I remember once to have read in some book that a man named Orlando Furioso used to drive a kind of winged monster through the air, fly over any countries he liked, kill unaided vast numbers of men and giants, and such like fancies, which from the point of view of reason are obviously absurd. A very similar story I read in Ovid of Perseus, and also in the books of Judges and Kings of Samson, who alone and unarmed killed thousands of men, and of Elijah, who flew through the air, and at last went up to heaven in a chariot of fire, with horses of fire. All these stories are obviously alike, but we judge them very differently. The first one sought to amuse, the second had a political object, the third a religious object. (p. 112)

Read within the context of the whole *Tractatus* (and particularly in light of the immediately preceding chapter, "Of Miracles," which argues that miracles are impossible) the passage is an example of shrewd obliquity. All three texts mentioned by Spinoza narrate obviously fantastic events. In Ariosto's case the purpose of such narration is openly to please, poetic fictions being "beautiful lies" devised to gratify the reader. In the case of Ovid, whatever one may say in favor of a possible allusive political meaning of the figure of Perseus in books 4 and 5 of *Metamorphoses,* what strikes the reader is the grand rhetoric used consistently and almost ostentatiously by the poet in his rendering of the myth. The three main episodes recounted by Ovid are the killing of the Gorgon Medusa, with the help of such magical objects as the winged sandals, which allow

. . .

Perseus to fly through the air, or the helmet of Hades, which had the property of rendering its wearer invisible; the rescue of Andromeda; and the disruption of Perseus's wedding to Andromeda by Phineus, followed by the fight in which Perseus defeats his enemies by showing them the fearsome head of Medusa and thus causing them to be suddenly metamorphosed into marble statues. Even if the story is meant also as a eulogy of Augustus, there appears to be nothing intrinsically political about Ovid's treatment of Perseus, nothing that would prompt us to interpret it any differently than Ariosto's treatment of Orlando. That the Biblical figures (Samson, Elijah) mentioned by Spinoza are evoked for a different, religious purpose is doubtless; but does not the commentator, by the mere fact of comparing them to such fictional/mythical beings as Perseus and Orlando suggest that the reader should be free after all to interpret them likewise, as pure fictions? And is not Spinoza's one of the earliest proposals—radically if almost invisibly demystifying—to read the Bible as literature, that is, as fiction?

Such an interpretation of the Spinoza passage is consistent with both the view that he remained a (philosophical) believer of sorts, at least insofar as belief was not incompatible with reason, and the view that he was a complete atheist. The latter view is defended by Leo Strauss, who, however, in keeping with his general theory of esotericism, argues that for Spinoza the Bible, including the New Testament, contained an "esoteric rationality" in contrast with its exoteric teachings; in other words, that for him the Bible consisted "partly of vulgar statements and partly of philosophical statements which deliberately and secretly contradict the vulgar ones" (*Persecution*, p. 182). But in making such a claim Strauss contradicts Spinoza's unambiguous assertion that what is rational in the Bible, namely, its moral teaching, is clear and distinct for anyone and is reaffirmed frequently, and that this rational moral core has little to do with the many undecidable passages or with the various fabulous accounts of miracles and supernatural events. For Spinoza rationality itself could not be esoteric—his model of a rational text was Euclid, and there could be nothing hidden or nontransparent about the principles of geometry—although the results of rational analysis under certain circumstances, particularly when bearing on delicate matters of faith and orthodoxy, could and should be communicated cautiously and obliquely. The reasons for Spinoza's prudence are thus circumstantial and political, and his broad ideal of writing, as a modern rationalist philosopher in the Cartesian tradition, is ultimate transparency and inclusiveness, not opacity and

· · ·

exclusiveness. Even the obliquities of the *Tractatus* contain all the elements for identifying the plain meaning or, as the case may be, the strategic ambiguities and the unanswered or unanswerable questions. Such questions are not necessarily of a "mystical" nature: there are demonstrably insoluble problems, after all, even in mathematics.

Are There Rules for Distinguishing Esoteric from Exoteric Statements?

Is there a universal method or set of methods or rules by which obliquity may be identified and the esoteric meaning separated from the exoteric? I would answer that there is not, nor can there be, a fixed method or set of rules for doing so. If there were, obliquity would become useless. As a good writer who addresses someone capable of reading between the lines will make use of a variety of procedures for disguising meaning—including all sorts of impromptu codes by which he or she will not only bypass the censor but also initiate successful coordination games with the likeminded reader—so a good reader between the lines will always be as flexible as possible and observe only one (negative) rule: Never cling to any fixed rules.

Writers who have fought censorship and who know its inner workings well are often aware of its ultimate ineffectuality in screening the truth that fiction can convey (this truth being of course completely different from what I called fictional truth in Part III). Thus, the South African novelist J. M. Coetzee wrote in 1987: "Storytelling can take care of itself. Is this true? Have censors been so ineffectual, century after century? Yes, they have. They are ineffectual because, in laying down the rules that stories may not transgress, and enforcing these rules, they fail to recognize that the offensiveness of stories lies not in their transgressing particular rules but in their faculty of making and changing their own rules. There is a game going on between the covers of the book, but it is not always the game you think it is" ("The Novel Today," p. 3).

Censorship can become singularly effective, however, when it ceases to operate by any rules itself. This rare case of a chaotic, totally unpredictable, indeed Kafkaesque censorship was realized in some of the former Communist countries of Eastern Europe, such as Nicolae Ceausescu's Romania. The psychological effects of such censorship on the writer are accurately described by the novelist Norman Manea. Speaking of his novel *The Black Envelope* (published in Bucharest in a heavily censored

· · ·

version in 1986), he confessed that no words of praise for it could "counteract the irritation I felt when I reread the book. It was not the disappearance from the edited version of various dark details of daily life that upset me, not the 'softening' of many passages. It was really the warping effect of all that encoding. Stylistic excess and opacity. Devitalization, circuitousness, waste" ("The Censor's Report," p. 105).

From a reader's point of view, even apparently simple rules of thumb for identifying and interpreting obliquity or secrecy, useful as they may be in certain cases, may become misleading: all depends on *how* and *when* they are applied and, more important, by *whom*. The interpreter's background knowledge, skill, general intelligence, and philosophical or ideological orientation must always be taken into account. No rules will prevent, for example, the follower of certain esoteric doctrines from reading all sorts of initiatory secrets *into* texts that are known for their difficulties, ambiguities, and veiled or allegorical modes. Such readers may even arrive at occasionally interesting insights (insights that are perversely dependent on their overall wrongheaded method of reading), although most of their interpretations will eventually look farfetched, cranky, and perhaps slightly paranoid. No commonsense rules of thumb, of course, will stop paranoid ideological extremists from projecting their conspiratorial conception of society onto what they read and from constantly "verifying" it. Such a projection is facilitated by the tendency in extremist ideological contexts for secrecy to lose its functional character and become purely symbolic, as the sociologist Edward Shils has observed.[4]

Symbolic secrecy, insofar as it is a measure not only of one's loyalty to the ideology of a given party or sect, but also of one's alertness to the subversive activities of a hidden and infinitely wicked enemy, fosters paranoid fantasies which are bound to influence one's reading. But symbolic secrecy is much older and more comprehensive than the modern forms of political paranoia might immediately suggest. Its traditions go back to ancient mystery cults, initiatory rites, secret societies, and various hermetic religious or quasi-religious practices in both the East and the West. It is not by chance that Umberto Eco, in writing his recent conspiracy-detective-esoteric novel *Foucault's Pendulum* (both a parody and an encyclopedia of esoterica through the centuries) has drawn on them in the same seriocomic manner as he has on modern political myths and types of paranoid imagination.

As for the rules for reading between the lines, the most one can say of them is that they cannot be better (or worse) than the interpreter who

. . .

applies them. At this point, it might be useful to take a closer look at some such rules that have been proposed. Leo Strauss provides a whole list of dos and don'ts derived from two "axioms": the first is that certain authors (including all the great classics) address only the very careful reader and that they exclude the superficial reader from understanding their true meaning; the second is that "a careful writer of normal intelligence is more intelligent than the most intelligent censor" (*Persecution*, p. 26). Here are some of the rules for reading between the lines suggested by Strauss (I have slightly reformulated them): (a) no reading between the lines is warranted unless it makes one's perception of a text more exact and clear than a straight reading would; (b) the reader must perfectly understand the context in which oblique statements occur, in light of the character and plan of the work as a whole (in this sense reading between the lines can only be *re*reading); (c) the reader must consider the possibility of irony; (d) obvious blunders, such "as would shame an intelligent high school boy," should be seen as intentional and as signaling that hidden meaning must be looked for; (e) the real views of an author are not necessarily those most frequently expressed in his works, nor should they be identified with the views of his characters; (f) internal contradictions within a corpus should not be automatically resolved by genetic hypotheses (for example, that the author must have changed his mind on the matter at hand), nor should contradictions found in older works—works that have come down to us from manuscript cultures—be attributed to spurious interpolations unless there is solid evidence; (g) of two flatly contradictory statements in the same work, one is intentionally false, the other is true— and it is the task of the reader to decide which is which;[5] (h) reading between the lines implies studious *re*reading—thus, in order to make sure that a book written in a period of persecution does indeed surreptitiously contradict the orthodox or official doctrine, "we must study [the] book all over again, with much greater care and much less naivete than ever before" (p. 32); (i) the secret truth must sometimes be looked for in places that belie its importance—in an easily missed parenthesis, in the small print of a footnote, in a haphazard comment; and (j) in certain cases the truth may be expressed by a silence or absence, from which the careful reader must infer it.

In summary, reading between the lines means being extremely attentive and refusing to take anything in the text at face value unless there is proof to the contrary. One may quibble that each of Strauss's rules is problematic, raising many more hermeneutical problems than it promises to solve.

. . .

Taken in combination, however, his recommendations look quite reasonable and, what is more, the way they are applied to the works discussed in *Persecution and the Art of Writing* displays a rare combination of erudition and intellectual brilliance.

The "secret truths" eventually disclosed by a Straussian reading, however, remain frustratingly elusive or ungraspably abstract. Maimonides' *Guide for the Perplexed,* Strauss argues, "is devoted to the explanation of an esoteric doctrine [hidden in the Bible]. But this explanation has itself an esoteric character. . . . Consequently it is a book with seven seals" (p. 55). Along similar lines, he sees the "purpose of the *Guide* . . . [as] not only to reveal the truth, but also to hide it. . . . [A] considerable number of statements are made in order to hide the truth rather than teach it" (p. 66). Curiously, Strauss himself seems to emulate rather than really explain Maimonides. Or is his conclusion (never stated as such) that the precise content of the vaunted secret truths of the Bible (which Maimonides attempted to reveal by hiding) is unimportant in itself and that what really counts is the "seven seals" under which it is locked? Or is he suggesting that such awesome secrets are revealed only in an act of absolute reading with absolute attention paid in absolute silence?

Or do my questions betray the inadequate, unphilosophical response of a merely literary reader to Strauss's philosophical argument? Be that as it may, I think that rereading for the secret—rereading for what a text conceals, holds away, means obliquely or allegorically, hints at but refuses to name, or names falsely, misleadingly, and tantalizingly—has its ultimate reward not in the discovery of a certain truth but in the quality of attention it achieves. This is so whether the text in question is philosophical, political, religious, or poetic. The major revelation produced by rereading for the secret is simply (but also mysteriously) the value of attention, of intense concentration, of focused ingenuity, of total absorption.

. . .

EPILOGUE

. . . .

The end is where we start from.
T. S. ELIOT
"Little Gidding"

. . . .

Since the time of reading is at once linear and circular, differences between beginnings and endings can be at once categorical and so relative as to vanish altogether. Beginnings and endings may therefore become interchangeable—less so in the case of narratives with a linear suspenseful plot and a surprising ending and much more so in the case of books of criticism like this one—while remaining important, privileged places where the articulate silence of reading actually starts or stops.

Some readers, myself included, are often tempted to begin with the epilogue and end with the preface or introduction. Indeed, many readers of a theoretical work will look first at the epilogue—if not directly at the bibliography—to decide whether they want to read it. Many others will take a quick look at the introduction and then leap straight to the conclusion, using the great freedom of movement forward and backward that reading allows. Only an ideal reader—a critical fiction—moves continuously through a text of some length from beginning to end. "Normal" readers skip, skim, swim back and forth, are happy to

. . .

have their attention caught but may lose interest at any point and drop the book.

Perhaps the best way to sum up the central argument of my essay is to tell a story—the story of how I came to write this essay on an intricate, difficult, and little-researched topic. What led me to it was an experience of rereading . . . for the secret. In the mid-1980s, after several "innocent" readings of certain texts by an author in whom I was interested at the time, I discovered that they contained carefully coded meanings that came to me as a total surprise. To refer in more detail to those texts would be both cumbersome and superfluous here. Suffice it to say that they confronted me with a number of theoretical problems in which all of a sudden I took great interest: How does one conceal meaning? What is the relationship between latent, hidden meaning and manifest, deceptive meaning? How can an outsider decipher concealed meaning? And how can an outsider become aware even of the existence of such meaning when it is well concealed?

Curiously, at first I was not concerned with a situation that was all too familiar to me as an émigré from Communist Romania, where I had been active as a writer, critic, and secret opponent of the regime between 1958, when I started publishing poetry and criticism, and 1973, when I came to the United States. The situation I am referring to is that of political censorship and includes the strategies adopted by writers to evade the censor and communicate with a reader capable of reading between the lines. The questions generated by the interrelationship of censorship, persecution, and secrecy in writing and reading imposed themselves on me later, and I have naturally dealt with them in this book; but I am not sure I have given them all the attention they deserve. I might get back to them on another occasion.

Anyhow, it was my perplexities in regard to secrecy and, more broadly, the enigmatic in literature that constituted the starting point of my reflection on rereading. Scrutinized with attention, intentionally concealed meaning in literary texts reveals a multiplicity of facets to the sensitive reader. Meaning can be hidden for purposes of serious communication—mystical, political, or metaphysical. Quite often, however, it is playfully concealed in order to create and manipulate reader interest (an enigma is posited and a solution is tantalizingly promised), or to achieve psychological suspense (narrative information is disclosed with unexpected twists, calculated delays, or strategic retractions), or to challenge the reader's

· · ·

ingenuity (the work itself may appear as a puzzle). Secrecy, in other words, frequently has a ludic dimension.

This raised for me the question of reading, rereading, and play. In what sense can reading be seen as a form of play, as an act of fantasy or imagining, a mode of impersonating, pretending, playing imaginary roles? More important, is it illuminating or productive to consider it from such a point of view? Reading, most obviously in the case of fictional texts, can be described as a way of playing games of make-believe that may lead to deep involvement and even to a sort of hypnosis or trance; it can also be seen, particularly in the case of reflective rereading, as playing games with rules, games that can be played more adeptly and more inventively by the experienced reader who will not only become deeply absorbed but will possibly cross the threshold from purely mental (re)writing to real creative writing. But beyond the distinction between involvement and absorption, the problem of play—including imaginary playacting—is relevant to my broader understanding of literary reading as *performance*. To read a literary work is to perform in several senses of the word. It is, first, to perform a role—the role of the reader as "scripted" in the text. The script, like the stage directions in most plays, is usually sketchy, and the reader is thus called upon to infer and improvise, guess and try, and eventually construct a role that gives a maximum of emotional and intellectual satisfaction. To read is, second, to perform in one's own mind the roles of major characters in a work of fiction—to become something of an *actor* who switches among various roles in an extended mental solo performance. But, in a third sense, to read is also a kind of mental stage directing, which includes, aside from coaching the fictive actors, designing the sets, selecting the costumes, and visualizing such expressive details as gestures, movements, and faces. To read is, in other words, to give voice, articulation, and shape to the text's silent language, to fill out its "spots of indeterminacy" (Ingarden), to give meaning and life to the printed page in one's imagination. And these are only some of the numerous possibilities of what I have called games of reading and rereading as they can be construed from various disciplinary perspectives ranging from cultural anthropology to sociology and game theory.

My tacit assumption throughout Part III was the standpoint of a contemporary reader, whether a highly skilled, experienced, and sophisticated player or a naive seeker after the daydream pleasures of reading for pure relaxation or escape. I worked on Part III, "Play" and Part II,

. . .

"History, Psychology, Poetics" during the same period, switching from one to the other. There are obvious continuities, if not overlappings, between these two parts. Questions posed in Part III required answers that went beyond the area of play, however generously defined. Readers of different ages may read to satisfy different psychological needs and have widely different patterns of reading, even if we consider only the case of reading for pleasure and exclude what might be called "work-reading" or reading to fulfill an obligation of whatever sort. Other differences in "places and situations of reading" and reader's background or gender also lead to sharply distinct, and on occasion diverging, constructions of the reading, and even more so the rereading, of one and the same literary text. Finally, the question of rereading had to be addressed also in the case of noncontemporary readers, that is, from the perspective of the history of reading. Hence the discussion of the distinction used by some historians of reading between intensive reading (actually rereading) and extensive, diversionary reading. One great historical paradox is that rereading as a practice preceded reading. To an early occurrence of the conflict between rereading and reading we owe the extraordinary Quixotic adventures in what I have called, with an awkward but perhaps not inaccurate term, misrereading.

Although the project to write this essay originated in my stumbling upon the unexpectedly esoteric meanings of certain innocuous-looking texts, I was not new to rereading. Actually, as a teacher of literature I had for many years been a professional rereader and a teacher of literary rereading. I suddenly recalled a witty remark made by Nabokov at Cornell in the introduction to his course on masterpieces of the novel: "One cannot *read* a book; one can only reread it." The chapter in which I dissect what I call "Nabokov's paradox" was in fact the one I wrote first. It led naturally to an exploration of the temporality of reading and rereading and of other paradoxes, such as the symmetrical opposite of Nabokov's paradox, namely, that one cannot read the *same* book twice. I then examined the way one might try to resolve such paradoxes, however unsatisfactorily: the conception of a circular, "mythic" time of (re)reading, a time in which, as Roland Barthes put it, there is no *before* or *after,* a time in which—to repeat—epilogues can become prologues and vice versa.

On a more conventional conclusive note, I wish to stress that rereading cannot be made into the clear univocal term of an ideally simple critical dichotomy, as one would wish. That is perhaps why a brief summation of

· · ·

the kinds of rereading considered in this book, in their dialectical relationship with reading, might be of some retrospective use. There are—and this is already an oversimplification—three basic ways of rereading stories. The first, and certainly the most frequent, is *partial rereading* (or backtracking) in order to recall more precisely certain significant textual details, or to take full cognizance of essential narrative information to which one has not paid, for whatever reason, sufficient attention the first time around. Such partial rereading, whose need arises from a fault in the mechanics of reading (insufficient concentration, absentmindedness, difficulty of comprehension, an unresponsive state of mind), has been of little concern in this essay.

Two other basic kinds of rereading stories have occupied centerstage: *simple (unreflective) rereading* or the repeating of a game of make-believe for the sheer pleasure of repeating it—the most important addition, the second time around, being a sense of psychological reassurance likely to accompany a game whose sequence and outcome are known, even if the player pretends not to know them; and *reflective rereading,* a meditative or critically inquisitive revisiting of a text one has already read. Reflective rereading can itself pursue a variety of purposes, such as rereading for replaying the original game of make-believe as a game with rules in order to enjoy it more intelligently, or even to study it and penetrate some of the secrets of its making; rereading with a view to improving one's understanding of the structure and inner logic of a given game by comparison with other games of the same type (such a rereading would be characteristic of the approach to fiction taken by poetics); rereading for the purpose of becoming more familiar with the fictional world of a particular work in view of interpreting it in a new manner (such an approach, characteristic of what we might call historical hermeneutics, involves a knowledge of earlier interpretations and a competitive attempt to best them); rereading with an introspective bent, in order to understand the nature of reading or rereading and to make it more self-conscious in all its complexity (this has been one of the main goals of this book; rereading (especially certain modernist and postmodernist works) for the purpose of establishing what might be fictionally true in their world; rereading for producing new fictional games of make-believe or fictional games with rules or both (this kind of *writerly* rereading or mental rewriting has come up again and again and has turned out to be one of the mainsprings of literary creativity); and rereading that attempts to decipher a potential secret or oblique reference in a text, to guess the hidden rules by which it has been produced

. . .

and, most important, to discern its possible explanations (from the pleasure of playing a game to the need to express heretical views covertly in a controlled culture).

If I were to point out that all the discussions of particular literary works in this book, whether shorter or analytically more detailed, try to account for experiences of rereading, I would be saying very little indeed. All criticism, good or bad, intelligent or obtuse, enlightening or obfuscating, impressionistic or systematic, prestructuralist or poststructuralist, presupposes rereading, even when it does not know it. What I think is less common about my discussion of these texts is the self-consciousness of their rereading, the attempt to deautomatize the mental operations involved in it, and the choice of specific frames within which the works are examined. These frames are derived from some of the fundamental questions a self-conscious rereader is likely to ask in order to understand *why* he or she rereads and *how*.

Thus Borges's "The Aleph," in chapter 1, was first framed in terms of these questions: How is a first-time (hypothetical) reader going to understand the story? What facts might he or she retain? What meaning could they have? The very form of these questions suggests that even the (theoretical) firstness of a first reading can be fully understood, in its transitoriness and fragility, only from the perspective of rereading. A second framing followed and, at that introductory stage it was meant to dramatize some of the main issues of rereading: the desire to replay the game of reading, the desire to understand its deeper rules, the desire to decipher its secrets. As the distinction between reading and rereading was elaborated theoretically, the framing of subsequent literary examples became more specific: historical in the case of Alonso Quijano/Don Quixote, who is our archetypal rereader (otherwise how would he know by heart the books of chivalry from which he quotes freely all the time?); broadly ludic in the case of *Pale Fire* (a crazy quilt of playful intertextuality being used here as a device for creating the need to reread and the sense of an infinite text); ludic again, but more nuanced and complex, in the case of *The Turn of the Screw* (which illustrates fictionally certain epistemological-legal puzzles derived from the question of the trustworthiness of a narrative testimony). The framing of Robbe-Grillet's early novels was also ludic (the game played by his texts consists of systematically flaunting the rules of the conventional, make-believe realistic novel) and illustrated what I called, paraphrasing Gérard Genette's "literature in the second degree," (re)reading in the second degree.

· · ·

In the final part of the book, Henry James's "The Private Life" was framed as a story about secrecy, privacy, and creativity. My main example of rereading for the secret, I realize, is perhaps not the most obvious. Using secrecy, however, as a frame for a rereading of James, one gains a subtle insight into the moral-psychological implications of secrecy—secrecy as a curse and a disease but also secrecy and privacy as a shield for the creative life of the imagination. One also becomes aware of certain problems raised by secret or oblique references—to the poet Robert Browning and the painter Frederic Leighton in the case of James's novella. Particularly the presence of the character of Browning in the text brought to mind a series of questions directly related to rereading and (overt or covert) intertextuality: How did James read Browning? How did he "read" his social personality in contrast with the literary one? In what sense is James's later reading of *The Ring and the Book* as a novel relevant to our understanding of "The Private Life," where Browning is portrayed as a novelist? How important is it to identify a secret or oblique reference and how does such an identification change the regime of (re)reading?

Was the choice of my literary examples arbitrary? In an essay, I think, one is given greater leeway to use one's own favorite examples than might be the case in other critical genres. Arbitrary, though, is the wrong word. As an inveterate rereader, I could not agree more with Georges Perec, a fellow rereader: "I re-read the books I love and I love the books I re-read." With few exceptions, the books I have mentioned or discussed here have haunted me for some time, and they will surely go on doing so: for there is no end to rereading. Still, I had to select, and I decided to limit myself to fiction, although poetry is more clearly designed for rereading than prose. But poetry is more resistant to simple, linear, "extensive" reading; at least in certain respects it resembles some modernist and postmodernist pieces of fiction that are not readable but only rereadable. Yet the pure re-readability of poetry, and not only of modern poetry with its deliberate ignorance of anecdote or any kind of story, would have confronted me with a different set of problems than the prose works I undertook to analyze in terms of (re)reading. Most of the central concepts I have used—fictionality, fictional truth, feigning, pretending, impersonating, playing roles, playing games of symbolic make-believe in contrast to games with rules—do not appear to be immediately applicable to most poetry. Nor could the linear and transparent readability of straight fiction (as in the case of the detective mystery) be so readily and conveniently evoked for purposes of contrast. Obviously, there are exceptions—Robert Browning,

. . .

for instance, whose *The Ring and the Book,* as we saw, could be read as a novel along the lines suggested by Henry James. But the question of reading poetry is separate and deserves separate treatment. The mental activities involved in rereading poetry—on which I touched only accidentally and indirectly—are clearly the subject of another book.

Within the area of fiction, I decided to focus on older or modern classics, that is, on works that one might wish to reread and that, even if one has not read them yet, one is almost forced to reread even the first time around. An added advantage is that these same works, on being reexperienced, can convey the sense of freshness associated with first readings, an apparent paradox which I have discussed at several junctures. As for the implied reader of this book, he or she is simply one who is ready to scrutinize himself or herself as a reader and, most emphatically, as a rereader. I have quoted in several contexts Proust's famous view of reading as self-reading. More narrowly, the reader postulated in these pages is invited to consider—in the same general mode of self-reading, but with a stress on his or her *literary* experiences—one of the major, if often ignored, possibilities opened up by reading: the act of rereading and its epiphanies.

. . .

One: Rereading Borges's "The Aleph"

1. The paradoxes and perplexities of the relationship between the two are wittily examined in the essay "Borges and I."

2. See Jerome Bruner, *Actual Minds, Possible Worlds.* In his attempt to construct a psychology of reading literature, Bruner naturally comes across the problem of the "virtual text" a reader creates, but considers it only in terms of a first reading and not of rereading. "In our research," Bruner writes, "we ask our readers to tell us back the story in their own words: to create, so to speak, a virtual text. . . . We did subject the 'told back' version of one of our readers, an experienced reader of fiction in his late teens who was reading the story for the first time. He told it back to us a day later. His version of [James Joyce's] 'Clay' was . . . typically shorter than the story." Bruner then discusses the main transformations to which Joyce's text had been submitted in the reader's "virtual text" (pp. 32ff.). In the appendix to *Actual Minds* Joyce's "Clay" is printed in a column facing the "virtual text" of the reader's retelling. It would be interesting to submit a critic's "virtual text" of a story—an extended commentary on "The Aleph," for example—to a similar transformational analysis. The "virtual text" in this last case would of course have to be considered the result of an indefinite number of rereadings.

3. See Gene H. Bell-Villada, *Borges and his Fiction,* p. 223. I find the whole section devoted to "The Aleph" in Bell-Villada's book one of the most careful critical (re)readings of the famous story (see pp. 219–29).

4. See Daniel Devoto, "Alephe et Alexis," p. 285.

. . .

5. For this observation see also Devoto, "Alephe et Alexis." But why did Borges choose Viterbo? Devoto offers no explanation. I chanced upon a possible answer during my visit to the Duomo of Siena, famous among other things for its floor mosaics. One of these displays the emblem of Viterbo: a unicorn. The unicorn embodies a feminine principle and symbolizes virginity, purity, and chastity. I thought immediately of Beatriz Viterbo and realized that her last name might be a fine example of cryptically erudite Borgesian irony.

6. Over the years, Borges wrote several essays on Dante, some of which are found in widely available Borges anthologies in English, for instance, "Paradiso XXXI, 108," in his *A Personal Anthology* or in *Labyrinths*; as for the essential "Meeting in a Dream," it was first translated in *Other Inquisitions* and is reprinted in *Borges: A Reader*. The essays on Dante are collected in Borges's *Nueve ensayos dantescos* (1982).

7. This point is made in an essay by Edna Aizenberg, who argues that Borges is the great precursor of Hebraizing—Kabbalistic and Midrashic—conceptions of reading and writing in contemporary literary theory. See her "Borges and the Hebraism of Contemporary Literary Theory," in Aizenberg, ed. *Borges and His Successors*, p. 257. Such Hebraism in contemporary theory is represented most prominently by Harold Bloom. The "miniaturization" of the *Divine Comedy* in "The Aleph," of the *Quixote* in "Pierre Menard, Author of the *Quixote*," or of More's *Utopia* in "Tlön, Uqbar, Orbis Tertius" is, Aizenberg notes, "strikingly reminiscent of Bloom's [application] of the Lurianic theory of creation to literature" (ibid.). The Lurianic model used by Bloom defines creation in terms of *zimzum* (concentration), *shevirat ha-kelim* (destruction or substitution), and *tikkun* (correction), which means, as Bloom puts it in his *Kabbalah and Criticism*, "creation through the contraction of an internalized precursor text" (a formula which is, by the way, perfectly applicable to "The Aleph"). See also Aizenberg's *The Aleph Weaver*.

8. See Jaime Alazraki, *Borges and the Kabbalah*, p. 45.

9. Ronald Christ, *The Narrow Act*, p. 12.

10. See *Borges: A Reader*, pp. 237–38, and the commentary on pp. 355–56, which underscores the parallelism between the secret code revealed to the pre-Columbian priest under torture and the Kabbalistic cipher of the universe.

11. Borges observes that if we take Scripture as the product of a "stellar intelligence" or of God's dictation, it becomes "an absolute text, where the collaboration of chance can be calculated to zero. . . . A book impenetrable by contingency, a mechanism of infinite purpose, of infallible variations, of revelations lying in wait, of superimposed light. . . . How could one not question it to absurdity, to numerical excess, as did the Cabala?" (p. 24).

12. For an authoritative account of *zimzum* and its place within "The Doctrine of Creation in Lurianic Kabbalah," see Gershom Scholem, *Kabbalah*, pp. 129–135. Borges was familiar with Scholem's works on Jewish mysticism, such as the

· · ·

classic *Major Trends in Jewish Mysticism* (first published in 1941 and reissued in numerous editions since) or his *On the Kabbalah and Its Symbolism* (first published in German in 1960, English translation 1965), and he even quotes Scholem's name in a poem. The same writings of Scholem have to a large extent inspired Harold Bloom's attempt to use Kabbalistic models for his theory of poetic influence.

13. See Edna Aizenberg, "Emma Zunz: A Kabbalistic Heroine in Borges's Fiction." On the exoteric, literal, "naturalistic" level, "Emma Zunz" is a detective-type story of revenge, in which a Jewish woman, Emma, kills the man responsible for her father's demise; on a deeper, esoteric, Kabbalistic level it is an allegorical retelling of the Kabbalistic myth of the *Shekhinah* (the tenth attribute of God, the female principle in God and God's power of justice); on the same archetypal level, the story also alludes to the Gnostic myth of *Sophia*.

14. In a seminar discussion of Borges's story, Elizabeth Starr pointed out that April 30 is the day of Hitler's death. Is it pure coincidence that April 30, the anniversary of Beatriz's birth, is also the day on which Hitler committed suicide in 1945? The publication history of "The Aleph" makes the "pure coincidence" theory rather unlikely. The story appeared in the literary magazine *Sur* in the issue for September 1945. It is known that Hitler committed suicide on April 30, 1945, and that Germany surrendered soon after that, on May 8, 1945. World War II formally ended with the surrender of Japan on August 14, 1945. All of these dates—and certainly many others—must have been fresh in the memory of the reader of late 1945. "The Aleph," one additionally notes, contains several other dates that might have some link to the history of the Third Reich and of World War II, including the Holocaust. The question is: Does Borges's story *really* contain oblique political-historical references to World War II? In other words, can it be read, in fact reread, also as a political-historical allegory? Of course it can, although a more precise and cohesive allegorical *interpretation* (as opposed to a looser, more tentative and more free-wheeling *rereading*) may be very difficult if not impossible to come by. This may explain why none of the commentaries of Borges's story I have read brings up the otherwise quite remarkable coincidence between Beatriz's anniversary and the day of Hitler's death or other possible allusions to World War II, including the history of Argentina during those years (Argentina under the quasi-fascist rule of Juan Perón was strongly in favor of the Axis powers, and after the war it became a haven for fugitive Nazi war criminals).

15. The meaning of fictional dates in fictional texts is notoriously hard to decode. It is usually very difficult even to distinguish between dates that may contain secrets and dates that are transparent. Consider James Joyce, who is certainly one of the most thoroughly studied authors of world literature: the possible reasons for his setting the action of *Ulysses* on Thursday, June 16, 1904 (a day which has subsequently become a national Irish holiday) have not been elucidated with certainty in the absence of an unambiguous authorial statement.

· · ·

This, to be sure, does not prevent the reader, and all the more so the Joyce scholar, from feeling that the choice of that date, in a work so rigorously thought-out in every detail, could not be arbitrary. But how was it chosen? Does it hide a purely personal secret—is it linked to a private anniversary, for example, as Richard Ellmann has suggested in his biography of Joyce? Ellmann notes that on the evening of June 16, 1904, Joyce had his first appointment with his future wife, Nora Barnacle, whom he had met a few days before and who had failed to show up for an earlier appointment on June 14: "To set *Ulysses* on this date was Joyce's most eloquent, if indirect tribute to Nora . . . . He would tell her later, 'You made me a man.' June 16 was the sacred day that divided Stephen Dedalus, the insurgent youth, from Stephen Dedalus, the complaisant husband" (*James Joyce,* p. 156). The private anniversary hypothesis is probably the best one we have, but it is no more than an hypothesis.

16. Daniel Devoto has dealt with some of the connotations of these toponyms in "Aleph et Alexis," pp. 283–84.

17. My views in this respect are close to the theory of reading developed by members of the Porter Institute for Poetics and Semiotics of the University of Tel Aviv such as Meir Sternberg and Menakhem Perry. For Perry, reading is "a process of constructing a system of hypotheses or frames which can create maximal relevancy among the various data of the text—which can motivate their 'co-presence' in the text according to models derived from 'reality,' from literary and cultural conventions, and the like" ("Literary Dynamics," p. 43). Or: "We cannot first determine the meaning of items and then seek the appropriate frame. The operation is simultaneous; hence the reading process is one of *guessing* frames (from 'sign-posts' and conventions) and selecting the one that works in the best way possible. . . . *Most of the information* a reader derives from a text is not explicitly written in it; rather it is the reader himself who supplies it by the mere fact of choosing frames" (pp. 44–45). Interestingly, Perry also addresses the question of rereading, if only as an afterthought. At the end of his analysis of Faulkner's "A Rose for Emily" (which constitutes the bulk of the article from which I have quoted), he broadly describes it as a "reconstructed first reading" or the result of a "retrospective repatterning" made possible only by a second and third reading. In fact, any critical, reflective, self-conscious reading is, or partici-pates in the nature of, rereading. But rereading is much more diverse and complex than its identification with a critical-reflective stance might suggest. Also, the relationship between reading and rereading is much less continuous, "natural," and harmonious than might appear at first sight.

Two: Temporal Flow or Spatial Form?

1. One might note that Nabokov's later fiction is explicitly composed not with the reader, but with the rereader in mind. The "dear reader" convention of older

. . .

novelists is appropriately (and playfully) replaced with a new "dear rereader" convention. In *Ada,* for instance, at the beginning of the story, "the modest narrator has to remind the rereader of all this" (p. 25).

2. For a polemical discussion of Frank's "spatial form" and of Genette's largely atemporal concept of reading, as well as for a broader critique of the anti-chronological/antitemporal bias in modern (French) poetics, see Meir Sternberg, "Time and Reader," pp. 75ff. and "Telling in Time," pp. 907–28. For Sternberg's larger argument in favor of a poetics sensitive to the temporal dimension of reading, see his *Expositional Modes and Temporal Ordering in Fiction* (1978). But Sternberg seems to ignore the fact that spatial concepts are—implicitly if not explicitly—applied to rereading, not to reading. Criticism, "New" and old, often overlooks the temporality of reading because it is itself the result of rereading. Evidently, rereading is a temporal process through and through and is in fact involved in a double temporality: linear and irreversible, on the one hand, like the temporality of the first reading; circular or cyclical, on the other (see the last part of chapter 4). It may be the case that in sustained but unself-conscious rereading what has been called "time's arrow" and what has been called "time's cycle" tend to cancel each other out, the effect being a (false) sense of "spatial form" or structure. The advantage of a critically sophisticated concept of rereading is that from its perspective one can understand and *explain* how the fallacy of spatial form came about, why it has been attractive for so long, and why, under certain circumstances, the notion of spatial form may even have some positive suggestive or heuristic value.

3. On the specific idea of the "cathedral-novel" and of Proust's profound understanding of architecture and architectural symbolism, see J. Theodore Johnson, Jr., "Marcel Proust and Architecture." Johnson writes on the spiritual meaning of the cathedral metaphor: "Like a cathedral, Proust's novel is not easy to read, all the more so as the reading we apply to this monument is less that of the plastic or linguistic surfaces than that of the depths hidden in ourselves, for 'Reading stands at the threshold of spiritual life; reading can lead us into it; reading does not constitute it' (Preface to *Sésame et les lys*). The mere fact of entering a cathedral does not necessarily constitute an entry into the spiritual life of the place or, for that matter, of oneself. . . . [A] cathedral-novel is a living thing as soon as the reader begins to read and discover the truths, the harmonies, and the great general plan which are to be found in the cathedral-novel and in himself. The miracle of reading occurs if one can say to oneself, 'I myself am the subject of this work' " (pp. 146–47).

4. This point is made in Ellen Eve Frank's perceptive discussion of Proust in her *Literary Architecture,* pp. 117–63.

5. Arnheim writes, "When the reader waits to see whether Stendhal's Fabrice will succeed in escaping from the prison before his enemies poison him, the two strands of action . . . grow as independent systems whose meeting in time is what matters" (*New Essays,* p. 88).

. . .

6. For an example of what Ingarden means by schematic structure, see his discussion of Thomas Mann's novella "Tristan," in *Cognition*, pp. 242–48. The schematic structure of the literary work of art is a consequence of the fact that fictional objects (characters, narrative situations, etc.), like real objects, cannot be fully determined in language: a fully determinate description of a fictional object would be infinite. The writer, then, must present his fictional entities "schematically," that is, selectively, indicating only some of their properties and leaving the reader to imagine, in more or less detail, the rest. For instance, the opening sentences of Thomas Mann's "Tristan" mention Einfried, the sanatorium where the action of the story is to take place ("A long, white, rectilinear building with a side wing," etc.), but they do not specify where Einfried is located: "This 'where'— e.g. in Europe, in Germany—constitutes a place of indeterminacy which may be . . . 'filled out' . . . in a more or less probable way" (p. 242). But, as Ingarden himself notes, this kind of elementary indeterminacy (leaving aside those countless indeterminacies which are "self-evident," such as, for instance, that Einfried is built on the surface of the earth) can be left unfilled. Other types of indeterminacy are less easily settled or ignored, such as those that are deliberately ambiguous and designed to give "the reader . . . a certain freedom in filling them out." Unfortunately, for these more interesting cases Ingarden offers no examples or only very vague ones. In the vast majority of cases, he concludes, "We can very well refrain from filling out the places of indeterminacy" (p. 241). A reading will be legitimate when the reader fills out whatever gaps he needs or chooses to fill out in a "permissible" manner and, more importantly, when he apprehends the schematic structure of the work with precision (desirably with "absolute precision"). As we have already seen, however, Ingarden's latter condition is inconsistent with his own notion of the absolute individuality of each act of reading: if there is such a thing as a fixed, unchanging, self-identical schematic structure of the work, which can and indeed should be apprehended correctly by the reader, by any reader, then Ingarden's whole subtle discussion of temporality and individuality becomes marginal, almost irrelevant. The truth is that Ingarden is of two minds on the question of concretization: concretization is both individual and general, both a process of filling out gaps without necessarily being conscious of them and a process of consciously, objectively identifying gaps without necessarily filling them.

7. For a contemporary discussion of this and other inconsistencies in Ingarden's aesthetic phenomenology, see William Ray, *Literary Meaning*, pp. 27–59; Robert C. Holub, *Reception Theory*, pp. 22–29; and Elizabeth Freund, *The Return of the Reader*, pp. 141–42.

Three: First-time Reading as Norm

1. In his book *The Fantastic*, Tzvetan Todorov notes that "the fantastic is a genre which emphasizes this convention [of irreversible reading time] more dis-

· · ·

tinctly than others. . . . Hence, the first and the second reading of a fantastic story produce very different impressions" (pp. 89–90). This feature is shared with detective novels and with jokes, "genres of emphatic temporality" whose existence depends on their ability to produce surprise. On jokes, Todorov quotes Freud's observation that jokes have a short life because their "very nature of surprising someone or taking him unawares implies that it cannot succeed a second time" (p. 90).

2. The apparent paradox is that in order to enjoy such a status, the first reading theorized by Ingarden must be of a text that also is—to repeat an earlier formulation—indefinitely rereadable.

3. Ingarden deems that longer works cannot be directly cognized as aesthetic wholes but only as a successive multiplicity of aesthetic objects, in which "the aesthetic object constituted in the final phase of the work is . . . only the aesthetic expression of a mere part of the work, e.g., the final scene of a drama or last chapter of a novel, where a more or less detectable echo of the previous parts of the work is only incidentally detectable in the background" (*The Cognition,* p. 316).

4. Fish uses such a model in *Surprised by Sin: The Reader in* Paradise Lost, and deals with some of its theoretical implications in essays collected in *Is There a Text in This Class?* (see particularly "What It's Like to Read *L'Allegro* and *Il Penseroso,*" "Facts and Fictions," and "Interpreting the *Variorum*").

5. See Michael Riffaterre, *Semiotics of Poetry,* pp. 5–7.

Four: Rereading as Norm

1. What distinguishes Barthes from most other literary semioticians is precisely his polemical stance against the first reading and his emphatic, almost partisan endorsement of rereading. Otherwise, the (methodological) importance of rereading is almost universally acknowledged in the field of literary semiotics. Speaking of reading as hypothesis-building and constant making of inferences, Umberto Eco notes in *The Role of the Reader* that "in reading literary texts one is obliged to look backward many times, and, in general, the more complex the text, the more it has to be read twice, and the second time from the end" (p. 26). More recently, in his article "The Interpretant in Literary Semiotics" (1985), Michael Riffaterre reformulates his imperative of rereading. To grasp the significance of a literary work, "the reader has to read twice" (p. 42). Without a second, comparative, reflective, and retroactive reading the significance of the work cannot be completely understood. Riffaterre writes: "Since the continuity of the semiosis is experienced in the circularity made possible by feedback from the interpretant to the text-sign, it takes only rereading to set the whole wheel of significance in motion" (p. 51).

2. The mere possibility of using the French Revolution as a metaphor for a cultural fashion, that of Lacanian psychoanalysis—consider the "cute" subtitle of

. . .

Sherry Turkle's book, *Psychoanalytic Politics: Freud's French Revolution*—gives an idea not only of the Parisian intellectual climate in the 1960s and early 1970s but also of the propensity of intellectuals to exaggerate the importance of their direct influence on society.

3. See *Le débat*, no. 50 (May-August 1988), p. 179.

4. For a broader discussion of the avant-garde, see the chapter "The Idea of the Avant-Garde" in my *Five Faces of Modernity*; for a discussion of Barthes's classicism/avant-garde dichotomy, of which the *lisible/scriptible* opposition is just a special case, see my article "Postmodernism and Some Paradoxes of Periodization."

5. See, for instance, my *Five Faces of Modernity*, pp. 51–52.

6. An interesting mechanical metaphor applied specifically to reading is I. A. Richards's notion that "a book is a machine to think with." In the introduction to *How to Read a Page* (1942), Richards recalled that twenty years before he had opened his *Principles of Literary Criticism* with that startling statement and added (speaking of himself in the third person): "Here he is trying to devise another sort of verbal machine: something which may be a help in using books as machines to *think* with. . . . Some books endeavor to transport their readers or to drag them passively hither and thither; others aim to stuff them, with facts or other supposedly fattening matter; others are microscopes, as it were, which can take the most familiar things and lay scraps and details of them before us, so transmuted by the new conditions under which we see them that we lose all power of recognizing them or putting them together again; others behave rather as pulverizers or consolidators" (pp. 1–2). Another famous mechanical metaphor of reading is Paul Valéry's view that a poem is a machine whose function is to produce poetic emotions in the reader (see "Poésie et pensée abstraite," in *Oeuvres*, vol. 1, p. 1337). As for textual metaphors applied to nontextual realities, they are not as new as some of their contemporary users think them to be; in fact they are largely modernized versions of such old *topoi* as "the book of nature" or the notion that the world is "the writing of God."

Five: To Read or to Reread?

1. "To Read, or Not to Read" (*The Critic as Artist*, p. 27). The movement through Dante's *Divine Comedy*, as described in the title essay (*The Critic as Artist*, pp. 375–78), is clearly a movement of rereading, set in contrast with the movement of life, which "is a failure from an artistic point of view . . . [since] one can never repeat the same emotion." Only art makes it possible to blissfully repeat the same emotion.

2. For a discussion of Cervantes and the *libros de caballerías*, see Daniel Eisenberg, *A Study of Don Quixote* (Newark, Del.: Juan de la Cuesta, 1987), pp. 3–44.

. . .

3. E. C. Riley argues in his *Don Quixote* that the reading public of the time of Cervantes was "in basic ways . . . similar to the modern mass market," even though the literate proportion of the population was only about 20 percent (p. 9).

4. See Keith Whinnom, "The Problem of the Best-seller in Spanish Golden-Age Literature." On Whinnom's best-seller list *Amadis* ranked after Fernando de Rojas's *La Celestina*, Mateo Alemán's picaresque novel *Guzmán de Alfarache*, and Montemayor's pastoral *Diana*, being an equal fourth with (interestingly) *Don Quixote*.

5. In his *Don Quixote*, E. C. Riley notes that "the chivalric hero is reborn in James Bond, suitably accoutred for the later twentieth century with a degree of cynical materialism; and reborn in purer form in the cosmic heroes of *Star Wars* and *Superman*" (p. 12).

6. Daniel Eisenberg, in the chapter "Who read the romances of chivalry?" in his *Romances of Chivalry in the Spanish Golden Age*, pp. 89–100, argues against the traditionally accepted view (whose main source is *Don Quixote* itself) that romances of chivalry were enjoyed by all classes of society, including peasants, and proposes the thesis of a mostly aristocratic readership. Keith Whinnom, in "The Problem of the Best-seller," agrees with D. W. Cruickshank's view in "Literature and the Book Trade in Golden-Age Spain." Cruickshank observes the emergence a new distinct lower-class audience at the beginning of the seventeenth century, an audience whose existence was deplored by good writers and booksellers. But he recognizes that writers like Cervantes, Lope de Vega, or Calderon tried and found it "possible to cater for both *discretos* and *vulgo*" (p. 821). And he remarks that the notion of *vulgo* could be applied to any occasional, idle, undiscriminating reader, even when he or she belonged to the nobility.

7. Frank Pierce, *Amadis de Gaula*, p. 107.

8. See the entry on "Allegory" in *Dictionnaire de spiritualité ascétique et mystique* (Paris: Beauchesne, 1937–), vol. 1, pp. 313–14.

9. See Daniel Eisenberg, *A Study of* Don Quixote, p. 23.

10. That such spiritual-symbolic implications of chivalric imagery may also be relevant to Cervantes is shown in Helena Percas de Ponseti's *Cervantes y su concepto del arte*, in her discussion (vol. 2, pp. 479–502) of the important episode of the cave of Montesinos in Part II of *Don Quixote*. Percas de Ponseti underscores the parallelisms between this episode and key images in the writings of Saint Teresa.

11. See Michel de Certeau, "La lecture absolue," in *Problèmes actuels de la lecture*, pp. 65–80. As Certeau notes, for Saint Teresa a book—a religious work, a treatise about how to pray, or something of that sort—"has the value of a necessary piece in a mental physics of attention" (p. 72).

12. The priest's statement on *Tirant lo Blanch* has enjoyed among Cervantes scholars the reputation of being "the most obscure passage of the *Quixote*" (Diego Clemencin). For a discussion and a scholarly bibliography, see Daniel Eisenberg,

. . .

"Pero Pérez the Priest and His Comment of *Tirant lo Blanch*," in his *Romances of Chivalry*, pp. 147–158.

13. For a recent discussion of the traditions as well as some contemporary versions of ethical criticism of fiction, see Wayne C. Booth, *The Company We Keep*.

14. We recall that in his pedagogical novel *Emile* (1762), Rousseau allowed his hero, once he had reached adolescence, to read and reread only one book, Defoe's *Robinson Crusoe*. In the process of Emile's education, as described from the moment of his birth to the age of twenty, learning from books was to be systematically avoided in favor of learning directly, instinctively, from nature and experience; Emile was not even supposed to be taught the unimportant or secondary skill of reading; he was to acquire it naturally, by himself, without any special instruction.

15. Stendhal, *Oeuvres complètes,* ed. Georges Eudes (Paris: Larrive, 1954), vol. 16, p. 27.

16. In a letter to Reynaldo Hahn dated Friday, January 18, 1895, Proust wrote: "This morning I shall go to the Bois if I get up soon enough, for I am still in bed, drunk with reading Emerson" (*Selected Letters*, p. 87).

17. In the Borgesian sense in which Kafka "created" his precursors, whose works would not have been linkable—or, in a different terminology, would not have displayed any intertextual and mutually enriching relationship—if Kafka had never existed (see the last part of chapter 4).

Six: Modernity and Reading

1. In *Hermeneutic Desire and Critical Rewriting* Marcel Cornis-Pope has argued convincingly that a critical pedagogy could benefit from exploiting the conflict between reading and rereading (see chap. 8, pp. 265–96). His interpretive pedagogy strives to create a contrast between first and second reading: readers are asked to consider how their response changes from one to the other, how their generic and cultural grids are readjusted in second reading. Although my essay deals only incidentally with pedagogical issues, I think that one interested in rereading should be aware of the possibilities (both theoretical and practical) offered by a pedagogy of rereading.

2. *The Cambridge History of the Bible*, vol. 3, p. 202.

3. See Victor Baroni, *La Contre-Reforme devant la Bible*, p. 204.

4. Raymond Williams, *The Long Revolution*, p. 159.

5. See the substantial entry on "*Lectio divina* et lecture spirtuelle," in *Dictionnaire de spiritualité ascétique et mystique*, vol. 9 (Paris: Beauchesne, 1976), esp. p. 494.

6. Commenting on the prologue of Bunyan's *Pilgrim's Progress*, in which the reader is addressed directly and promised the opportunity to "read thyself . . . and

· · ·

know whether thou art blest or not," Wolfgang Iser writes in *The Implied Reader*: "The book is meant to appeal to each individual reader . . . and its aim is to lead the believer to recognize himself. . . . And so the gradual acquisition of *certitudo salutis* puts a subjective slant on the objective events" (p. 7); "The monologues in the *Pilgrim's Progress* were of particular interest to Puritan readers, for Christian's search for reassurance offered them a guideline as to how they should examine themselves" (p. 19).

7. In a recent discussion of the relationship between midrash, interpretation, and allegory, Gerald L. Bruns writes in "Midrash and Allegory": "As the rabbis, Augustine, and Luther knew, the Bible, despite its textual heterogeneity, can be read as a self-glossing book. One learns to study it by following the ways in which one portion of the text illumines another" (p. 626). On midrash and literary interpretation, see Geoffrey H. Hartman and Sanford Budick, eds., *Midrash and Literature*.

8. For a commentary on this passage from *La nouvelle Héloïse* (letter of Claire to Julie) in the context of a discussion of Engelsing's intensive/extensive reading dichotomy, and more generally of the emergence of a new kind of tender, sensitive, and empathetic reader (a reader who is actually the opposite of Engelsing's extensive reader), see Roland Galle, "*La nouvelle Héloïse* ou le commencement d'une nouvelle lecture," pp. 216–28.

9. See J. Paul Hunter, " 'The Young, the Ignorant, and the Idle': Some Notes on Readers and the Beginnings of the English Novel."

10. See, for instance, Margaret Spufford, *Small Books and Pleasant Histories*.

Seven: Ages, Places, and Situations

1. Actually, they may produce just the opposite effect, as Michael Steig notes in *Stories of Reading* in his response analysis of Kenneth Grahame's *The Wind in the Willows*: "My adult response to this [passage] upon the first rereading was a mixture of empathy and revulsion; no doubt this was what my colleague referred to as 'that awful religious stuff,' with its too obvious paralleling of Pan and Christ" (p. 89). For the ten-year-old, as Steig remembers, this same paralleling had triggered a positive fantasy "of being completely taken care of by an adult," a fantasy the mature reader, a teacher of literature and a professional critical rereader, could certainly do without.

2. "J'ignore ce que je fis jusqu'à cinq ou six ans: je ne sais comment j'appris à écrire. Je ne me souviens que de mes premières lectures et de leur effet sur moi: c'est le temps d'où je date sans interruption la conscience de moi-même" (*Confessions*, p. 8).

3. See Charles Grivel, "Les premières lectures," p. 137.

4. Proust, *A la recherche du temps perdu*, vol. 1, pp. 41–42; *Jean Santeuil*, pp. 309–16, 366–68.

· · ·

5. The newspaper analogy was suggested to me by C. S. Lewis's *An Experiment in Criticism,* in which he describes those who "never read anything twice" as follows: "The sure mark of an unliterary man is that he considers 'I've read it already' to be a conclusive argument against reading a work" (p. 2). The argument of Lewis's book is interesting in that he uses rereadability and the actual occurrence of rereading as the ultimate criterion of good literature: "Where there is passionate and constant love of a book and re-reading, then, however bad we think the book and however immature or uneducated we think the reader," we cannot dismiss the work as trash and we have no right to speak of "unliterary reading" (pp. 114–115).

6. By and large, this metaphorical view of a child/adolescent reader who survives and manifests himself or herself in the adult person is confirmed by empirical psychological approaches to the question of reading for pleasure, or "ludic" reading. An experimental psychologist of ludic reading, Victor Nell, believes that "earlier tastes do not wither and die as more refined appetites develop. . . . New systems do not replace older ones but are superimposed on them. . . . Psychoanalysis . . . also suggests that earlier and more primitive needs and desires are not rooted out by maturation and education but merely overlaid and that they remain active in disguised or flamboyant ways throughout life (*Lost in a Book,* p. 5).

7. The rationale of bibliotherapy for children who are faced with a serious problem or crisis (a death or disabling illness in the family, divorce, and so on) has been aptly summarized by Betsy Hearne, professor of children's literature at the University of Chicago: "Sometimes fantasy is the best way of dealing with reality" (quoted by Carol Lawson in "Once Upon a Time in the Land of Bibliotherapy," *New York Times,* November 8, 1990, B2).

8. This argument is homologous to the classical Marxist argument that proletarian class consciousness cannot be achieved except through commitment to the cause of the proletariat—that is, the struggle for a transparent, classless, communistic society. The cause of the proletariat is scientifically defined and mapped out by theoretical Marxism itself, or by the avant-garde of the working class (the Marxist-Leninist party), or by its advanced revolutionary elite. The mere fact of being a member of the working class does not insure access to class consciousness. Unenlightened proletarians (the vast majority) cannot articulate their experiences and class interests, because they are unwitting mental prisoners of the categories of bourgeois ideology, a particularly pernicious form of "false consciousness."

Eight: Notes for a Poetics of Reading

1. See Tzvetan Todorov, "Reading as Construction." The view of reading as "performance" has been convincingly advanced by Lowry Nelson, Jr., in "The Fictive Reader: Aesthetic and Social Aspects of Literary Performance."

. . .

2. For a discussion of Trilling's essay "The Fate of Pleasure: Wordsworth to Dostoevsky," see my essay "Modernity and Popular Culture," in *Sensus Communis*.

3. The successful critical anthology *The Reader in the Text*, edited by Susan Suleiman and Inge Crosman, has popularized this label, although in fact only some of the essays included in the volume deal with the reader in the text or inscribed reader proper.

4. The notion of fictive reader has been proposed by Lowry Nelson, Jr., who in his "The Fictive Reader and Literary Self-Reflexiveness" sees the fictive reader as being under a sort of "contractual duty in the very act of reading to assume provisionally a fictive role, not as an outsider but as an accomplice, communicant, collaborator, or willing suspender of disbelief" (p. 173).

5. The formula used by Menachem Perry in "Literary Dynamics" might be applied to most "readers in the text": "What I term reader is . . . a metonymic characterization of the text" (p. 43).

6. See Jean Rousset, *Le Lecteur intime,* the whole section entitled "Un genre ambigu, le journal intime," and particularly the chapter "Pour une poétique du journal intime," pp. 155–70.

7. See Béatrice Didier, "Le Lecteur du journal intime." She notes that since keeping a journal does not involve any competence, "tout lecteur de journal intime est tenté de devenir lui-même auteur d'un journal intime." This kind of mimetic relationship between author and reader is less evident in the case of reading poems or novels (p. 249).

Nine: Preliminaries

1. At the end of his 1962 diary, as quoted in Brian Boyd's *Vladimir Nabokov,* the writer noted for possible use in an interview, "I wonder if any reader will notice the following details: 1) that the nasty commentator is not an ex-king and not even Dr. Kinbote, but Prof. Vseslav Botkin, a Russian and a madman . . ." (vol. 2, p. 709).

2. In this reading, Botkin would also be a creation of Shade.

3. Even though I use the concept of fictional truth rather freely, I wish to acknowledge my debt for it, as well as for the conception of a certain way of reading fiction as a playing a game of make-believe, to Kendall Walton's seminal ideas as expressed in a series of articles published in the 1970s and 1980s and ultimately set out in a book, *Mimesis as Make-Believe: On the Foundations of the Representational Arts* (1990). Simply put, works of fiction contain various "props" and "prescriptions to imagine" certain things as true (fictionally true) and are meant to offer the reader an opportunity to play a "game of make-believe." See particularly chapter 1, section 5, "Props and Fictional Truths" (pp. 35–43), and chapter 4, "The Mechanics of Generation" [of fictional truths] (pp. 138–74).

. . .

4. For a useful overview of the play concept in modern philosophical and scientific discourse, see Mihai I. Spariosu, *Dionysus Reborn* (1989). Spariosu's more recent *God of Many Names* (1991) analyzes the concept of play in Hellenic thought, with important chapters on Plato and Aristotle. See also his earlier *Literature, Mimesis, and Play* (1982), which deals primarily with questions of literary theory.

Ten: The Ludic Dimension

1. I should like to emphasize again that my use of the adjective *ludic* is different from the one adopted by Victor Nell in *Lost in a Book*; it encompasses *all* the pleasures of reading and rereading, including those derived from concentration, absorption, and the ability to respond elegantly to an intellectual challenge.

2. Fred Waitzkin, in *Searching for Bobby Fischer* (1988), describes well the combination of natural talent, work, and addiction-like passion that often goes into professional chess careers: "The best practitioners live tragic, deprived lives. . . . They are treated as if they are naughty curiosities, children who never grew up. . . . Professional players . . . are bitter about their poverty and lack of recognition, but they don't do much to improve their image. Failure seems to beget failure. Even at the best tournaments the players are a ragtag group, sweaty, gloomy, badly dressed, gulping down fast food, defeated in some fundamental way" (p. 58). In reading Waitzkin, I was made conscious of an intriguing potential relationship between play and addiction (or addictive behavior), particularly in adults. Such addictive behavior extends to fans, in the case of chess kibitzers, those "persistent kibitzers" who, according to Waitzkin, are "hooked on observing games in the same way some are addicted to baseball or bridge or spy novels" (p. 103).

3. The relevance of Schelling's views to literature, and specifically to the question of literary reading, has been noted in Elizabeth W. Bruss, "The Game of Literature and Some Literary Games." The theoretical first part of this essay contains interesting suggestions, but the examples in support of the theory, discussed in the second part (Plato's *Meno* as a game of full cooperation, Faulkner's *The Hamlet* as a mixed-motive game, and Melville's *The Confidence-Man* as a game of full competition), are arbitrary and unconvincing.

4. Georges Perec observes in the "Preamble" to his masterpiece, *Life: A User's Manual* (a novel itself constructed like an elaborate puzzle), that when jigsaw puzzling is truly an art, when the maker of the puzzle "undertakes to ask himself all the questions the player will have to solve . . . one can make a deduction which is quite certainly the ultimate truth about jigsaw puzzles: despite appearances, puzzling is not a solitary game: every move the puzzler makes, the puzzle maker has made before; every piece the puzzler picks up, and picks up again, and studies and strokes, every combination he tries, and tries a second time, every blunder and

. . .

every insight, each hope and each discouragement have all been designed, calculated, and decided by the other" (p. 3).

5. In 1988 I discussed the main points of my scenario of playful professional reading with Professor Peter Constantin of the Department of Mathematics of the University of Chicago, whom I am pleased to acknowledge here. He confirmed my initial intuitions concerning the play element in reading for professional purposes and helped me to articulate them more lucidly.

6. See also the passages about art and nature as sources of "nonutilitarian delights" and as "a game of intricate enchantment and deception" (*Speak Memory,* p. 125).

7. Solomon Marcus, *Poetica matematica* (Bucharest: Editura Academiei, 1970).

Eleven: Psychological Approaches

1. Transposed to the context of the dichotomy between play and games, the question of involvement versus absorption recalls the way the psychologist L. S. Vygotsky deals with the developmental change from what he calls very aptly "games with an overt imaginary situation and covert rules" to "games with overt rules and a covert imaginary situation." See his *Mind and Society* (1975), p. 96.

2. Marcel Proust, *A la recherche du temps perdu,* vol. 1, *Du côté de chez Swann,* pp. 180–81.

Twelve: Fictionality

1. On the topic of fictionality, see Evans's critique of Frege's notion of fictionality, pp. 28–30, and chapter 10, "Existential Statements," pp. 343–72.

2. For the broad area of what Goffman calls "expression games" and games of "strategic interaction," see his *Strategic Interaction* (1969).

3. The example of "dozens" comes from a study by the linguist William Labov, "Rules for Ritual Insults," in David Sudnow, ed., *Studies in Social Interaction* (New York: Free Press, 1972), pp. 120–169; and William Labov, *Language in the Inner City* (Philadelphia: University of Pennsylvania Press, 1973).

4. This chapter was written before the publication of Kendall Walton's *Mimesis as Make-Believe* (1990), into which his 1978 article "Fearing Fictions" has been assimilated. All subsequent page references in this section are to the article as it appeared in the *Journal of Philosophy,* January 1978.

Thirteen: A "Christmas-Tide Toy"

1. For the historical details and meanderings of the dispute, see the Norton Critical Edition of *The Turn of the Screw* (1966); Jane P. Tompkins, ed.,

· · ·

Twentieth-Century Interpretations of "The Turn of the Screw" and Other Tales (Englewood Cliffs, N.J.: Prentice-Hall, 1970); and Gerald Willen, ed., *A Casebook on Henry James's "The Turn of the Screw"* (New York: Crowell, 1967). A review of the main arguments in support of the two theories, including the most characteristic misreadings, fallacious arguments, and inadmissible extratextual inferences, is found in chapter 6, " 'The Turn of the Screw' and Its Critics: An Essay in Non-methodology," of Christine Brooke-Rose's *A Rhetoric of the Unreal* (1981), pp. 128–57. For a more recent review of the claims to validity of conflicting interpretations of James's story, see chapter 5, "History, Epistemology, and the Example of the *The Turn of the Screw*," in Paul B. Armstrong, *Conflicting Readings* (1990), pp. 69–108.

2. Pp. 311–316. In the row about *The Turn of the Screw,* Booth himself supports, rather unsubtly, the governess's version, which he thinks corresponds to James's "conscious intentions" (pp. 311–16).

3. See Caillois's *Images, images . . .* (1966), specifically his emphasis on the fantastic as an exploration of the derealizing and hence terrifying powers of certain images.

4. See Jacques Lacan, *Ecrits 1,* p. 16.

5. The main pieces in the dossier of the "Purloined Letter" debate are Jacques Lacan, "Le Séminaire sur 'La Lettre volée,' " trans. Jeffrey Mehlman as "Seminar on 'The Purloined Letter,' " in *French Freud: Structural Studies in Psychoanalysis, Yale French Studies* 48 (1972), pp. 38–72; Jacques Derrida's critique of Lacan's reading, "Le Facteur de vérité," trans. Willis Domingo et al. as "The Purveyor of Truth," in *Graphesis: Perspectives in Literature and Philosophy, Yale French Studies* 52 (1975), pp. 31–113; Barbara Johnson, "The Frame of Reference: Poe, Lacan, Derrida" (1977), reprinted in *The Critical Difference* (Baltimore: Johns Hopkins Univ. Press, 1980); Norman Holland, "Re-Covering 'The Purloined Letter': Reading as a Personal Transaction," in Suleiman and Crosman, eds., *The Reader in the Text,* pp. 350–70; and John T. Irwin, "Mysteries We Reread, Mysteries of Rereading: Poe, Borges, and the Analytic Detective Story; Also Lacan, Derrida, and Johnson," in *Modern Language Notes* 101 (1986), pp. 1168–1215.

Fourteen: Mysteries for Rereading

1. See Michael Holquist's "Whodunit and Other Questions" (1971), in which Borges, Robbe-Grillet, and Nabokov receive particular attention. Another early essay is Frank Kermode's *Novel and Narrative* (1972), in which Raymond Queneau, Robbe-Grillet, and Michel Butor serve as examples. Robert Champigny, in his *What Will Have Happened* (1977), points out some of the intriguing links between certain types of mystery stories and what he calls "pseudonarratives" (or narratives of inconclusive investigations), citing such modern authors as Kafka,

· · ·

Maurice Blanchot, Michel Butor, Ionesco, and Beckett (see Part III of his essay, "Cryptogram," and particularly pp. 139–148). See also David I. Grossvogel's *Mystery and Its Fictions* (1979), which discusses, along with Poe's "Purloined Letter" and Agatha Christie's novels, works by Dostoevsky, Camus, Kafka, Pirandello, Borges, and Robbe-Grillet.

2. See Dennis Porter, *The Pursuit of Crime,* particularly the chapter "The Detective Novel as Readable Text," pp. 82–99.

3. In Glenn W. Most and William W. Stowe, eds., *The Poetics of Murder,* p. 12.

4. A. S. Burack, ed., *Writing Detective and Mystery Fiction,* p. 82.

5. For a philosophical approach to reading detective stories as games, see Bernard Suits's "The Detective Story: A Case Study of Games in Literature." Suits distinguishes three aspects: first, the literary work (the detective story) is *constructed* as a game; second, the work-as-game is *played,* that is, actively played, by the reader; and third, the game proposed by the work is *viewed* by a nonplaying reader (the response of such a reader would be comparable to the reactions of a baseball fan to a game he is watching). Suits does not speak of rereading, but clearly rereading is involved in appreciating the way the game is constructed; it is also involved, but to a lesser degree, in playing the game actively; and it is only marginally relevant to mere watching, in which straight reading and make-believe have the major role.

6. "Transposition," or "serious transformation," Genette writes, "is without any doubt the most important of the hypertextual practices," after which he offers some of the same examples (*Faust, Ulysses,* Tournier's *Vendredi*) that he had earlier cited as cases of "serious parody." For the definition of transposition, see *Palimpsestes,* p. 237; for "parodie sérieuse," a term used only in passing and with due caution ("pour l'instant"), see p. 37. In fact, I am in essential agreement with Genette on the intellectual hazards involved in a generalized concept of parody, however tempting it may be at times. I made my position on the question clear in my review article on Linda Hutcheon's *A Theory of Parody,* "Parody and Intertextuality," *Semiotica* 65 (1987), pp. 183–90.

7. Oulipo (from Ouvroir de littérature potentielle, or Workshop of Potential Literature) is the collective name of an association of writers, founded in 1960 by Raymond Queneau and François Le Lionnais, and devoted to experimentation with explicitly ludic literary techniques in transforming older (famous) texts or in creating new ones. Among the procedures used by the Oulipo writers are extended puns or plays on words (*calembours*), permutations of letters or words according to arbitrary rules, anagrams, lipograms, palindromes, rebuses, and a variety of other strictly defined constraints. Aside from the founders, the membership of Oulipo consisted, among others, of Italo Calvino, Marcel Duchamp, Harry Mathews, Georges Perec, and Jacques Roubaud. For a presentation of Oulipo in English, see Warren F. Motte, Jr., ed., *Oulipo: A Primer of Potential Literature* (Lincoln: University of Nebraska Press, 1986).

. . .

8. For a discussion of the Borges story, mainly as a rewriting of Poe's "Purloined Letter," see John T. Irwin, "Mysteries We Reread, Mysteries of Rereading" (1986). Irwin's discussion raises the question of what I would call a *secret* rewriting, a rewriting that becomes so unrecognizable that Irwin's arguments do not completely convince me that Borges did in fact rewrite Poe's story.

9. As down-to-earth, unimaginative Inspector Treviranus correctly suggests. But Lönnrot rejects the accidental explanation: "Possible, but not interesting. . . . You'll reply that reality hasn't the least obligation to be interesting. And I'll answer you that reality may avoid that obligation but that hypotheses may not. In the hypothesis that you propose, chance intervenes copiously. Here we have a dead rabbi; I would prefer a purely rabbinical explanation" (Borges, *Labyrinths*, p. 77). It is precisely such an "explanation" that Scharlach sets out to provide in order to tempt Lönnrot to come at a precise time to the precise place of his death.

10. In his recent autobiography, *Le Miroir qui revient* (1984), Robbe-Grillet declares, "I write first of all against myself, . . . and therefore against the public" (p. 40), and then goes on to describe his writing as "a trap for the humanist reader, one for the politico-Marxian or Freudian reader, etc., and finally a trap also for the searcher of structures devoid of meaning" (p. 41).

Fifteen: Introducing Secrecy

1. The reader might usefully ponder legal definitions of secrecy, including attempts to distinguish between secrecy and privacy. Here is one such definition (offered by Kim Lane Scheppele in *Legal Secrets*): "A secret is a piece of information that is intentionally withheld by one or more social actor(s) from one or more social actor(s)" (p. 12). Privacy, on the other hand, is "a condition in which individuals can, temporarily, free themselves from the demands and expectations of others. Secrecy is one of the methods that an individual may use to attain this condition. But privacy and secrecy describe different entities. Secrecy describes information, and privacy describes individuals" (p. 13).

2. The passage I am referring to reminds me of Georg Simmel's notion of sociability as an elaborate form of social play. See *The Sociology of Georg Simmel*, pp. 40–57. Simmel insists on the importance of unreality (a condition of play), tact, and impersonality (implying a drastic "reduction of personal poignancy," p. 45) in the construction of "the artificial world of sociability" (p. 48). The center of sociability is the art of conversation. Talk, in sociability, is "the fulfillment of a relation that wants to be nothing but relation. . . . Hence even the telling of stories, jokes, and anecdotes, though often only a pastime if not a testimonial of intellectual poverty, can show the subtle tact that reflects the elements of sociability. It keeps the conversation away from individual intimacy and from all purely personal elements" (p. 53).

3. In his *Notebooks* James wrote on July 27, 1891, that he had chosen the title

· · ·

"The Private Life" for "the little tale founded on the idea of F. L. and R. B.,"
adding on August 3 that "the idea of rolling into one story the little conceit of the
private identity of a personage suggested by F. L. and that of a personage suggested
by R. B., is of course a rank fantasy, but as such may it not be made amusing and
pretty? It must be very brief—very light—very vivid." See *The Complete Notebooks of Henry James,* p. 60. The editors note that F. L. was Sir Frederic Leighton
(1830–1896), a painter and sculptor and, at the time, president of the Royal
Academy. R. B. was Robert Browning. For the biographical background of "The
Private Life," including details about James's relations with the real-life models of
Vawdrey and Lord Mellifont, see Leon Edel, *Henry James: The Conquest of
London* and *Henry James: The Middle Years,* the latter of which contains a
discussion of "The Private Life," pp. 274–77. For a discussion of the relationship
between Henry James and Robert Browning, see Robert Posnock, *Henry James
and the Problem of Robert Browning,* which reviews the relevant bibliography,
including biographical studies of Browning which accept and use James's view of
Browning as a double personality.

4. James writes specifically: "To express his inner self—his outward was a
different affair!— . . . was clearly, for his own measure and consciousness of that
inner self, to *be* poetic" (p. 468; James's emphasis). The secretiveness of this
allusion is easily understood, given the celebratory occasion for which James
conceived his Browning lecture.

5. See, for instance, his letters to Mrs. Humphrey Ward, July 26, 1899 and Mrs.
W. K. Clifford, May 18, 1912; see also his letter to H. G. Wells, September 21, 1913.

6. For the parallelisms between gossip and fiction, see Patricia Meyer Spacks,
Gossip (1985). Spacks quotes Margaret Drabble's observation that "much fiction
operates in the spirit of inspired gossip: it speculates on little evidence, inventing
elaborate and artistic explanations of little incidents and overheard remarks that
often leave the evidence far behind" (p. 10). Among many other literary examples,
Joseph Conrad's *Chance* is cited by Spacks as "a novel using gossip as a subject and
as a narrative technique" (ibid.).

Sixteen: Understanding Texts with Secrets

1. See James Atlas, "The Case of Paul de Man," in *The New York Times
Magazine,* August 28, 1988. For a recent review of the debate, see Part II of David
Lehman's *Signs of the Times,* "The Fall of Paul de Man," pp. 141–268.

2. See also Sissela Bok, *Secrets: On the Ethics of Concealment and Revelation*
(1983). She writes: "I shall take concealment, or hiding, to be the defining trait of
secrecy." A secret is not simply something unknown, but something deliberately,
"studiously hidden" (Samuel Johnson's first meaning for "secret" in his *Dictionary,* cited by Bok); secrecy then is typically definable as "intentional concealment"
(pp. 5–10).

. . .

3. Some secrets are carried, consciously or unconsciously, as one carries a disease. A repressed secret may be, as Henry James suggests, a "painless disease" (see the discussion of Lady Mellifont in the previous chapter), but the painlessness is not an indication of its degree of seriousness: fatal diseases may be painless. It is worth mentioning that some psychoanalysts, both in the Freudian and in the Jungian traditions, have seen certain types of secrets as pathogenic agents. In their theory of cryptonymy and cryptonyms, Nicolas Abraham and Maria Torok go so far as to claim that "crypts" and "phantoms" can be unconsciously transmitted over generations, so that certain individuals may be the unconscious bearers of the unspeakable secrets of their great-grandfathers. However, the explanation of how unconscious secrets (for instance the sense of guilt and shame associated with secret crimes) may be communicated unconsciously from parents to their children and so on through successive generations remains obscure if metaphorically appealing.

4. In his famous article "The 'Uncanny'" (1919) Freud characterizes the uncanny (quoting Schelling) as that which "ought to have remained hidden and secret, and yet comes to light" (*Collected Papers,* vol. 4 [London: The Hogarth Press, 1949], p. 376) and notes that "an uncanny effect is often and easily produced by effacing the distinction between imagination and reality, such as when something that we have hitherto regarded as imaginary appears before us in reality. . . . The infantile element in this . . . is the over-accentuation of physical reality—a feature closely allied to the belief in the omnipotence of thoughts" (p. 398).

5. See *The Sociology of Georg Simmel,* pp. 332–34.

6. Goffman discusses questions of secrecy and privacy from various angles or "frames," such as role playing (in *The Presentation of Self* and other works) or deviant behavior that is stigmatized by society and is for that reason kept secret (*Stigma: Notes on the Management of Spoiled Identity* [Englewood Cliffs, N.J.: Prentice-Hall, 1963]). For Edward Shils's views, see his *The Torment of Secrecy* (1956).

7. By "philosophical" here I mean only to stress that at least in some types of deciphering, the reader may ask broader questions, such as: Is the literary text the carrier of a secret doctrine, of historically heretical views? Is the text the bearer of a certain ideology, of which its author might have been partly or even totally unconscious? Is the text an expression of individual or collective unconscious wishes, complexes, and archetypes? With the last two questions it may seem that I am contradicting my earlier statement about the intentional and conscious nature of secrecy. But I have already qualified that statement by saying that certain secrets (such as those of the skeleton-in-the-closet type) may be "forgotten," that is, repressed. I might add here that from the (re)reader's point of view, which is the point of view in which I have placed myself here, the procedures used for deciphering what the psychoanalysts call enigmas (the riddle of the unconscious, the enigmatic meanings of dreams, and so on) as opposed to secrets (which are deliberately hidden) are very similar. For a more detailed discussion of the psycho-

. . .

analytic distinction between enigma and secrecy, see Victor N. Smirnoff's "Le Squelette dans le placard" (1976).

8. The originator of modern esoteric interpretations of Dante is Gabriele Rossetti (1783–1854), the father of Dante Gabriel Rossetti and Christina Rossetti. An Italian political exile in London since the mid-1820s, Gabriele Rossetti devoted to Dante several important studies, from his early analytical commentary to the *Inferno* (published in London in 1825–26), through his five-volume *Il mistero dell'Amor platonico del Medioevo* (London, 1840) and *La Beatrice di Dante* (1842), to the posthumously published commentary to *Purgatorio*. His impressive scholarship was put in the service of overinterpretation along political-conspiratorial and esoteric-initiatory lines. Every figure, verbal detail, even syllable in Dante's text was given a cryptographic significance accessible only to the few who knew the secret language. The influence of masonic modes of thought, secret rites, and symbolism is obvious. Some of Rossetti's controversial ideas about Dante's secret language were developed by Luigi Valli (1878–1931), particularly in his *Il linguaggio segreto di Dante e dei Fedeli d'Amore* (Rome, 1928–30), in which he argued that Dante belonged to the sect of the Fedeli d'Amore, whose adepts had developed a secret language. A more recent view of Dante along the lines of the secret tradition of esotericism is René Guénon's *L'esotérisme de Dante* (Paris: Gallimard, 1957).

9. The main problem of uncensored speech is that it appears to be less vitally meaningful than speech that evades or, more heroically, defies censorship. Western writers have sometimes envied their fellows in old Communist Eastern Europe for the double attention paid to their word: the attention of the censor (which seemed to mean that their word could indeed change the world) and that of the public seeking the hidden, subversive message. But of course the other, less glamorous part of the story is the frequent duplicity of the officially tolerated writer (a duplicity that the censor may perversely encourage) and the deceptive dramatization of what is sometimes no more than the utterance, courageous under the circumstance, of essential banalities and truisms.

10. Speier, in "The Communication of Hidden Meaning," notes: "The critics [of a totalitarian regime] have the choice of leaving the profession or becoming hypocrites. . . . The critics who do not abandon their work must behave in public like zealots. Different from dissenters . . . , they are compelled by the nature of their work to advocate rather than merely tolerate beliefs they do not share. . . . After prolonged compliance with official regulations . . . , the journalist may attribute to his readers an understanding of meanings hidden in his writings which they either no longer possess or have ceased to be interested in: or else the hidden meaning may be so faint as to pass unnoticed" (pp. 488–89).

11. I rely on the article "Literary Quotations in Perec's *La Vie: mode d'emploi*" (1987), by Perec's English translator, David Bellos. See also Gabriel Josipovici, "Georges Perec's Hommage to Joyce (and Tradition)" (1985).

. . .

12. For a discussion of Broch's statement and, more broadly, of kitsch, see my essay entitled "Kitsch" in *Five Faces of Modernity*.

13. See, for instance, Nicholas Rand's "Translator's Introduction: Toward a Cryptonymy of Literature," in Abraham and Torok, *The Wolf Man's Magic Word*, pp. il–lxix; see also Esther Rashkin, "Tools for a New Psychoanalytic Literary Criticism: The Work of Abraham and Torok," in *Diacritics*, Winter 1988, pp. 31–52.

Seventeen: The Language of Secrecy and the Politics of Interpretation

1. See "Privacy as a Social and Historical Phenomenon," chapter 2 in Joseph Bensman and Robert Lilienfeld, *Between Public and Private* (1979). On the question of literacy and privacy, the authors express a consensus view when they note, "Reading makes privacy both respectable and tolerable, and so literate classes have always had opportunities to legitimate and express their inclinations for privacy" (p. 33).

2. An interesting illustration of this is offered by Simmel, in his reference to the secret order of Gallic Druids: "The content of their secrets lay, particularly, in spiritual songs which every Druid had to memorize. But because all this was so arranged—above all, probably, because of the prohibition to write the songs down—it required an extraordinarily long time, even up to twenty years." See *The Sociology of Georg Simmel*, p. 350. I would add here that an atmosphere of "diffuse secrecy" surrounds any tradition that is orally handed down, including oral instructions about what to read, when to read, how to read, and how to refer (in various contexts) to what one has read. We tend to forget that a "well-educated" person—a product, say, of a prestigious university—is in possession of an orally acquired lore about what is important to know and what kind of reading is necessary to deal with a certain subject, even on the level of social conversation. In this sense, we can say with Proust that distinction, in the order of intelligence and reading (and handling what one has read socially), consists "in a kind of freemasonry of customs, and in an inheritance [and oral communication, I might add] of traditions" (*On Reading Ruskin*, p. 125).

3. For an anthropological study of secrecy in primitive oral societies, see Jean Jamin, *Les Lois du silence: essai sur la fonction sociale du secret* (1977). Although Jamin does not seem to be aware of Simmel's work on secrecy, his general thesis that the function of secrecy is connected to the "educative processes" whose aim is the retention of speech and the teaching of how to be silent ("à savoir se taire") echoes Simmel, to whose insight he brings documentary confirmation.

4. "Such [functional] secrecy is a far cry from the secrecy which is required by paranoid ideological extremism. The latter secrecy is not functional but symbolic. It is part of the war of fantasy which the pure and the good conduct incessantly with corruption and evil until the Last Judgment" (Edward Shils, *The Torment of Secrecy*, p. 235).

· · ·

5. One such example in Spinoza's *Tractatus,* brought out by Strauss, is the self-contradiction that there can be a suprarational truth (that is, a revelation), but that suprarational truth is impossible and that "belief in invisible things which cannot be demonstrated by reason is simply absurd, or that what are said to be teachings 'above reason' are in truth dreams or mere fictions and 'by far below reason.'" (*Persecution,* p. 170).

. . .

BIBLIOGRAPHY

. . . .

Abraham, Bernard. "A propos de la relecture." In *Semen 1: Lecture et lecteur*, pp. 83–103. Annales Littéraires de l'Université de Besançon, 278. Paris: Belles Lettres, 1983.

Abraham, Nicolas, and Maria Torok. *The Wolf Man's Magic Word: A Cryptonymy*. Translated by N. Rand. Foreword by Jacques Derrida. Minneapolis: University of Minnesota Press, 1986.

Aizenberg, Edna. *The Aleph Weaver: Biblical, Kabbalistic and Judaic Elements in Borges*. Potomac, Md.: Scripta Humanistica, 1984.

———. "Emma Zunz: A Kabbalistic Heroine in Borges's Fiction." In Daniel Walden, ed., *Studies in American Jewish Literature 3*, pp. 223–35. Albany: State University of New York Press, 1983.

Aizenberg, Edna, ed. *Borges and His Successors*. Columbia: University of Missouri Press, 1990.

Alazraki, Jaime. *Borges and the Kabbalah*. New York: Cambridge University Press, 1988.

Alter, Robert. *The Pleasures of Reading in an Ideological Age*. New York: Simon and Schuster, 1989.

Alter, Robert, and Frank Kermode, eds. *The Literary Guide to the Bible*. Cambridge, Mass.: Harvard University Press, 1987.

Altick, Richard D. *The English Common Reader*. Chicago: University of Chicago Press, 1957.

. . .

305

Appel, Alfred, Jr., and Charles Newman, eds. *Nabokov*. Evanston, Ill.: Northwestern University Press, 1970.

Appleyard, J. A. *Becoming a Reader: The Experience of Fiction from Childhood to Adulthood*. New York: Cambridge University Press, 1990.

Armstrong, Paul B. *Conflicting Readings: Variety and Validity in Interpretation*. Chapel Hill, N.C.: University of North Carolina Press, 1990.

Arnheim, Robert. *Art and Visual Perception*. Berkeley and Los Angeles: University of California Press, 1969.

————. *New Essays in the Psychology of Art*. Berkeley and Los Angeles: University of California Press, 1986.

Auden, W. H. *The Dyer's Hand*. New York: Random House, 1962.

Bachelard, Gaston. *Poétique de la rêverie*. Paris: Presses Universitaires de France, 1961.

Bakhtin, M. M. *Rabelais and His World*. Cambridge, Mass.: MIT Press, 1968.

Baroni, Victor. *La Contre-Reforme devant la Bible*. 1943. Geneva: Slatkine Reprints, 1986.

Barthes, Roland. *The Pleasure of the Text*. Translated by Richard Miller. New York: Farrar, Straus and Giroux, 1975.

————. *The Rustle of Language*. Translated by Richard Howard. New York: Hill and Wang, 1986.

————. *The Semiotic Challenge*. Translated by Richard Howard. New York: Hill and Wang, 1988.

————. *S/Z*. Translated by Richard Miller. Preface by Richard Howard. New York: Hill and Wang, 1974.

Bateson, Gregory. *Steps to an Ecology of Mind*. San Francisco: Chandler, 1972.

Beauvoir, Simone de. *The Second Sex*. Translated by H. M. Parshley. New York: Knopf, 1952.

Bellman, Beryl L. *The Language of Secrecy: Symbols and Metaphors in Poro Ritual*. New Brunswick, N.J.: Rutgers University Press, 1984.

Bellos, David. "Literary Quotations in Perec's *La Vie: mode d'emploi*." *French Studies* 41, no. 2 (April 1987): 181–194.

Bell-Villada, Gene H. *Borges and His Fiction*. Chapel Hill: University of North Carolina Press, 1981.

Bensman, Joseph, and Robert Lilienfeld. *Between Public and Private*. New York: Free Press, 1979.

Benveniste, Emile. "Le jeu comme structure." *Deucalion—Cahiers de philosophie* 2 (1947): 161–67.

Berberova, Nina. "The Mechanics of *Pale Fire*." In Alfred Appel, Jr., and Charles

· · ·

Newman, eds., *Nabokov,* pp. 147–159. Evanston, Ill.: Northwestern University Press, 1970.

Bloom, Harold. *The Anxiety of Influence.* New York: Oxford University Press, 1973.

Bloom, Harold, ed. *Vladimir Nabokov.* New York: Chelsea House, 1987.

Bok, Sissela. *Secrets: On the Ethics of Concealment and Revelation.* New York: Vintage Books, 1983.

Booth, Wayne C. *The Company We Keep.* Berkeley and Los Angeles: University of California Press, 1988.

———. *The Rhetoric of Fiction,* 2d ed. Chicago: University of Chicago Press, 1983.

Borges, Jorge Luis. *Borges: A Reader.* Edited by Emir Rodriguez Monegal and Alastair Reid. New York: Dutton, 1981.

———. *Borges at Eighty.* Edited by Willis Barnstone. Bloomington: Indiana University Press, 1982.

———. *Labyrinths.* Edited by D. A. Yates and J. Irby. New York: New Directions, 1964.

———. *Nueve ensayos dantescos.* Introduction by M. R. Baratán and J. Arce. Madrid: Espasa-Calpe, 1982.

———. *Other Inquisitions.* Translated by Ruth L. C. Simms. Austin: University of Texas Press, 1965.

———. *A Personal Anthology.* New York: Grove Press, 1967.

Boyd, Brian. *Vladimir Nabokov.* 2 vols. Princeton, N.J.: Princeton University Press, 1990, 1991.

Brooke-Rose, Christine. *A Rhetoric of the Unreal.* Cambridge: Cambridge University Press, 1981.

Bruner, Jerome. *Actual Minds, Possible Worlds.* Cambridge, Mass.: Harvard University Press, 1986.

Bruner, Jerome, Alison Jolly, and Katy Sylva, eds. *Play: Its Role in Development and Evolution.* New York: Basic Books, 1976.

Bruns, Gerald. "Midrash and Allegory: The Beginnings of Scriptural Interpretation." In Robert Alter and Frank Kermode, eds., *The Literary Guide to the Bible,* pp. 625–46. Cambridge, Mass.: Harvard University Press, 1987.

Bruss, Elizabeth W. "The Game of Literature and Some Literary Games." In *New Literary History* 9, no. 1 (Autumn 1977): 153–72.

Burack, A. S., ed. *Writing Detective and Mystery Fiction.* Boston: The Writer, 1967.

Caillois, Roger. "The Detective Novel as Game." In Glenn W. Most and Wil-

· · ·

liam W. Stowe, eds., *The Poetics of Murder,* pp. 1–13. New York: Harcourt Brace
Jovanovich, 1983.

———. *Images, images . . .* Paris: José Corti, 1966.

———. *Man, Play, and Games.* Translated by M. Barash. New York: Shocken
Books, 1979.

Calinescu, Matei. *Five Faces of Modernity: Modernism, Avant-Garde, Deca-
dence, Kitsch, Postmodernism.* Durham, N.C.: Duke University Press, 1987.

———. "Modernity and Popular Culture." In János Riesz, Peter Boerner, and
Bernhard Scholz, eds., *Sensus Communis,* pp. 221–26. Tübingen: Gunter Narr,
1986.

———. "Parody and Intertextuality." *Semiotica* 65, no. ½ (1987): 183–90.

Calinescu, Matei, and D. W. Fokkema, eds. *Exploring Postmodernism.* Amsterdam: John Benjamins, 1987.

Calvino, Italo. *The Uses of Literature.* Translated by Patrick Creagh. San Diego:
Harcourt Brace Jovanovich, 1986.

The Cambridge History of the Bible. 3 vols. New York: Cambridge University
Press, 1975.

Camus, Albert. *Carnets.* Vol. 2. Paris: Gallimard, 1964.

Certeau, Michel de. *The Practice of Everyday Life.* Translated by S. Rendall.
Berkeley and Los Angeles: University of California Press, 1984.

Cervantes, Miguel de. *Don Quixote.* Translated by Samuel Putnam. New York:
Modern Library, 1969.

Champigny, Robert. *What Will Have Happened.* Bloomington: Indiana University Press, 1977.

Charles, Michel. *Rhétorique de la lecture.* Paris: Seuil, 1977.

Chartier, Roger. *The Cultural Uses of Print in Early Modern France.* Translated by
Lydia G. Cochrane. Princeton, N.J.: Princeton University Press, 1987.

Chartier, Roger, ed. *Pratiques de la lecture.* Marseille: Rivages, 1985.

Christ, Ronald. *The Narrow Act: Borges' Art of Allusion.* New York: New York
University Press, 1969.

Coetzee, J. M. "The Novel Today." *Upstream* 6 (1988): pp. 2–5.

Cohen, David. *The Development of Play.* New York: New York University Press,
1987.

Cornea, Paul. *Introducere in teoria lecturii.* Bucharest: Minerva, 1988.

Cornis-Pope, Marcel. *Hermeneutic Desire and Critical Rewriting: Narrative Interpretation in the Wake of Poststructuralism.* London: Macmillan, 1991.

Crawford, Mary, and Roger Chaffin. "The Reader's Construction of Meaning:
Cognitive Research on Gender and Comprehension." In Elizabeth Flynn and

· · ·

Patrocinio Schweickart, eds. *Gender and Reading,* pp. 3–30. Baltimore: Johns Hopkins University Press, 1986.

Crosman, Robert. *Reading* Paradise Lost. Bloomington: Indiana University Press, 1989.

Cruickshank, D. W. "Literature and the Book Trade in Golden-Age Spain." *Modern Language Review* 73 (1978): 799–824.

Csikszentmihalyi, Mihaly. *Beyond Boredom and Anxiety.* San Francisco: Jossey-Bass Publications, 1977.

Culler, Jonathan. *On Deconstruction.* Ithaca: Cornell University Press, 1982.

———. *Structuralist Poetics.* Ithaca: Cornell University Press, 1975.

Darnton, Robert. "Readers Respond to Rousseau: The Fabrication of Romantic Sensitivity." In *The Great Cat Massacre and Other Episodes in French Cultural History,* pp. 215–56. New York: Basic Books, 1984.

———. "What Is the History of Books?" In Cathy N. Davidson, ed., *Reading in America,* pp. 27–52. Baltimore: Johns Hopkins University Press, 1989.

Davidson, Cathy N., ed. *Reading in America.* Baltimore: Johns Hopkins University Press, 1989.

De Man, Paul. *Allegories of Reading.* New Haven: Yale University Press, 1979.

Demetz, Peter, Thomas Greene, and Lowry Nelson, Jr., eds. *The Disciplines of Criticism.* New Haven: Yale University Press, 1968.

Devoto, Daniel. "Alephe et Alexis." In *L'Herne,* special issue on Jorge Luis Borges. Paris: Editions de l'Herne, 1981.

Dictionnaire de spiritualité ascétique et mystique. Paris: Beauchesne, 1937–.

Didier, Beatrice. "Le lecteur du journal intime." In Michel Picard, ed., *La Lecture littéraire,* pp. 229–55. Paris: Clancier-Guénaud, 1987.

Du Secret. Nouvelle Revue de Psychanalyse 14 (1976).

Eco, Umberto. *The Limits of Interpretation.* Bloomington: Indiana University Press, 1990.

———. *The Role of the Reader: Explorations in the Semiotics of Texts.* Bloomington: Indiana University Press, 1979.

Edel, Leon. *Henry James.* 2 vols. Philadelphia: Lippincott, 1962, 1963.

Ehrmann, Jacques. "*Homo ludens* Revisited." *Yale French Studies* 41 (1968): 31–57.

Eisenberg, Daniel. *Romances of Chivalry in the Spanish Golden Age.* Newark, Del.: Juan de la Cuesta, 1982.

———. *A Study of* Don Quixote. Newark, Del.: Juan de la Cuesta, 1987.

Eliot, T. S. *Selected Prose.* Edited by Frank Kermode. New York: Harcourt Brace Jovanovich, 1975.

· · ·

Ellmann, Richard. *James Joyce.* New and revised edition. New York: Oxford University Press, 1982.

Emerson, Ralph Waldo. *The Collected Works of Ralph Waldo Emerson.* 3 vols. Cambridge, Mass.: Belknap Press, Harvard University Press, 1971, 1979, 1983.

Engelsing, Rolf. *Der Bürger als Leser. Lesergeschichte in Deutschland, 1500–1800.* Stuttgart: Metzler, 1974.

Evans, Gareth. *The Varieties of Reference.* Oxford: Oxford University Press, 1982.

Faguet, Emile. *L'Art de lire.* Paris: Hachette, 1912.

Felman, Shoshana. "Turning the Screw of Interpretation." *Yale French Studies* 55–56 (1977): 94–207.

Ferry, Luc, and Alain Renaut. *La pensée 68: Essai sur l'antihumanisme contemporain.* Paris: Gallimard, 1985.

Fetterley, Judith. *The Resisting Reader.* Bloomington: Indiana University Press, 1978.

Fish, Stanley. *Is There a Text in This Class?* Cambridge, Mass.: Harvard University Press, 1980.

———. *Surprised by Sin: The Reader in* Paradise Lost. 2d ed. Berkeley and Los Angeles: University of California Press, 1971.

Flynn, Elizabeth A., and Patrocinio P. Schweickart, eds. *Gender and Reading.* Baltimore: Johns Hopkins University Press, 1986.

Frank, Ellen Eve. *Literary Architecture.* Berkeley and Los Angeles: University of California Press, 1989.

Frank, Joseph. "Spatial Form: An Answer to Critics." *Critical Inquiry* 4, no. 2 (Winter 1977): 231–52.

———. "Spatial Form: Some Further Reflections." *Critical Inquiry* 5, no. 2 (Winter 1978): 275–90.

———. *The Widening Gyre.* Bloomington: Indiana University Press, 1968.

Freud, Sigmund. *The Standard Edition of the Complete Psychological Works of Sigmund Freud.* Edited under the direction of James Strachey. 24 vols. London: Hogarth Press, 1953–1974.

Freund, Elizabeth. *The Return of the Reader.* London: Methuen, 1987.

Furet, François, and Jacques Ozouf. *Reading and Writing: Literacy in France from Calvin to Jules Ferry.* Translation of *Lire et écrire,* 1977. Cambridge: Cambridge University Press, 1982.

Gadamer, Hans-Georg. *Truth and Method.* Translated by Garrett Barden and John Cumming. New York: Crossroad, 1988.

Galle, Roland. "*La nouvelle Héloise* ou le commencement d'une nouvelle lecture."

. . .

In Michel Picard, ed., *La Lecture littéraire*, pp. 216–28. Paris: Clancier-Guénaud, 1987.

Game, Play, Literature. Yale French Studies 41 (1968).

Genette, Gérard. *Narrative Discourse.* Translation by Jane E. Lewin of *Figures III*, 1972. Ithaca: Cornell University Press, 1980.

———. *Palimpsestes: La littérature au second degré.* Paris: Editions du Seuil, 1982.

Gide, André. *The Journals of André Gide, 1889–1949.* Edited and translated by Justin O'Brien. Vol. 2. Evanston, Ill.: Northwestern University Press, 1987.

———. *Pretexts: Reflections on Literature and Morality.* Edited by Justin O'Brien. Translated by Angelo P. Bertocci. 1959. Reprint. Freeport, N.Y.: Books for Libraries Press, 1971.

Goffman, Erving. *Frame Analysis.* Cambridge, Mass.: Harvard University Press, 1974.

———. *The Presentation of Self in Everyday Life.* Garden City, N.Y.: Doubleday, 1959.

———. *Strategic Interaction.* Philadelphia: University of Pennsylvania Press, 1969.

Gombrich, E. H. *Art and Illusion.* Princeton, N.J.: Princeton University Press, 1969.

Gombrowicz, Witold. *Diary.* Translated by Lillian Vallee. Vol. 1. Evanston: Northwestern University Press, 1988.

Goodman, Kenneth. "Reading: A Psycholinguistic Guessing Game." *Journal of the Reading Specialist,* 1967:126–35.

Grivel, Charles. "Les premières lectures." In Michel Picard, ed., *La Lecture littéraire,* pp. 128–60. Paris: Clancier-Guénaud, 1987.

Grossvogel, David I. *Mystery and Its Fictions: From Oedipus to Agatha Christie.* Baltimore: Johns Hopkins University Press, 1979.

Guerard, Albert J. *The Triumph of the Novel: Dickens, Dostoevsky, Faulkner.* Chicago: University of Chicago Press, 1976.

Harding, D. W. "Psychological Processes in the Reading of Fiction." In Margaret Meek et al., eds., *The Cool Web: The Pattern of Children's Reading,* pp. 58–72. New York: Atheneum, 1978.

Hartman, Geoffrey, and Sanford Budick, eds. *Midrash and Literature.* New Haven: Yale University Press, 1988.

Hilgard, Josephine R. *Personality and Hypnosis.* Chicago: University of Chicago Press, 1975.

Hoesterey, Ingeborg. "The Intertextual Loop: Kafka, Robbe-Grillet, Kafka." *Poetics Today* 8, no. 2 (1987): 373–92.

. . .

Holland, Norman. *The Dynamics of Literary Response.* New York: Oxford University Press, 1968.

———. *5 Readers Reading.* New Haven: Yale University Press, 1975.

Holland, Norman, and Leona Sherman. "Gothic Possibilities." In Elizabeth Flynn and Patrocinio Schweickart, eds., *Gender and Reading,* pp. 215–33. Baltimore: Johns Hopkins University Press, 1986.

Holquist, Michael. "Whodunit and Other Questions: Metaphysical Detective Stories in Post-War Fiction." *New Literary History* 3 (1971): 131–56.

Holub, Robert C. *Reception Theory: A Critical Introduction.* London: Methuen, 1984.

Huizinga, Johan. *Homo ludens.* Boston: Beacon Press, 1955.

Hunter, J. Paul. " 'The Young, the Ignorant, and the Idle': Some Notes on Readers and the Beginnings of the English Novel." In A. C. Kors and P. J. Korshin, eds., *Anticipations of the Enlightenment in England, France, and Germany,* pp. 259–82. Philadelphia: University of Pennsylvania Press, 1987.

Hutcheon, Linda. *A Theory of Parody: The Teachings of Twentieth-Century Art Forms.* London: Methuen, 1985.

Hutchinson, Peter. *Games Authors Play.* London: Methuen, 1983.

Ingarden, Roman. *The Cognition of the Literary Work of Art.* Translated by R. A. Crowley and K. R. Olson. Evanston, Ill.: Northwestern University Press, 1973.

———. *The Literary Work of Art.* Translated by G. Grabowicz. Evanston, Ill.: Northwestern University Press, 1973.

Irwin, John T. "Mysteries We Reread, Mysteries of Rereading: Poe, Borges, and the Analytic Detective Story; Also Lacan, Derrida, and Johnson." *Modern Language Notes* 101 (1986): 1168–1215.

Iser, Wolfgang. *The Act of Reading: A Theory of Aesthetic Response.* Baltimore: Johns Hopkins University Press, 1978.

———. *The Implied Reader.* Baltimore: Johns Hopkins University Press, 1974.

James, Henry. *The Art of Criticism.* Edited by William Veeder and Susan Griffin. Chicago: University of Chicago Press, 1986.

———. *The Art of the Novel: Critical Prefaces.* Foreword by R. W. B. Lewis. Introduction by R. P. Blackmur. 1934. Boston: Northeastern University Press, 1984.

———. *The Complete Notebooks of Henry James.* Edited by Leon Edel and Lyall H. Powers. New York: Oxford University Press, 1987.

———. *Letters.* Edited by Leon Edel. 4 vols. Cambridge, Mass.: Belknap Press, Harvard University Press, 1974–1984.

———. "The Private Life." In *The Altar of the Dead,* vol. 17 of the New York Edition of *The Novels of Henry James.* New York: Scribner's, 1909.

. . .

———. *The Turn of the Screw*. Edited by R. Kimbrough. New York: Norton, 1966.

Jamin, Jules. *Les Lois du silence: Essai sur la fonction sociale du secret*. Paris: Maspéro, 1977.

Jauss, Hans Robert. *Aesthetic Experience and Literary Hermeneutics*. Translated by M. Shaw. Introduction by W. Godzich. Minneapolis: University of Minnesota Press, 1982.

———. *Toward an Aesthetic of Reception*. Translated by T. Bahti. Introduction by Paul de Man. Minneapolis: University of Minnesota Press, 1982.

Johnson, Theodore J., Jr. "Marcel Proust and Architecture: Some Thoughts on the Cathedral Novel." In Barbara J. Bucknall, ed. *Critical Essays on Marcel Proust*, pp. 133–61. Boston: Hall, 1987.

Josipovici, Gabriel. "Georges Perec's Homage to Joyce (and Tradition)." *Yearbook of English Studies* 49 (1985): 180–200.

Kappeler, Susanne. *Writing and Reading in Henry James*. New York: Columbia University Press, 1980.

Kermode, Frank. *The Genesis of Secrecy*. Cambridge, Mass.: Harvard University Press, 1979.

———. *Novel and Narrative*. Glasgow: University of Glasgow Publications, 1972.

Klinger, Eric. *Structure and Functions of Fantasy*. New York: Wiley, 1971.

Kors, A. C. and P. J. Korshin, eds. *Anticipations of the Enlightenment in England, France, and Germany*. Philadelphia: University of Pennsylvania Press, 1987.

Lacan, Jacques. *Ecrits 1*. Paris: Editions du Seuil, Collection Points, 1966.

Lawson, Carol. "Once Upon a Time in the Land of Bibliotherapy." *New York Times*, November 8, 1990, B2.

Leavis, Q. D. *Fiction and the Reading Public*. 1932. Reprint. New York: Russell & Russell, 1965.

Leenhardt, Jacques, and Pierre Jozsa. *Lire la lecture*. Paris: Le Sycomore, 1982.

Lehman, David. *Signs of the Times*. New York: Poseidon Press, 1991.

Lewis, C. S. *An Experiment in Criticism*. New York: Cambridge University Press, 1961.

———. "On Stories." In Margaret Meek et al., eds., *The Cool Web: The Pattern of Children's Reading*, pp. 76–90. New York: Atheneum, 1978.

Lorenz, Konrad. "Psychology and Phylogeny." In Jerome Bruner et al., eds., *Play: Its Role in Development and Evolution*, pp. 84–94. New York: Basic Books, 1976.

Mailloux, Steven. *Interpretive Conventions: The Reader in the Study of American Fiction*. Ithaca, N.Y.: Cornell University Press, 1982.

Manea, Norman. "The Censor's Report." *Formations* 5, no. 3 (1990): 90–107.

. . .

Marcus, Solomon. *Poetica matematica.* Bucharest: Editura Academiei, 1970.

Marino, Adrian. *Biografia ideii de literatura.* Cluj: Dacia, 1991.

————. "Lecture." In *Dictionnaire international des termes littéraires,* edited by Robert Escarpit. The Hague: Mouton, 1973.

Marino, James A. G. "An Annotated Bibliography of Play and Literature." *Canadian Review of Comparative Literature,* June 1985:306–53.

Meek, Margaret, Aidan Warlow, and Griselda Barton, eds. *The Cool Web: The Pattern of Children's Reading.* New York: Atheneum, 1978.

Mercier, Louis-Sébastien. *Dictionnaire d'un polygraphe.* Edited by G. Bollème. Paris: Union Générale d'Editions, 1978.

————. *Memoirs of the Year 2500.* Translated by W. Hooper. 1795. Reprint. Clifton, N.J.: Kelly, 1973.

Meyer, Patricia. *Gossip.* New York: Knopf, 1985.

Meyer, Priscilla. *Find What the Sailor Has Hidden: Vladimir Nabokov's* Pale Fire. Middletown, Conn.: Wesleyan University Press, 1988.

Miller, J. Hillis. *The Ethics of Reading.* New York: Columbia University Press, 1987.

Millet, Kate. *Sexual Politics.* New York: Avon Books, 1970.

Montalvo, Garcia Rodriquez de. *Amadis of Gaul.* Translated by E. B. Place and H. R. Behn. 2 vols. Lexington: University of Kentucky Press, 1974.

Montaudon, Alain, ed. *Le Lecteur et la lecture dans l'oeuvre.* Clermont-Ferreand: Faculté des Lettres et Sciences Humaines, Fascicule 15, 1982.

Morrisette, Bruce. *The Novels of Robbe-Grillet.* Ithaca, N.Y.: Cornell University Press, 1975.

Most, Glenn W., and William W. Stowe, eds. *The Poetics of Murder.* New York: Harcourt Brace Jovanovich, 1983.

Motte, Warren F. *Oulipo: A Primer of Potential Literature.* Lincoln: University of Nebraska Press, 1986.

Nabokov, Vladimir. *Ada.* Greenwich, Conn.: Fawcett, 1969.

————. *Lectures on Literature.* Edited by Fredson Bowers. Introduction by John Updike. New York: Harcourt Brace Jovanovich, 1980.

————. *Pale Fire.* New York: Putnam's, 1962.

————. *Speak Memory.* New York: Putnam's, 1966.

————. *Strong Opinions.* New York: McGraw-Hill, 1973.

Nell, Victor. *Lost in a Book: The Psychology of Reading for Pleasure.* New Haven: Yale University Press, 1988.

Nelson, Lowry, Jr. "The Fictive Reader: Aesthetic and Social Aspects of Literary Performance," *Comparative Literature Studies* 15 (1978): 203–10.

. . .

————. "The Fictive Reader and Literary Self-Reflexiveness." In Peter Demetz, Thomas Greene, and Lowry Nelson, Jr., eds., *The Disciplines of Criticism*, pp. 173–91. New Haven: Yale University Press, 1968.

Ong, Walter J. *Orality and Literacy*. London and New York: Methuen, 1982.

Pavel, Thomas G. *Fictional Worlds*. Cambridge, Mass.: Harvard University Press, 1986.

Percas de Ponseti, Helena. *Cervantes y su concepto del arte*. 2 vols. Madrid: Gredos, 1975.

Perec, Georges. *Life: A User's Manual*. Translated by David Bellos. Boston: Godine, 1987.

————. *Penser/Classer*. Paris: Hachette, 1985.

————. *W, or the Memory of Childhood*. Translated by David Bellos. Boston: Godine, 1988.

Perry, Menakhem. "Literary Dynamics: How the Order of a Text Creates Its Meaning. With an analysis of Faulkner's 'A Rose for Emily.'" *Poetics Today* 1, no. 1 (1979): 35–64, no. 2 (1979): 311–61.

Piaget, Jean. *Play, Dreams, and Imitation in Childhood*. Translated by C. Gattegno and F. M. Hodgson. New York: Norton, 1951.

Picard, Michel. *La Lecture comme jeu*. Paris: Editions de Minuit, 1986.

Picard, Michel, ed. *La Lecture littéraire*. Colloque de Reims 1984. Paris: Clancier-Guénaud, 1987.

Pierce, Frank. *Amadis of Gaula*. Boston: Twayne, 1976.

Porter, Dennis. *The Pursuit of Crime*. New Haven: Yale University Press, 1981.

Posnock, Robert. *Henry James and the Problem of Robert Browning*. Athens, Ga.: University of Georgia Press, 1985.

Preston, John. *The Created Self*. London: Heinemann, 1970.

Prince, Gerald. "Introduction à l'étude du narrataire." *Poétique* 14 (1973): 178–96. (English version in Tompkins, ed., pp. 7–25.)

————. "Notes on the Text as Reader," in Susan Suleiman and Inge Crosman, eds., *The Reader in the Text*, pp. 225–40. Princeton, N.J.: Princeton University Press, 1980.

Problèmes actuels de la lecture. Colloque de Cerisy, sous la direction de Lucien Dällenbach et Jean Riacardou. Paris: Clancier-Guénaud, 1982.

Proust, Marcel. *A la recherche du temps perdu*. Pléiade edition. 3 vols. Paris: Gallimard, 1954.

————. *Contre Sainte-Beuve*. Pléiade edition. Paris: Gallimard, 1971.

————. *Jean Santeuil*. Pléiade edition. Paris: Gallimard, 1971.

————. *On Reading Ruskin*. Translated and edited by Jean Autret, William

· · ·

Burford, and Phillip J. Wolfe. Introduction by Richard Macksey. New Haven: Yale University Press, 1987.

———. *The Past Recaptured*. Translated by Andreas Mayor. New York: Vintage Books, 1971.

———. *Selected Letters (1880–1903)*. Edited by Philip Kolb. Translated by Ralph Mannheim. Garden City, N.Y.: Doubleday, 1983.

Quintilian, *Institutio Oratoria*. Vol. 4. Translated by H. E. Butler. Loeb Classical Library. Cambridge, Mass.: Harvard University Press, 1936.

Rabinowitz, Peter. *Before Reading: Narrative Conventions and the Politics of Interpretation*. Ithaca, N.Y.: Cornell University Press, 1987.

Racine, Jean. *Théâtre*. Paris: Fernad Hazan, 1947.

Ray, William. *Literary Meaning: From Phenomenology to Deconstruction*. Oxford: Blackwell, 1984.

Richards, I. A. *How to Read a Page*. New York: Norton, 1942.

Riffaterre, Michael. "The Interpretant in Literary Semiotics." *American Journal of Semiotics* 3, no. 4 (1985): 41–56.

———. *Semiotics of Poetry*. Bloomington: Indiana University Press, 1978.

Riley, E. C. *Don Quixote*. London: Allen and Unwin, 1986.

Rimmon, Shlomith. *The Concept of Ambiguity: The Example of Henry James*. Chicago: University of Chicago Press, 1977.

Rimmon-Kenan, Shlomith. *Narrative Fiction: Contemporary Poetics*. London: Methuen, 1983.

Robbe-Grillet, Alain. *The Erasers*. Translated by Richard Howard. New York: Grove Press, 1964.

———. *Last Year at Marienbad*. Translated by Richard Howard. New York: Grove Press, 1962.

———. *Le miroir qui revient*. Paris: Editions de Minuit, 1984.

———. *The Voyeur*. Translated by Richard Howard. New York: Grove Press, 1958.

Rousseau, Jean-Jacques. *Les Confessions,* Pléiade edition. Paris: Gallimard, 1933.

Rousset, Jean. *Le Lecteur intime*. Paris: José Corti, 1986.

Ruskin, John. *The Bible of Amiens*. Vol. 33 of *The Library Edition of the Works of John Ruskin*, ed. E. T. Cook and Alexander Wedderburn. London: George Allen, 1907.

———. *Munera pulveris*. Vol. 19 of *The Library Edition*. London: George Allen, 1905.

———. *The Queen of the Air*. Vol. 17 of *The Library Edition*. London: George Allen, 1905.

· · ·

————. *Sesame and Lilies.* Vol. 18 of *The Library Edition.* London: George Allen, 1905.

Schelling, Thomas C. *The Strategy of Conflict.* Cambridge, Mass.: Harvard University Press, 1963.

Scheppele, Kim Lane. *Legal Secrets.* Chicago: University of Chicago Press, 1988.

Scholem, Gershom. *Kabbalah.* New York: New American Library, 1974.

Scholes, Robert. *Protocols of Reading.* New Haven: Yale University Press, 1989.

Schweickart, Patrocinio. "Reading Ourselves: Toward a Feminist Theory of Reading." In Elizabeth Flynn and Patrocinio Schweickart, eds., *Gender and Reading,* pp. 31–62. Baltimore: Johns Hopkins University Press, 1986.

Shils, Edward. *The Torment of Secrecy.* Glencoe, Ill.: Free Press, 1956.

Sidney, Philip. *A Defence of Poetry.* Edited by J. A. Van Dorsten. London: Oxford University Press, 1966.

Simmel, Georg. *The Sociology of Georg Simmel.* Edited by Kurt H. Wolff. Glencoe, Ill.: Free Press, 1950.

Singer, Jerome L. *The Child's World of Make-Believe.* New York: Academic Press, 1973.

————. *Daydreaming: An Introduction to the Experimental Study of Inner Experience.* New York: Random House, 1966.

————. *Daydreaming and Fantasy.* Oxford: Oxford University Press, 1981.

Slatoff, Walter J. *With Respect to Readers: Dimensions of Literary Response.* Ithaca, N.Y.: Cornell University Press, 1970.

Smirnoff, Victor N. "Le Squelette dans le placard." *Nouvelle Revue de Psychanalyse* 14 (1976): 27–54.

Smith, Frank. *Understanding Reading.* 3d ed. New York: Holt, Rinehart and Winston, 1982.

Spacks, Patricia Meyer. *See* Meyer, Patricia.

Spariosu, Mihai I. *Dionysus Reborn: Play and the Aesthetic Dimension in Modern Philosophical and Scientific Discourse.* Ithaca, N.Y.: Cornell University Press, 1989.

————. *God of Many Names: Play, Poetry, and Power in Hellenic Thought from Homer to Aristotle.* Durham, N.C.: Duke University Press, 1991.

————. *Literature, Mimesis, and Play.* Tübingen: Gunter Narr, 1982.

Speier, Hans. "The Communication of Hidden Meaning." *Social Research* 44, no. 3 (Autumn 1977): 471–501.

Spinoza, Benedict de. *A Theologico-Political Treatise,* Translated by R. H. M. Elwes. New York: Dover Publications, 1951.

. . .

Spolsky, Ellen, ed. *The Uses of Adversity: Failure and Accommodation in Reader Response*. Lewisburg, Pa.: Bucknell University Press, 1990.

Spufford, Margaret. *Small Books and Pleasant Histories: Popular Fiction and Its Readership in Seventeenth-Century England*. London: Methuen, 1981.

Steig, Michael. *Stories of Reading: Subjectivity and Literary Understanding*. Baltimore, Md.: Johns Hopkins University Press, 1989.

Sternberg, Meir. *Expositional Modes and Temporal Ordering in Fiction*. Baltimore, Md.: Johns Hopkins University Press, 1978.

———. "Telling in Time (1): Chronology and Narrative Theory." *Poetics Today* 11, no. 4 (Winter 1990): 901–48.

———. "Time and Reader." In Ellen Spolsky, ed., *The Uses of Adversity: Failure and Accommodation in Reader Response*, pp. 49–89. Lewisburg, Pa.: Bucknell University Press, 1990.

Stevenson, Robert Louis. *Essays Literary and Critical*. Tusitala Edition. Vol. 28. London: Heinemann, n.d..

Strauss, Leo. *Persecution and the Art of Writing*. Glencoe, Ill.: Free Press, 1952.

———. *Spinoza's Critique of Religion*. New York: Shocken Books, 1965.

Suits, Bernard. "The Detective Story: A Case Study of Games in Literature." *Canadian Review of Comparative Literature*, June 1985: 200–219.

Suleiman, Susan. "Malraux's Women: A Re-vision." In Elizabeth Flynn and Patrocinio Schweickart, eds., *Gender and Reading*, pp. 124–46. Baltimore: Johns Hopkins University Press, 1986.

Suleiman, Susan, and Inge Crosman, eds. *The Reader in the Text*. Princeton, N.J.: Princeton University Press, 1980.

Teresa of Avila. *The Collected Works of St. Teresa of Avila*. translated by K. Kavanaugh and O. Rodriguez. Vol. 1. Washington, D.C.: Institute of Carmelite Studies, 1976).

Thiem, Jon. "Borges, Dante, and the Poetics of Total Vision," *Comparative Literature* 40, 2 (1988): 97–121.

Todorov, Tzvetan. *The Fantastic: A Structural Approach to a Literary Genre*. Ithaca, N.Y.: Cornell University Press, 1975.

———. "Reading as Construction." In Susan Suleiman and Inge Crosman, eds., *The Reader in the Text*, pp. 67–82. Princeton, N.J.: Princeton University Press, 1980.

Tompkins, Jane P., ed. *Reader-Response Criticism: From Formalism to Post-Structuralism*. Baltimore: Johns Hopkins University Press, 1980.

Turkle, Sherry. *Psychoanalytic Politics: Freud's French Revolution*. New York: Basic Books, 1978.

Tylliard, E. M. *Poetry Direct and Oblique*. London: Chatto & Windus, 1945.

· · ·

Valéry, Paul. *Oeuvres*. Pléiade edition. 2 vols. Paris: Gallimard, 1957.

Vigny, Alfred de. *Journal d'un poète*. Edited by Louis Ratisbonne. Paris: Calmann Lévy, 1882.

Vygotsky, L. S. *Mind in Society*. Edited by Michael Cole et al. Cambridge, Mass.: Harvard University Press, 1978.

Waitzkin, Fred. *Searching for Bobby Fischer: The World of Chess Observed by the Father of a Child Prodigy*. New York: Random House, 1988.

Walton, Kendall L. "Fearing Fictions." *Journal of Philosophy* 75, no. 1 (January 1978): 5–26.

———. *Mimesis as Make-Believe: On the Foundations of the Representational Arts*. Cambridge, Mass.: Harvard University Press, 1990.

Wat, Aleksander. *My Century*. Edited and translated by Richard Lourie. Berkeley and Los Angeles: University of California Press, 1988.

Watt, Ian. *The Rise of the Novel*. Berkeley and Los Angeles: University of California Press, 1957.

Whinnom, Keith. "The Problem of the Best-Seller in Spanish Golden-Age Literature." *Bulletin of Hispanic Studies* 57 (1980): 189–98.

Wilde, Oscar. *The Artist as Critic*. Edited by Richard Ellmann. Chicago: University of Chicago Press, 1969.

Williams, Raymond. *The Long Revolution*. New York: Columbia University Press, 1961.

Wimmers, Inge Crosman. *Poetics of Reading: Approaches to the Novel*. Princeton, N.J.: Princeton University Press, 1988.

Winnicott, Donald W. *Playing and Reality*. London: Tavistock, 1971.

Wittgenstein, L. *Lectures and Conversations on Aesthetics, Psychology, and Religious Belief*. Edited by Cyril Barrett. Berkeley and Los Angeles: University of California Press, 1967.

Woolf, Virginia. *Collected Essays*. Vol. 2. London: Hogarth Press, 1966.

———. *The Common Reader*. London: Hogarth Press, 1984.

———. *The Second Common Reader*. New York: Harcourt Brace Jovanovich, 1986.

. . .

. . .

· · ·

. . .

· · ·

· · ·

. . .

· · ·